Occasional Papers on Antiquities, 3

Greek Vases

In The J. Paul Getty Museum

THE J. PAUL GETTY MUSEUM   MALIBU, CALIFORNIA
VOLUME 2/1985

GREEK VASES 2 / 1985

Information about other Getty Museum publications
may be obtained by writing to the Bookstore, The
J. Paul Getty Museum, P.O. Box 2112, Santa Monica,
California 90406.

Edited by Jiří Frel and Sandra Knudsen Morgan;
designed by Patrick Dooley; typography by Freed-
men's Organization, Los Angeles; printed by Gard-
ner/Fulmer Lithograph, Los Angeles.

The paper and binding in this book meet the guidelines for permanence and durability of the Com-
mittee on Production Guidelines for Book Longev-
ity of the Council on Library Resources.

Photographs in this book have been provided by
the institution that owns the object unless otherwise specified. Every effort has been made to reproduce fragments 1:1.

Cover: Loutrophoros with scenes from the myth of
Niobe. Malibu, The J. Paul Getty Museum 82.AE.16.
Detail of obverse. See article p. 129.

Library of Congress Cataloging in Publication Data
(Revised for volume 2)

J. Paul Getty Museum.
     Greek vases in the J. Paul Getty Museum.

     (Occasional papers on antiquities; v. 1,   )
     English and German.
     Includes bibliographies.
     1. Vases, Greek—Addresses, essays, lectures.
2. Vase-painting, Greek—Themes, motives—Addresses,
essays, lectures. 3. Vase, Etruscan—Addresses, essays,
lectures. 4. Vase-painting, Etruscan—Themes, motives—
Addresses, essays, lectures. 5. Vases—California—
Malibu—Addresses, essays, lectures. 6. J. Paul Getty
Museum—Addresses, essays, lectures. I. Title.
II. Series: Occasional papers on antiquities; v. 1,
etc.
     NK4623.M37GJa7   1983   738.3'82'0938074019493   82-49024

ISSN 8756-047X
ISBN 0-89236-070-4

THEODORICO DE BOTMARE
MUSEI GETTIANI AMICO
XIII LUSTRIS PERACTIS

Contents

Mycenaean Vases in the J. Paul Getty Museum

Sinclair Hood

The thirteen Mycenaean vases which belong to the Getty Museum form an interesting collection. They are said to have been acquired from two different sources, Nos. 1–11 forming one group and Nos. 12 and 13 another. The two vases of this second group are alleged to have come from a different part of Greece than those of the first, and the clay of No. 13 in particular looks sufficiently unlike the clay of the vases of the first group as to be in harmony with the idea of a separate place of manufacture.

The relatively complete condition of all the vases suggests that they were found in tombs. This is in any case highly probable, and the character of the vases themselves supports this view: all of them are closed vessels, jugs or jars of one kind or another, and they are mostly of types standard in Mycenaean tombs on the Greek mainland. The vases of the first group consist of a narrow-necked jug (No. 1), three squat alabastra (Nos. 2–4), three squat jars with angular profiles (square-sided alabastra) of a type related to the squat alabastron (Nos. 5–7), three small handleless jars (Nos. 8–10), and the unusual if not unique handleless jar (No. 11), which may have been a small drum related to a type of ritual vase that is also found in tombs. The two vases of the second group are a piriform jar (No. 13) and a stirrup vase (No. 12). There are no open bowls or drinking vessels of any kind among the vases of either group.

All the vases seem to be assignable to Late Helladic III; none of them need be dated in Late Helladic I–II. The vases of the first group (Nos. 1–11) cover a wide range in probable date within Late Helladic III, from the earliest phase of it, Late Helladic III A 1, to Late Helladic III C.

This does not mean that the vases of this group could not all have come from the same tomb, since many Mycenaean chamber tombs are known to have been used for burials over an extended period of time. Over half of the eleven vases of the first group, six in all (Nos. 2, 5, 8–11), appear to be of Late Helladic III A 1. The probable date for two of the three square-sided alabastra (Nos. 6 and 7) is Late Helladic III A 2–B, and for the jug (No. 1) it is Late Helladic III B 1. Two of the three squat alabastra (Nos. 3 and 4) seem to be the latest vases in the group and to date from early in Late Helladic III C. The two vases of the second group (Nos. 12 and 13) are best assigned to Late Helladic III A 2.

Without an analysis of the clay from which they are made, it is only possible to guess where the vases are likely to have been found. The appearance of the vases of the first group, however, is not inconsistent with a source of manufacture in the Argolid, and the types can mostly, it seems, be paralleled from sites there. But in many other areas, such as Attica, Boeotia, and Achaia, Mycenaean tombs are known to have been discovered in the past; and the vases of both groups might have come from one of these or from elsewhere. Mrs. Susan Sherratt has suggested to me that the Late Helladic III C squat alabastra, and especially the shape of No. 3, may point to Achaia as the area from which the first group of vases came.

CATALOGUE

1. Narrow-necked jug with handle attached below rim (figs. 1–2).
Beveled rim; torus base. Complete and unbroken, except

I am very grateful to the J. Paul Getty Museum for inviting me to be a Visiting Scholar during the winter of 1981–82 and to Dr. Jiří Frel for bringing these vases to my attention and asking me to study and publish them. Dr. Frel and Miss Marit Jentoft-Nilsen kindly arranged for the excellent photos of the vases to be taken by the museum's Photographic Department. The drawings were made by Martha Breen Bredemeyer. I am much obliged to Mrs. Susan Sherratt for suggestions about the interesting Late Helladic III C squat alabastra (Nos. 3 and 4).

Abbreviations other than those in normal use in the Journal:

Asine	O. Frödin and A.W. Persson, *Asine, Results of the Swedish Excavations 1922–1930* (Stockholm, 1938)
BMA	E.J. Forsdyke, *Catalogue of the Greek and Etruscan Vases in the British Museum I, Part 1, Prehistoric Aegean Pottery* (London, 1925)
FLMV	A. Furtwängler and G. Loeschcke, *Mykenische Vasen* (Berlin, 1886)
Mycenae ChT	A.J.B. Wace, *Chamber Tombs at Mycenae (Archaeologia 82)* (Oxford, 1932)
MP	A. Furumark, *The Mycenaean Pottery, Analysis and Classification* (Stockholm, 1941)
Papadopoulos 1979	T.J. Papadopoulos, *Mycenaean Achaea (Studies in Mediterranean Archaeology 55)* (Göteborg, 1979)
Perati	S.E. Iakovidis, Περατή (Athens, 1970)
Prosymna	C.W. Blegen, *Prosymna* (Cambridge, 1937)
Tiryns V, VI, VIII	U. Jantzen, *Tiryns V* (1971), VI (1973), VIII (1975) (Mainz am Rhein: Philipp von Zabern)

Figure 1. No. 1. Narrow-necked jug. Malibu, The J. Paul Getty Museum 81.AE.61.10.

Figure 2. No. 1 from above.

Figure 3. No. 2. Squat alabastron. Malibu, The J. Paul Getty Museum 81.AE.61.8.

for slight chips and a crack on the body. Height 16.1 cm. Diameter of body 13.5 cm, of rim 4.8 cm.

Surface orange-buff, smoothed; decoration in lustrous red-brown: thin band around inside of rim; band below top of rim outside; band around neck, continuing down top of handle which is therefore solid; wide band around base of neck. Shoulder with six "Mycenaean III flowers." Three wide bands below these but above the belly; one wide band on the lower part of the body. The vase corresponds to *MP* shape 120 with a range of LH III A 2–B, but it is smaller than average. The Mycenaean III flowers on the shoulder belong to varieties current in LH III B according to Furumark (cf. *MP* motif 18 nos. 128–132): they are all of the same type but show a considerable variation in detail. Flowers of a comparable type appear to be at home at Mycenae at the time of the destruction identified by E. French as dating from LH III B 1, which is the earlier of the two destructions there in LH III B (*BSA* 61 [1966] 218 fig. 1:17f.; 62 [1967] 160 fig. 10:8).

Probable date: LH III B 1.

2. Squat alabastron with three handles (figs. 3–5).
Broken, but virtually complete. Height 7.5 cm. Diameter of body 14.4 cm., of rim 6.7 cm.
Surface orange-buff, well smoothed; cf. No. 11. Decoration in lustrous red-brown: rim solid, band around top of

shoulder, handles solid. Standard Mycenaean rock pattern on body, with bold quirks above in the spaces between the handles. Base with three sets of concentric circles.

The vase seems to correspond to *MP* shape 84 assigned to LH III A 1, and the decoration is in harmony with this date. The continuous rock pattern on the body belongs to Furumark's Rock Pattern I, as *MP* motif 32 no. 5, with a range of LH I–III B. Motifs comparable with the quirks in the spaces between the handles are regularly associated with this type of rock pattern on alabastra of *MP* shape 84. The design on our vase is closest to *MP* motif 13 no. 6, assigned to LH III A 1. Furumark derived motifs of this kind from the Ogival Canopy of LH II; but they seem more likely to be descended from the seaweed associated with rock-work on Cretan LM I B Marine Style vases, as suggested by Forsdyke under *BMA* 1041. The earliest known Aegean vases of the squat alabastron shape assignable to LM I B (or LH II A if they were made on the Greek mainland) include some with Marine Style decoration that incorporates rock-work and seaweed (e.g. Phylakopi on Melos: *BSA* 17 [1910–11] 15, pl. 11, no. 137, regarded as an import from Crete. Egypt: *BMA* 651, which may also be Cretan in spite of claims for a mainland origin).

There are a number of close parallels for the shape of the Getty vase with decoration of a similar kind from sites in

Figure 4. No. 2 from below, showing rings underneath base.

Figure 5. Drawing of the rim of No. 2 by Martha Breen Bredemeyer.
Scale 1:1.

Figure 6. No. 3. Squat alabastron. Malibu, The J. Paul Getty Museum 81.AE.61.6.

Figure 7. Side view of No. 3.

Figure 8. Drawing of No. 3 by Martha Breen Bredemeyer. Scale 1:2.

the Argolid, including Mycenae itself: Mycenae, Atreus bothros deposit, datable to LH III A 1 (*BSA* 59 [1964] 247f., 244 fig. 1:2, pl. 69 [b]). *Asine* 413, no. 27b, assigned by Furumark to shape 84 dated LH III A 1. Argos, Aspis hill (*BMA* 1041, assigned by Furumark to shape 84 dated LH III A 1). *Prosymna* I 445 and II fig. 431 no. 159, from Tomb II. Also comparable, *Prosymna* II fig. 454 nos. 112, 117, from Tomb III; fig. 260 no. 627, from Tomb XXXIV Cist IV; fig. 367 no. 898, from Tomb XLII; fig. 712 no. 49, from Tomb XIII, assigned by Furumark, *MP* 657, to shape 84 but with a date in LH III A 2 *early*. Cf. Berbati: G. Säflund, *Excavations at Berbati 1936–1937* (Stockholm, 1965) 32 fig. 15 no. 3. Argos: J. Deshayes, *Argos – Les Fouillles de la Deiras* (Paris, 1966) pl. xc:5, bottom right. Athens: P. A. Mountjoy, *Four Early Mycenaean Wells from the South Slope of the Acropolis at Athens* (Ghent, 1981) 28 fig. 13 no. 144, assigned to LH III A 1.

Concentric circles are regularly found under the bases of squat alabastra and vases of allied types from the beginning of LH III (Wace, *Mycenae ChT* 158, 171; Blegen, *Prosymna* I 420).

Probable date: LH III A 1.

3. Squat alabastron with three handles (figs. 6–8).
Broken but complete except for chips missing from rim. Height 7.3 cm. Diameter of body 9.8 cm, of rim 4.8 cm. Surface orange, smoothed, but not as well as in the case of No. 2. Decoration in lustrous red-brown: rim solid, wide band around neck. Bold stemmed spirals crudely painted on the body in the spaces between the handles; the stems of the spirals continue on the tops of the handles. A large tassel under each handle. Underneath of base undecorated.

The vase appears to correspond to *MP* shape 85 of LH III A 2–B date and to some of the examples listed under *MP* shape 86 assigned to LH III C 1 *early*. The tassels below the handles are *MP* motif 72 no. 7, characteristic of LH III C 1 according to Furumark, and the careless rendering of the spirals is consistent with a date in LH III C rather than earlier. A squat alabastron from Mycenae resembling No. 3 in shape and also with three handles (*FLMV* pl. xliv:118) is listed by Furumark as LH III C 1 (*MP* shape 86 no. 1). Tassels appear in the same position under the handles of a squat alabastron from Achaia comparable in size and shape to No. 3 (Papadopoulos 1979, 207 fig. 130 [d] PM. 339); but the tassels here are akin to those of *MP* motif 72 no. 6 assigned by Furumark to LH III B, and the vase is dated by Papadopoulos in LH III B 2.

Probable date: LH III C *early*.

4. Squat alabastron with two handles (figs. 9–11).
Complete and unbroken except for half of rim and one handle missing; some damage to the side below the missing handle. Height 6.5 cm. Diameter of body 8.3 cm, of rim 4.3 cm.

Like No. 3 in shape but rather better made. Surface orange, smoothed, cf. No. 3. Decoration in lustrous red: rim solid, three thin bands around top of shoulder, handles solid. A pair of solid semicircles on each side in the spaces between the handles, with two wide bands below. Underneath of base undecorated.

The vase resembles No. 3 in shape, except that it was provided with two instead of the more usual three handles. An alabastron covered with a red wash, apparently from the area of Mycenae, is similar in shape and has two handles but is somewhat larger than No. 4; it is dated by Furumark in LH III B (*BMA* 1053. *MP* shape 85 no. 7). Even more comparable perhaps was an alabastron with two handles but with the rim missing, assignable to LH III C from Tomb 16 of the Kolonaki cemetery at Thebes (*ADelt* 3 [1917] 166 no. 10, 163 fig. 121:8). Another LH III C alabastron found with this (*ibid.* 106 no. 11) is taller and different in shape, as are three alabastra with rounded bodies from the LH III C cemetery at Perati in Attica (*Perati* II 207 fig. 79A nos. 484, 898, 1093).

The decoration on No. 4 with pairs of solid semicircles is LH III C in character (cf. *MP* 345, fig. 58, motif 43: Isolated Semicircles: Late [III C] Series: a). When solid semicircles appear on the shoulder of a squat alabastron like No. 4, it is tempting to believe that they must be connected in some way with continuous rock pattern of the kind found on our No. 2 and standard on vases of this type throughout earlier Mycenaean times into LH III B (*MP* motif 32: Rock Pattern I no. 5). An alabastron from Achaia, also apparently with only two handles and comparable in shape to No. 4 although a good deal larger, has a rock pattern which might be regarded as a transitional stage in the direction of solid semicircles (Papadopoulos 1979, fig. 128 [i] PM. 18): the humps of the rock pattern on this piece are separated from each other instead of forming continuous waves as on our No. 2; the vase is dated by Papadopoulos 1979, 199, to LH III B 2. Another alabastron from Achaia of taller shape with three handles is decorated with isolated solid semicircles like No. 4: both Vermeule and Papadopoulos assign it to late in LH III C (E. Vermeule, *AJA* 64 [1960] 8 no. 18. Papadopoulos 1979, 202 figs. 134 [d], 234 [c], 235 no. 9 for the decoration, PM. 153).

Probable date: LH III C *early*, like No. 3.

5. Squat jar with angular profile (square-sided alabastron) (figs. 12–14).

Three handles; beveled rim; rounded base. Complete and unbroken, except for one handle and a small part of the rim missing; some damage to the sides, which are cracked in places. Height 10.5 cm. Diameter of body 14 cm, of rim 8.2 cm.

Surface buff, well smoothed, cf. No. 2. Decoration in lus-

Figure 9. No. 4. Squat alabastron. Malibu, The J. Paul Getty Museum 81.AE.61.7.

Figure 10. Reverse of No. 4.

Figure 11. Reconstruction drawing of No. 4 by Martha Breen Bredemeyer. Scale 1:2.

Figure 12. No. 5. Squat jar with angular profile (squaresided alabastron). Malibu, The J. Paul Getty Museum 81.AE.61.5.

trous red-brown: rim solid inside and outside, apart from the beveled top, which was left plain except for a thin band along the middle. The shoulder decorated with a rather careless lattice pattern (*MP* motif 57: Diaper Net no. 2) below three thin horizontal bands. Handles solid. Wide bands around the carinated top and bottom of the sides, with four thin bands in the space between them. Three sets of concentric circles underneath base.

This vase seems to correspond to *MP* shape 93 with usually tapering sides current in LH III A 1 rather than to the later version (*MP* shape 94) with concave sides as Nos. 6 and 7. The lattice pattern on the shoulder is very characteristic. For examples of this shape with similar decoration assignable to LH III A 1, see, e.g., Nauplia (*FLMV* pl. xv:95); Skinokhori also in the Argolid (*BCH* 47 [1923] 218f., 222f. fig. 37 right, from Tomb E); Thebes (*ADelt* 3 [1917] 83 nos. 1–2 fig. 59, from Ismenion Tomb 2); Trypa in Euboia (G. A. Papavasileiou, Πέρι τῶν ἐν Εὐβοίᾳ Ἀρ-

χαίων Τάφων [Athens, 1910] 23, 27 fig. 18). A vase from the Profitis Ilias cemetery at Tiryns is comparable in shape and has exactly the same system of decoration (*Tiryns* VI 34 pl. 15:2, Grave IV no. 1). Some vases from Prosymna are also comparable in shape and decoration (*Prosymna* I 446 fig. 572 no. 1188, from Tomb LI. Cf. *ibid.*, fig. 357 no. 771, from Tomb XLI). For the shape and system of bands decorating the sides compare also the Atreus bothros deposit at Mycenae dated to LH III A 1 (*BSA* 59 [1964] 248, 244 fig. 1:1).

Probable date: LH III A 1.

6. Squat jar with angular profile (square-sided alabastron) (figs. 15–17).

Three handles; beveled rim; base rounded with a slight sinking in the center. Unbroken and complete, except for chips from one of the handles. Height 5.9 cm. Diameter of body 8 cm, of rim 4.2 cm.

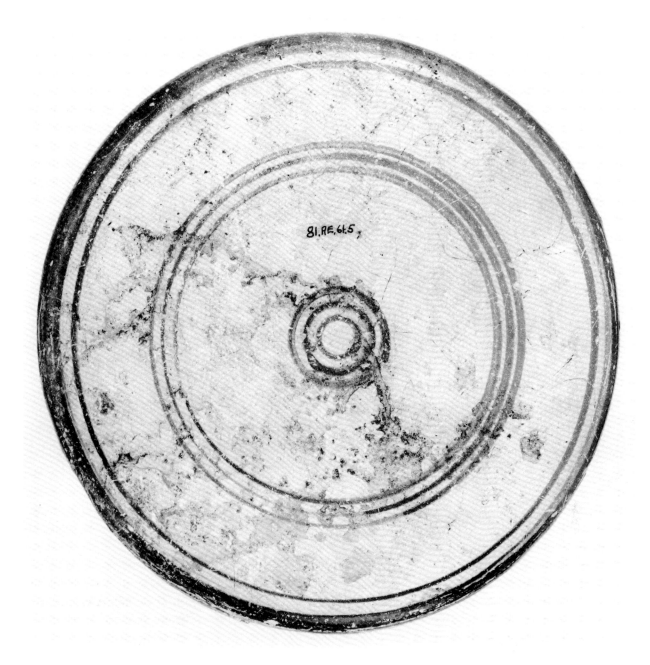

Figure 13. No. 5 from below, showing rings underneath base.

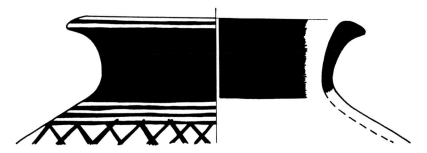

Figure 14. Drawing of the rim of No. 5 by Martha Breen Bredemeyer. Scale 1:1.

Figure 15. No. 6. Squat jar with angular profile (square-sided alabastron). Malibu. The J. Paul Getty Museum 81.AE.61.4.

Figure 18. No. 7. Squat jar with angular profile (square-sided alabastron). Malibu, The J. Paul Getty Museum 81.AE.61.3.

Figure 16. No. 6 from below, showing rings underneath base.

Figure 19. No. 7 from below, showing rings underneath base.

Figure 17. Drawing of the rim of No. 6 by Martha Breen Bredemeyer. Scale 1:1.

Figure 20. Drawing of the rim of No. 7 by Martha Breen Bredemeyer. Scale 1:1.

Surface orange, smoothed. Decoration in red-brown: rim solid inside and outside, apart from a reserved strip along the beveled top. The shoulder decorated with groups of vertical lines below a pair of thin horizontal bands. Handles solid. Wide bands around the carinated top and bottom of the concave sides, with a group of three thin bands in the space between them. A set of four concentric circles rather carelessly drawn in the center of the underneath of the base.

This vase with its concave sides corresponds to *MP* shape 94 current in LH III A 2 and LH III B. The simple decoration on the shoulder as *MP* motif 64 no. 21 is derived by Furumark from the Foliate Band of earlier times and dated by him to LH III A 2–B. A vase of this shape from Achaia with comparable decoration is assigned by Papadopoulos to LH III B 1 (Papadopoulos 1979, 210 fig. 137 [d], PM. 467.

Probable date: LH III A 2–B.

7. Squat jar with angular profile (square-sided alabastron) (figs. 18–20).

Three handles; rounded rim; base rounded. Unbroken and complete, except for one handle missing. Height 7.1 cm. Diameter of body 8.8 cm, of rim 4.3 cm.

Orange clay; surface with a buff slip, smoothed but rather worn. Decoration in red-brown to red: rim apparently painted solid. The shoulder decorated with groups of parallel diagonal lines flanked by pairs of thin bands above and below. Handles solid. Wide bands around the carinated top and bottom of the concave sides, with three thin bands (two above and one below) in the space between them. Two sets of concentric circles underneath base.

This vase resembles No. 6 in shape and decoration, but is somewhat larger and has a rounded instead of a beveled rim.

Probable date: LH III A 2–B.

8. Small handleless jar (figs. 21–22).

Rounded to beveled rim; concave-splaying neck; flat base. Unbroken and complete except for a small chip missing from the rim. Height 9 cm. Diameter of body 10.1 cm, of rim 5.8 cm. Surface orange, smoothed.

Decoration in red-brown: rim painted solid on top and outside, but left plain inside. Four thin neat bands above a wide band on the shoulder corresponding to four similar thin bands flanked by wide bands around the base; the body in the space between covered with stipple pattern.

This vase corresponds to *MP* shape 77 dated by Furumark to LH II B – III A 1. E. French, *BSA* 59 (1964) 247, observes that the shape is not known to occur in LH III A 2. But C. Mee, *Rhodes in the Bronze Age* (Warminster, 1982) 15 pl. 12:4, suggests that one from New Tomb 51 in the Ialysos cemetery on Rhodes with a more globular body

Figure 21. No. 8. Small handleless jar. Malibu, The J. Paul Getty Museum 81.AE.61.13.

Figure 22. Drawing of the rim of No. 8 by Martha Breen Bredemeyer. Scale 1:2.

than the Getty vase but with similar stipple decoration from its associations should be LH III A 2 rather than LH III A 1 in date. Closely comparable to our No. 8 in shape are three vases assigned by Furumark to LH III A 1: *Mycenae ChT* 71, 151 pl. xxxiii no. 9, from Tomb 517; *BMA* 755, from Enkomi in Cyprus; *Asine* 297 fig. 205:1. Examples of this shape were recovered from the Atreus bothros deposit at Mycenae dated to LH III A 1, and it was noted that the large number decorated with stipple pattern was very striking (*BSA* 59 [1964] 247, 244 fig. 1:5). Papadopoulos 1979, figs. 124–126 illustrates many vases of this shape from Achaia: one of these (*ibid.* 203 figs. 126 [a], 231 [a], [f], PM. 170) assigned to LH III A 1 is close to No. 8 in shape and has similar decoration. Compare also vases from Palaiokhori in Kynouria (*ADelt* 9 [1924–25, pub. 1927] 18, 19 fig. 4, third from left); Kopreza in Attica (F. Stubbings, *BSA* 42 [1947] 47 pl. 12:7); Chalkis in Euboia (V. Hankey, *BSA* 47 [1952] 74 pl. 22 no. 471); Tolo on

Figure 23. No. 9. Small handleless jar. Malibu, The J. Paul Getty Museum
81.AE.61.11.

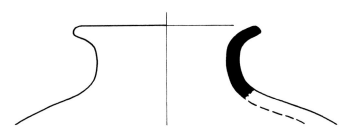

Figure 24. Drawing of the rim of No. 9 by Martha Breen
Bredemeyer. Scale 1:2.

Rhodes (*Clara Rhodos* 6–7 [1932] 49 fig. 46, left).

The stippling on the body of No. 8 corresponds to *MP* motif 77 no. 2, which Furumark thought was copied from a fresco pattern, probably representing sands. Another suggestion is that the stipple motif of decoration originated from the imitation of the surface of an ostrich egg (e.g. Forsdyke, under *BMA* 635, in connection with a vase of this shape but with stipple pattern as *MP* motif 77 no. 1). Vases made from ostrich eggs, especially it seems rhyta for libations, were used in Crete in Late Minoan I and on the Greek mainland in early Mycenaean times. Jars like our No. 8 may be descended from copies in clay of such

ostrich-egg vessels. A derivation from ostrich-egg vessels is suggested by Blegen in the case of a pair of vases of this shape with stipple pattern from Tomb XVIII at Prosymna (*Prosymna* I 58, 405f., 416 figs. 109, 110, 669 nos. 210, 219): Blegen describes these as rhyta, but it is not entirely clear from his account that either of them had a hole in the base.

Probable date: LH III A 1.

9. Small handleless jar, like No. 8 but larger (figs. 23–24). Concave neck; base roughly flat. Complete and unbroken, except for chips on body and parts of rim missing. Height 12.4 cm. Diameter of body 12.6 cm, of rim 5.2 cm. Surface orange, apparently without a slip, well smoothed.

MP shape 77, current in LH II B and LH III A 1. For a vase of this shape with a comparable plain finish but much smaller in size, see V. Hankey, *BSA* 47 (1952) 70 pl. 22 no. 454, from Chalkis in Euboia.

Probable date: LH III A 1.

10. Small handleless jar (figs. 25–26).
Like No. 8 but of depressed globular somewhat biconical shape. Neat flat-topped rim; splaying neck; base slightly hollowed. Complete and unbroken, but with surface

Figure 25. No. 10. Small handleless jar. Malibu, The J. Paul Getty Museum
81.AE.61.12.

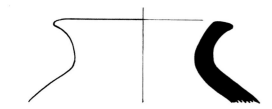

Figure 26. Drawing of the rim of No. 10 by Martha Breen
Bredemeyer. Scale 1:2.

rather worn in places. Height 9.3 cm. Diameter of body 9.9 cm, of rim 4.9 cm.

Surface coated with a lustrous red-brown wash, continuing on top of rim (but not inside rim and not under base).

MP shape 77, like Nos. 8 and 9. Some handleless jars of depressed globular shape and with an overall wash like No. 10 appear to come from late LH III B and LH III C contexts (e.g. *Tiryns* V 69 pl. 38 no. 37; *ibid.* VIII 67 pl. 47 no. 38, about the same size as our No. 10 and rather comparable in shape but with a heavier rim, dated by context to LH III B – C 1. Cf. *Perati* I 191 no. 493 pl. 56a, from Tomb 56, which looks comparable in shape but is somewhat smaller and has a heavier rim and ring base). It has

indeed been suggested that the tendency toward a biconical shape of this kind is a sign of late development (*Tiryns* V 69). But there are also earlier examples of small handleless jars of this general shape. One that looks very close in shape to our No. 10 and has a similar kind of rim, although it is smaller in size and is described as handmade, comes from the Ayios Ilias cemetery at Tiryns, where it was evidently found in association with the earlier burial in the grave pit on the north side of Tomb VII along with vases assignable to LH II B or LH III A 1 at the latest (*Tiryns* VI 49 – 51 fig. 6 pl. 26:2, Tomb VII no. 2). The seven small handleless jars of comparable depressed globular shape illustrated by Papadopoulos from Achaia are all similarly dated by him in LH III A 1 (Papadopoulos 1979, 202 PM. 156, 157; 203 PM. 167, 168; 207 PM. 333; 212 PM. 692; 219 AM. 22): the three of these which seem closest in shape to No. 10 are said to have a monochrome wash (Papadopoulos 1979, 202 fig. 124 [b], PM. 157; 203 fig. 126 [k], PM. 168; 212 fig. 126 [i], PM. 692).

Probable date: LH III A 1.

11. Small handleless jar (figs. 27–29).

Comparable in shape to No. 8, but with a rather irregular

Figure 27. No. 11. Handleless jar. Malibu, The J. Paul Getty Museum 81.AE.61.9.

Figure 28. No. 11 from above, showing holes in shoulder and decoration.

Figure 29. Drawing of No. 11 by Martha Breen Bredemeyer. Scale 1:2.

flat-topped rim, slightly spreading collar neck, raised hollowed base, and six small holes (each approx. 3 mm in diameter) at fairly regular intervals high on the shoulder. The holes were made before the vase was decorated and fired: traces of paint are visible running down inside some of them. Complete and unbroken except for a few small chips from the body. Height 7 cm. Diameter of body 8.4 cm, of rim 4.4 cm.

Surface orange-buff, well smoothed, cf. No. 2. Decoration in lustrous red-brown: rim solid, with four bands around the neck and the top of the shoulder. On the upper part of the body, four pieces of "sacral ivy" with triple stalks, above three bands. Base solid with a band above.

This vase does not exactly correspond to any shape listed by Furumark in *MP*. It is reminiscent of a class of early handleless jars decorated with "sacral ivy" and perhaps intended for ritual use. These jars are comparable to our No. 11 in size, but their mouths are narrower and their necks are concave or splaying like those of Nos. 8 – 10 (e.g. *Prosymna* I 401, II fig. 664 no. 1001, with "sacral ivy" akin to *MP* motif 12 nos. 9 and 10 dated by Furumark in LH II A. Cf. *ibid*. I 68f., II fig. 137, top left, from Tomb WI, the first excavated by Sir Charles Walston). At least one of these vases from Prosymna (no. 1001) has a hole through the base suggesting that it was used as a rhyton for libations.

Dr. Elizabeth French has kindly drawn my attention to some jars with holes in their rims from wells at Athens dated to LH II B – III A 1 (P. A. Mountjoy, *Four Early Mycenaean Wells from the South Slope of the Acropolis at Athens* [Ghent, 1981] 19 nos. 3 – 5 fig. 3 pl. 1:b, from Well E; 35 no. 212 fig. 19, from Well Z). The holes in this case were evidently meant for tying lids in place over the jar mouths; but they are set just below the tops of the rims, not in the shoulder as on No. 11. Moreover, the jars themselves are considerably larger in size and of a rather different shape,

Figure 30. No. 12. Stirrup vase. Malibu, The J. Paul Getty Museum 81.AE.61.2.

Figure 31. Reverse of No. 12.

with two horizontal handles on the shoulders, as well as being of a totally different fabric (plain burnished ware).

The holes on the Getty vase, however, certainly look as if they were meant to help in tying something in place over the open mouth. Set as they are in the shoulder they are wrongly situated for securing a lid. Perhaps what was tied in place over the mouth was a membrane, and the vessel was a small drum intended for ritual use. This would explain the "sacral ivy" decoration on it, and would be in harmony with its resemblance to a class of probable rhyta as noted above. A clay drum of this kind seems to be exceptional if not unique in the repertory of Mycenaean pottery; but drums of clay, although of a different shape, are attested before this in Anatolia (e.g. S. Lloyd and J. Mellaart, *Beycesultan* II [London, 1965] 12, 93, 97 fig. P. 8:17, pl. VI [*a*]. Cf. *ibid.* 117, 121).

The curve-stemmed ivy with triple stalk on No. 11 is akin to *MP* motif 12 nos. 25–27 assigned to LH II B – III A 1. The actual leaves are very much like those in the design on a jug from Nauplia dated by Furumark in LH III A 1 (*BMA* 784. *MP* motif 12 no. 12).

Probable date: LH III A 1.

12. Small squat false-necked jar (stirrup vase) (figs. 30–32). Raised base. Complete and unbroken. Height 8 cm. Diameter of body 10.5 cm.

Surface orange, well smoothed. Decoration in dark red-brown: top of false spout with a solid blob inside a circle; tops of handles solid; bands around top and bottom of spout. Upper part of shoulder decorated with five "sea anemones" consisting of open circles with strokes radiating from them; three of the circles have an inner ring of

Figure 32. Side view of No. 12.

dots; a half circle at the back of the vase between two of these has a ring of dots around the outside; a fill motif consisting of parallel lines decreasing in size is adjacent to the third dot-filled "sea anemone" on the front of the vase to the left of the spout. The lower part of the shoulder is decorated with six neat thin stripes flanked by wide bands; there are four similar stripes flanked by wide bands on the lower part of the body, and a band around the base with a thin stripe above it.

The vase seems to be closer to *MP* shape 178 at home in LH III A than to shape 179 characteristic of LH III B. The blob inside a circle on top of the false spout corresponds to *MP* motif 41 no. 12, assigned to LH III A – B.

Figure 33. No. 13. Piriform jar. Malibu, The J. Paul Getty
Museum 81.AE.61.14.

"Sea anemones" of one kind or another (*MP* motif 27)
are not infrequent as decoration on the shoulders of small
Mycenaean stirrup vases throughout LH III and into LH
III C (e.g. Papadopoulos 1979, figs. 210 – 211, from Achaia.
Cf. *BSA* 62 [1967] 160 fig. 10:19; 64 [1969] 77 pl. 18 [a] no.
18: both from Mycenae, and dated to LH III B; *Perati* II 165
fig. 35, assignable to LH III C). The outer circles of
radiating lines of the "sea anemones" on the Getty vase
suggest that they are not far removed in time from examples listed by Furumark as LH II – III A 1 (*MP* motif 27 nos.
11–13). But four "sea anemones" resembling the two
without an inner ring of dots on No. 12 appear on the
shoulder of a stirrup vase of more globular shape assigned
by Papadopoulos to the beginning of LH III C (LH III C 1
a) (Papadopoulos 1979, 208 figs. 110 [d], [e], 210 [f], PM.
388). There is an isolated example of the same motif on the

shoulder of another stirrup vase from Achaia dated by
Papadopoulos in LH III B 2 (Papadopoulos 1979, 208 figs.
91 [d], [e], 210 [e], PM. 402).

Fill ornament consisting of parallel lines decreasing in
size, like the isolated motif on the shoulder of No. 12,
appears among argonauts dated by Furumark to LH III A
2 *late* (*MP* motif 22 no. 13). A number of such fill ornaments are the only decoration on the shoulder of a stirrup
vase from Achaia resembling No. 12 in shape and similarly
dated to late in LH III A 2 (Papadopoulos 1979, 204 figs.
116 [b], 202 [a], 209 [f], PM. 232).

Probable date: LH III A 2.

13. Small conical piriform jar (three-handled amphora)
(fig. 33).
Beveled rim; three horizontal handles; hollowed splaying
base. Complete and unbroken, except for chips from rim
and half of one handle missing. Height 8.1 cm. Diameter
of body 6.9 cm, of rim 4.3 cm, of foot 2.9 cm.
Soft fabric; pale orange clay. Decoration in dark red-
brown: rim solid inside and outside, apart from a reserved
strip along the beveled top (cf. No. 6); tops of handles
solid. Three thin stripes around the top of the shoulder,
above groups of diagonal lines flanked by wide bands in
the handle zone. Below the handle zone, two stripes above
a wide band. Outside of base solid, with three stripes and a
wide band above.

This is an unusually small example of *MP* shape 45 common in LH III A 2 – B. A good many vases of this shape
have simple decoration of this kind (*MP* motif 64 no. 21)
on the shoulder (e.g. *Mycenae ChT* 91 pl. xlv no. 7, from
Tomb 525, assigned by Furumark [*MP* shape 45 no. 2] to
LH III A 2 *late*: larger than No. 13 but with a comparable
scheme of decoration. Cf. *Tiryns* VI 34 pl. 15:3, from the
Profitis Ilias cemetery, Tomb IV no. 3. *Prosymna* I 447, II
fig. 714 no. 18, from Tomb XI; fig. 134 no. 369, from Tomb
XXII; fig. 174 no. 296, from Tomb XXIV; fig. 256 no. 644,
from Tomb XXXIV; fig. 473 no. 924, from Tomb XLIII.
Chalkis in Euboia: V. Hankey, *BSA* 47 [1952] 82 pl. 21 no.
532 Gamma. Achaia: Papadopoulos 1979, 206 fig. 121 [f],
PM. 325).

Probable date: LH III A 2.

Great Milton
Oxford

Mass Production and the Competitive Edge in Corinthian Pottery

J. L. Benson

When I undertook in my dissertation to analyze the factors which led to the decline of the Corinthian ceramic hegemony[1] of the late seventh-early sixth centuries B.C., I could not have foreseen that I would experience the principal factor in a most personal way, through being chosen, about a decade later, to complete the study[2] of the vast pottery finds from the Potters' Quarter in Corinth itself, which Agnes Stillwell had begun. That principal factor was "mass production"—a new experience for the Mediterranean world and possibly for all of mankind. One might see the ceramic production of Mycenae as a kind of dry run for this, but that may have lacked the geographical concentration and above all the element of industrial competition which existed between Corinthian and Attic entrepreneurs.

In considering such phenomena we must try to avoid the danger of reading too much of the mentality of our own times into the practices of early times. This has been stressed recently by A. Snodgrass[3] and must also apply to the operation of state coinage which I formerly thought of as a factor in the Corinth-Athens relationship. Nevertheless, it is obvious that some combination of factors, however little we can isolate them, did produce specialization in the ceramic industry; and this is inextricably connected with wide overseas distribution of the resulting products. The whole process can, and indeed I think must, be called mass production in the sense of a prototype of what that term means today. To quote Derry and Williams, "First at Corinth and later at Athens pottery manufactured for a wide overseas market achieved a degree of industrial concentration which almost rivals that of modern times."[4] This intensification was the means, or at least part of the means, by which Corinth and Athens respectively coped with problems in an industrial situation which had arisen between them. To what extent it was also a direct commercial situation there is no way of knowing, but in either case it is not amiss to recall that encouragement of the competi-

tive spirit was built into Greek culture in general through cultic games.

In a recent article[5] entitled "Corinth Kotyle Workshops" I reviewed the results of my study of the masses of kotyle fragments found in the Potters' Quarter at Corinth and tried to place the workshops specializing in this shape in the larger context, first of workshops represented by finds from Corinth elsewhere than the Potters' Quarter and then in the still larger context of workshops represented by finds from places outside ancient Corinth. That inquiry concentrated on Middle Corinthian production of kotylai, since it appears that one of the important decisions of Corinthian entrepreneurs in meeting the rising Attic challenge to their products in the late seventh century was to redesign the kotyle shape as an article for mass distribution. The modified shape bore a characteristic decoration of certain favored combinations of animals: mostly panthers and goats, with a liberal sprinkling of birds and *Mischwesen*. This systematization seems to have entailed a reduction in the number of artists who created quasi-luxury products (such as those of the Royal Library Painter) in favor of assembling a core of merely competent draughtsmen (in my dissertation I had isolated this movement in a very general way as *Gruppe des polychromen Skyphos*) to produce large quantities of kotylai. These artists in turn had around them imitators ranging from slightly less than competent to totally incompetent.

Those kotylai found in the city of Corinth by artists whose work is not represented specifically in the Potters' Quarter confirm the general impression that from the end of Early Corinthian onward the more distinguished artists only occasionally decorated this shape—possibly as a luxury article—while a class of less talented kotyle specialists plied their trade constantly.

Great numbers of kotylai have been found entirely outside of Corinth and even of Greece. The painters of some of these have been isolated, and they have everything in

1. *Die Geschichte der korinthischen Vasen* (Basel, 1953) 100–109.
2. *Corinth* XV,3 (forthcoming).
3. *Archaic Greece* (London, 1980) Ch. IV "Economic Realities," esp. 134–36, 145.

4. T.K. Derry and T.I. Williams, *A Short History of Technology* (Oxford, 1961) 78.
5. *Hesperia* 52 (1983) 311–326.

common with that group of Potters' Quarter painters characterized above as merely competent draughtsmen. Moreover, the greater number of these pieces are the work of imitators of the last mentioned. Because of the stifling mediocrity, or sub-mediocrity, of their work, it is difficult to sort it out in terms of connoisseurship.

On the basis of these results a certain amount of reasoning can be undertaken. First, the striking similarity of the finds at the Potters' Quarter and the finds outside of Corinth, particularly in the colonial cities of Magna Graecia, makes it likely that the latter originated essentially in the Potters' Quarter under the direction of the same entrepreneurs. This further confirms the Potters' Quarter as the heart of the Corinthian experiment with mass production.[6] These entrepreneurs took a large chance in solving the mass production problem by putting quality at total risk: nowadays we would call it working for the short-term advantage. The extent of the exports shows that it worked at first. But the precipitous decline in volume (and quality) of Late Corinthian I kotylai in the absence of any known external catastrophes (other than Attic competition) leaves us with no other probable conclusion than that the experiment failed for internal reasons: inspiration dried up at the source as the merely competent painters became bored with their routine tasks, while their hangers-on were such a shifting, unsteady lot that they could not survive alone. Thus we do not even have to ask whether the former customers of Corinth found something better; some had continued to buy wretched products as long as they were available, but even these were no longer there. The fact that the Corinthian ceramic industry tended to turn local after Late Corinthian I and developed patterned wares as a mainstay confirms this reasoning. It could not produce the figural vases which were still required, but Athens and a few other competitors could. From the first decades of the sixth century the industry at Corinth could not or did not invest in top quality artists with the imagination and ingenuity to meet changing market conditions, and thus craftsmen (or craftswomen) pure and simple who did—often fine—pattern decoration inherited the Potters' Quarter.

This is a seemingly merciless analysis based on one shape alone, and I am the first to admit that it needs supplementation and refinement from a study of other shapes. Yet the general outlines can hardly be wrong.

In order to pursue another line of reasoning it is now necessary to return briefly to the category of kotylai by artists whose works were found in the city of Corinth but not in the Potters' Quarter itself. First of all this is numerically a

Figure 1. Middle Corinthian export kotyle. Detail of bird. Malibu, The J. Paul Getty Museum 77.AE.57.

much smaller group, and, secondly, these artists *could* also have been employed at the Potters' Quarter. But they might not have been—a possibility which is strengthened by the potters' dump deposit found in the Anaploga Well, which is some fifteen minutes' walk from the Potters' Quarter. The editor of this material[7] stressed that the pottery contained in this dump differed "strikingly" from that of the Potters' Quarter and concluded that it was the spoiled work of "rather unpretentious artisans who catered to home trade." One must mention here also the site of Vrysoula, closer to the Potters' Quarter, even though what was found there points to a period long after the one in question.[8] What Anaploga and Vrysoula tell us is that conditions may have been favorable for small independent entrepreneurs to locate in various parts of the western section of the city. This circumstance, together with the fact that the entire region of the main Potters' Quarter can hardly be said to have been exhaustively explored by the excavations which took place there in the late 20's and early 30's, can tentatively offer refuge for any Corinthian style pottery—of any period—examples of which have not been documented at manufacturing sites in Corinth itself.

Nevertheless, this logically leads to another aspect: was everything which looks Corinthian necessarily made at Corinth? In order to introduce this problem, it seems appropriate to focus attention briefly on an actual example of the standard variety of Middle Corinthian export kotylai, one which has found its way into the collections of the J. Paul Getty Museum (figs. 1–3; 77.AE.57; presented by Gordon McLendon). It is complete except for minor restorations on the inside bottom of the base and a few places on the body. It has the characteristic light buff surface and chocolate brown, slightly lustrous paint of Corinthian

6. See n. 2.

7. *Corinth VII 2 Archaic Corinthian Pottery and the Anaploga Well* (Princeton, 1975) by D.A. Amyx and P. Lawrence, p. 69.

8. *Hesperia* 38 (1970) 265–307.

Figure 2. Malibu 77.AE.57. H: 13.5 cm.

Figure 3. Malibu 77.AE.57.

wares—lighter brown in places but generally even—enhanced decoratively with red applied to parts of the animal representations. It is decorated with the standard kotyle-formula "squiggles" in the handle zone, upward rays at the foot, and a frieze bordered by two heavy circumferential lines above and below. In the frieze is a grazing goat, left, flanked by standing panthers. A bird, right, occupies the rest of the space and forms a kind of pendant to the goat as the two creatures face off at opposite sides of the frieze. The tight interlocking in the arrangement of the animals is underlined by the carefully incised rosettes and blobs placed in the field to create a fairly dense background pattern.

The total effect, especially when one sees the original colors, is quite pleasing. The rather prominently horizontal shape, emphasized by the frieze, is balanced by the rays and, above all, the squiggles, which provide a dynamic vertical quality. The drawing of the animals, economical of effort through their elongation, is nevertheless neat and careful, as are the amply spaced rays. Quite apart from whatever religious overtones the animals may have carried for the people of ancient times, the sheer visual effect makes this a product of which no factory need be ashamed, despite its modest artistry.

Further interest attaches to the identification of the kotyle. It is by an artist whom I designate as the Painter of Taranto 50284 and is to be added to four attributions listed in my *Hesperia* study.[9] These latter kotylai were all found in Taranto itself, but the style of their painter is rather closely related to that of one of the Potters' Quarter Well I inner core of artists, viz., the Painter of KP 17. Two works by the latter were found in the Potters' Quarter but none among exported materials. Probably the best, certainly the easiest, explanation for this situation is that

these two painters were benchmates in the Potters' Quarter, so that the finding of works by one only in Italy and works by the other only at the place of manufacture is due simply to chance. In fact, there can be no doubt that the Painter of Taranto 50284 at least *learned* his craft in the Potters' Quarter.

Nevertheless, we may also recall that from time to time Italian scholars have isolated a few vases among the legions in Corinthian style found at Taranto as being of local manufacture; the shapes vary from kotylai to an oinochoe.[10] In general this hypothesis seems to have arisen from a notion of inferior quality, exactly the factor which we have isolated as a fatal tendency operating in the Potters' Quarter. Since there is as yet no guaranteed native ceramic school with which to compare the suspected vases, the suspicions themselves remain subjective. This is not to say that a renewed study from this viewpoint of the large number of Corinthian vases found in Taranto would not be worthwhile, but there is simply no way to verify the hypothesis as it now stands. Yet, if one takes the find places of the works of the Painter of KP 17 (Corinth) and of those of the Painter of Taranto 50824 (Taranto) at full face value, another admittedly slim possibility arises.

From this evidence one could construct a scenario in which not the poorest nor oddest vases of Corinthian style were made in Taranto by local botchers—for the excavations at Corinth prove that the Potters' Quarter had its own share of botchers—but in which Corinthian vases of decent style were made at Taranto. By this account the painter of Taranto 50284 might have been sent to Taras by one of the Potters' Quarter entrepreneurs to open or oversee a branch establishment. If, indeed, there was such an establishment, *some* Corinthian artists must have gone there *in corpore*, for none of the kotylai I saw there has any

9. Cf. n. 5, p. 325.
10. R. Bartoccini, *NSc* (1936) 133; C. Drago, *NSc* (1940) 321 and fig.

12; F.G. LoPorto, *ASAtene* 21-22 (1959-60) 188.

characteristics that set them off from the great mass of Potters' Quarter kotylai. In favor of the plausibility of such a hypothesis is the fact that the group of artists I am referring to as the Well I associates (including the Painter of KP 17) have demonstrable connections with Taras, whereas there is no demonstrable pattern of this kind involving any other Potters' Quarter groups with any other Italian cities. Admittedly, this statement rests on material which can constitute only a small fraction of the numbers of objects actually in commerce; but with that proviso it can generate some reasoning about the likelihood of its being valid.

Taras had a good port and perhaps always tended to foster industrial as much or more than agricultural activities.[11] If the Corinthians were looking for a convenient transshipping point for their wares, they could hardly have found a more conveniently located one. It was closer than their own colonial dependency Syracuse and better suited as a first station for overland transport of their products to any of the Italian and Etruscan markets. Being Dorians, the Tarantines would perhaps have had a predisposition to admire Corinthian products; in any case they obviously siphoned off a goodly part of the imports for their own use and thus avoided further transportation charges that must have accrued to more distant buyers. It would help in our interpretation if something could be said about the effect of politics on Corinthian industry and shipping. One is, for example, tantalized by the legend of Demaratos.[12] If such a person did actually relocate in Etruria, that would show that upper class Corinthians with energy and imagination did on occasion go to Italy for political reasons. Such a person might well have opened a branch factory in Taranto by hiring a few competent artists away from the Potters' Quarter.

However speculative this may be, there are scarcely any technical impediments to the idea. The building of appropriate kilns could certainly have been managed by a few transplanted technicians. The shipment of clay should have been possible; in any case the acquisition of just the right kind of clay is generally a first consideration with pottery makers. Entrepreneurs, whether tribes, towns, or industrialists, have never refused to contemplate whatever efforts are necessary. Various examples of this could be given,[13] but the rather extreme one of Josiah Wedgwood's importation of clay from North Carolina will amply demonstrate the point.[14] Again, artists with their brushes and paints can certainly move around if the inducements are right.

It is only at this point that certain doubts begin to arise in my mind. Comparable situations in the history of the decorative arts suggest that artists or artisans who leave their motherland and work in a colony soon betray the effect of the new environment in their work, whether in the exact way materials are handled or subtle nuances in the way they treat styles. Examples of this can be found in the American colonies of the seventeenth century. While a *particular* artifact made in the colonies could be difficult to distinguish from its European counterpart, a group of such artifacts taken together will certainly be distinguishable, and this will only heighten as time goes on and a local tradition begins to form.[15] I am inclined to believe that if a Corinthian branch had existed in Taras from, say, 600/590 to about 570 B.C. some "Tarantine" characteristics would manifest. Admittedly, the routine level of style in what might have emerged locally might make these hard to distinguish. But I do not think that a strong case can be made at present. Particularly in the case of the Getty kotyle, my intuition is that it is a genuine product of the Potters' Quarter. Let future research that takes into account more subtle factors than we have been accustomed to in the past decide!

University of Massachusetts at Amherst

11. So J.B. Bury, *A History of Greece* (New York, Modern Library n.d.). How much this applies to the middle Archaic period can hardly be known.

12. Cf. C. Ampolo, "Demarati Osservazioni sulla mobilità sociale arcaica," in *Dialoghi di Archeologia* IX–X (1976–77) 333–345. Particularly interesting in this connection are the small bronzes considered to be of provincial Corinthian style which may have been manufactured at Taras: cf. T.J. Dunbabin, *The Western Greeks* (Oxford, 1948) 290.

13. Examples of this cited by C. Singer, J. Holmyard, A.R. Hall, *A His-*tory of Technology* I (Oxford, 1954) 406.

14. Anthony Benton, *Josiah Wedgwood* (New York, 1976) 68. After importing five tons of "Cherokee Clay," which he found to be just what he wanted, Wedgwood nonetheless found no way around immense shipping costs and gave up using it. The authors mentioned in n. 13 point out (p. 409) that sea-transport was expensive in antiquity.

15. For a close study of how this worked in furniture, cf. J.T. Kirk, *American Furniture and the British Tradition to 1830* (New York, 1982).

Giants at the Getty

Mary B. Moore

In Greek mythology, there is no divine battle more important than the one between the Olympian gods and the giants who challenged them for the supremacy of the universe. Born of Earth (Gaia), these aggressive upstarts fought long and hard before Olympian might prevailed to banish them forever.[1] In literature, giants are mentioned as early as Hesiod, who describes them as the offspring of Earth,[2] and the story of their battle with the Olympians may have been known this early as well.[3] In Greek art, the earliest representations appear on Attic vases during the latter part of the second quarter of the sixth century B.C.[4] Though all surviving early examples are fragmentary, they depict large battles with most of the Olympians present and share certain features. Most notable are the following: Zeus, thunderbolt in raised right hand, mounting his chariot drawn by four horses who gallop to right over a fallen giant; Herakles in the chariot leaning forward, his left foot on the chariot pole, about to finish off the fallen giant with one of his arrows; Athena striding alongside the team toward one or two opponents. In three scenes, Gaia begs Zeus to spare her sons.[5] The rest of the gods and their giants are arranged to right and left of the central group. These early examples have enough in common with one another to suggest that they are based on a single prototype. They were all dedicated on the Athenian Akropolis shortly after the Panathenaic Games were reorganized in 566 B.C. Part of the ceremonies of this festival in honor of Athena, which took place every four years, was to drape the cult statue of the goddess with a new peplos. Woven into this garment was a composition showing the gods fighting giants, and it is tempting to think that these early examples from the Akropolis reflect this composition.

Recently, the J. Paul Getty Museum acquired a fragmentary Attic black-figure dinos that depicts a large Gigantomachy in its main zone with the names of most of the figures inscribed in red letters.[6] Below the battle is a lotus-palmette-festoon, and below that is a frieze of animals. Then comes a zone of black glaze and, on the very bottom, a reserved medallion decorated with a whirligig whose reserved segments alternate with ones painted either black or red. Above the Gigantomachy on the shoulder there is a tongue pattern, and on the topside of the mouth, a chain of palmettes. A dinos is a large handleless bowl with a low, slightly overhanging rim and a rounded bottom that fits into a stand. Fragments of the stand for this dinos (not illustrated) have also survived. The inside of the receptacle is glazed. The outside of the rim is decorated with a border of esses between a torus molding top and bottom. The stand contracts until it reaches a flat, projecting disc, then there is a spherical pommel and another disc. The pommel has a lotus-palmette-festoon, the same ornament that appears between the Gigantomachy and the animal frieze on the bowl. Below the pommel, the stand widens, and on what remains of the spread of the foot are two zones of animals: 1) siren (body, legs, outspread left wing, start of right wing) and feline (body, legs), both to right; 2) feline (tail) to left, swan (neck, body) to right, facing a goat (muzzle, most of left foreleg and right hind leg missing). A thick torus foot supported the stand.

Jiří Frel has attributed this dinos and its stand to the Tyrrhenian Group, several painters who flourished during the second quarter of the sixth century B.C.[7] These painters stand somewhat apart stylistically and iconographically from their contemporaries, among whom are

I wish to thank Dr. Jiří Frel, Curator of Antiquities at the J. Paul Getty Museum, for inviting me to publish this dinos. I studied the fragments first hand when I was a Guest Scholar at the museum in March 1983, and for this opportunity I wish to thank Dr. Laurie Fusco, Director of Academic Affairs. I also wish to thank Evelyn B. Harrison and Joan R. Mertens for discussing with me the various problems that arose in reconstructing the composition. Thanks, as always, go to Dietrich von Bothmer for allowing me to write much of the text in his department and to consult his photo archive.

1. The basic bibliography for the Gigantomachy is still the two monographs by Francis Vian: *Répertoire des gigantomachies figurées dans l'art grec et romain* (Paris, 1951) and *La guerre des géants. Le mythe avant l'epoque hellénistique* (Paris, 1952).

2. Hesiod, *Theog.* 183.

3. Vian, *La guerre*, p. 184.

4. Akropolis 1632 c-d (Graef, *Die antiken Vasen von der Akropolis zu Athen* [Berlin, 1925-33] pl. 82); Akropolis 2134 and Akropolis 2211 (both, Graef, pl. 94).

5. *Supra* n. 4.

6. Accession number 81.AE.211; a fragment was reproduced by D. Williams in *Greek Vases in the J. Paul Getty Museum. Occasional Papers in Antiquities* 1 (Malibu, 1983) 34, fig. 36. See also p. 13.

7. *ABV* 94-105; *Para.* 34-43.

Figure 1. Attic black-figure dinos, fragment *a*. Malibu, The J. Paul Getty Museum 81.AE.211. H: 22 cm.

Kleitias, Nearchos, Lydos, and the young Amasis Painter. To judge by the proveniences of their vases, painters of the Tyrrhenian Group worked almost exclusively for the Etruscan market.[8] The shape preferred by these painters is the ovoid neck amphora, though they have left us one or two examples of other shapes: column kraters, hydriai, dinoi, an oinochoe, and a plate. The Tyrrhenian painters were imaginative artists who enjoyed endowing their figures with exaggerated postures and bold gestures and using liberal amounts of decorative incision and accessory red and white. The effect is quite different from the

restrained results achieved by their companions working in the Athenian Kerameikos.

Twenty-five fragments preserve part of the figured decoration of the dinos that is the subject of this study. Examination of these fragments yields enough information to calculate the height and circumference of each decorated zone and to make a reconstruction drawing of both the Gigantomachy and the animal frieze. The procedure was first to establish the basic measurements, then to ascertain the sequence of the animals. Here, the spacing between the units of the lotus-palmette-festoon was helpful in deter-

8. Here are two exceptions: a fragment found in the Kerameikos in Athens (*ABV* 104, 122) and Akropolis 696 (*ABV* 104, 125).

Figure 2. Malibu 81.AE.211, fragment *b*. Max. L: 7.3 cm.

Figure 3. Malibu 81.AE.211, fragment *d*. Total H: 7 cm.

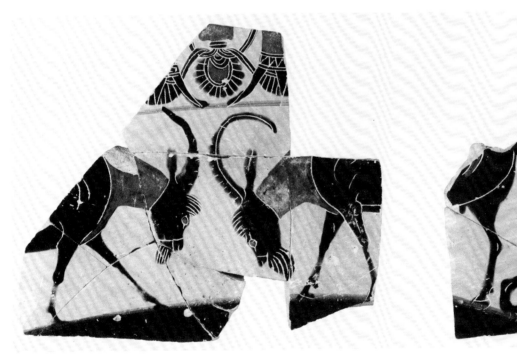

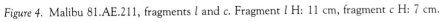

Figure 4. Malibu 81.AE.211, fragments *l* and *c*. Fragment *l* H: 11 cm, fragment *c* H: 7 cm.

Figure 5. Malibu 81.AE.211, fragment *e.* H: 14.5 cm.

mining the position of several fragments. Working upward from the animals allowed me to reconstruct on paper most of the Gigantomachy composition. Other criteria besides the animal frieze and the lotus-palmette-festoon that helped to ascertain the position of the Gigantomachy fragments were the character of the glaze on the inside, the lines left by the potter's fingers, and the color of the glaze on the outside, which in places misfired slightly. Still, there is one gap in this zone where there simply was not enough information from the dinos itself nor adequate parallels to enable me to draw a plausible composition. In the drawing, the perimeter of each fragment is indicated by a dotted line. The height of the Gigantomachy frieze is 9.5 cm. Its upper circumference is 1.00 m; its lower 1.30 m. The height of the animal zone is 6.5–7.0 cm. Its upper circumference is 1.28 m; its lower 1.11 m. The height of the lotus-palmette-festoon is 5.0 cm. In order to avoid distortion of the figures, I have "stretched" each frieze so that its top and bottom lengths are the same. Thus, the animal frieze was "stretched" at the rate of 1.0 cm every 7.5 cm to equal 1.30 m, and the Gigantomachy 1.0 cm every 13.0 cm to equal 1.30. The results appear in foldout illustration 1.

I shall begin with the large fragment (*a*: fig. 1) that preserves parts of four animals: a boar to left between panthers, and a bull. Of the left panther, only its chest and part of the left foreleg remain here, but a small fragment (*b*:

fig. 2) preserves its ears and the top of its head, while a third (*c*: fig. 4) gives its body and hindquarters. The head and most of the neck and shoulders of the right panther are lost. Fragment *d* (fig. 3) preserves a bit of its neck. On the far right of fragment *a* are the hindquarters and tail of a bull to right. Accessory red is applied to the chests and necks, ribs, markings on hindquarters, and the eye of the boar. The lowered head of the bull is preserved on the next fragment (*e*: fig. 5) where it confronts a second bull whose hindquarters are not preserved. The missing parts of each bull are reconstructed from what remains of the other. Eyes, necks, ribs, and markings on hindquarters are covered with accessory red. Next comes a panther confronting a ram (*f*: fig. 6). Much of the body, all of the legs, and part of the tail of the panther are missing. More of the ram (belly, hind legs, scrotum) appears on fragment *g* (fig. 7), as well as the left hind leg of a lion to right who confronts a boar. Fragments *h-k* (fig. 8) give more of these two: hindquarters, tail, part of the body, and the forelegs of the lion; the neck, shoulder, part of the body, and forelegs of the boar. Accessory red is applied to necks and manes, markings on hindquarters of the lion, and the eye of the ram. The positions of these fragments are provided chiefly by the amount of space required for the missing parts of the beasts, but the placement of some of them may be double-checked by the spacing necessary for the units of lotus-palmette-festoon. The length of the boar on *h-k* is also estimated by the size of the boar of fragment *a* (fig. 1). The last animals in our frieze are two confronted goats that appear on fragment *l* (fig. 4), which preserves their heads, necks, and foreparts, and on fragment *c* (fig. 4), which shows the hindquarters and tail of the right goat. Eyes, necks, and markings on the right goat's hindquarters are covered with accessory red. The animal frieze, then, is composed of eleven beasts (ill. 1): a boar between panthers; two confronted bulls; a panther facing a ram; a lion facing a boar; and two confronted goats.

I began the reconstruction of the Gigantomachy with the group directly above the boar between two panthers on fragment *a* (fig. 9), for here the two figured friezes are linked by the lotus-palmette-festoon, and thus the position of the human figures is certain. At the very top of fragment *a* there is the lower right quadrant of a round shield emblazoned with a Gorgoneion and to its right, both feet and the left greaved calf of a giant who has fallen backward to the right. The greave and the face of the Gorgoneion are white. Fragment *m* (fig. 10) gives the upper left quadrant of the shield, most of the right arm, and part of the right thigh of the giant to whom it belongs, and much of Herakles, his opponent. The hero's face above his mouth, his right forearm and hand, part of his torso, all of his right leg, and the left leg from the knee down are miss-

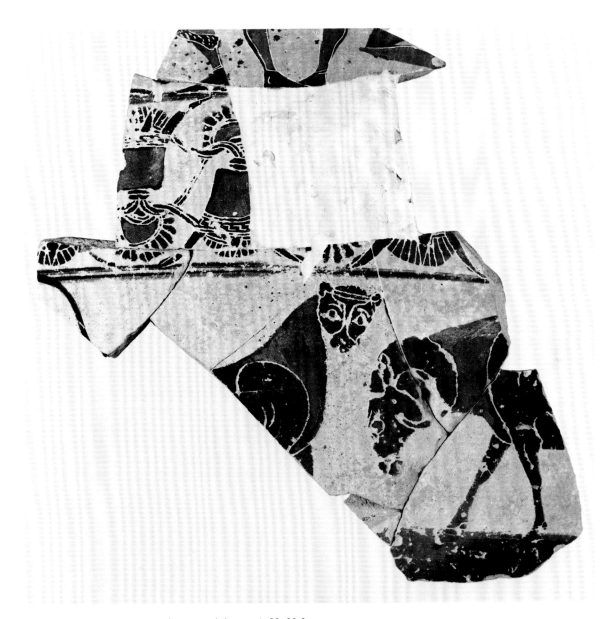

Figure 6. Malibu 81.AE.211, fragment *f* (bottom). H: 23.3 cm.

Figure 7. Malibu 81.AE.211, fragment *g*. H: 5.2 cm.

ATHENA   HERAKLES   ZEUS

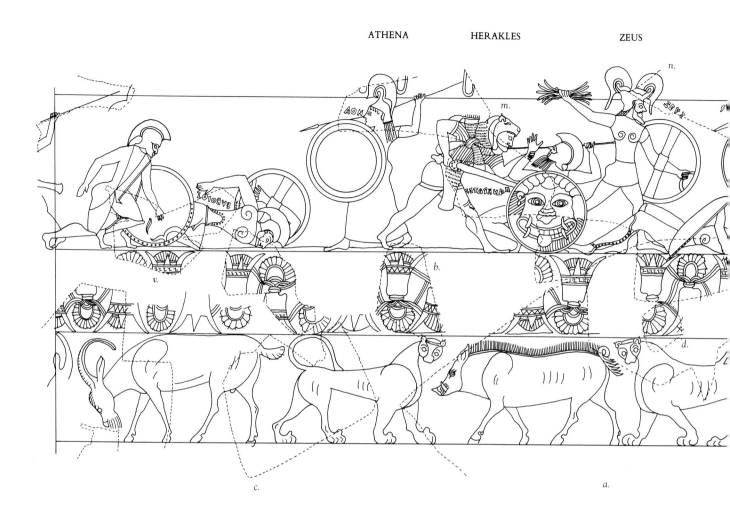

Illustration 1. Reconstruction drawing of dinos by the author.

POSEIDON   DIONYSOS   ARES   HERMES   APOLLO   ARTEMIS

Figure 8. Malibu 81.AE.211, fragments *h–k*. H of bottom fragment (*j*): 6 cm.

ing. Clad in a short white chiton under his lionskin, a quiver full of arrows projecting above his right shoulder, Herakles strides to right, a large sword with a red blade in his right hand, his left seizing his opponent by the wrist. The name of this giant is inscribed: ΠΑΝΚΡΑΤΕS, retrograde. Though falling backward and very much on the defense, Pankrates is still armed, for just a bit of the shaft of his spear drawn in dilute glaze appears at the break in front of Herakles' mouth and beard. An oddity is that Pankrates does not hold his shield. Apparently, he released his grip on it when Herakles bore down on him. Between Pankrates' raised forearm and the rim of his shield, at the break, are traces of red that look like the ends of a long beard.[9] If so, then his head is probably thrown backward, the position for which I have opted. If the interpretation of this small bit of added red is correct, it gives this giant a much longer, shaggier beard than those of the other giants preserved in this composition. Athena appears in back of Herakles striding to left, spear poised, her round shield held on her left arm. White dots decorate

its rim, and part of its exterior is red. The head of the goddess, protected by a high-crested red helmet, and her right arm remain on this fragment; on fragment *b* (fig. 2) at the very top is one foot, probably her right. Her flesh was covered with accessory white which has flaked. In front of her face appear the last three letters of her opponent's name:]ΑΟΝ. Nothing of him is preserved (see *infra*).

Fragment *d*, which gives a bit of the neck of the panther to the right of the boar, is, like fragment *a*, linked to the Gigantomachy frieze by the lotus-palmette-festoon. At the top of fragment *d* (fig. 3), there is more of the fallen giant whose feet and greaved calf appear on the right of fragment *a*: part of his left buttock and his torso protected by a corslet, also part of his round shield seen in profile. White dots decorate its rim; the rest of it is red. Just to the left of the shield is the foot of a male to right that we shall see belongs to Zeus. The high crest of the Olympian's helmet, together with a bit of its crown, appears on the very left of the next fragment, *n* (fig. 11). The crown and the front half of the crest are red; the back half and the tail are black,

9. The bits of red are too high to be blood.

Figure 9. Malibu 81.AE.211, fragment *a* (detail). H: 22 cm.

Figure 10. Malibu 81.AE.211, fragment *m*. Max. L: 13 cm.

Figure 11. Malibu 81.AE.211, fragments *n–p*. Max. L: *n* 9.2 cm, *o* 6.2 cm, *p* 5.1 cm.

probably because of the manner in which the crest over-laps the tongues above. To the right of the helmet, Zeus' name is inscribed: **IEVꞄ**. The position of the helmet crest with its tail hanging down suggests that the god's head faced to left, but the left-to-right direction of his name as well as the narrative content indicate otherwise. It would make no sense for him not to look directly at the two giants who confront him with spears poised. Therefore, Zeus should stride to right, and confirmation of this inter-pretation is given by fragments *a* and *d* (figs. 1 and 3), each of which preserves one foot of the god. The foot on frag-ment *d*, mentioned above, is probably the god's left foot, the one with which he leads. The toes of his right foot may be seen on fragment *a* between the rim of Pankrates' shield and the left foot of the fallen giant. The only way to

explain the position of Zeus' helmet crest, which would normally belong to a helmet worn by someone who faces to left, is that this is a helmet with a double crest. A good parallel for this may be seen on an unattributed ovoid neck amphora in the Louvre which shows a large Giganto-machy (fig. 21).[10] Here, Zeus, his name inscribed, strides to left wearing a double-crested helmet, his thunderbolt aimed at two giants, one of whom also has a double crest on his helmet. They rush in to rescue a fallen companion, and the composition shares certain affinities with the one on our vase. Equipping Zeus with a double-crested helmet increases his stature and gives him the importance he deserves. I suggest that in addition to his thunderbolt, he also carried a shield which would nicely fill the space above the fallen giant.

10. Louvre E 732 (Vian, *Répertoire*, pl. 22, no. 96).

11. For this type of cheekpiece, cf. G.S. Korre, Τὰ μετὰ κεφαλῶν κριῶν κράνη (Athens, 1970).

12. Cf. Apollodorus I, 6, 2. For Polybotes as the opponent of Poseidon, cf. Vian, *La guerre*, 77–79.

13. For a good photograph, cf. P. de La Coste-Messelière, *Dèlphes*

(Paris, 1943) fig. 83; or R. Lullies, *Greek Sculpture* (New York, 1957) fig. 46.

14. Beazley, *Development*, 43; *ABV* 107, 1. Pausanias VIII, 32, 5 and 36, 2 mentions a giant by this name who was friendly to Rhea when she was pregnant with Zeus and feared that Kronos would attack her.

15. Here are just a few examples: the long legs of the second warrior

The first of Zeus' two attackers appears on the right of fragment *n*. Only his face, colored red, and a little of the ram's horn cheekpiece of his helmet remain,[11] along with a small part of his round shield and the end of his spear. The small bit of glaze next to the last tongue divider at the break above is not part of a black tongue because there is a little of the reserved ground between it and the break. It is more likely that this represents the tip of the helmet crest. The rim of his shield is white, then comes a broad circle, followed by a very narrow one of white dots. This giant's name is Polybotes (ΠΟLVƁΟΤΕꙄ, inscribed in red, retrograde). He traditionally fights Poseidon who crushed him to death with a huge rock broken off from Kos that later became the island Nisyros.[12] In the lower right of the fragment at the break is the red rim of a round shield belonging to Polybotes' companion. More of Polybotes' shield and his left leg protected by a red greave appear on fragment *o* (fig. 11). What remains of the center of his shield is white with incised lines that look like they might represent feathers, in which case the device could be an eagle.

In the lower left corner of fragment *o* is a curved black form with incised contour that represents the helmet crest of the fallen giant; to the left of Polybotes' leg are the last three letters of his name ꟼΜΑꙄ. From what remains of this giant, it seems that he should prop his shield with his left arm, that his right arm was raised above his head, similar to that of a giant carved some decades later on the north frieze of the Siphnian Treasury.[13] His eyes were probably closed, or nearly so, as death draws near. His name may have been Hopladamas, a name Beazley suggested for the giant being speared by Apollo on fragment *c* of the big dinos by Lydos, Akropolis 607.[14] The crowding of the last two letters of his name on the Getty fragment suggests that the name was a long one that probably began close to the rim of his shield. Hopladamas would fit quite well here. More of the shield of Polybotes' companion and his left leg, its calf encased in a white greave, appear at the top and on the right of fragment *o* respectively. His shield is emblazoned with a whirligig, its elements alternating white, red, white, black, white. In the lower right corner of fragment *o*, just above the groundline, is a bit of glaze with incision that looks like the hand of a fallen giant. Fragment *p* (fig. 11) preserves the head and raised right forearm with spear of Polybotes' companion. This giant's face is black (his eye is red) and he wears a cap (mostly red) decorated with a spiral that projects in back. At the break, just in front of

his face at eye level, is a trace of red that may be the end of the tail of Polybotes' helmet crest. Were there more space between him and Polybotes, it might be part of this giant's name, but this can hardly be the case; thus the end of the helmet crest seems a surer interpretation.

The amount of space between the group of Zeus and his giants and the next section of the Gigantomachy frieze that is preserved may be calculated by working upward from the animal frieze. On fragment *a* (fig. 1), the animal frieze ends with part of the hindquarters and tail of a bull to right. The lowered head of this bull appears on fragment *e* (fig. 5) where it confronts another that is preserved except for its hindquarters. The missing parts of each bull may be reconstructed from what is preserved, and the amount of space they take up is confirmed by the amount of space required for the units of the lotus-palmette-festoon above. At the top of fragment *e* lies a giant who has fallen to left. Part of his head, the start of each arm, his torso, and legs to the knees remain. He wears a low-crested helmet, a red corslet over a short chiton, and red greaves. A sheathed sword is suspended from a baldric over his right shoulder. The small bit of glaze in the lower right corner of fragment *o* (fig. 11) that looks like the hand of a fallen giant probably belongs to this one. This makes his right arm very long, but such deviations from proper human scale occur elsewhere in the work of the Tyrrhenian Group.[15] The fallen giant's left arm was raised and surely held a shield for protection. On the far side of this giant is the greaved (red) lower left leg of a companion who comes in to help, and the lower part of his shield appears just above the fallen giant's buttocks. The segment of its rim does not seem quite circular, so I have opted for a Boeotian shield, the type normally reserved for heroes but which occurs a little further on in the frieze for both gods and giants (see *infra*). The presence of the companion coming in to help implies an Olympian opponent directly in back of the giant who is the companion of Polybotes and wears the cap with the projecting spiral. I suggest a god here rather than a goddess, for in this Gigantomachy the gods outnumber the goddesses by a large margin.[16] (Here, only the presence of Athena and Artemis [see *infra*] may be accounted for.) Nothing is preserved of this necessary, but hypothetical, god. I suggest that he is Poseidon, since Zeus, Dionysos, Ares, Apollo, and Hermes appear elsewhere. He is unlikely to be Hephaistos, for usually he has bellows or tongs and fights near his forge;[17] there is not

from the left on the reverse of Berlin 1704, the name piece of the Kyllenios Painter (*ABV* 96, 14; *Para.* 36, 14); Polyxena on London 97.7-27.2 by the Timiades Painter (*ABV* 97, 27; *Para.* 37, 27); the disparate scales of the figures on Villa Giulia 74989 attributed by Bothmer to the Prometheus Painter; the fallen figure on the amphora in the Tokyo market attributed by Bothmer to the Castellani Painter

(Sotheby's, 1–2 October 1969, pp. 92–93, lot 89); or some of the figures on the Louvre dinos, E 875 (*ABV* 104, 123).

16. The only goddesses that appear for certain are Athena and Artemis. Of the male deities, Zeus, Dionysos, Ares, Hermes, and Apollo are accounted for, all but the last with his name inscribed.

Figure 12. Malibu 81.AE.211, fragment *f* (top). Joins with fig. 6. H: 23.3 cm.

space enough in this part of the composition for bellows and a forge. Thus, Poseidon seems to be the best choice, and this may be strengthened by his proximity to Dionysos, who appears in the next section, for in other mid-sixth-century Gigantomachies that depict a large battle with most of the Olympians present, the two appear near one another.[18] In these battles, Poseidon is equipped with his trident and holds Nisyros on his left arm, about to hurl it at his adversary. This is likely to be the way he appeared in the Getty composition.

The amount of space between the group of this fallen giant and the next section may be determined once again by working upward from the animal frieze, this time from

fragment *f* (fig. 6), which shows a panther confronting a ram. Directly above is a large section of the Gigantomachy that shows Ares (inscribed in red: APEⳌ) attacking a giant who is almost down on one knee (fig. 12). In back of Ares, Oranion fights Dionysos (both names inscribed in red: OPANION and ΔIONVⳌOⳌ). Below Dionysos' name is part of a large snake (its upper jaw and beginning of its neck). More of this snake (a bit of its body with white underbelly, its lower jaw with beard, and its red forked tongue) as well as parts of two others appear on fragment *q* (fig. 13). This fragment also preserves the left forearm and hand of Dionysos holding a large black snake, part of a panther attacking Oranion, a little of this giant's torso protected by a red

17. For Hephaistos in archaic Gigantomachies, cf. Vian, *La guerre*, 90–92.

18. For the proximity of Poseidon and Dionysos, cf. Vian, *La Guerre*, 98. They appear near each other on the following vases, all from the

Akropolis: Akropolis 2211 (Graef, pl. 94; Vian, *Répertoire*, pl. 23, no. 104); Akropolis 2134 (Graef, pl. 94; Vian, *Répertoire*, pl. 25, no. 106); and Akropolis 1632 (Graef, pl. 84; Vian, *Répertoire*, pl. 23, no. 111).

19. For representations of the snake of Dionysos, cf. Akropolis 2211

corslet, the pommel of his sword and the start of its sheath, his round white shield seen in profile, and the tip of his spear aimed at Dionysos. At the very bottom of the fragment, at the break, is some accessory red, which is part of the greave covering Oranion's left calf. Fragment *f* (fig. 12) gives more of Oranion: his raised right arm with spear and his right calf encased in a red greave. This leg is attacked by a second feline, probably a lion; the part that remains, its right foreleg, is incised with short strokes to indicate a different sort of pelt from that of a spotted panther. Its head may have been turned around, about to bite Oranion. Just below Oranion's arm is more of the third snake, which has a spotted back and red underbelly divided by pairs of lines to indicate segments. More of this snake appears on fragment *q* to the left of the panther's neck and just beneath its belly. The curved object with incised contour, which appears just below Oranion's elbow, is not part of the snake but the flap of a quiver.

This is a very dense, complicated composition; it is rather difficult to figure out how each part, especially the snakes, ought to be reconstructed. Their appearance in the drawing may be just mere approximations of how they looked originally.[19] Dionysos was surely wreathed and wore a pantherskin over a chiton, his standard costume in the Gigantomachy, and he was very likely armed with a spear.[20] In spite of the ferocity of the feline and serpentine attack, Oranion has a remarkable amount of fight left in him.

On fragment *f* (fig. 12), all of Ares except for his right leg is preserved. He wears a high-crested Corinthian helmet that is red except for its crest; he also has red thigh guards and red greaves. He is armed with a spear, a sheathed sword, and a Boeotian shield seen from the inside, its interior covered with accessory red. His opponent is clad in a short chiton worn under a red corslet, red greaves, and a Corinthian helmet with a low crest colored red. A sheathed sword hangs at his left side, and he aims his spear at Ares while holding out his shield to try to ward off the Olympian's attack. In the upper right corner of fragment *f* is the raised right elbow of a giant who attacks Hermes.

Up to this point, the animal frieze has established the sequence of the gods and giants; so far about 75 cm, or more than half, of the Gigantomachy composition has been reconstructed. The sequence of the remaining 55 cm of this frieze and the positions of the rest of the Gigantomachy fragments were established in the following manner. After tracing each of these fragments, *r–v*, I reconstructed

Figure 13. Malibu 81.AE.211, fragment *q*. Max. L: 8.3 cm.

as much of each figure as possible. Fortunately, the figures are striding, falling, or fallen, so their postures could be established from others in the frieze. When these preliminary drawings were finished, it became clear that the remaining portion of the Gigantomachy ought to look more or less the way it does in illustration 1. In the discussion below, I shall continue the description from left to right.

The giant whose raised right elbow appears in the upper right corner of fragment *f* (fig. 12) should be one who strides purposefully to right, probably in a posture similar to that of Polybotes and his companion on fragments *n–p* (fig. 11). A little more of this giant appears on fragment *r* (fig. 14), which shows his upper torso protected by a white corslet and the start of his left arm holding his round shield seen in profile. The rim of the shield is red with white dots; the rest is red. This giant is coming to the rescue of a companion who is about to get the worst of it from Hermes. They appear on fragment *s* (fig. 15). Here, Hermes strides to left grasping firmly the incurving rim of his opponent's Boeotian shield as he prepares to thrust his spear into the giant's chest. The crown of Hermes' head, his right forearm, buttocks, and right leg are missing. An incised line in front of his forelocks just at the break represents the brim of his petasos. In front of his face is the beginning of his name inscribed in red: ΗΕⱤΜΕ϶, retrograde. The god wears a short chiton decorated with scales, a spotted nebris, and boots. Some of the scales are

and 1632 (*supra*, n. 18); also, Akropolis 607 by Lydos (*ABV* 107, 1; *AJA* 83 [1979], pl. 11, fig. 4 and ills. 1–2, opp. p. 99). An early fifth-century kyathos in Berlin by the Oinophile Painter (*ARV²* 333, 3; Vian, *Répertoire*, pl. 41, no. 373) shows one of Dionysos' giants fallen to the ground

with a very large snake twined around him.

Figure 14. Malibu 81.AE.211, fragment *r*. Max. L: 3.4 cm.

Figure 15. Malibu 81.AE.211, fragment *s*. Max. L: 8.4 cm.

large Gigantomachies, each Olympian fights one or at most two giants. Allowing Zeus to fight three giants as he does here is fitting, since he is the chief Olympian. But to show Hermes, who is not particularly warlike, fighting three giants and thus seeming to equal Zeus, does not seem quite acceptable. Therefore, I should like to insert a fallen giant as a foreground figure in the space between the giant being speared by Ares and the one attacked by Hermes and to suggest that he is a giant who has been slain by Ares. His appearance could be comparable to that of Hopladamas on fragments *d* and *o* (figs. 3 and 11).

In the lower right corner of fragment *s* (fig. 15) between the falling giant's greaved left calf and Hermes' boot, there is the booted foot of a god striding to right. The identity of this god as Apollo is made certain by what remains of the Gigantomachy on fragment *t* (fig. 16), a large rim fragment. On the left are the crests of two helmets belonging to a pair of gods who fight a giant named Ephialtes, for his head appears on the right of the fragment as well as his name inscribed in red letters: ΕΦΙΑΛΤ[ΕΣ, retrograde. Traditionally this giant is the opponent of Artemis and Apollo, the only Olympians who fight as a closely knit pair. Thus, they may be identified with the two helmet crests, and the booted foot on fragment *s* (fig. 15) would then belong to Apollo. He would be slightly in back of his sister, a sequence not often seen but which may be paralleled on a slightly later cup found on the Athenian Akropolis.[21] Each helmet crest is supported by a snake with an open, bearded mouth. Apollo's crest is white; Artemis' black, and the snake red. Apollo probably wore a short chiton, perhaps with a nebris over it; Artemis would wear a long chiton, possibly also with a nebris.[22] One would expect the pair to fight with bows and arrows, but if this were so, Apollo's bow would overlap Artemis' face and the result would be unpleasing. Therefore, I have equipped Apollo with a shield and spear, weapons that he uses in the battle painted by Lydos on the Akropolis dinos.[23] Artemis was surely armed with a bow and arrows, for not only would her bow fit nicely in the space in front of her, but also one of her arrows has found its mark in the chin of a giant further to the right. Ephialtes is bareheaded and may have been nude or clad in a short chiton. To help fill the space between him and the twins, I have given him a round shield, and he very likely had a spear. Just below the Ⴑ and Τ of his name, at the break, are small traces of accessory red with incision that are thus far unexplained.

Fragment *u* (fig. 17) preserves more of the opponents of

red, as are the god's face and boots. A sheathed sword hangs at his left side; his round shield, seen in profile and colored white, is suspended from a baldric over his right shoulder. All that remains of his opponent is part of his bent left leg and his right knee, which almost touches the ground. Red greaves protect his calves; his shield is red except for its rim.

This section of the composition, between the giant attacked by Ares and Hermes fighting his giants, looks a little empty without another figure, especially when compared with other sections of the battle, such as the one just discussed. Therefore there ought to be another figure, either a giant striding to right attacking Hermes or a fallen giant who has been vanquished by Ares. A review of how many giants each Olympian fights in this battle helps to answer the question of whether the giant should be an opponent of Ares or of Hermes: Zeus fights three giants; Poseidon two; Dionysos one; Ares one (certain); Hermes two; Artemis and Apollo four (two each). Normally, in

20. Cf. the example *supra* n. 18.

21. Akropolis 1632 d (Graef, pl. 84). Here, the pair moves from right to left.

22. On Akropolis 2134 b, Artemis wears a long chiton (Graef, pl. 94; Vian, *Répertoire*, pl. 25, no. 106). On the Akropolis dinos by Lydos (*ABV* 107, 1; *AJA* 83 [1979], pl. 12, fig. 6 and ills. 1–2, opp. p. 99), and on the

Figure 16. Malibu 81.AE.211, fragment *t*. H: 7.3 cm.

Apollo and Artemis. One is a giant named, oddly enough, Euphorbos, a name usually reserved for a Trojan hero. He has fallen flat on the ground, and all that remains of him are his calves (red greaves) and part of one arm bent at the elbow. Above this is all but the first letter of his name inscribed in red: Ε]ΥΦΟΡΒΟΣ. The end of the round shield seen in profile should belong to him. Two more giants, each armed with a spear and a Boeotian shield, rush in to assist Ephialtes. The head, torso, and feet of the leading one are missing; his companion's right forearm and leg are lost. The first three letters of his name remain, in red: ΟΡΑ[, another Oranion? Both giants wear red greaves. The left has white thigh guards and a cloak as well, and presumably he was helmeted. His shield is red but for its rim. A thin line between its rim and Euphorbos may be an arrow, and short brush strokes of added red that appear below the rim of the leading giant's shield look like streams of blood; thus he is wounded, though not mortally, given his strong, lively posture. The giant whose name is partly preserved wears a Corinthian helmet with a high black crest and cheekpieces edged with white dots, a red chiton

that has no skirt, and a white nebris. A sheathed sword is suspended from a baldric over his right shoulder. An arrow shot by Artemis is about to pierce his chin or mouth. On the far right of fragment *u* appears some black glaze next to accessory red that looks as if it should belong to a giant fighting from left to right.

At this point, considerable difficulties arise in working out the rest of the reconstruction; there is a space of about 15 cm between the giants who fight Apollo and Artemis on fragment *u* and the figure of Athena on the far left of fragment *m* (figs. 17 and 10). Fragment *v* (fig. 18) belongs in this space and preserves parts of two giants. The left giant stumbles and falls forward. His hand has loosed its hold on his round shield, which is seen from the inside and covered with added red except for its white grip and black rim decorated with white dots. The end of this giant's cloak (white with red borders) as well as part of his left thigh and calf with red greave, a bit of his right thigh, and his left fingers are all that remain. The next giant, Euboios, whose name appears above his torso inscribed in red (ΕΥΒΟΙΟΣ, retrograde), has fallen face downward. His right foot,

unattributed band cup from the North Slope (Vian, *Répertoire*, pl. 28, no. 144) she is clad in a long chiton with a lionskin worn in the manner that Herakles wears his. The presence of a helmet on fragment *t* rules out a

lionskin on our vase.
23. Akropolis 607 (*ABV* 107, 1; *AJA* 83 [1979], pl. 12, fig. 8 and ills. 1–2, opp. p. 99.

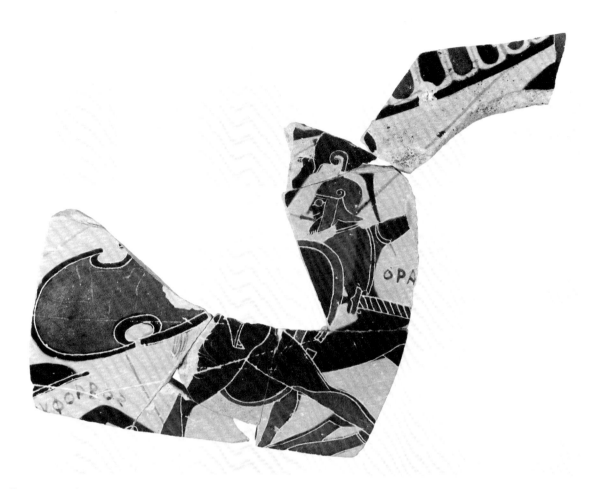

Figure 17. Malibu 81.AE.211, fragment *u*. Max. L: 11.8 cm.

thighs, greaved (red) left calf, torso protected by a red corslet, and part of his face remain. The rim of his shield, decorated with white dots, appears just to the right of his name and again next to his nose. Above his name at the break is a bit of glaze. The head of the stumbling giant was probably bent downward somewhat, and he very likely wore a helmet. Whether and how he held a spear is questionable. Considering the position of Euboios' torso and head, his left arm has probably released its grip on the shield. It is more difficult to determine the position of his right arm. For want of a better solution, I am opting for the possibility that it was simply raised and bent at the elbow.

This still leaves to be interpreted the black glaze next to the accessory red on the far right of fragment *u* (fig. 17) and the bit of glaze above the letters of Euboios' name on fragment *v* (fig. 18). These two problematic areas are best discussed in connection with two of our last three fragments, *w* and *x* (fig. 19). These are almost but not quite joining,

and the character of the glaze on the inside indicates that they belong in the section under discussion; but because I have not been able to fit them into the composition satisfactorily, I have drawn them separately, merely showing their relationship to one another and extending the lines a little outside the perimeter of the sherds (ill. 2). Fragment *w* preserves a raised forearm and hand that does not appear to hold anything. In back of it is a slender object terminating in a finial or knob that is partly covered with added white. This object looks a little like a scabbard, an interpretation that does not seem quite correct, however.[24] On the right of the fragment is part of an object, covered with added red, from which spring the heads of four snakes with open mouths. Fragment *a* gives more of the tongue pattern above the Gigantomachy and on the right, at the break, the tip of a snake's mouth.

If the arrangement of the fragments and their reconstruction presented above is correct, then this last section of the composition will show Athena fighting her giants.[25]

24. Compare the scabbard of the fallen giant on fragment *e* (fig. 5) or on fragment *f* (fig. 12).

25. For this central group, cf. Vian, *La guerre*, 96–97.

Figure 18. Malibu 81.AE.211, fragment *v*. Max. L of left fragment: 9 cm, right fragment: 7.9 cm.

The goddess' name does not appear, but her identity on the left of fragment *m* is assured because in the big battles she fights near Zeus and Herakles; here they appear to the right of her on fragments *m* and *n* with their names inscribed (figs. 10–11).[25] Zeus fights three giants, and it would make a pleasing composition if Athena did too. Two of her giants have already been conquered; and to justify the goddess' aggressive posture, she must have a threatening adversary. This is where the problem arises: how to include in the space available a fighting giant, and how to interpret and fill out fragments *w* and *x* as well as the problematic bits of glaze on fragments *u* and *v*.

The problems with the reconstruction of the figures in this space may perhaps be best understood by proceeding from left to right, beginning with the black glaze and accessory red on the far right of fragment *u* (fig. 17). The red looks like the edge of a helmet crest, and at first I thought that it and the black glaze belonged to a giant striding toward Athena; but this cannot be the case because such a figure would be overlapped too much by the stumbling giant on fragment *v* (fig. 18). Closer examination of the added red reveals that it stops just short of the break rather than continuing as it would have to if it were

a helmet crest. Next comes the small area of black glaze just above Euboios' name. This looks like it could be the knee of another giant who is stumbling (as a kind of pendant), but this small form is too high in the composition to be a knee. It could be the elbow of a fallen or falling figure, but it is difficult to link it with Euboios because his shield overlaps it; and one would not expect another fallen figure so close to him. As for the hypothetical giant fighting Athena, ideally one would like to see him as a back-up for his stricken companion, similar to Polybotes or to Poseidon's giant; but this is difficult to support, as we have seen. The last three letters of this giant's name appear,]ΛΟΝ, written right to left next to Athena's face. In view of this, one would expect to see him closer to his name.[26] Using one of the other striding giants as a model, it is impossible to insert a similar giant into the composition on the left-hand side of Euboios' shield, chiefly because part of his legs and feet would have to overlap the preserved background on fragment *v*, and there is no trace of a giant here.

This brings us to the two problematic fragments, *w* and *x*: what is represented on them and how do they fit into the composition? The raised forearm and empty hand

26. His name might be ΓΑΙΩΝ, misspelled, which is the name of Artemis' opponent on the late-fifth-century cup by Aristophanes in

Berlin (F 2531: *ARV*² 1318, 1; *Para.* 478, 1; Vian, *Répertoire,* pl. 43, no. 388).

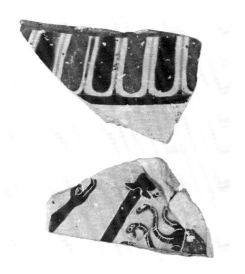

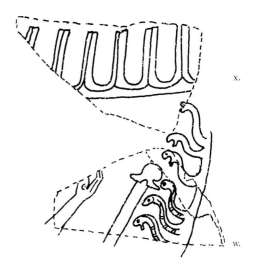

Illustration 2. Drawing of fragments *x* and *w* by the author.

Figure 19. Malibu 81.AE.211, fragments *x* and *w*. Max. L of top fragment: 5.3 cm, bottom fragment: 4.5 cm.

Figure 20. Malibu 81.AE.211, fragment *y*. Max. L: 3.8 cm.

ought to belong to a giant who is falling backward, at least to judge by its position in the frieze. It is difficult to make it the right arm of Euboios, for then the scabbard-like object and the snakes will overlap Athena's shield. Nor may one easily reconstruct Euboios holding the scabbard-like object. At first glance, the snaky object looks like it could be part of Athena's aegis, but there is no trace of this shawl over her right shoulder, and from what remains of Athena on fragment *m* (fig. 10), it is difficult to make this strange object into an aegis. The outer contour from which the snakes emerge is slightly concave, so this eliminates the possibility that the rim of her shield was fringed with snakes, as on Zeus' shield in the nearly contemporary Gigantomachy on the unattributed ovoid neck amphora in the Louvre (fig. 21).[27]

In the Gigantomachy, snakes appear in very specific places. Besides decorating Athena's aegis and on occasion threatening her adversary, only Dionysos has snakes, usually just one, yet in this battle he has three large ones. The shield of Zeus with its snakes on the Louvre amphora just mentioned (fig. 21) seems to be without another parallel in known representations of the Gigantomachy. In any case, our fragments with snakes cannot be associated with Zeus in this battle, because the tongue pattern between him and Polybotes is preserved.

Our last fragment, *y* (fig. 20), preserves part of a lotus and a palmette, and above it a bit of the figure decoration; exactly what is uncertain. The upper left corner is chipped,

and there is a bit of black glaze. Next to it are three vertical lines that might possibly be the end of the tail of one of Dionysos' snakes, perhaps the spotted one. The ornament below would fit in here, but this fragment could also fit in to the right of Ares, and for this reason I decided not to try to include it in a specific place in the reconstruction drawing.

This is a splendid big battle with most of the Olympians taking part. The composition does not follow the conventional one for this period, the second quarter of the sixth century, for Zeus and Herakles fight on foot, not from the god's chariot, and Athena fights to left instead of to right.[28] Clearly this painter was bold and imaginative in his conception of the battle.

Frel attributed the Getty dinos to the Tyrrhenian Group and saw that it was by the same hand as the fragmentary one in Ostermundigan (fig. 22), which Bothmer gave to the Kyllenios Painter.[29] It has the same system of decoration in its main zone as ours: figured frieze, lotus-palmette-festoon, animals. The drawing of the goat, especially the short incised lines that articulate the front contour of the horn, is nearly the same, and the face of the panther compares

27. Cf. *supra*, n. 10.

28. Cf. *supra*, n. 25.
29. *Para.* 42.

Figure 21. Attic black-figure ovoid neck amphora. Paris, Louvre E 732.

Figure 22. Fragmentary black-figure dinos. Ostermundigan, private collection.

well with the one on fragment ƒ (fig. 6). The boar on each vase has a double line between back and bristles and a pair of lines on its shoulder. The greater amount of incison on the Kalydonian Boar on the Ostermundigan dinos is due no doubt to its larger size. This scene, though very fragmentary today, was surely as ambitious and complicated as our Gigantomachy. The fallen Ankaios shows the same twisted, contorted posture as some of the giants, and the short strokes indicating the texture of the lionskin reappear on Atalante's pantherskin. Also, the names are inscribed, and on each vase the sigmas are reversed. These two dinoi are associated with a third, also fragmentary, which is in the Freiburg art market. The main zone shows a Centauromachy. Below is a horse race with the goal post, and tripods set up as prizes. Then comes a frieze of animals, and on the very bottom a whirligig. A tongue pattern borders the Centauromachy at the top, and on the topside of the mouth there is an animal frieze. The drawing on this dinos is as careful as it is on the Getty vase, and it has the same liberal use of accessory red. Other works by the Kyllenios Painter that go well with these are his name piece,[30] Frankfurt Univ. 136,[31] and Louvre E 832.[32] These three neck amphorae have colorful, lively compositions and together with the three dinoi form the nucleus of the painter's best work. In the Getty Gigantomachy, the Kyllenios Painter has left us one of his most spirited and memorable compositions.

Hunter College
New York

30. Berlin 1704 (*ABV* 96, 14; *Para.* 36, 14).
31. *Para.* 39.
32. *ABV* 100, 74.

Some New and Little-Known Vases by the Rycroft and Priam Painters

Warren G. Moon

Known primarily for decorating large vases in a variety of shapes and for their comparatively neat and quiet styles, the Rycroft and Priam Painters are mentioned in the scholarly literature largely because of their association with Psiax, a more famous contemporary who may have been their teacher. The Rycroft and Priam Painters decorated their vases in the black-figure technique which had become rather old-fashioned by 510 B.C., the period of their best production. Thus these painters have often been relegated to the "old guard" by scholars more enthusiastic to study the innovative red-figure style. The new attribution of several vases to these painters is occasion enough to reconsider their careers, particularly since one of these attributions has been made to a red-figure (not a black-figure) hydria now in a German private collection (figs. 8a–c).

Each of the two vase painters emerges as an independent talent, responding separately to the challenge of keeping black-figure competitive and flexible, in its eleventh hour, to changing markets and tastes. The Rycroft Painter seems to exhibit a more refined graphic sense, and is more keenly aware of the intrinsic spatial advantages and increased naturalism and animation of the red-figure style. In his drawing the Rycroft Painter was doubtless inspired by Psiax, who worked both in black- and red-figure and may have been influenced by the "Pioneers" of red-figure; it is he who may have tried his hand at this technique. The Priam Painter, on the other hand, appears to have made more of a mark as an imagist and may have inspired other painters, for instance some members of the Leagros Group, to repeat his designs. His artistic associations then seem to have been more directly with black-figurists. One

may begin the discussion with the Rycroft Painter because his vases can be found in California collections—three from private collections, three fragments of a calyx krater and a type B amphora (on loan from the Bareiss collection) at the J. Paul Getty Museum.

A black-figure kalpis in a Los Angeles private collection (figs. 1a–b) is of rather rare type and class and was given to the Rycroft Painter some fifteen years ago, though it has not been listed with the painter in Beazley's *Paralipomena*.[1] The shape is one of those compact, unified, more curvilinear designs, new around ca. 510 B.C., which were thrown in a continuous movement of the potter's hands. Beazley himself attributed one kalpis to the Rycroft Painter, and a pelike, another of these innovative shapes, has been placed "near" his hand. Fine black-figure kalpides are uncommon in the archaeological record; the new shape quickly became a favorite of red-figure painters as the artistic power of the older technique began to fade. The Los Angeles kalpis, which is an attractive vase, belongs to a small class of kalpides which includes a vase in Montreal and another in the Lyman Wright Art Center of Beloit College.[2]

The picture panel on the Los Angeles kalpis, which occupies the upper half of the body to below the handles, depicts, as does the Beloit vase, a driver starting his chariot. The horses on the Beloit and Los Angeles vases, in the rendering of the tails and other specifics, are not far from those drawn on side B of a type B amphora sold in Lucerne in 1964 and which Beazley attributed to a member of the Leagros Group (*Para.* 166, no. 108 bis).[3] Although neither the Rycroft nor the Priam Painter is Leagran, one compares their stride with the Leagran period and some-

This was a lecture at the J. Paul Getty Museum, October 7, 1982, and it is presented here essentially as it was given. I thank Jiří Frel for including it in a volume dedicated to Dietrich von Bothmer, who has helped me on numerous occasions.

1. A. Emmerich Gallery, Inc., New York, *Art of the Ancients: Greeks, Etruscans and Romans* (February 7 – March 13, 1968) no. 16, where the vase is described and its attribution and class set forth. One hesitates to give the kalpis to the Rycroft Painter (*infra* n. 2).

2. W.G. Moon and L. Berge, eds., *Greek Vase-Painting in Midwestern Collections*, exhibition catalogue (Chicago, 1980) 121, no. 68. Infor-

mally by letter Bothmer assigned this kalpis to the class and disagreed with the attribution to the "manner of the Antimenes Painter," which had been made by Charles Seltman. The acquisition of the vase is mentioned, *Parnassus* (May 1931) 15 and front cover ill. (Bothmer).

3. Ars Antiqua A.G., *Antike Kunstwerke* Auktion V (7 November 1964) no. 122. Side B with goddess mounting chariot displays an overall stylistic similarity to certain scenes by the Rycroft Painter and convinces us that the Potters' Quarter in Athens was small in area, thus affording an easy exchange of designs and styles.

Figures 1 a–b. Kalpis by the Rycroft Painter. Los Angeles, private collection. Photo: D. Widmer.

times their style with the "calmer" members of that group. The charioteer, bearded and wearing his traditional long robe, holds a kentron or goad in his right hand. The driver has flexed his knees and is about to tug on the reins; the near pole horse has already begun to pull, with its head lowered and its right leg raised. The bent back of the charioteer sensitively repeats the sloping shoulder of the vase immediately adjacent. The groundline is deliberately high to give added separation of the design from the black field. The panel is bounded at the top with a net pattern in three rows, a subsidiary motif used rather infrequently by the Rycroft Painter.

Such scenes of driver and team deal with chariot racing, a featured event at Olympic and other games, reminiscent of an "early heroic" mode of warfare which fostered the agonistic milieu for this sport. Racing was the delight of the aristocracy which bred horses, and such equestrian scenes are depicted less frequently as affection for the leisured class began to change after the expulsion of the Peisistratid tyranny in 510 B.C. Parenthetically a similar design of single chariot (with driver and rider) can be seen

on side B of the name vase (a type A amphora) by the Painter of Tarquinia RC 6847, a particularly close artistic companion of the Rycroft Painter.[4] The scene of driver and chariot appears regularly in black-figure, and we will encounter it again.

A black-figure hydria (figs. 2a–c) in the collection of Mr. and Mrs. Arthur Silver of Beverly Hills is one of the better vases of the Rycroft Painter's later period, ca. 500 B.C.;[5] it helps confirm the attribution of a column krater in the Basel market (figs. 3a–b).[6] In the main panel on the far left a man is mounting a chariot, and a veiled woman, presumably his bride (Peleus and Thetis: *hieros gamos*), is at his side in the car. Apollo plays the cithara, and there are two goddesses attending, one holding a torch—the flame is indicated, quite remarkably one should note, in yellow wash. Compositionally the scene can be compared to many others by the Rycroft Painter, e.g. to side A of a type B amphora in the Ashmolean, Oxford 1911.256 (fig. 4), which Beazley has also placed late,[7] and to side A of the name vase, also in the Ashmolean, a type A amphora, Oxford 1965.118 (fig. 6).[8] Such dependence on formulae, it

4. *ABV* 338, no. 1; *Para.* 150, no. 1; *Addenda* 44.

5. Height: 45.1 cm; diameter of mouth: 22.9 cm.

6. Bothmer has written me (November 3, 1982): "The column krater was no. 79 at the Basel Fair of 1972 and was later offered at Sotheby's (London) on December 9, 1974, lot no. 279, where however it remained unsold. The attribution to the Rycroft Painter was already published in

the Sotheby catalogue on p. 168. The attribution was first made by Herbert Cahn and Mrs. Perry, though it did not appear in the mimeographed checklist for the exhibition, March 9–19, 1972, stand 29."

7. *ABV* 336, no. 11; Moore, *Horses,* A 784, pl. 60.2 (see *infra* n. 10).

8. *ABV* 335, no. 1; *Para.* 148, no. 1; *Addenda* 44; Moore, *Horses,* A 775 (see *infra* n. 10).

Figures 2 a–c. Hydria by the Rycroft Painter. Beverly Hills, collection of Mr. and Mrs. Arthur Silver.

Figures 3 a–b. Column krater by the Rycroft Painter. Basel market. Photos: D. Widmer.

might be added, is not uncommon in late black-figure; and we have already implied that the Rycroft Painter is not exceptional in the variety of subject matter that he treats or creates. Likewise the scene on the shoulder of the Silver hydria, Herakles' battle with the Nemean lion, in many aspects of the design recalls the larger versions of the tale seen on side A of a type B amphora, Orvieto Faina 74, and on an amphora of similar shape, Berlin 3214, which is close to but perhaps not by the painter.[9]

There are characteristic areas of applied red on the vases—alternate tails of the horses, the stripe at the base of the mane and along the hems of garments—and other features which are criteria for attribution to the hand, especially the cheekstrap which cuts the mane at the poll.[10] The horses' bodies are free of inner markings (the Priam Painter's horses are rather similar in this regard), giving them a certain lady-like appearance as Beazley himself described.[11] The long hairs at the outer edge of the mane and inner contour of the tail are rendered in short, feathered incisions; and in his later work the outer profile of the tail is occasionally drawn hastily in a continuous wavy line.

9. The vase is not sufficiently close to give to the painter.

10. These points are discussed by M.B. Moore, *Horses on Black-Figured Greek Vases of the Archaic Period: Circa 620 – 480 B.C.* (unpublished diss. New York University, 1971) 113–115, particularly 278–279.

11. M.H. Swindler, "The Worcester Vase by the Rycroft Painter and Its Boston Companion," *Worcester Art Museum Annual* 6 (1958) 3. "The style of the Rycroft Painter as revealed on the Worcester vase is characterized by very careful drawing and by a fine understanding of the anatomy of the horse which he renders almost without inner details," as Swindler adds.

Figure 4. Type B amphora by the Rycroft Painter. Oxford, Ashmolean Museum 1911.256.

Figure 5. Detail of a type A amphora by the Rycroft Painter. Worcester Museum of Art 1956.83.

Figure 6. Type A amphora by the Rycroft Painter. Oxford, Ashmolean Museum 1965.118.

One can identify different body types for his horses: the "locomotive-like" animals on the Silver hydria appear on the painter's very latest vases. The belly-line here is even more horizontal, the body more tubular than one observes on the other "late" vases, for instance, Oxford 1911.256[12] (fig. 4) and Worcester 1956.83[13] (fig. 5). On these latter examples the type is less convincing than the steed one finds earlier, for example, on the name vase, Oxford 1965.118 (fig. 6), where the silhouettes seem more carefully descriptive of the horses' powerful anatomy. A few of the painter's horses are particularly delicate and can be found on the important hydria in Hamburg (fig. 7).[14] It is this

type which is closest to the horses drawn on the two fine hydriai (one red-figure) recently attributed to the Rycroft Painter, which will be discussed later (figs. 8a–c).

Describing the horses on the Worcester amphora, Mary Swindler has commented in a flourish of appreciation, "the delicately executed legs of the horses, to quote a layman's words, are like a fugue."[15] The arrangement of the horses' legs in the main panel of the Silver hydria is certainly harmonious, four legs raised front and back. One immediately notices the similarity with the team on side A of the Ashmolean amphora (fig. 4). The shape of the bodies and the stance and conformation of the horses' legs

12. See n. 7 *supra*.

13. *ABV* 335, no. 5 bis where it is called "Late"; *Para.* 148, no. 5 bis; *Addenda* 44. The horses' bodies have begun to attenuate but not to the degree that will signal his very latest work.

14. *ABV* 337, no. 25; *Addenda* 44. Moore, *Horses*, A 795, pl. 63.1. The Rycroft Painter inherits his delicacy from Psiax; on the closeness of their styles, Beazley's comment, *Para.* 128 referring to *ABV* 337, no. 2 and p. 692, which is also *Addenda* 44.

Figure 7. Detail of a hydria by the Rycroft Painter. Hamburg, Museum für Kunst und Gewerbe 1917.476.

compare with the Rycroft Painter's column krater still on the Basel market (figs. 3a–b). The scheme of raised legs from the Silver hydria can additionally be observed on other vases: on the red-figure hydria in Germany (fig. 8), on the shoulder of the recently attributed hydria on the London market (figs. 9a–c), and as we have already mentioned on side B of the Luzern amphora given by Beazley to a member of the Leagros Group.[16]

On the largest of the three fragments at the Getty, a figure—there seems to be only one—mounts a chariot; the vine branch near the figure suggests Dionysos is either the intended driver of the chariot or an immediate bystander

(fig. 10b). The figure next to the car in all probability is Apollo. Details of drapery, disposition of figures (and theme?) can be compared to the frieze on a calyx krater formerly on the Swiss market (fig. 12).[17] The two remaining Getty fragments go together and show a high-stepping draped youth playing the pipes (figs. 10a, c). One is reminded of figures on another of the Rycroft Painter's big vases, a calyx krater in the Toledo Museum of Art (figs. 11a–b). Frel attributed these fragments, and Bothmer has recently mentioned them.[18]

Two more vases by the Rycroft Painter are related to each other by their scenes and are in California. Both are

15. Swindler, *op. cit.*

16. See n. 1 *supra.*

17. Münzen und Medaillen A.G., Basel, Auktion 51 *Kunstwerke der Antike* (March 14–15, 1975) no. 131.

18. Moon and Berge, *Midwestern Vases,* 108–109, no. 62. And too the painter's high-stepping satyrs on the B side of the Vanderlip column krater: *ABV* 337, no. 23[5] and *Para.* 149, no. 23[5]. Bothmer's mention of the fragments: Moon-Berge, 113, no. 64.

Figures 8 a–c. Hydria by the Rycroft Painter. German private collection. Photos: D. Widmer.

Figures 9 a–c. Hydria by the Rycroft Painter. London market.

Figures 10. a–c. Fragments from a calyx krater attributed to the Rycroft Painter. Malibu, The J. Paul Getty Museum 75.AE.14a–c. Max. L: a
17.5 cm, b 12 cm, c 8.3 cm.

Figures 11 a–b. Calyx krater by the Rycroft Painter. The Toledo Museum of Art 63.26.

Figure 12. Calyx krater by the Rycroft Painter. Swiss market. Photo: D. Widmer.

type B amphorae. The first, from the Brundage collection (figs. 13 a–b), was destroyed in the tragic fire at Merlo (*Para.* 149, no. 15 *ter*);[19] and it is illustrated here with the kind permission of the Beazley Archive. The second is from the Bareiss collection which is on loan to the J. Paul Getty Museum (figs. 14 a–b).[20]

Each amphora has on side A a rider and driver in a chariot wheeling round and on side B Dionysos riding a donkey flanked by satyrs. The instances of these themes recurring in the painter's work are numerous, especially in the late period, and there is little variation. As on the Brundage amphora, the chariot may sometimes be shown with an archer running ahead (also Cab. Méd. 208; Rhodes 13447)[21] or with one before and after (Laon

37.977).[22] The wheeling chariot motif seems dramatically more forceful, however, when it stands alone, without attendant figures, as one sees it on the Bareiss vase (fig. 14a). There may be much or little added color in these scenes; the Bareiss amphora stands apart from the rest because of the white used on side A for the rim of the warrior's shield, the charioteer's traditional robe, and the white stars on the horses' heads, and, on side B, for the donkey's undercoat.

In Attic vase painting the motif of the war chariot wheeling around appears first near the middle of the century in the workshop of Group E, perhaps the invention of the Geryon Painter or someone near him. The horses' curving bodies and the movement of the chariot and team help emphasize the swelling contours of the panel

19. *Para.* 149, no. 15 ter; Moore, *Horses*, A 788. This is discussed in a letter from Dr. Jane Nelson, the M.H. de Young Memorial Museum: "the de Young Museum does not have any of the remaining fragments of Greek vases from the Brundage collection. I have talked to the chief curator of the Asian Museum, which houses the Brundage collection, and he tells me that they do have what pieces remain from the fire which destroyed some of the collection, and that their conservation department

has worked on those fragments. However, a check on the Asian Museum records indicates that no identifiable fragments remain of the neck-amphora, no. 3/196, the vase which was no. 40 in the 1963 Santa Barbara catalogue" (letter dated 26 August 1980).

20. *Para.* 149, no. 15; Moore, *Horses*, A 790 bis. The development of this iconography is discussed by Moore, 416–420, particularly 419.

21. Moore, *Horses*, A 785 and A 787 respectively, with bibliography.

Figures 13 a–b. Type B amphora by the Rycroft Painter. Brundage Collection. Photos: Beazley Archives.

amphora itself. E. E. Bell has recently commented on the motif: "When it first appears, the wheeling chariot turns to the right; in late black-figure, it faces left. This change in direction probably occurred because vase painters wanted to display the shield blazons of the hoplite and charioteer."[23] In all five or so examples of the scene on vases by the Rycroft Painter, the chariot wheels to the right, as it had in Group E. In fact, the chariot in the Bareiss amphora echoes a similar scene, at some distance in time, on a type B amphora in the Toledo Museum of Art, which Bell has given to the Geryon Painter.[24] The Rycroft Painter's choice of this time-honored theme may have been influenced by his workshop affiliations. The spirit of the scene and its strong spatial reference seem not

to have been incompatible and may have been reinvoked in this large format to compete with the advantages of the new red-figure technique, with the latter's bold foreshortenings and heightened narrative effects.

Two hydriai newly given to the Rycroft Painter merit special attention. The black-figure hydria (figs. 9a–c) on the London market (now Stuttgart?) and attributed by Robert Guy is equal in period and quality to the painter's best vases, among which are his type A amphorae in Toledo (fig. 15), London (figs. 16a–b), and Worcester (fig. 5); his psykter in Bloomington;[25] and, particularly close, the lovely neck amphora in Basel (figs. 17a–b).[26] The hydria is in fine preservation, with restoration in the large figure scene chiefly confined to Herakles' mouth and nose.

22. *Para.* 148, no. 14 and Moore, *Horses*, A 786.

23. E.E. Bell, "An Exekian Puzzle in Portland: New Light on the Relationship between Exekias and Group E," *Ancient Greek Art and Iconography*, Warren G. Moon, ed. (Madison 1983) 81–82, and 85.

24. *Ibid.*

25. Moon and Berge, *Midwestern Vases*, no. 64 (Bothmer). The Rycroft Painter's design of the ransom of Hector's body (Toledo, Ohio 72.54: fig.

15) is perhaps his most powerfully narrative. With outstretched arms King Priam rushes close to Achilles' couch. A youthful attendant brings payment for the body and Hermes with winged hat approaches on the far left. Certain elements of this scene appear in those of contemporaries in the broad sphere of the Leagros Group: W. Basista, "Hektors Lösung," *Boreas* (1979) V 10, 11 and V 9, 7.

26. *Para.* 149, no. 16 bis.

Figures 14 a–b. Type B amphora by the Rycroft Painter. Bareiss Collection 3, on loan to The J. Paul Getty Museum
S.82.AE.238. H: 38.5 cm.

Figure 15. Detail of a type A amphora by the Rycroft Painter. The Toledo Museum of Art 72.54.

Figures 16 a–b. Type A amphora by the Rycroft Painter. London, The British Museum C 678. Photos: Courtesy of the Trustees of The British Museum.

nose. The main panel shows a favorite scene of the Rycroft Painter, Apollo and Herakles struggling over the Delphic tripod; the shoulder scene is of a driver mounting a chariot, attended by hoplites. The red-figure hydria (figs. 8a–c), now in a German private collection and attributed by Mrs. Rita Perry, is the sole example known in the new technique by this painter who was thought to have worked exclusively in black-figure.[27] Almost by definition its association with the Rycroft Painter, a member of the

old guard, has some problems (not so for the attribution of the companion black-figure hydria which seems certain). The main panel here has a driver mounting a chariot (fig. 8a); the shoulder scene seems to show a younger and an older man bringing horses to harness (fig. 8b). Since the Rycroft Painter is noted for his sensitive treatment of drapery, the missing portion of the charioteer's robe on this vase is therefore the more regrettable; otherwise this vase too is in fine condition. The two hydriai share aspects

27. Münzen und Medaillen A.G., Basel, *Kunstwerke der Antike Auktion 56* (19 February 1980) no. 91. This is not to imply that this hydria and the one on the London market are the only vases which are new attributions to the Rycroft Painter. Besides some additions which Moore makes, *Horses,* A 798 (A 798 and A 800), several others are made: W.G. Moon, "The Priam Painter: Some Stylistic and Iconographic Considerations," in *Ancient Greek Art and Iconography,* ed. W.G. Moon

(Madison, 1983), 115, n. 10, by R. Guy and by myself. Another fine hydria by the painter has recently been published (see n. 28). There are graffiti under the foot of the painter's hydria on the London market: XII, and on the slope opposite: X and a circle that is divided into six parts. It scarcely needs mentioning that the scene of driver and chariot on the Rycroft Painter's red-figure hydria (in Germany) is far more popular in the black-figure tradition.

Figures 17 a–b. Details of a neck amphora by the Rycroft Painter. Basel, Antikenmuseum BS 409.

of iconography and style. One notices that the lip and side handles of both vases are reserved, a scarce occurrence, which may show a connection with the "Pioneer" workshop and with the introduction of red-figure painting itself.[28] The horses' gaits, their poised hooves, and their fine-boned proportions are quite similar; and it seems an odd coincidence that a palm tree—an uncommon motif—appears in the two main pictures.

Of the more than 175 examples in vase painting of the struggle over the Delphic tripod, Bothmer has found the palm included in the story only three times as a determinant of locale.[29] The palm on the London hydria (fig. 9a) thus is extraordinary; the Rycroft Painter depicts the theme of the Delphic tripod at least five times, but only on the latter vase does he include the motif. He had added the tree, however, at least as many times in a variety of other iconographical circumstances: along with the olive in the

battle of Herakles and the Nemean lion (*ABV* 336, no. 10); between profile heads on the painter's oinochoe at Eaton (*ABV* 337, no. 30); twice with Ajax and Achilles playing dice (fig. 12a) on either side of the scene (*Para.* 149, no. 23 *bis* and *Addenda* 44); with Apollo and Artemis on side B of his name vase now at Oxford (*ABV* 335, no. 1; *Para.* 148, no. 1 and *Addenda* 44); and , if one accepts the attribution of the red-figure hydria (fig. 8a), the palm appears in a scene of driver mounting a chariot. Our painter's enthusiasm for the palm may have been aligned with that of the Antimenes Painter who included the plant in his own designs nearly as often. A recent Berkeley dissertation discusses the iconography of the palm in Greek art.[30]

The date palm was rare in Greece. "It was ill-suited for cultivation on the northern shores of the Mediterranean where its fruit ripened inconsistently, maturing badly or

28. Joan R. Mertens, "A Black-Figure Hydria of Red-Figure Date," *Indiana University Art Museum Bulletin* (1979) 6–15, especially 11–12.

29. Dietrich von Bothmer, "The Struggle for the Tripod," *Festschrift*

für Frank Brommer (Mainz, 1977) 51–63, particularly 53, nos. 30–32.

30. Helena Fracchia Miller, *The Iconography of the Palm in Greek Art: Significance and Symbolism* (unpublished diss., University of California,

infrequently, and further north the tree lives but will not flower."[31] The tree does figure in Greek myth, as midwife to Leto on Delos in the birth of Apollo (or of Apollo and Artemis), and is represented in Greek art infrequently just after the middle of the sixth century B.C. A few isolated instances actually appear a century or so before. For instance, a large-scale palm dedication may have been offered at Delphi by Kypselos, and much later there was one at Delos from Nikias. Mrs. Miller shows convincingly that the palm may just as easily designate Delphi as Delos and that the tree fittingly becomes an attribute of Apollo or of Apollo and Artemis. The inclusion of the palm on the reverse of the Rycroft Painter's name vase at Oxford and in the panel of the London hydria (fig. 9a) is thus readily explained. Coincidentally, moreover, the palm on the latter hydria may also symbolize victory, that high measure of discipline and courage needed for success. A fragment of

a black-figure oinochoe from Como, which is attributed to the Antimenes Painter, may corroborate these references to Delphi and to victory.[32] Certainly toward the end of the sixth century the plant's botanical characteristics were beginning to give rise to its symbolic use in art.

"The equality of the leaves of the palm is similar to a contest or race, because they spring up in opposition to each other and run along together," one ancient source testifies.[33] "The palm possesses unique ability to resist imposed weight, is long-living, and in its vigor makes a suitable athletic token," Mrs. Miller concludes.[34] As early as ca. 540–520 B.C. the palm had become an accepted victory token; this can be argued from the appearance of taeniae and palm on an amphora by the Swing Painter (*ABV* 305, no. 24; *Addenda* 40) and from the palm in a scene of the pankration on a Panathenaic amphora which she dates to the late sixth or early fifth century.[35] Furthermore, the

Berkeley, 1979).

31. *Ibid.*, 4–6, 6–18.
32. *Ibid.*, 7, cat. no. 26, with bibliography.

33. *Ibid.*, 35.
34. *Ibid.*
35. *Ibid.*, 36, cat. no. 97: Naples 81294.

Rycroft Painter seems to have been aware of the victory palm, as one may conclude from a scene of Ajax and Achilles playing dice on side A of his fine calyx krater in the Toledo Museum of Art (fig. 11a).[36] Each hero is flanked by a palm tree; the one near Achilles, the victor, has *five* lateral pairs of fronds, while his opponent's tree displays only *four*. The viewer is informed about the outcome of the contest (locale and other symbolism understood). The tree is clarion of areté and athletic discipline, which is ever triumphant over brute force and blind action. This certainly applies to many of the Rycroft Painter's designs which have the tree, including the struggle over the tripod. Perhaps this explains the palm on the red-figure hydria recently attributed to our painter.[37] And the palm may lend the spirit of success (along with the olive) to the painter's scene of Herakles' battle with the Nemean Lion (*supra*).

Though depicted similarly on these two new hydriai, the palm is admittedly less elegant than one finds on the Rycroft Painter's calyx krater in Toledo (fig. 11a) or between the heads in *anodos* on his oinochoe at Eaton College. This brings us to the issue of attribution. R. Guy's of the London hydria needs no lengthy defense; it is so obviously the Rycroft Painter's hand. It is customary for the painter to have Herakles wear the tripod around his body like a garment (a borrowing perhaps from red-figure). The tripod's bowl is especially shallow and made of bronze, which is suggested by the applied red. The profile of Apollo's face and the cut and decoration of his chiton are, among other details, hallmarks of the painter's style. Mrs. Perry's attribution of the red-figure hydria is much less easy to prove. After many reversals of opinion, I think it may be the Rycroft Painter.

The composition and draughtsmanship on this intriguing red-figure hydria (figs. 8a–c) are plain, stiff, and in some places awkward. On the shoulder of the vase the clothing of the grooms exhibits nothing of the care for detail that was the painter's usual delight. The displacement of the elements of the design, the relationship of the solids to voids, and some of the secondary decorative motives initially remind one of a cup painter, perhaps from the "Coarser Wing," or of painters of bigger pots, like the Gallatin Painter or Hypsis. In fact, the scene on the shoulder recalls another in the same position on the well-

known Munich hydria by this latter painter (*ARV*² 30, no. 1; 1583, 1621; *Addenda* 75). The drawing of the palm tree immediately reminds one of the plant represented on a type A amphora in Boston which is in the broad circle of the Euthymides Painter (MFA 63.1515).[38] On this latter amphora it should be noted that Herakles' silhouette and movement, the hero's wearing of the tripod, and the design of the tripod itself bear close comparison to the Rycroft Painter's rendition of the hero on the neck amphora in Basel (figs. 17a–b) and the hydria on the London market (fig. 9a). Furthermore, the disposition and nudity of Herakles on this Boston "Pioneer" amphora compare favorably with other vases by the Rycroft Painter, which have similar scenes of the Delphic struggle: on the reverse of an amphora of type A in Boston (MFA 98.919: *ABV* 335, no. 3; *Para.* 148, no. 3; *Addenda* 44)[39] and around a very fine lekythos in Würzburg (381: *ABV* 337, no. 31).[40] Herakles' twisting torso and abdominal musculature in each case demonstrate the painter's awareness of the innovative red-figure technique.

Mrs. Perry has catalogued specific points of similarity and comparison between the red-figure hydria and other works by the Rycroft Painter.[41] One is particularly salient: the turned, foreshortened head of the further pole horse (fig. 8a) is close to the corresponding detail from the main panel on the important hydria in Hamburg (1917.476; *ABV* 337, no. 25; *Addenda* 44) (fig. 7).[42]

Additionally, the Rycroft Painter's most *modern* conception is the central figure from the main panel on this hydria now in Hamburg. The sense of the mass of the handler's body, the indication of musculature, and the foreshortened bicep and lower arm, among other details in the scene, go far beyond the expectations and limitations of black-figure. It is not too surprising that at such a juncture in his career the Rycroft Painter might have accepted the challenge of the red-figure technique and that the stiffness of line on the red-figure hydria might be the result of his lack of familiarity with the brush.

As he has shown on the hydria in the Museum für Kunst und Gewerbe, Hamburg, the Rycroft Painter seems to have understood the artistic objectives and possibilities of red-figure in many ways better than some practitioners of the new technique itself. The Priam Painter, to whom we now turn, was on the other hand a much less gifted

36. This observation was made by Kurt Luckner, in Moon and Berge, *Midwestern Vases*, 109, no. 62.

37. Does this suggest the site of Delphi and success at the Pythian games? That the scene might refer to the Dokimasia, to the fields of Dionysos, to more complex iconographies is indeed possible. The Rycroft Painter uses the palm, it should be recalled, between the heads of Dionysos and Ariadne (or Semele) on the Eaton College oinochoe. There may be a simpler solution to the scene, on the other hand, than Mrs.

Perry has put forth.

38. *ARV*² 1705; *Para.* 324, no. 7 bis; Bothmer, "Struggle for the Tripod," *Brommer*, no. 30.

39. *ABV* 335, no. 3; *Para.* 148, no. 3; *Addenda* 44.

40. *ABV* 337, no. 31.

41. *Kunstwerke der Antike* (1980) no. 91.

42. *ABV* 337, no. 25; *Addenda* 44.

43. To some degree the discussion here on the Priam Painter is a

Figures 18 a–b. Details of the Lerici-Marescotti type B amphora by the Priam Painter. Photos: DAI, Rome.

draughtsman.[43] One need only compare his four scenes of harnessing,[44] his grooms or heroes in side-turning attitude, with the central figure from the main panel of the Rycroft Painter's hydria just discussed. Similarly, the Priam Painter seems much less imaginative in the vase shapes he decorates, which are chiefly hydriai and amphorae (and one calyx krater), at least as the archaeological record has so far preserved. The Priam Painter is not to be thought of, however, as inflexible. He is a talented imagist using gesture to convey and heighten his narrative, and is a painter with some humor, when he contrasts, for instance, Triptolemos and Dionysos, bread and wine, on a neck amphora in Compiègne (*ABV* 331, no. 13; *Addenda* 43) or satyrs laboring at the vintage with a scene of nymphs bathing on his charming Lerici-Marescotti type B amphora (*Para.* 146, no. 8 *ter*) (figs. 18a–b). Stylistically linked to Psiax, some of his scenes, particularly the last mentioned, put him in the vicinity of the Andokides Painter; and many others establish his connection with the Leagrans, as I hope to show.

Though I have discussed the Lerici-Marescotti vase at length elsewhere,[45] it may still be useful here to reiterate some significant points. On side A (fig. 18a) seven dwarfed satyrs collect grapes as Dionysos sits in the center of the composition beneath a canopy of feathery vines that are laden with fruit. The vase-like baskets for the produce (and

those on another of his vases with a scene of women in an orchard: Munich 1702 A) and the tenor and other elements of the scene recall a similar design in the tondo of a cup decorated by a member of the Leagros Group: Cabinet des Médailles 320: *ABV* 389 middle and *Para.* 171 bottom). Young people had a part in the Oschophoria, Dionysos' October celebration of wine-making; and these pictures may pertain, perhaps in parody.[46] The Priam Painter's scene has only one parallel, so far as I know, on side B of an amphora of type A in the Museum of Fine Arts, Boston 63.952, which is earlier and close to the hand of Exekias. As has been shown, the picture is a hybrid of two conventional black-figure scenes: Dionysos sitting and satyrs vintaging.[47]

On the reverse of the Lerici amphora (fig. 18b) seven nymphs swim in a cool country grotto, depicted by the Priam Painter in an extraordinarily painterly style. They may have been part of a Bacchic entourage who are relaxing after a day's service to the god. In Greek art and literature references to swimming are unexpectedly rare; again only one contemporary comparison comes to mind, the scene of Amazons swimming in the open sea by the Andokides Painter on the reverse of his amphora in Paris (Louvre F 203), which is late in the artist's "early" period. During his "transitional" period the Andokides Painter treats Exekian themes, perhaps influenced by the Lysip-

reiteration of a paper on the artist which has recently appeared: W. G. Moon, "The Priam Painter: Some Stylistic and Iconographic Considerations" (*supra*, n. 27).

44. Oxford 212 (*ABV* 331, no. 5; *Para.* 146, no. 5; *Addenda* 43); Florence 94355 (*ABV* 331, no. 6); Madrid 10920 (*ABV* 332, no. 17; *Para.* 146, no. 17; *Addenda* 44).

45. M. Moretti, "Tomba Martini Marescotti," *Quaderna di Villa Giulia 1* (Milan, 1966) I. and L. Vanoni, "La Tomba Martini Marescotti,"

Prospegioni Archeologiche (1966) 18. *Para.* 147, no. 30 and *Addenda* 44. The vase is discussed in Moon, *Ancient Greek Art and Iconography*, 110–113 and 115, n. 5. In that article I said incorrectly that applied white slip was used to indicate the breeze-blown water.

46. E. Simon, *Festivals of Attica* (Madison, 1983) 89–92.

47. *CVA* Boston 1, pl. 12.3.

pides Painter,[48] and it is in this context that the Priam
Painter, at slightly later date, begins his career. Two of the
earliest depictions of Aeneas carrying his father Anchises
are painted by Exekias and the Priam Painter and share
some essentials in presentation. Psiax, the Priam and
Rycroft Painters' companion or teacher, has ties with the
Andokidean workshop at this time.[49] Oddly enough, one
of the Priam Painter's designs for the story of Herakles and
the giant Alkyoneus, newly attributed to the painter by
Bothmer, was thought by one scholar to be the work of
the Andokides Painter himself.[50] We will have more to say
about this type A amphora in Paris, Louvre F 208.

The Priam Painter has most to do with the Leagros
Group, the black-figure counterparts of the Pioneer
Group. This is easy enough to demonstrate. His scene of
Achilles dragging the body of Hektor around the tomb of
Patroklos, on a type A amphora in the British Museum,
London 99.7–21.3 (figs. 19, 20), is similar in its iconographic
peculiarities to two paintings by members of the Leagros
Group: the shoulder scene on a hydria in Munich (1719:
ABV 361, no. 13) and that on a lekythos from Delos (546:
ABV 378, no. 257; *Para.* 163, no. 257; *Addenda* 48) (fig. 20).
Unlike most other versions of the scene, the action in these
three pictures oddly moves to the *left* with a slow surge and
the tomb of Patroklos is on the extreme right. A snake
whose body is roughly in the shape of an omega is painted
on it. Above the tomb is the *eidolon* of the dead Patroklos,
running left. Achilles stands, facing right, above Hektor's
body which is in front of or near the tomb. At Achilles'
back is the charioteer and car. On the Delos and London
vases Iris is immediately at the car, while on the Munich
hydria she stands at the head of the team. These three pictures seem to illustrate *Iliad* XXIV.12 where Zeus dispatches
Iris to Thetis, Achilles' mother, so that the latter might persuade her son to stop the excessively brutal and inhuman
treatment of Hektor's body. All three vases show the same
conflation of the story, having Iris speak directly to Achilles.
This presupposes a strong workshop affiliation and perhaps
prototype or common sketch.

"The half-seen chariot team is a favorite motive in the
Leagros Group,"[51] Beazley wrote; and such a device appears several times on the Priam Painter's vases, among
them the hydria Boulogne 406 (fig. 21); the Civitavecchia
fragment of a hydria (fig. 22 on left); and side B of a type A
amphora in Paris, Louvre F 208 *bis* (fig. 23), where the
border cuts the body of the centaur Pholos.[52] This trunca-
tion of elements using the side of the picture panel creates
a window effect which makes the viewer look onto a scene

Figures 19 a–b. Type A amphora by the Priam Painter.
London, The British Museum 99.7–21.3.
Photos: Courtesy of the Trustees of the
British Museum.

progressing in the distance. Somewhat toward similar ends
the Priam Painter, the Rycroft Painter, and others extend
important elements of their designs beyond the sides of the
picture panel; to mention only two notable instances: the
horse being led to harness on the Priam Painter's name
vase in Madrid (Archaeological Museum 10920) and an
Amazon's mount on side B of the painter's fine type A amphora in the British Museum (London 99.7–21.3; fig. 19b).
The latter design successfully conveys, by overlapping and
with the alternation of color, the sense of the bustle and
dispatch of queen Andromache's Amazons on patrol.

The tale of Herakles killing the giant Alkyoneus appears
during the Leagran period and is popular with members of
that group and, to some degree as well, with the Priam
Painter. The Civitavecchia-Munich fragments (fig. 22)
have the giant on the porch of a building with Doric

48. Beth Cohen, *Attic Bilingual Vases and Their Painters* (New York,
1978) 156, pl. XXIX.2 and discussion on 153–157.

49. Moon and Berge, *Midwestern Vases*, 104, no. 60 (Mertens).

50. B. Andreae, "Herakles und Alkyoneus," *JdI* 77 (1962) 174–176, p.
174, no. 1.

51. J. D. Beazley, *The Development of Attic Black-Figure* (Berkeley and

columns. Alkyoneus sits, full face, and is asleep. Though my drawing of the scene may not convey it very well, at first glance the giant seems of human scale, but in fact sitting on the floor he is nearly as tall as Herakles. To my knowlege, the addition of the building is the personal variation of the Priam Painter and is unique in the more than thirty examples of the scene now known.[53] As mentioned, a type A amphora in Paris (Louvre F 208) (fig. 24) has been attributed to the Priam Painter, and its rendition of the Alkyoneus story is quite different. The giant is out of doors. The painter has put him on a mountain, as in Pindar, *Isthmian* VI.32, where he is asleep, with his eyes tightly closed, head down-turned, and his arms hanging limp. The body is properly massive, stretching across much of the panel. Behind Alkyoneus is a small-leafed tree. Herakles approaches on the left, his body tensed, his

bow aimed, soon to deliver his arrow. The moment is genuinely dramatic, powerful in its simplicity, akin to the temperament of Exekias. A painting, comparably strong and direct, by a member of the Leagros Group seems to substantiate further the working proximity of the Priam Painter with that group. On a fine lekythos in the Toledo Museum of Art (Toledo, Ohio, 52.66)[54] (figs. 25a–b) Herakles advances on the left toward the giant, with a bow in his left hand and sword in his right. The Leagran design has the giant full-face, the small-leafed tree, the mountain, and, additionally, a winged personification of Sleep.

The Priam Painter also has had an important vase recently attributed to his hand, a type B amphora in an American private collection. Since I have not seen the vase in person, I can only comment from photographs. Side A has a scene of harnessing, which in many of its par-

Los Angeles, 1951) 83.

52. Louvre F 208 bis: *ABV* 331, no. 7; *Para.* 146, no. 7.

53. *ABV* 332, no. 22; *Para.* 146, no. 22; *Addenda* 44; Andreae,

"Herakles und Alkyoneus," (*supra* n. 50) 174, no. 7.

54. My thanks to Kurt Luckner for sending me these photographs.

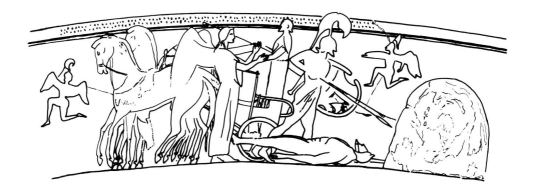

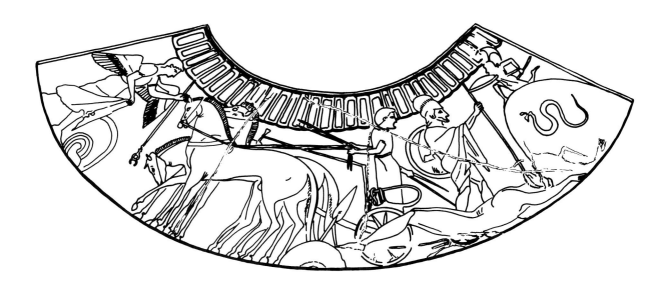

Figure 20. Comparative drawings of lekythos in Delos, hydria in Munich by members of the Leagros Group, and the type A amphora by the Priam Painter in London. Drawings after K.P. Stähler, *Grab und Psyche des Patroklos* (Münster, 1967).

Figure 21. Hydria by the Priam Painter. Boulogne 406. Photo: Devos.

Figure 22. Drawing after a fragmentary hydria by the Priam Painter. Munich and Civitavecchia.

Figure 23. Detail of a type A amphora by the Priam Painter. Paris, Musée du Louvre, F 208*bis*.

Figure 24. Detail of a type A amphora by the Priam Painter. Paris, Musée du Louvre, F 208.

Figures 25 a–b. Lekythos by a member of the Leagros Group. The Toledo Museum of Art 52.66.

ticulars brings to mind three other renditions of the theme by the painter. In all his work this is closest in time and style to the painter's name vase in Madrid (Archaeological Museum 10920). This, coupled with inscriptions, indicates an early date in the painter's career. Curious additions to the composition include on the extreme left a Scythian carrying a spear and, on the opposite side, a little boy who seems to be quieting the team. With regard to such iconography I have argued in a paper that the painter's occasional use of formulae (as in these harnessing scenes) seems to preclude any possibilities for political symbolism as has been in vogue to proclaim, particularly concerning the Priam Painter's controversial type A amphora in the Ashmolean Museum, Oxford 212.[55] Side B of this type B amphora from a private collection has Herakles battling the Nemean lion in a crouched attitude, with Iolaos, Athena, and Hermes in attendance. This is the only example known to me by the Priam Painter of this scene in large format, and as such it provides iconographic links with his companion the Rycroft Painter and with Psiax, with type

B amphora Orvieto Faina 74 (*ABV* 336, no. 9; *Addenda* 44) by the former painter and with the latter's great design of the crouching pair struggling on side A of the type A amphora in Brescia (*ABV* 292, no. 1; *Para.* 127, no. 1; *Addenda* 38). Scholarship has recently found that the *Liegekampf* design comes from Exekias and thrives in the ambit of the Andokides Painter. Our Rycroft and Priam Painters descend from that tradition, through Psiax, proud exponents near the conclusion of a time-honored technique. Psiax increasingly, it has been said, seems to be a "brother" to the Andokides Painter; and some designs of the Rycroft and Priam Painters, although at a distance and in varying degrees, may eventually help to justify that claim.[56] Both general and specific points of stylistic comparison notwithstanding, the artistic personalities of the two painters are individually fascinating and are also indicative, each in its own way, of the complex inner workings of the Athenian Potters' Quarter at a crucial time in its illustrious history.

University of Wisconsin
Madison

---

55. Moon, in *Ancient Greek Art and Iconography*, 102–106.
56. See n. 49. For Psiax and the rival Nikosthenic workshop: M.

Eisman, "Nikosthenic Amphorai: The J. Paul Getty Amphora," *Getty Mus J* 1 (1974) 48–49.

New Fragments of an Early Cup by Douris

Diana Buitron

The J. Paul Getty Museum recently acquired three fragments, two of which join, of a cup attributed to the early career of Douris (fig. 1).[1] The larger fragment preserves on the inside the head and shoulders of a bearded man. He wears a chiton of thin material with a scalloped neckline; it is fastened at the shoulder and along the arm with pins. Numerous wavy lines in dilute glaze indicate fine folds that converge toward the center of the garment. These lines are especially close, indicating crinkles, near the pin heads. He also wears a himation of heavier, stiffer material that stands up a little behind his neck. Binding his hair is a fillet rendered in added red paint, the loops and ends of the knot of which hang down the back of his neck. Above his head is the single letter sigma Ϟ rendered in added red. A few fingers of the man's left hand are preserved at the lower edge of the fragment. Relief contour lines outline the figure and are also used to delineate the beard. Thin relief lines are used for the facial features, fingers, and the larger folds of drapery. On the left side of the sherd is what Frel has suggested may be a pair of greaves or shin guards on a ledge.

The smaller fragment preserves part of a carved folding stool with an embroidered cushion on it; its pattern of lattice and dots is rendered in dilute glaze. The relative position of the two fragments to one another—fixed as we shall see by the picture on the exterior—shows that the man is seated on the stool. Above the cushion the folds of the man's garment are visible.

The scene on the exterior shows warriors arming (fig. 2). The larger fragment preserves the edge of a helmet resting on a shield placed flat on the ground and a pair of greaves on a shelf, as well as five human legs: two pairs and one odd leg. The frontal leg second from the right should perhaps be interpreted as a greave. Tied around the ankles of three of the legs are ankle guards rendered in added red—these guards, made of a soft material, protected the

ankle from chafing caused by the metal greaves. The smaller fragment preserves the other end of the shield, the toes of another foot, and two short lines in added red that might be the tassels of an ankle guard for a pair of greaves. Relief contour lines outline the figures and armor; the details are rendered in relief lines. There are traces of preliminary sketch lines on the legs.

The ornament that forms the lower frame for the outside scene consists of three trapped maeanders alternating with checkerboards. The trapped maeander is a specialty of Douris and appears on at least seven cups attributed to or signed by him, which are dated to his early period ca. 505–500 B.C.[2] The maeander originates in the upper right corner of the framed area and turns inward eight to twelve times, penetrating to the middle of the maze but not coming out again: a false maeander. Vertical lines separate the maeander units, thus trapping or boxing them in. Generally, the trapped maeander does not alternate with any other kind of ornament. The checkerboards, each made up of thirty-five alternating black and white squares carefully drawn with relief lines, are also found on a cup in Vienna showing warriors arming,[3] one of the earliest cups signed by Douris as painter. On the cup in Vienna the checkerboards consist of twenty alternating black and white squares punctuating sets of running maeander triplets—a rhythm of light and dark similar to that on the Getty fragments.

The ornament has been dwelt upon at length because of its importance as a clue in determining attribution to a particular painter. Within the work of the painter, the ornament can often help in narrowing the date. Douris demonstrates the value of this method because his ornamental schemes were individualistic and painstaking, as in the many little squares of the checkerboards drawn with relief lines. Although his contemporaries occasionally copied them, their results were less careful and precise. For

1. The attribution to Douris was first suggested by Jiří Frel, to whom I am grateful for permission to publish these fragments. Accession numbers 82.AE.146.19 and 83.AE.35 (the latter presented by D. von Bothmer), two joined fragments, and 81.AE.192.1 (presented by D. von Bothmer, who recognized that his fragments belonged).

2. Louvre G 127 (ARV² 427, 1); Louvre G 128 (ARV² 442, 211); Louvre Cp 12143; Tübingen E 19; and a fragment, once Rome, Giglioli (ARV²

442, 212 and 214)—these three joined by Bothmer in 1976; Geneva, Koutoulakis; Baltimore, The Johns Hopkins University (ARV² 442, 215); Athens, North Slope AP 2267 (ARV² 428, 8); and Louvre G 122 (ARV² 428, 10). For a discussion of the date, see Buitron, *Douris*, diss., 1976 (University Microfilms, Ann Arbor, Michigan) 210.

3. Vienna 3694, ARV² 427, 3.

Figure 1. Fragments of a cup attributed to Douris. Interior. Malibu, The J. Paul Getty Museum 82.AE.146.19
     and 83.AE.35 (joined), 81.AE.192.1. Max. L of large fragment 8.7 cm, of small fragment 4.3 cm.

example, of Douris' contemporaries who employed the trapped maeander in their ornamental borders, the Triptolemos Painter generally drew his less densely—the line makes only seven or eight turns to the center of the maze.[4] Onesimos' checkerboards are less precise and lose their square quality because of hastier rendering.[5]

The ornament of the new fragments at the Getty is similar in its complexity and in the spacing of lighter and darker elements to that of the arming cup in Vienna. Other parallel features are: the preserved portion of the helmet suggests that the head piece was elaborately decorated with a pattern similar to the overlapping scales seen on many of the helmets on the cup in Vienna. That cup is characterized by a variety of linear detail contrasting with dark areas and with dilute glaze areas, thin wavy lines for drapery as on the Getty fragments, and washes as well,

4. For example: Leipsic T 504 (*ARV*[2] 363, 35); Leipsic T 513 (*ARV*[2] 364, 43); Leipsic T 509 (*ARV*[2] 1647). Cab. Méd. 657, 800, 669, 761, 642, 635 frr. (*ARV*[2] 363, 36) is more like the Dourian examples.
5. For example, Perugia 89 (*ARV*[2] 320, 8).

6. *ARV*[2] 442, 215 and 428, 13.
7. *ARV*[2] 427, 2.
8. *ARV*[2] 428, 12.
9. *ARV*[2] 428, 6 and 14.

Figure 2. Exterior of the same cup as in figure 1. Malibu, The J. Paul Getty Museum.

creating a richly patterned and crowded composition. A hint of similar composition on the Getty fragments is seen in the decorated helmet, the dilute glaze and added red details, and in the number of figures indicated by the overlapping feet within a small space on the cup.

Details of the drawing support the comparison. The legs and feet on the outside scene are long and narrow. The curved outline of the toes, rendered with several strokes of the brush, gives them a somewhat exaggerated importance, indicating a concern for detail. Other early cups show the same interest; compare, for example, the cups in the archaeological collection of the Johns Hopkins University and in Berlin-Charlottenburg.[6] The man seated on a stool on the inside of the cup has a long almond-shaped eye with a light iris, the inner corner left open to approximate a true profile rendering. The long eye and light iris is typical of Douris in his early period and continues; the open corner of the eye becomes more frequent in his later work. The schematic rendering of the ear is paralleled on the Vienna cup and on an early cup in the Vatican.[7] The scalloped neckline of the chiton is similar to the neck and arm holes of the chitoniskoi worn by the youths arming on the Vienna cup and to the neckline of the flute girl on a cup in Berlin.[8] For the rendering of the stiff folds of the himation, compare the cup fragments in Tübingen and the Cabinet des Médailles.[9]

The man on the Getty fragment sits on a folding stool, one corner of which is visible. This type of stool could have a cloth or leather seat or a seat of firmer material. There are pivotal pins on each side of the seat rails—one is visible—and at the junction of the legs which in this type of stool are crossed and usually end in hooves or lion's paws.[10] The seat itself must be of a firm material, since it seems to be bearing the weight of the man. It is ornamented with carved decoration and has on it a cushion embroidered with a lattice pattern and dots rendered in dilute glaze. This emphasis on linear detail is consistent with what has been noted on the outside of the fragments.

The folding stool is less common in Douris' work than the stool with four perpendicular legs, but it does appear on at least one vase of his Early Middle period, a white lekythos in Switzerland with an arming scene,[11] and on several cups of the Middle period, in one of which the subject on the inside is a warrior seated, and the subject on the outside is the voting on the arms of Achilles.[12] It would seem that the folding stool was considered appropriate for scenes in army camps. In this case, the scene on the inside of the Getty fragments might be related to the scene on the outside, which must represent warriors arming since at least two of them already have their ankle guards on.

The ornament, delight in linear detail, and style of drawing all suggest that the new Getty fragments should be

10. G.M.A. Richter, *The Furniture of the Greeks, Etruscans, and Romans* (London, 1966) 43–45.

11. *Art Antique, Collections Privées de Suisse Romande* (Geneva, 1975) no. 205.

12. Vatican, Astarita 132 (*ARV²* 433, 72).

placed very close to the Vienna arming cup in the sequence of Douris' works. The Vienna cup is exceptional in the early work of Douris because of the richness of linear patterning, the elaborate ornamental schemes, the lavish use of dilute glaze contrasted with patterned and dark areas, and the full composition achieved by overlapping figures and objects. It has been suggested that the Vienna cup was painted under the influence of another vase painter.[13] The characteristics we have noted occur in the work of one of the greatest Attic vase painters, who in his later years was also a potter—Euphronios. Douris, in his early period, painted several cups attributed to Euphronios as potter,[14] and it is probable that Douris was apprenticed in the workshop of Euphronios. The Getty fragments, by reason of their similarity to the Vienna cup, give us another cup that reflects the period of Euphronios' influence in Douris' work.

Chevy Chase, Maryland

13. A Furtwängler, K. Reichhold, *Griechische Vasenmalerei* (Munich, 1904-1932) 53; J.D. Beazley, *Attic Red-Figured Vases in American Museums* (Cambridge, 1918) 98, note 1.

14. Louvre G 127 (*ARV²* 427, 1); Vatican (*ARV²* 427, 2); and Berlin 3168 (*ARV²* 428, 13). On the attribution of these three cups to Euphronios as potter, see H. Bloesch, *Formen attischer Schalen* (Berlin, 1940) 70, 71, 77.

A Fragmentary Hydria by the Berlin Painter

Mark Kotansky, Karen Manchester, Jiří Frel

The remains of an Attic red-figure hydria were among a large set of vase fragments presented anonymously to the J. Paul Getty Museum in 1981 (figs. 1–10).[1] Although incomplete, parts of the pot have been sufficiently mended from the surviving fragments to reconstruct the characteristic wide mouth, broad horizontal shoulder, and ovoid body of the traditional black-figure shape.

Above a softly flaring neck, the overhanging lip is distinguished by a central rib, creating two narrow registers. The upper zone broadens toward its base and is decorated with eggs and dots, while the reserved band below angles inward toward the neck. On the flat surface inside the rim, an Etruscan graffito is scratched into the glaze (fig. 1).

ε Λ ο/Λ

The vertical handle has a central rib and is flanked by two rotellae on the rim.

Just below the point of attachment to the body, two narrow incised lines precede the foot (fig. 3), whose ogee contour flares out toward a toroid base. Inside are splashes of black that apparently dripped from the brush as the glaze was applied to the mouth area.

Numerous black sherds from the body of the vase are preserved, but only a few fragments of the figural decoration have survived. Except for the subsidiary decoration on the rim and the palmette beneath the upright handle (fig. 2), all painting was confined to the area on the obverse between the two carrying handles. One fragment (fig. 4) shows the lower legs of a draped male figure facing left. The contour of his outer leg can be seen through his himation, the hemline of his garment terminating in a point or tassel. Behind him, the end of a knobbed stick rests on the ground. Below, providing a groundline for the figure, is a stopt maeander pattern alternating with boxed and dotted saltire squares. A second fragment (fig. 6) depicts the right termination of the maeander band and above the remains of a second pair of feet. Broken across the instep, the lower leg and heel of the left foot are illustrated as well as the partly raised foot of the figure as he steps forward. A third group of sherds has been joined to produce another frag-

ment (fig. 5) with an elegant figure wearing a himation. The profile head, set off from the background by a narrow reserved zone, is canted slightly downward; individual ringlets of hair fall from beneath an added-red wreath and fillet bound around his head. Behind the figure's ear, relief lines distinguish three reserved tear shapes.

In addition, there are several minor fragments from the figural zone. One, from the shoulder of the hydria (fig. 7), has a section of a knobbed stick; another (fig. 8), only the tiny point or tassel from the corner of a garment; and a third sherd (fig. 9) appears to depict a small section of a draped figure. The arcing black line that bisects the reserved section of the fragment possibly represents a fold in a garment. Nearby a faint line of dilute glaze is introduced from one edge. The last figural fragment (fig. 10), almost entirely black, is intersected at one corner by a narrow curving band in reserve that is distinguished by a central black line. In the upper left limits of the figural zone not enough remains to identify the context.

Even with such minimal remains, it is possible to recognize the hydria as an early work by the Berlin Painter from the first decade of the fifth century. Certain distinctive trademarks of his style support the attribution, such as the eye with its medial opening and the parallel contour of the brow above, as well as the use of a pair of curving black lines to designate the helix of the ear. Also important is the use of dilute glaze to render the musculature of the lower leg. At first these faint lines seem to indicate the preliminary sketch, but careful examination reveals that the bulging calf muscle just below the hem is also lightly defined. At the juncture of leg and foot a pair of black hooks articulates the protuberances of the ankle bones. The feet are carefully contoured, each toe individually defined with the largest digit markedly shorter than the next. With its arced kneecap, the profile of the near leg is visible beneath the drapery. These, plus the small tassels at the ends of the drapery, are usual additions; parallels for each of these features can be found on other pots decorated by the Berlin Painter during his early period. The brush strokes preserved in the glaze, as well as the placement of the carrying handle, clearly indicate that the cloaked man is the terminal figure to the right of the composition. The upraised foot on another fragment certainly

---

1. Malibu, The J. Paul Getty Museum accession number 81.AE.206.B1.

Figure 1. Rim of a fragmentary Attic red-figure hydria attributed to the Berlin Painter. Malibu, The J. Paul Getty Museum 81.AE.206.B1. Diam. 22.3 cm.

Figure 2. Fragment of Malibu 81.AE.206.B1. Max. length 18.7 cm.

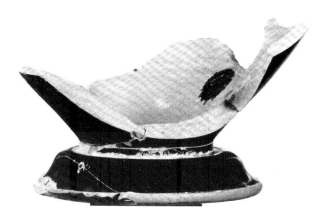

Figure 3. Base of Malibu 81.AE.206.B1. Diam. 15.3 cm.

Figure 4. Fragment of Malibu 81.AE.206.B1. Max. length 15.1 cm.

Figure 5. Fragment of Malibu 81.AE.206.B1. Max. length 16.5 cm.

Figure 6. Fragment of Malibu 81.AE.206.B1. Length of top
edge 5.1 cm.

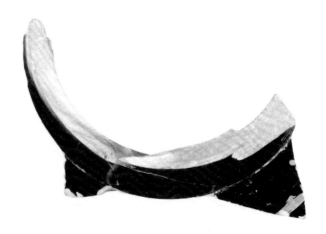

Figure 7. Fragment of Malibu 81.AE.206.B1. Distance
from point to point 10.7 cm.

Figure 8. Fragment of Malibu 81.AE.206.B1. Length of left edge 1.7 cm.

Figure 9. Fragment of Malibu 81.AE.206.B1. Length of top edge 2.2 cm.

Figure 10. Fragment of Malibu 81.AE.206.B1. Length of right edge 3.8 cm.

belongs to him, as the right extreme of the maeander is visible below. Facing left, he probably held the upper end of the stick that angles diagonally up from behind the legs of the other figure. Closely compacted, these two figures were probably joined by a third who approached from the left, resulting in an even distribution of the scene over its allotted area. It is possible that the fragment illustrating what appears to be a fold in a garment and the piece from the shoulder with the section of a knobbed stick may also have belonged to this third figure, who is otherwise lost. In addition to the characteristic drawing, the unusual shape of the vase fits into the Berlin Painter's known oeuvre and serves to substantiate the attribution. With its contour corresponding exactly to the Vatican hydria, it seems probable that the Getty vase was fashioned by the same hand that threw other pots for the Berlin Painter as well.[2]

Beazley lists seven hydriai of the stately black-figure shape that the artist decorated; five are from his early period.[3] With the discovery of the Getty hydria, the recorded number is now brought to eight. It is unfortunate that no more of this handsome vase remains.

Malibu

2. Particularly good comparisons are Athens Akr. 742 (G24) and London E 459, from Athens (*ARV²* 205.117, *Der Berlin Maler*, pl. 32); and NY 56.171.38 (ex Hearst), from Nola (*ARV²* 197.3, *Berl.*, pl. 21).

3. *ARV²* 209.162–168.

A New Meidian Kylix

Marion True

A large late fifth century kylix in the Getty Museum has recently focused attention on the Meidias/Meidian question (figs. 1–4).[1] In his discussion of late fifth century Attic vase painting, Walter Hahland wrote that the artist called the Meidias Painter was one of the most skillful draughtsmen in history.[2] His tableaux on large vases that show gardens filled with elegant women, erotes, and sometimes mythological heroes, obviously appealed to a population which was tired of the incessant Peloponnesian War and probably enjoyed some relief in these pleasant fantasies. More intimate scenes of erotes and women adorning themselves and conversing decorated the smaller vase shapes intended for personal use.

As the Meidias Painter was very popular, he was also widely imitated. His influential style presents some serious problems to the students of vases who try to separate his work from that of his contemporaries. Similar compositional elements that would usually be considered strong evidence for a specific attribution—such as details of costume and drapery, poses, the shape of feet, the gestures of hands, or the treatment of the hair—appear not only on the artist's own vases but also on works by even the most original of his immediate circle of associates. Because of this, the corpus of work attributed to the hand of the Meidias Painter changes, often significantly, with every new publication on late fifth century vase painting. Beazley began with a list of 61 vases attributed to the Meidias Painter;[3] he finished with only 21, possibly 29.[4] However, he listed some 13 other artists and groups of artists as subdivisions of the Meidias Painter's manner, and another 130 vases were assigned to the artist's manner, sundry.[5] F. Hauser once suggested that the Meidian vase painter who signed himself as Aristophanes should be identified with the Meidias Painter;[6] and recently Ursula

Knigge proposed that the Meidias Painter is none other than Aison, another of the few artists working in the Meidian manner who actually signed his name.[7] The Getty cup does not, in my opinion, offer support for these interesting hypotheses, but it may add some new dimensions to the corpus of work attributed to the Meidians.

The Getty cup is well preserved, though it was broken and repaired already in antiquity[8] and has suffered more extensive damage since these original repairs were made. Overall losses are small, and the surface is generally intact. The graceful appearance of the wide, shallow bowl (fig. 1) is deceptive, for the cup is actually quite heavy to the hands and clumsily potted. The underfoot is glazed with a single black band, centered between the outer edge and the inner stem, which leaves most of the footplate reserved.

On the inside (fig. 2), a dense left-handed maeander set between reserved lines frames the tondo. The pattern is interrupted after every third square by a checkered square with dotted reserved areas (kreuzblatt), and the odd fellow is just above the center of the left side of the frame, where half a maeander is suppressed. The tondo has an empty exergue separated by a relief line from the three figures who stand and sit above, but this reserved space was not intended to serve as a groundline. Rather, the setting here is a rocky landscape whose roughness was originally indicated with fine lines added in red paint. Now worn away, these lines are still traceable as dark shadows on the milky green-black surface. The only element that touches the exergue is a delicate plant with three branches.

At the left side of the medallion, a woman stands in profile facing the center. Her left foot is raised high on the irregular ground, and she bends forward, gesturing with her right hand to the woman who sits before her. The transparent belted chiton enhances her attractive pose. Its tiny

1. The cup is Getty accession number 82.AE.38. Height: 12.4 – 13 cm. Diameter of the bowl: 35.4–5 cm. Width with handles: 47.2 cm. Diameter of the foot: 13.5 cm. Since my first seminar with Dietrich von Bothmer was entitled "Attic Red-Figure Kylikes," the publication of a newly acquired Attic cup seems an appropriate offering to the much-deserved volume in his honor. I wish to express my thanks to Jiří Frel, not only for permission to publish the cup but also for his invaluable suggestions for improvement of the text and bibliographic references.

2. W. Hahland, *Vasen um Meidias* (2nd ed., Mainz, 1976) 5.

3. J. D. Beazley, *Attische Vasenmaler* (Tübingen, 1925) 459ff., quoted in

W. Real, *Studien zur Entwicklung der Vasenmalerei im ausgehenden 5. Jahrhundert v. Chr.* (Münster, 1973) 58 n. 78.

4. ARV² 1312–1314; Para. 477.

5. ARV² 1315–1332, Para. 477–480.

6. Real (*supra* n. 3) 73 n. 93.

7. U. Knigge, "Aison, der Meidiasmaler?" AM 90 (1975) 123–143, taf. 43–51.

8. There are the remains of five bronze rivets in the bowl, two of which form a pair. In addition, there are two empty holes connected by a deep channel for another type of repair.

Figure 1. Attic red-figure kylix. Side A. Malibu, The J. Paul Getty Museum 82.AE.38. H: 12.4–13 cm.

folds cling to her legs in impossible patterns which empha-size the roundness of the thighs and calves, while the dark parallel woven stripes running down the side ignore the folds and follow the curve of her back and knee. Behind her right shoulder, a bunch of the soft fabric has escaped the dark cord which is tied around the shoulders to hold the sleeveless bodice in place. Her hair is pulled up in a krobylos, wrapped around with an elaborate apicate band. The stephane is lozenge-patterned, with a broad extension under the krobylos decorated with a volute. She also wears a necklace and an earring that was once painted white.

The central figure is seated in three-quarter view with her head, slightly bowed, in profile to the left. Her left foot is drawn up to a ledge somewhat above her right, her right hand rests quietly in her lap, and her left hand is ex-tended, palm down, behind her on the rocky seat to pro-vide support. She wears a sleeved chiton of fine fabric, belted at the waist and fastened with cord at the shoulders, and around her legs she has wrapped a himation of thicker, starred material. One thin dark stripe is woven into the lower edge of her chiton, and another runs irreg-ularly just across the midriff. Although the back of her head is damaged, enough survives to show that part of her hair is bound up at the nape of the neck. Another part is gathered into a sort of bun over the left temple, and across the front of her head is set an apicate stephane decorated with maeander pattern. Her jewelry consists of a necklace, bracelet, and earring.

On the left shoulder of the seated woman rests the hand

of the Eros who stands behind her. His nude body is fron-tal, but his outspread wings and his head are turned to the left as he observes the pair before him. His hair is pulled up into a topknot.

The presence of Eros in combination with the pose of the standing woman provides a clue to her identification. She must be Peitho, goddess of Persuasion, counseling the modest central figure about love. The identity of this seated woman is not a problem, for the artist has carefully inscribed her name above her head in painted letters which have left ghosts: ΔΕΜΩΝΑ૬Α૬ (Demonassa).

A Demonassa appears on at least two other late red-figure pieces, one a hydria in Florence indisputably attri-buted to the Meidias Painter and dated around 410 B.C. (fig. 6),[9] the other a fragment of a pyxis in the Agora from the time of the Jena Painter, that is, about 400 B.C.[10] Unlike the pyxis fragment, the Florentine vase preserves a context for the woman. There she is the companion of Phaon, the ferryman of Lesbos who won Aphrodite's grat-itude for giving her passage on his boat when she was dis-guised as a poor old woman. Phaon's reward was the woman of his choice, and in a version of the myth popular at this time, he apparently rejected the poetess Sappho, with whom he is often linked, in favor of Demonassa.[11] On the hydria, Phaon plays the lyre for Demonassa beneath an arch of laurel leaves, surrounded by erotes and gods in a rocky garden.

The drawing in the tondo of the Getty cup is careful and controlled, with nearly all details of the figures and the

9. Florence 81947, *ARV²* 1312, 2. Inscribed: ΔΗΜΩΝΑ૬.

10. J. D. Beazley, "Some Inscriptions on Vases, V," *AJA* 54 (1950) 320. Inscribed: ΔΗΜΩΝΑ૬૬A.

11. *Ibid.* Real's explanation (*supra* n. 3) of Demonassa as a personi-fication of the female population of Lesbos seems unnecessary. The name was already known in mythology and vase painting in the sixth century

when a Demonassa, daughter of Amphiaraos, was represented as a child with her name inscribed on a Corinthian krater once in Berlin and now destroyed (*RE* vol. 5.1, col. 143, Demonassa). Beazley also notes that a hetaira of this name is mentioned by Lucian. The inconsistency in the spelling of the name, most specifically in the use of E instead of H shows simply that the artist was aware of both letters.

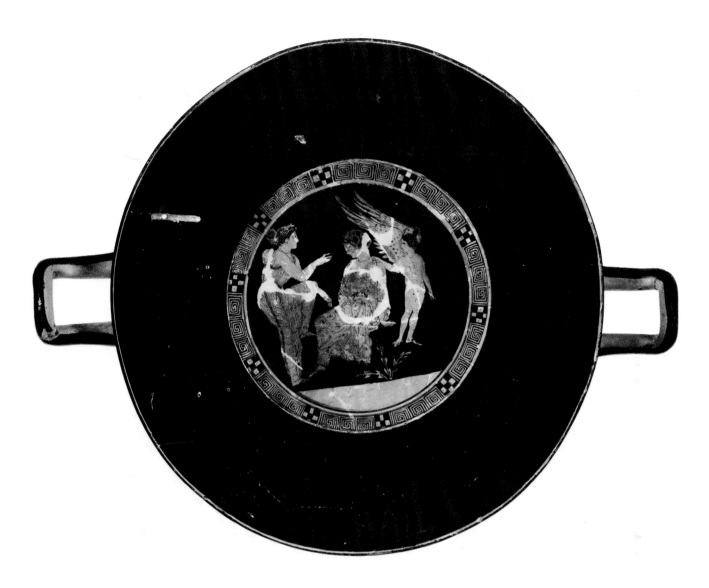

Figure 2. Malibu 82.AE.38. Interior. Diam: 35.5 cm.

plant executed in extremely fine relief line; the vase may be dated to about 410 B.C., close to the Florence hydria. Of the entire design, only the maeander pattern is not in relief line. Dilute glaze has been added for the irises, the wash beneath the individual strands of hair on each head, and for the shading on the upper row of feathers in Eros' wings. Evidence of preliminary sketches can be found on Peitho's right leg and face profile (which was moved to the right), on Demonassa's himation, and on Eros' profile, along the left side of his torso, and on his left arm. Still, there is a certain sloppiness in the application of the slip which fills the background, and a carelessness which is in marked contrast to the precise contours of the figures and drapery. Unintentional specks appear on Peitho's chiton, on Eros' body, and in the maeander border, and a close inspection of the black ground under raking light reveals obvious spots where the loaded brush was lifted, leaving ir-

regularities in the otherwise smooth surface.

This carelessness is more apparent on the outside. In addition to the obvious brushwork of the background, the cyma pattern which runs around the entire rim has a large smear across it over the head of the right end figure on one side (B) (fig. 4). Several of the female subjects on the same side are actually disfigured with awkward splotches of black (note that these irregular smears seem to follow a pattern: from the left arm of the first figure on the left to the almost totally defaced visage of the last figure on the right—that looks like the path of a brush accidentally dragged across the surface). In many places, the background has encroached on the outlines of the figures, obscuring edges of drapery and outlines of projecting fingers.

Each side of the bowl presents a group of women, conversing and adorning themselves, composed of five stand-

Figure 3. Malibu 82.AE.38. Detail of side A.

ing figures gathered in various poses around a more or less central seated figure. On side A (fig. 3), the first woman on the left stands in profile facing right, holding a wreath of laurel leaves out in front of her. The leaves were added in red or white which has now faded. Next to her stands a woman, her body frontal and her head in profile to the right, holding out a mirror in her left hand. The third figure is seated on a klismos, her legs to the left but her shoulders frontal and her head turned back toward the trio who stand behind her on the right. Her left hand is raised in an awkward, meaningless gesture. Of the remaining three women, two face each other in conversation and the last figure on the right end stands frontally, looking back to the left, holding a long painted cord (now faded) with tasseled ends in her outspread hands.

Side B (fig. 4) offers a variation of the same subject. Here, the first two women on the left converse, the leftmost with one hand on her companion's shoulder. The third woman bends attentively over the fourth, who is seated to the right on a klismos. On this side, the gesture of the seated figure's left hand is not an affectation, for she holds in it a painted flower, now faded. Before her on the right stand two more women, both with raised right hands, appar-

ently in conversation.

On each side, the seated figure and one of the standing women wear transparent chitons wrapped around with heavier himatia. The other four women wear girded or ungirded versions of the Doric peplos in which the artist has gone to some pains to distinguish different types of fabric. Some fall in brittle folds, others flow more gracefully with dark linear patterns woven into the materials. But in no case is the drapery drawn with the care lavished on the garments of the two figures inside the cup. A comparison between the fine lines that describe the paths of the crinkly fabric over Demonassa's breasts and shoulders and the more coarsely rendered folds that follow the contours of the breasts of the women in chitons on the exterior may demonstrate the difference. Nowhere on the outside do the contours of the drapery conform so closely to the rounded forms of the lower body beneath as in the figure of Peitho.

Several of the women on both sides wear bracelets, and six have elaborate hair ornaments. On two (figure 1 on side A and figure 4 on B), the hair is bound up in sakkoi; a third woman (figure 4 on side A) wears a spiral-patterned apicate stephane with thick white paint, once overlaid

Figure 4. Malibu 82.AE.38. Detail of side B.

with gilding, on the three points across the front of her head. On the fourth (figure 3 on side A), a series of three narrow bands ornamented with little leaves is tied around the head; the fifth wears an all-black apicate stephane (figure 2 from left, side A), difficult to distinguish from her hair; and the sixth (figure 2 on side B) has a stephane decorated with cyma pattern fastened into a large sort of bun over her ear, similar to the style of Demonassa. Two of the women without hair ornaments (figure 5 on side A and figure 1 on side B) once had long fillets of added red tied around their krobyloi.

The artist has offered no clue to the identities of the figures. The only complete inscription, added in red over the head of the seated woman on side A, is KALH, "beautiful." The subject is apparently as simple as it appears, with the only possible distinctions being those of social position. The seated women, those dressed similarly in himatia over chitons, and figure 4 on side A who wears the elaborate stephane apparently are attended by the other women gathered around them. The interpretation of a fragmentary inscription on side B of the exterior will be considered below.

Though certain details, such as the hair ornaments, are done with care and there is abundant evidence of preliminary sketchwork in most of the drapery, none of these exterior figures is distinguished by fine drawing. The relief lines in many cases are coarse, the feet barely distinguishable, and the hands often ill-proportioned and poorly drawn (figures 3 and 5 on side A; figure 1 on side B especially). In the drapery, consideration is given to distinctions of fabric, but large areas are rendered with summary indications of folds and gathers. Especially the patterns of folds in the himatia of figure 3 on side A and figure 6 on side B have no relationship to natural appearance.

Still, in comparison with the drawing on the inside, certain important similarities in minor details are visible. The eye of Peitho is very close in appearance to the eye of the seated woman in the center of side B. In both cases, the profile eye is carefully delineated with two fine lines joined at the inner corner for the upper lid, a curving lower lid which is only half as long as the upper, and an iris indicated in dilute glaze with a black pupil and relief outline. Also, the right foot of Peitho can be compared with the right foot of the seated woman on side B. Both show long delicate toes, the large toe separated distinctly from the others, and the small toe, much tinier than the rest, set

Figure 5. Malibu 82.AE.38. Detail of floral pattern around handle B/A.

down somewhat on the side of the foot. The unusual square-ended folds visible around Demonassa's right knee appear again in the peploi of figures 1, 3, and 4 (side B). Finally, the tiny folds of the sleeved chitons worn by the women outside follow similar horizontal patterns across the shoulders and across the breasts as those on Demonassa's garment. Though the lines of Demonassa's chiton are much finer, the erratic alternations of horizontal and vertical fold patterns in all of the chitons are inspired by the same notion.

Such comparisons suggest that the interior was drawn with care by a master. The exterior figures are either rapid products of the same hand, drawn with far less interest, or they are the efforts of a close follower working in the master's style and perhaps over his preliminary sketches. I opt for the latter explanation because the interior is so different from the exterior in spirit.

The question of the number of hands involved in the decoration of this kylix becomes more complicated, however, with the ornamental patterns. Beneath the figural

12. The closest parallel for these florals known to me appears on two fragments of a large volute krater in Würzburg, H4729 a and b, attributed to the circle of the Pronomos Painter and dated ca. 400 B.C The suggestion that these fragments belonged to the same krater as Würzburg frag-

ments H4781 (*ARV*² 1690) has now been replaced with the suggestion that the two groups of fragments come from the principal sides of two very similar kraters from the same workshop (F. Holscher, *CVA* Deutschland 46, Würzburg fasc. 2, [Munich, 1980] 56–58, pl. 40).

decoration is a maeander pattern with checkerboard interruptions, similar in every way to the border around the tondo except that the maeanders are simpler. Yet if this particular pattern is common in this period and uninspired, the explosion of floral motives beneath the handles is wonderfully unique (fig. 5).[12] At each side of the bowl, a large irregular cluster of palmettes with ribbed fronds, spiraling volutes, acanthusizing lotus buds, acanthus leaves, single fronds, and little bull's eye dots fill the space between the figural compositions. Some of these elements, the addorsed acanthusizing lotus buds, for example, are unusual, but what is most remarkable about these patterns is the complete lack of symmetry. Unlike the ornamental patterns on nearly every other surviving vase of this period, these motives are not centered or balanced in any regular way. Rather, the whole complex seems to grow in natural luxuriance. Still, the density of the elements dispersed around the handles is fairly uniform, and the impression of the whole composition is that of a refreshingly original and harmonious design.

Adrienne Lezzi-Hafter has convincingly demonstrated that the floral patterns of many Attic late-fifth-century vases were executed quite independently of the figural decoration, and they may be assigned to a small group of artists who specialized in ornament.[13] In fact, every individual element of the unusual florals on the Getty cup is to be found in the acanthusizing group of her Hand Three, the last of the painters of "Shuvalov florals."[14] And not only do the individual floral elements accord with those attributed to Hand Three, so also does the left-handed maeander pattern with checkerboard interruptions. What makes the Getty kylix's ornamentation exceptional is the asymmetrical way in which the floral elements have been combined. If not the work of Hand Three, the ornamental patterns on the Getty kylix are an important variation by one of his immediate associates.[14bis]

Patterns painted by Hand Three are most often found on vases attributed to figure painters from the Meidian circle and on at least one by the Meidias Painter himself.[15] Thus the florals, following the inscription Demonassa, are the second piece of evidence to link the cup with the Meidian circle. And with this connection established, the details of drapery and costume on the Getty kylix, poses, the feminine subject matter, and the general grace that distinguishes the drawing, especially in the tondo, can serve to confirm an attribution to the Meidian manner.[16]

But is the artist Meidian or is he the Meidias Painter himself? The answer to this question requires more than consistency of the widely imitated details; it requires specific parallels.

Perhaps the Florence hydria provides the most important evidence for this problem and not just with its inscription. The name Demonassa is the fortunate connection to the vase on which are other compositional elements more significant for attribution. To the left of the Phaon-Demonassa group are two women, one seated and one standing, labeled respectively Chrysogeneia and Leura (fig. 6), who offer some interesting comparisons with the two women in the tondo of the Getty cup (fig. 8). The two are situated in a rocky landscape, similar to that around Peitho and Demonassa, with its irregularity indicated by fine painted lines. The ribbed leaves of the laurel branch beside them, which arcs over the heads of Phaon and Demonassa, recall those of the Getty cup's plant that grows below the seated Demonassa.

Seated Chrysogeneia is dressed like the Getty Demonassa in a belted, long-sleeved chiton which is wrapped at the hips with a starred himation. The folds of her bodice are similarly irregular—roughly horizontal around the neck and over the breasts, then vertical over the midriff—and a similar woven stripe runs through the vertical folds, a little higher and straighter in its course than on Demonassa's chiton. Chrysogeneia wears her hair in the style of the Getty Demonassa, with the bun over the temple distinguished from the rest of the hair by the same circular pattern of its wavy strands. The only difference in costume is the apicate stephane, decorated here with a cyma pattern rather than the maeander.

However, the more important figure for the purpose of attribution is Leura. Like Peitho, she wears a transparent sleeveless chiton belted at the waist and bound around the shoulders with a black cord. An edge of drapery has escaped the cord and flutters behind her back under the right arm, recalling the wisp that billows out behind Peitho's back. But the most striking similarity to the figure of Peitho appears in the pattern of folds which models Leura's right leg. The fine diagonal lines across the thigh that subtly change to shallow horizontal curves around the knee and calf are almost identical on the two figures, as are the profiles of the legs and the proportions of the bodies.

Virtually the same formula for drapery appears on yet

13. A. Lezzi-Hafter, *Der Schuwalow-Maler* (Mainz, 1976) 41–51.

14. *Ibid.,* 46–49.

14bis. Dr. Lezzi-Hafter has noted in correspondence (7-24-84) that she does not believe that the florals are by Hand Three, although they are

inspired by those of Hand Three, or vice versa.

15. *Ibid.,* 46.

16. For the general features of the Meidian style, see W. Hahland, *op. cit.* and G. Becatti, *Meidias, un manierista antico* (Firenze, 1957) 16–19.

Figure 6. Detail of red-figure hydria attributed to the Meidias Painter. Florence 81947. Photo: Soprintendenza Archeologica per la Toscana.

Figure 7. Detail of red-figure hydria by the Meidias Painter. London E 224.

Figure 8. Malibu 82.AE.38. Detail of interior.

another figure by the Meidias Painter, this time on the hydria in London which is the name piece of the artist.[17] In the center of the lower register, the scene in the Garden of the Hesperides, a figure labeled Asterope leans on the shoulder of Chrysothemis who reaches out to pick an apple from the sacred tree (fig. 7). Asterope wears the sleeveless, belted chiton of Peitho and Leura. Again, a corner of the bodice forms a graceful frill behind the right shoulder. The filmy fabric clings to her right leg in a pattern which repeats that on the figures on the other two vases almost line for line, emphasizing the fact that the outlines and proportions of thigh and calf are also similar.

It is true that the Meidias Painter was widely imitated, and one of the most notable features of his drapery is this sort of pantaloon-like arrangement of folds. Yet no identifiable artist in the Meidian circle uses exactly this pattern of folds on legs of precisely these contours and proportions.[18] Neither does any imitative example of the leg-hugging drapery on a workshop piece show the sensitivity to the modeling of volumes found in the figure of Peitho. She is drawn with the same confidence and ease as Leura and Asterope in contrast to the rigidity and self-consciousness that generally distinguish a copy.

The drapery of the Peitho figure is the compositional ele-

17. London E 224; *ARV²* 1313, 5.

18. Mention must be made here of the Palermo krater, attributed by Beazley to the manner of the Meidias Painter, sundry (*ARV²* 1321, 9). The subject on side A is again Phaon, and before him stands an unnamed woman whose pose is very similar to that of Leura and Asterope. The pattern of folds around her right leg is very close to the formula found in the figures of Peitho, Leura, and Asterope, but the heavy proportions of the figure are quite different. Similar to the Getty cup also are the square-

ended folds in the drapery around the leg of the female figure behind this woman, and the position of Phaon's left hand is basically the same as that of Demonassa's. Furtwängler had actually attributed the Palermo vase to the Meidias Painter as a late work (*ARV²* 1321), and Real has recently suggested that it is the vase most closely related to the artists' hydriai (*supra* n. 3, p. 68). In spite of these similarities, I consider the krater still to be manner of the Meidias Painter.

ment most specifically related to the works of the Meidias Painter, but the other details of costume, poses, facial features, feet, and hands of Peitho and Demonassa, mentioned before as more generally Meidian, serve to support the attribution of the tondo to this artist with numerous parallels among the figures on his best-known vases.[19] Only the figure of Eros, larger than most Meidian erotes, has no known counterpart. Still, individual details of his figure—the double vertical line over his sternum and over his midriff, his clumsy feet, and the general contours of his wings—can be found among the Meidias Painter's compositions.[20]

There are, of course, objections to be raised to this attribution. For one, there is no other kylix now attributed to the artist. Given the odds against the survival of any Greek vase, this fact should not be so much an objection as an observation. But, in consideration of the Getty tondo composition, it might be added that the artist of this cup was not adept at filling a circular frame, a fact which may account for the dearth of cups from his hand.[21] The vacant reserved exergue does nothing to improve the unbalanced design, heavily weighted to the left side of the bowl and too empty to the right. Another objection is the fact that although the Meidias Painter frequently employed the three-quarter view of the face on his other

vases, every head on this cup, inside and out, is in profile, even when a three-quarter view would have been more effective and appropriate to the figure. However, every Meidian artist was capable of rendering a three-quarter face, so the choice was intentional. It may simply reflect the same lack of interest shown in the general execution of the exterior figural compositions.

In conclusion, there is one final piece of evidence that must be mentioned, although its meaning is certainly not clear. On side B (fig. 4), over the heads of the last two figures on the right end are the remains of an inscription: E ΔA. It seems unlikely that the letters are part of a reference to one of the figures in the scene, since the only other inscription on the exterior is the banal ΚALH. However, it is possible, in terms of space, to restore MEIΔIAℲ, though the intervals between the letters would be somewhat wide and irregular, especially since a head intrudes between the E and Δ. There is also room on the same side of the handle to restore a verb, though no apparent justification to do so. But since the only other signature of Meidias the potter appears on the London hydria mentioned above as the name piece of the Meidias Painter, it may not be too presumptuous to propose this name as one possible interpretation for an inscription on a cup now attributed to the painter with whom Meidias is known to have collaborated.

Malibu

19. Among the figures on the two hydriai in Florence (81948 and 81947, ARV² 1312, 1 and 2), the hydria in London (E 224, ARV² 1313, 5), and the New York pelike (Metropolitan Museum 37.11.23, ARV² 1313, 7) are many parallels for the garments and headdresses of Peitho and Demonassa. There also can be found the eyes with irises rendered in dilute glaze; the unbroken line of the profile from hair to tip of nose; the delicate slit of the mouth with its tiny oblique corner; the double lines for the helix of the ear; the elongated toes with carefully separated large toes and tiny small toes; and the wavy relief lines of hair laid over a dilute glaze wash, arranged in variations of the hairstyles of the Getty figures. For the pose of Peitho and the gesture of her right hand, the closest parallel is found with the figure of Klytios in the Garden of the Hesperides scene on the London hydria. Demonassa's seated pose is presented in a number of variations, as is the rocky terrain around her. For the square-ended folds found in Demonassa's himation, the best comparison is on a recently discovered fragment from the Kerameikos attributed to the Meidias Painter (B. von Freytag gen. Löringhoff, "Neue Frühattische Funde aus dem Kerameikos," AM 90 [1975] 75, taf. 21. fig. 3), where the square-ended folds have actually been shaded with dilute wash.

20. The double line between the breasts and again below them appears on the figure of Adonis on the Florence hydria 81948. The awkward frontal foot with foreshortened big toe, more curled middle toes, and hooked little toe is found on the figure of Leto to the right of Demonassa on the Florence hydria 81947 and on the figures of Klymenos and Demophon in the Hesperides scene on the London hydria E 224. These two figures are also similarly posed, though the articulation of the bodies is almost impossible to compare from available reproductions. The elongated profile of Eros' left foot recalls the left foot of Herakles on the New York pelike 37.11.23; the line drawn parallel to the instep is found here as well as on many other figures. The wings of the Eros repeat only the general outlines of the right wing of Pothos on the Florence hydria 81947; however, the articulation of the coverts and the individual feathers is a cruder version, without parallel, of the same wing.

21. It should be noted that there is a plate attributed to the Meidias Painter; though only partially preserved, its figured composition is more successfully adapted to the circular frame. See D. Cramers and E. Simon, "Ein neues Werk des Meidias-Malers," AA 93 (1978), 67–73.

A Parthenonian Centaur

Katherine A. Schwab

Among the vases painted in Athens during the second half of the fifth century B.C., there is a group whose figured compositions were inspired by the sculptures of the Parthenon. Many of these vases are attributed to well-known artists, such as the Niobid Painter, Polygnotos, the Kleophon Painter, the Pronomos Painter, and the Suessula Painter. The painters of other vases, however, have not yet been identified. In the latter category is a red-figure squat lekythos in Malibu (fig. 1).[1] Although it is by a minor painter, perhaps a follower of Polygnotos, it is nevertheless important for what it illustrates. The decoration on this vase is a lone centaur standing on a ground-line facing to right and threatening an unseen opponent with a weapon in his raised right hand. The weapon is not the pine tree or boulder so often associated with centaurs but the upper half of a broken vessel. The use of a vessel as a weapon by centaurs occurs during one specific event in Greek mythology: the wedding feast of the Lapith hero Peirithoos.[2]

The painter of the Malibu vase had available to him in Athens two monumental representations of the centauromachy at the wedding feast as possible sources of his painting. The earlier is the famous wall painting from the 470's, now lost, in the Theseion, which may have shown centaurs hurling vessels. The second is on the south metopes of the Parthenon, finished by about 442, which illustrate the event extensively and include the motif of centaurs hurling vessels.[3]

Of the original thirty-two metopes on the south side of the Parthenon, metopes 1–12 and 21–32 include a centaur either fighting a Lapith or assaulting a Lapith woman, while the middle group participates in an event that is not yet fully understood.[4] Turning to the metopes with duels, there are three in particular that may be the source for the motif of the centaur on the Malibu vase (fig. 1). These are metopes 5, 11, and 28.[5] Metopes 5 (fig. 2) and 11 (fig. 3) are related in composition in that they both have the centaur at left attacking to right while the opposing Lapith is standing at right and attacking to left. The centaur in metope 28 (fig. 4) is also facing to right; but in contrast to the other two examples, he is rearing triumphantly over the body of a Lapith lying on the ground, a unique composition among the metopes.

By comparing the sculptural compositions of these three metopes with those in vase painting, one can isolate a group of painted duels that share one element: a centaur hurling a vessel. Among the painted examples of the vessel-hurling motif there are two categories. The centaur either holds the unbroken vessel overhead with both hands[6] or he holds the upper half of a broken vessel (hydria or pointed amphora) in his raised right hand while extending his left arm in front of him.[7] This left arm is

I offer this essay in honor of Dr. von Bothmer who as a teacher has so generously shared his expertise and enthusiasm for vase painting with his students.

1. Accession number 71.AE.216. I would like to thank Dr. Jiří Frel for inviting me to publish this vase. Height 14.6 cm; diameter of mouth 3.8 cm; diameter of body 9.5 cm; diameter of base 6.9 cm; numerous sketch lines visible on the centaur. It is close to Oxford 1925.69 (*ARV*[2] 1132, 189); see Wolf W. Rudolph, *Die Bauchlekythos* (Bloomington, Ind., 1971) 94 and pl. XVIII.

2. Ancient literary sources: Homer, *Od.* XXI 289–311; Pindar fr. 166 (Schroeder); Paus. I 17.3; Ovid, *Met.* XII 182–535. For a thorough treatment of this centauromachy, see Brian B. Shefton, "Herakles and Theseus on a Red-Figured Louterion," *Hesperia* 31 (1962) 330–368.

3. Before the Parthenon, this centauromachy appeared on the West Pediment of the Temple of Zeus at Olympia by 458/57, but here the centaurs did not use vessels as weapons. On the three later sculpted examples from the second half of the fifth century, vessels again were not used as weapons: the examples are the West Pediment of the so-called Theseum, frieze of the Temple of Poseidon at Sounion, and the interior frieze of the Temple of Apollo at Bassai.

4. Frank Brommer, *Die Metopen des Parthenon* (Mainz, 1967), hereafter

Brommer. For recent interpretations of the middle metopes, see Erika Simon, "Versuch einer Deutung der Südmetopen des Parthenon," *JdI* (1975) 100–120; Martin Robertson, "Two Question-Marks on the Parthenon," *Studies in Classical Art and Archaeology* (Locust Valley, N.Y., 1979) 78–87; and Evelyn Harrison, "Apollo's Cloak," *Studies in Classical Art and Archaeology* (Locust Valley, N.Y. 1979) 92–94, 96–98.

5. Brommer, pls. 178–180, 199, 221–223; Carrey drawings in Brommer, pls. 149–152; and for discussion, see pp. 83–84, 93–94, and 120–121. Metope 32 is related to the other three only in general composition. It is not discussed in the text because its reflection in vase painting indicates that the Lapith holds a sword overhead in his right hand while the centaur counters with a lampstand. For examples see *ARV*[2] 1043,1; 1319,2; 1319,3; and probably 1408,2 and Florence 12220.

6. *ARV*[2] 541,1; Ferrara VP T.136, *CVA*, pl. 13. Whole vessels thrown by both hands overhead all derive from south metope 4; Brommer, pl. 173.

7. An exception is an unbroken pointed amphora held by one hand in the duel at right on Ferrara VP T. 136. See *CVA*, p. 7, where it is noted that the vase may possibly be South Italian. Also see the Faliscan fragmentary amphora in Tübingen, F 16; C. Watzinger, *Griechische Vasen in Tübingen* (Reutlingen, 1924) pl. 46.

Figure 1a. Centaur hurling a broken vessel, detail from a squat lekythos. Malibu, The J. Paul Getty Museum 71.AE.216.

Figure 1b. Malibu 71.AE.216.

Figure 2a. South metope 5. Photo: Brommer, pl. 178.

Figure 2b. Carrey drawing of south metope 5. Photo: Brommer, pl. 149.

Figure 3a. South metope 11. Photo: Brommer, pl. 199.

Figure 3b. Carrey drawing of south metope 11. Photo: Brommer, pl. 150.

Figure 4a. South metope 28. Photo: Brommer, pl. 221.

Figure 4b. Carrey drawing of south metope 28. Photo: Brommer, pl. 152.

Figure 5a. Centaur hurling a broken vessel, detail from side A of a cup by Aristophanes. Boston, Museum of Fine Arts 00.345. Photo: A. Furtwängler-K. Reichhold, *Greichische Vasenmalerei* 3 (1932) pl. 129.

Figure 5b. Centaur hurling a broken vessel, detail from side B of the cup in figure 5a. Photo: Furtwängler-Reichhold 3, pl. 129.

Figure 6. Centaur hurling a broken vessel, detail from a fragmentary pelike in Barcelona, Museo Arqueológico 33. Photo: Furtwängler-Reichhold 3, fig. 25.

often covered by an animal skin for protection. Examples of a centaur hurling a broken vessel occur on the following vases:

> Malibu 71.AE.216, squat lekythos (fig. 1)
> Boston 00.344, cup, by Aristophanes
> Boston 00.345, cup, by Aristophanes (figs. 5a, b)
> Barcelona 33, pelike (fig. 6)

All of the painted examples except the Malibu squat lekythos illustrate a duel in which the opposing Lapith attacks either by thrusting a short sword into the equine chest of the centaur (fig. 5a)[8] or by swinging an axe overhead with both hands (figs. 5b, 6).[9] The stabbing motif derives from the composition in metope 11 (fig. 3). The motif in metope 5 remains inconclusive because the Lapith's arms are not preserved (fig. 2).

A more fruitful result is revealed when comparing metope 28 (fig. 4) with the Malibu squat lekythos (fig. 1). Several important similarities become apparent. Both centaurs move to the right, each with the extended left arm protected by an animal skin. In his raised right hand each holds a vessel in a threatening gesture.[10] A distinctive feature in both cases is that neither is confronted by an attacking Lapith.

There are differences between the centaurs, such as the type of animal skin on the left arm and the position of the tail and right foreleg, but these discrepancies are minor. The feature that is noticeably absent on the Malibu vase is the fallen Lapith so beautifully rendered in the metope. Despite these differences, the similarities between metope 28 and the Malibu squat lekythos single out that vase from the other painted examples. The combination of a centaur who holds a vessel in his raised right hand while facing to the right, the customary direction of the victor in archaic and classical Greek art, and who wears an animal skin protectively over the extended left arm suggests that metope 28 was the source for the motif. The absence of an attacking Lapith, which is unique among the metopes, and the triumphant bearing of the centaur confirm the source as metope 28.

The painter of the Malibu vase can now be added to the group of painters who turned to the Parthenon for inspiration. Although not remarkably talented, this painter was no less ambitious than his contemporaries, for he was perhaps the only one to choose metope 28 for the motif of the triumphant centaur, a unique composition among the south metopes of the Parthenon.

Institute of Fine Arts, NYU
New York

8. Boston 00.344 and 00.345 (fig. 5a), *ARV²* 1319,2; 1319,3.

9. Boston 00.344 and 00.345 (fig. 5b); probably Barcelona 33 (fig. 6), where the centaur is in backview, and for the Lapith at right on Ferrara VP T. 136.

10. A.H. Smith, *British Museum. The Sculptures of the Parthenon* (London, 1910) 36, "large bowl"; and P.E. Corbett, *The Sculpture of the Parthenon* (London, 1959) pl. 3, "remains of a great wine bowl."

A Representation of the *Birds* of Aristophanes

J. R. Green

One of the most fascinating documents for the staging of classical theatre ever to come to light is an Attic red-figure calyx-krater recently acquired by the J. Paul Getty Museum.[1] The vase is reconstructed from a number of large fragments, but, apart from the foot, little of importance is missing. To take the reverse first (figs. 1–2), a youth stands in the center of the scene, facing right. He is nude but for a short cloak which seems to hang over his left arm and shoulder. He holds a spear in front of him with his left hand, and in his right he carries a crested Corinthian helmet. The bronze of the helmet is indicated with a yellow-brown wash. In front of the youth stands another, who wears an enveloping himation and holds a curly stick in his right hand. His hair is remarkably straggly. At the left of the scene is a woman dressed in chiton and himation. Her right hand is concealed within the himation, but her left is extended. The groundline on which the figures stand is a little above the pattern-band that runs between the handles; the pattern comprises three groups of three maeander squares, separated by saltires. Above the scene, on the under-face of the lip and running all around the vase, is a band of laurel. No traces of added colour remain, although one may guess that white was used for stems joining the leaves to the central branch and perhaps for dot-buds between the leaves. A fragment of the rim is missing from the centre of this side and so are adjoining fragments which would have given the top and back of the central youth's head, his neck, and his right shoulder. Relief con-

tour was used only intermittently: on the figure on the right for the back of his shoulders; not at all on the woman; on the central youth for the triangle of the back of his chest and the inner face of his right arm, for the drapery below the helmet, for the spear above his left hand, for the upper side of his left arm and hand, for his nose, and for his legs but not his feet. There are some slight traces of preliminary sketch, the most interesting being a series of lines radiating from the central figure's right elbow, as if the painter had toyed with the idea of having drapery there. The drawing is not particularly competent; notice the crude, out-sized hands of all the figures, or the feet and arm of the youth on the right. The painter clearly expended most of his effort on the central figure, with a fuller use of relief contour, a much better drawn face, and a great deal of internal detail.

The scene on the obverse is more remarkable (fig. 3). A piper stands, frontal, between two dancing men dressed as birds. He is bearded and wears a chiton elaborately decorated with representations of a charioteer (on the left of his chest), winged horses, deer, and hares amid a profusion of crosses, dots, pi-shaped motifs, and a maeander that runs around the skirt. The pipes are also carefully drawn, with their turned bulbs near the mouthpiece.[2] The dancing men apparently wear spherical masks (washed with dilute glaze) with vicious hooked beaks and pronounced combs or crests. On their bodies they wear all-over tights or leotards which terminate at wrist and ankle. They have

1. Malibu, The J. Paul Getty Museum, accession number 82.AE.83. Preserved height 18.7 cm; diameter of lip 23 cm. My first and very warm thanks go to Dr. Jiří Frel for inviting me to publish the vase. I am also indebted to many other friends who have discussed the vase and its associated problems with me, in particular Ann Ashmead, J.-P. Descoeudres, E.W. Handley, Suzanne MacAlister, W. Ritchie, and M. Robertson. I am grateful too to the following for photographs and/or permission to publish them here: A. Andriomenou, G. Beckel, R.S. Bianchi, D. von Bothmer, N. Boukides, H.A. Cahn, B.F. Cook, Chr. Grunwald, U. Kästner, U. Knigge, K.H. Lee, C.W. Neeft, A. Pasquier, N. Schimmel, U. Sinn, V. Tusa, M.J. Vickers, F. Wolsky, and the Trustees of the British Museum.

special abbreviations:

Bieber, *Theater*	M. Bieber, *The History of the Greek and Roman Theater* (¹1939, ²1961)
DFA²	A.W. Pickard-Cambridge, *The Dramatic Festivals of Athens* (2nd ed., rev. by J. Gould and D.M. Lewis, 1968)
DTC²	A.W. Pickard-Cambridge, *Dithyramb, Tragedy and Comedy* (2nd ed., rev. by T.B.L. Webster, 1962)
Ghiron-Bistagne	P. Ghiron-Bistagne, *Recherches sur les acteurs dans la Grèce antique* (1976)
GTP	T.B.L. Webster, *Greek Theatre Production* (¹1956, ²1970)
IGD	A.D. Trendall and T.B.L. Webster, *Illustrations of Greek Drama* (1971)
MMC³	T.B.L. Webster, *Monuments Illustrating Old and Middle Comedy* (3rd ed., rev. and enlarged by J.R. Green, BICS suppl. 39, 1978)
Russo	C.F. Russo, *Aristofane autore di teatro* (1962)
Sifakis *Parabasis*	G.M. Sifakis, *Parabasis and Animal Choruses* (1971)

2. The form is normal for the period: see Landels, BSA 58 (1963) 118; *Hesperia* 33 (1964) 394.

Figure 1. Calyx-krater. Malibu. The J. Paul Getty Museum, 82.AE.83. Reverse.

wings attached between the shoulders, spurs at the backs of the ankles, and shoes on their feet. They also wear short drawers with tails attached at the back and erect phalloi at the front. Their costumes are decorated with dot-filled circles and on the drawers with solid black circles at the hip on which there remain traces of added white. There also seems to have been white on the shoes of the right birdman but not on those of the left.

The use of relief contour is again erratic. For the right-hand figure it was used for the phallos, the face and beak, the upper chest, the shorts, his right leg and the spur behind it; there is also a ring of relief line around the black/white circle on his hip. The piper has relief contours

only down the left side of the chiton's overfall; the left-hand figure has none. Similarly, the painter omitted to draw the toes of the piper's left foot; yet, as on the reverse, the face of the central figure was painted with some care. A curious feature of the drawing of the hands is the use of dots for the knuckles. The pattern-band below the scene comprises two groups of three and one group of two maeander squares, the groups separated by saltires. An area of the wall behind the left-hand figure has misfired.

The uneven character of the drawing does not make the vase easy to date. The painter's style seems most closely related to that of the Painter of Munich 2335,[3] as can be seen in a number of details of drawing and in the way that

3. *ARV*² 1161ff. He too can exhibit a range of quality on a single piece, as on his name vase.

Figure 2. Detail of figure 1.

Figure 3. Malibu 82.AE.83. Obverse.

both derive similar elements from the later, more ordinary work of the Achilles Painter. There can be no doubt that the Painter of Munich 2335's later work runs on to the end of the fifth century even though it was relatively little affected by the Rich Style,[4] and several elements in the drawing of our vase, for example the face of the young warrior on the reverse, the decoration of the piper's chiton, the use of added white, and the form of the laurel or myrtle around the lip (surely also once with added white) all suggest a date towards the later part of the fifth century although not near its end.[5] The form of the vase would also be consistent with such a date.

If such a date is acceptable, the equation of the obverse with the *Birds* of Aristophanes is, to say the least, difficult to avoid. It is one of the plays for which we have a firm date, 414 B.C. As the *hypotheses* tell us, it was produced for Aristophanes at the City Dionysia by Kallistratos in the archonship of Chabrias and won second prize.[6]

The iconographic type of the scene belongs to a tradition going back well over a century, a type in which a piper provides music for a chorus that dances in the guise of animals or particular categories of men, the chorus that so often provided the title for a comedy. A list of examples will perhaps be useful, although most of them are well

4. See Robertson in *Kition* IV, 67, who points out that he leads straight into much of the Plainer Group of early-fourth-century painters. The Berlin Painter, the Achilles Painter, and the Painter of Munich 2335 each seem to have had remarkably long working lives. For a note on the Achilles Painter's chronology, see Cornelia Isler-Kerenyi, "Chronologie und 'Synchronologie' attischer Vasenmaler der Parthenonzeit," *AntK*

Beih. 9 (*Festschrift Bloesch*, 1973) 22–33, esp. 24.

5. On the wreath about the lip, see the useful discussion by Adrienne Lezzi-Hafter, *Der Schuwalow-Maler* (*Kerameus* 2, 1976) 33–34. She also has a good discussion of chronology, pp. 1–4. For the face of our young warrior, compare her fifth (late) sub-group of the Shuvalov Painter, p. 109 (dated ca. 420–415/10 B.C.). It is also worth comparing for style some

Figures 4a–b. No. 1. Siana cup. Amsterdam, Allard Pierson Museum 3356.

known. The order is roughly chronological; the references are selective.[7]

1. Black-figure cup (Siana cup) (figs. 4a–b). A and B:

Piper and six men dancing. On each side the men are divided into half-choruses to either side of the piper, each half wearing different dress and dancing different steps. Some wear feathers.

of the earlier work of the Academy Painter, *ARV*[2] 1124–25, such as the Athens hydria, *BCH* 92 (1968) 595, fig. 47. His late work belongs to the early fourth century: see Beazley, *JHS* 59 (1939) 26, no. 62. By the later fifth century, a scene with departure of a warrior is an old-fashioned one: see Elizabeth G. Pemberton, *JWalters Art Gallery* 36 (1977) 65.

6. Ameipsias' *Komastai* came first, Phrynichus' *Monotropos* third.

Kallistratos also produced the *Banqueters, Babylonians, Acharnians* and *Lysistrata*. See Ghiron-Bistagne 128–129, 134. If, as I hope to demonstrate below, the equation of the scene with the *Birds* can be proved rather than merely supposed in the absence of other evidence and rival claimants, the Getty vase gives a not unimportant fixed point in the development of later-fifth-century red-figure.

Figure 5. No. 2. Detail of hydria. Sweden, private collection. Photo: Widmer.

Figure 6. No. 3. Detail of amphora. Berlin, Staatliche Museen F 1697.

Figure 7. No. 4. Detail of amphora. Christchurch, University of Canterbury 41/57. Photo: Author.

Amsterdam 3356, from Greece.
ABV 66, 57; *CVA* (3) pl. 2, 4; Webster, *Bull. John Rylands Library* 36 (1954) 574, 585; *DTC²* pl. 6b; Webster, *Greek Chorus* pl. 3; *IGD* no. I, 8; *Gods and Men in the Allard Pierson Museum* (1972) pl. 41; *Istoria tou ellenikou ethnous* III, 2, 354 (colour); Ghiron-Bistagne fig. 124.
Ca. 560 B.C. By the Heidelberg Painter. The only clear use of half-choruses in this series. For the costume, compare No. 2 below.

  2. Black–figure hydria (fig. 5). On the shoulder, piper in short striped chiton; four men dancing, wearing peploi with varied decoration and animal ears in their headbands. Sweden, private collection.

Münzen und Medaillen (Basel), *Auktion* 34 (1967) lot 121. Ca. 560 B.C. The piper also wears the animal ears. Their nature and function are unclear; perhaps they represent horse, perhaps deer, ears. If horse, there is no other hint that the men mimic satyrs. This and the previous vase stand apart as the earliest certain examples of the tradition. They are not unlike each other in many respects.

3. Black-figure amphora (fig. 6). Piper and three men dressed as knights on "stage" horses. The knights each have different crests on their helmets.
Berlin F 1697, from Cerveteri (?)
ABV 297, 17; *Para.* 128; Bieber, *Theater*² fig. 126; V. Ehrenberg, *People of Aristophanes* (1951, 1962) pl. 2b; Koller, *Musik und Dichtung* fig. 19; *DTC*² pl. 7; Sifakis, *Parabasis* pl. 1; *Istoria tou ellenikou ethnous* III, 2, 410 (colour); J. Boardman, *Athenian Black Figure Vases* (1974) fig. 137; Ghiron-Bistagne fig. 113.
Ca. 540–530 B.C. By the Painter of Berlin 1686.

4. Black-figure amphora (fig. 7). Five bearded men on stilts wearing corselets and pointed hats, each corselet of the same type but decorated differently.
Christchurch (N.Z.), University of Canterbury 41/57.
Para. 134, 31 *bis*; *DTC*² pl. 8a; *AA* (1962) 755 fig. 8; *AntK* 11 (1968) pl. 15,1; A.D. Trendall, *Greek Vases in the Logie Collection* (1971) pls. 20–21 and frontispiece (colour); *IGD* no. I, 10; *Istoria tou ellenikou ethnous* III, 2, 411 (colour); Boardman, *op. cit.* fig. 144; CVA New Zealand (1) pl. 8; Böhr, *Schaukelmaler* 86 no. 53, pl. 56.
Ca. 530 B.C. By the Swing Painter. Although there is no piper, the identification as a comic chorus seems certain.

5. Black-figure hydria (fig. 8). On the shoulder: three (men dressed as) minotaurs, holding stones.
London B 308, from Vulci.
CVA (6) pl. 81, 1; L.B. Lawler, *The Dance in Ancient Greece* (1964) 71, fig. 27.
Ca. 520 B.C. Compare No. 7. There is no piper and the dress is not obviously artificial, but the pose suggests a chorus. Minotaurs regularly hold stones; so too do the Ram Jug Painter's "trolls" and some padded dancers.

6. Red-figure psykter (fig. 9). Six bearded men riding dolphins, wearing corselets and helmets and carrying shields and single spears.
Kings Point, Norbert Schimmel Collection (on loan to New York, The Metropolitan Museum of Art, L.1979.17.1).
*ARV*² 1622, 7 *bis*; *Para.* 259, 326; Greifenhagen, *Pantheon* 23 (1965) 1–7; Sifakis, *BICS* 14 (1967) 36–37, pl. 6; Sifakis, *Parabasis* pl. 5; H. Hoffmann, *Collecting Greek Antiquities* (1971) colour pl. 9; *IGD* no. I, 15; O.W. Muscarella (ed.), *Ancient Art. The Norbert Schimmel Collection* (1974) no. 57; Boardman, *Archaic Rf* (1975) fig. 58; J. Settgast (ed.), *Von Troja bis Amarna* (1978) no. 76.
Ca. 510 B.C. By Oltos. The costume varies only in the shield-devices (cup, kantharos, and volute–krater alternating with whirligigs). ἐπὶ δελφῖνος comes from the riders' mouths: as Sifakis showed, the words are from their anapaestic entry song. Beazley, *ARV*² 1622, was unsure of the connexion with a chorus because of the absence of a piper, but Sifakis' argument that he would be out of place when the vessel sat in water is cogent. The dress is to be distinguished from the later production on the same theme, Nos. 13–17 below.

7. Black-figure cup (Droop cup) (figs. 10a–b). A: Three men dressed as bulls in spotted costumes, dancing right. B: Two similar men.
Oxford 1971.903.
Ashmolean Museum. Report of the Visitors 1970–71, 30; *Arch. Reports* 1974–75, 30 no. 15, fig. 4.
Ca. 510–500 B.C.. Perhaps by the Wraith Painter. No piper. The men of A dance a different step from those of B. It is hard to judge given the quality of the drawing, but the painter may have tried to show that masks are worn; see the backs of the heads of the left and centre figures on A. Compare No. 5 above.

8. Black-figure oinochoe (figs. 11a–c). Piper with two men dressed as birds.
London B 509.
Haspels, *ABL* 214 no. 187; *ABV* 473; *Para.* 214; V. Ehrenberg, *People of Aristophanes* (1951, 1962) pl. 2c; Bieber, *Theater*¹ fig. 76, ²fig. 123; Koller, *Musik und Dichtung* fig. 20; *DTC*² pl. 9a; Sifakis, *Parabasis* pls. 7–8; *IGD* no. I, 12; *Istoria tou ellenikou ethnous* III, 2, 413 (colour); Ghiron-Bistagne fig. 115.
Ca. 500–490 B.C. By the Gela Painter.

9. Black-figure amphora (figs. 12a–b). A: Two pairs of helmeted men with long hair moving right and holding up their highly decorated himatia. B: Two similar figures.
Brooklyn 09.35, said to be from Thebes.
Sotheby *Sale Cat.*, 19–20 July 1895, lot 55; Fifth Avenue Art Galleries *Sale Cat.* 16 January 1909, lot 104.
Towards 490 B.C. Compare No. 10.

10. Black-figure oinochoe (fig. 13). Three men in large cloaks and helmets.
Würzburg L. 344.
ABV 434, 5; *Para.* 295; Langlotz no. 344, pl. 103; Brommer, *AA* (1942) 74 fig. 10; Beazley, *Attic Vases in Cyprus* 37–38.
Towards 490 B.C. By the Painter of Villa Giulia M. 482. There is no piper, but the men's movement and dress suggest a chorus. Compare No. 9.

11. Black-figure amphora (fig. 14). A: Piper leading two men in large cloaks and cock-masks. B: Herakles (without lion-skin) running.
Berlin F 1830, from Vulci.
Bieber, *Theater*¹ fig. 77, ²fig. 124; Bethe, *Die Antike* 15 (1939) 334 fig. 11; *DTC*² pl. 9b; Sifakis, *Parabasis* pl. 6; Koller, *Musik und Dichtung* fig. 18; *Istoria tou ellenikou*

Figure 8. No. 5. Detail of hydria. London B 308. Courtesy of the Trustees of the British Museum.

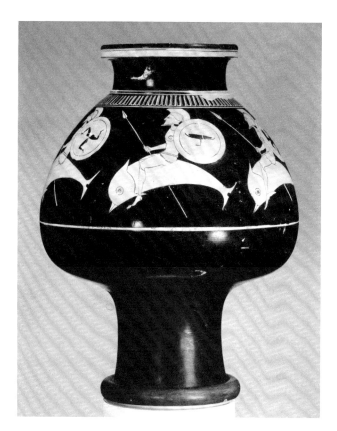

Figure 9. No. 6. Psykter. New York, Norbert Schimmel collection. Photo: The Metropolitan Museum of Art L.1979.17.1.

ethnous III, 2, 358 (colour); Ghiron-Bistagne fig. 114; *CVA* (5) pls. 43,1–2, 47,5 (with full refs.).
Ca. 480 B.C. It is possible that the scenes of A and B are connected. A should be the entry of the chorus.

12. Black-figure skyphos (figs. 15a–b). A: Piper followed by six old men in cloaks with sticks or torches. B: Piper and six old men in chitoniskoi standing on their heads.
Thebes B.E. 64.342, from Thebes.
IGD no. I, 13.
Ca. 480 B.C. Side A should be the entry of the chorus. It is hard to say if side B is a different performance or the same after the old men have put aside their cloaks (cf. *Wasps*). If one knew of a philosopher who had supposed the world to be round, side B could be a parody with the first European representation of antipodeans. However, there must be other reasons for standing on one's head. *IGD* recalls the case of Hippokleides (Herod. 6, 129).

13. Black-figure lekythos (figs. 16a–b). Piper with two bearded dolphin-riders wearing corselets, helmets, and cloaks; each rider carries two spears.
Athens, Kerameikos 5671, from the Kerameikos.
ABV 518; Brommer, *AA* (1942) 71 figs. 4–5.
Ca. 490–480 B.C. By the Theseus Painter. The cloaks are decorated with red.

14. Black-figure lekythos (fig. 17). Piper with two dolphin-riders, dressed as on No. 13 above.
Palermo CAT 2816, from Selinus.
Arch. Reports 1966–67, 40 fig. 19b–d; *IGD* no. I, 14; V. Tusa (ed.), *Odeon* (1971) pl. 51a–c and colour pl. XII.
Ca. 490–480 B.C. By the Athena Painter.

Figures 10a–b. No. 7. Details of droop cup. Oxford, Ashmolean Museum 1971.903.

15. Black-figure cup fr. (fig. 18). I: Dolphin-rider dressed as on No. 14 above.
Basel, Collection H.A. Cahn, 849.
Das Tier in der Antike (exhib. cat., Zurich 1974) no. 244.
Ca. 490–480 B.C.

16. Black-figure cup (figs. 19a–c). A and B: Piper with eight bearded dolphin-riders wearing helmets and corselets and each carrying two spears.
Paris, Louvre CA 1924.
ARV² 1622, foot; *Para.* 259; Brommer, *AA* (1942) 71 fig. 3; Ghiron-Bistagne figs. 111–112.
Ca. 490–480 B.C. Preyss Cup, near the Theseus Painter. Without cloaks or shields.

17. Black-figure skyphos (figs. 20a–b). A: Piper before six dolphin-riders dressed as on Nos. 13–15 above. B: Piper and small bearded figure before six ostrich-riders.
Boston 20.18.
Haspels, *ABL* 108, 144, 163; Bieber, *Theater*¹ fig. 78, ²fig. 125; Brommer, *AA* (1942) 70 figs. 1–2; *DTC²* pls. 7b and 8b; Sifakis, *Parabasis* pls. 2–4; *IGD* no. I, 11; *Istoria tou*

ellenikou ethnous III, 2, 359 (side B; colour); Ghiron-Bistagne figs. 109–110.
Ca. 490–480 B.C. Side B is the only scene to have a figure resembling an actor with the chorus: see Sifakis, *Parabasis* 91–92.

18. Black-figure lekythos (fig. 21). Three men in short chitons, helmets, and greaves running right, sword in right hand, helmetted head in left.
London B 658.
Haspels, *ABL* 269 no. 67; *ABV* 586; Brommer, *AA* (1942) 74 figs. 6–8; Boardman, *Athenian Black Figure Vases* fig. 279; Vermeule, *Aspects of Death* 107, fig. 24.
Second quarter of the fifth century B.C. By the Beldam Painter. There is no piper, but the movement suggests a chorus. The subject is so far unexplained.

The Getty vase stands very much at the end of this series, although it is not the last representation of members of a comic chorus in vase-painting. The little bell-krater in Heidelberg, of the early fourth century, shows them before or after their performance, in a different, more recent,

Figures 11a–c. No. 8. Oinochoe. London B 509. Courtesy of the Trustees of the British Museum.

Figures 12a–b. No. 9. Amphora. The Brooklyn Museum 09.35, gift of R.B. Woodward.

iconographic tradition.[8] As with the scene on the reverse, departure of a warrior (?), the scheme of a piper with dancers is not a little old-fashioned by this date. Even the parallel (and in the mid-fifth century much more popular) representations of satyr-players were dying out by this period, as the formal scenes of them in action were replaced by the less formal scenes of preparation before or relaxation after a performance.[9]

An inevitable question concerns the reliability of the representation on the Getty vase and on these vases in general. Any answer can, of course, only be in terms of probabilities, but these are not insignificant. First, it seems that in vase-painting comic scenes are shown more literally than tragic scenes. This is especially true where representations of actors are concerned: contrast the so-called phlyax vases, whether of Attic, other mainland, or South Italian Greek manufacture, with those representing tragedy. The vase-painter (and by extension the audience as a whole) remained aware of the conventions of staging, just as playwrights were capable of standing back and making "objective" comments about their stagecraft or about the costume worn.[10] These conventions could indeed be a source of humour in themselves.

The whole tradition of scenes of comic choruses rests on

Figure 13. No. 10. Detail of oinochoe. Würzburg, Martin von Wagner Museum L. 344.

Figure 14. No. 11. Amphora. Berlin, Antikenmuseum, Staatliche Museen Preussischer Kulturbesitz F 1830.

7. I have listed only those which seem to me more certainly to represent comic choruses or their unofficial predecessors of earlier than 486 B.C., the supposed date of the formal recognition at the City Dionysia. (It may have been earlier at the Lenaia: *DFA*[2] 40.) Some other possible examples are discussed in T.B.L. Webster, *The Greek Chorus* (1970) 14ff., 93-94. I should perhaps have included the lekythos by the Beldam Painter showing three women in pointed hats moving right (Paris, Louvre CA 2925, *ABV* 587, 4; von Bothmer, *Amazons* 110 no. 200; *AntK* 8 (1965) pl. 10, 3-5; *Para.* 292). Webster took them as Amazons, von Bothmer was not certain, Beazley justifiably wrote "not Amazons." They are painted against a background of ivy, like the London Birds, No. 8 in the list. Note also the red-figure cup with old men dancing, *ARV*[2] 837, 10 (Sabouroff Painter); Münzen und Medaillen (Basel) *Auktion* 56 (19 Feb. 1980) lot 103; E. Simon, *The Ancient Theatre* (1982) pl. 6, 2. Simon takes it as a comic chorus, but these choruses normally dance with a uniform step. The phallos-pole on B and their dress remind one of Semos' description of the *ithyphalloi*: *DTC*[2] 137, also *DFA*[2] 60ff. Beazley described the scene as a komos. Also to be considered is the cup by the Codrus Painter in Cambridge, GR.2.1977, *Annual Report of the Fitzwilliam Museum Syndicate* (1977) pl. 2.

8. *MMC*[3] 61, AV 16 with references. Note, however, the fragments of a stone commemorative monument from the Agora, *MMC*[3] 118, AS 3, pl. 9, dating to the third quarter of the fourth century. It has two sets of males dancing with staffs over their shoulders, each set wearing identical dress; the two sets are closely related.

9. See in general Brommer, *Satyrspiele*[2] (1959) with additions in *Getty MJ* 6-7 (1978-79) 139ff. and *Greek Vases in The J. Paul Getty Museum* 1 (1983) 115ff. Erika Simon, "Satyr-Plays on Vases in the Time of Aeschylus," *The Eye of Greece. Studies in the Art of Athens* (D. Kurtz and B.A. Sparkes, eds., 1982) 123–148, is a major step forward in the discussion of scenes derived from satyr-play. She is mostly concerned with that category which has the satyrs taking a direct part in the action rather than simply represented as a chorus, a category which the vase-painter tends to translate into "real" terms as he does tragic scenes (see n. 10).

Figures 15a–b. No. 12. Skyphos. Thebes B.E. 64.342.

Figures 16a–b. No. 13. Lekythos. Athens, Kerameikos 5671. Photos: DAI, Athens.

Figure 17. No. 14. Lekythos. Palermo CAT 2816.

Figure 18. No. 15. Cup fragment. Basel, H.A. Cahn collection, 849.

formance is reflected on the Brooklyn amphora and the Würzburg oinochoe (Nos. 9–10, figs. 12–13). Despite the differences between the two (the apparent wearing of long chitons on the Würzburg vase, the style of the helmets), they share the critical features that distinguish them from ordinary men: the full beards and the very long hair that falls from under the helmet, the use of the helmet without other evidence of arms or armour, the very elaborate decoration of the himatia, and, most of all, the gesture of grabbing the himation from the inside and holding it up, a gesture which is so far unexplained. It is almost as if they were exclaiming about the nature of their dress, and this is what the turned head of the right-hand figure in figure 13 also seems to imply. These too are by quite different painters. By contrast, Nos. 5 and 7 (figs. 8 and 10) have choruses on a similar theme, but the hydria seems to be earlier than the cup; the dress of each version is different.

The whole point of these representations must have been to give a depiction accurate enough to make it distinct from other choruses with a similar theme, especially given the propensity in Attic Old Comedy to have recurrent themes in title and chorus character. It is also possible that as time went on, it became an important element in *production* to add something new, interesting, or different in costuming in a traditional chorus, and therefore that the audience, including the vase-painter, would also be particularly conscious of this aspect. It is at least an hypothesis that is worth bearing in mind.

In terms of subject-matter, the closest parallel for our piece is the Birds oinochoe in London, No. 8 above, figs. 11a–c; although it is over a half century earlier than Aristophanes' production, this is the way most scholars and indeed modern producers have envisaged his chorus was dressed. Yet our familiarity with the London vase has perhaps prompted us to overlook how special this costume in fact is. The scene has two birdmen dancing right before a piper against a background of ivy, which of course emphasizes the Dionysiac context.[12] Their human faces have red beards and large pointed noses; on their heads are pronounced red crests or combs. They wear body tights decorated for the most part with arcs or circles, probably to indicate feathers, although the one nearer the piper simply has short strokes on his body, right arm, and right

careful representation of costume. None of the scenes is identified by inscription, and yet individual choruses/plays seem quite clearly to have been intended.[11] A good example is the series of representations of dolphin-riders, Nos. 6 and 13–17 above. No. 6 (fig. 9), the dolphin-riders painted by Oltos, is distinct from the others in that the men carry shields and only a single spear. It is also earlier, by ten or twenty years. The four pieces listed as Nos. 13–15 and 17 (figs. 16–18 and 20a) seem to be contemporary with each other so far as our knowledge permits a conjecture. The riders in these four wear identical costumes, and they should therefore derive from the same play, yet the four seem to have been drawn by different hands. They are four independent views of the same thing. The Louvre cup (No. 16, fig. 19) lacks the cloaks, but it is likely that it reflects the same performance. It is also arguable that a single per-

10. On the representation of tragic as opposed to comic scenes, see most recently E. Simon, *The Ancient Theatre* (1982) 8, and Green, *RevArch* (1982) 247–248. With tragic scenes there is a greater tendency to interpret or translate the performance into a representation of the myth or story "retold" by the poet. Although particular plays are detectable in vase-paintings, particular costuming is only sometimes clear, and it is only rarely that we are given much idea of the technicalities of the staging. For comic poets' comments on stagecraft, see for example the explicit use of the *mechane* in Aristophanes' *Peace* 80ff., *Clouds* 218ff., and the references in *POxy* 2742 (Austin *CGFP* no. *74), or the comment on the *mechane* as

used by tragic poets in Antiphanes fr. 191, 15; the use of the *ekkyklema* in Aristophanes' *Acharnians* 408ff., *Thesmo.* 95ff.; the well-known reference to mask-makers, Aristophanes' *Knights* 231–232; on costume, Aristophanes' *Clouds* 538–539. For the breaking of dramatic illusion as a feature of comedy, see *RE* suppl. xii (1970) 1538ff. (Gelzer), K.J. Dover, *Aristophanic Comedy* (1972) 55–59, and Sifakis' useful discussion, *Parabasis* 7–14.

11. Ἐπὶ δελφῖνος is not a title on the psykter by Oltos: see list, No. 9.

12. I am deeply grateful to Professor E.W. Handley and Mr. J.M. Murphy who carefully re-examined the vase for me and patiently

thigh—whether a deliberate variation by the painter or through boredom with incising arcs it is difficult to say.[13] Their wings, by contrast with those of the Getty vase, seem to be relatively loose and pliable. The left figure has his chest toward us so we clearly see their underside; they fall over the arm and are gripped by a strap or cord near their ends (clearly visible at the dancer's right hand). The pose of the right dancer is more difficult to make out; he must have his back towards us, and we see the back of his wings.[14] The black of the wings here has misfired slightly brown, and it is just possible to make out, even in the photographs, two lines of a purer black which come down his left (rear) wing showing the outline of his arm. They must be where the added white has worn away. There are actual traces of white remaining at the edge of the other wing, and there are lines continuing from them which also seem to have shown the outline of the arm, but they are less clear. There are also "ghosts" of white touches by the upper and lower edges of the wing. That we can see the outline of the arm through the wing suggests that the wings were somewhat transparent and certainly light-weight, easily flapped with the arms but also tending to float.

A curious feature of the dress of the men on the London vase is the protrusion at each knee. Webster took them for feathers,[15] but if so, it is difficult to see their supposed function. The left figure has three red strokes from his left (rear) knee, but from his right (forward) knee four strokes, now two red and two black, alternating. The surface is worn here. It seems that, as with the combs, the red here was added over black; so there were three black strokes, each with red over, and a fourth red stroke was added. The fact that these strokes were red seems to me to strengthen the possibility that they represent birds' feet. They are above ground level as the dancers move: the "bird" is therefore in its natural state of movement, flying. If the birds are to rest, it would not be difficult for the chorusmen to kneel, and a kneeling position would be a suitable imitation of birds at rest.

The remainder of the costume is obscure. There seems to be no evidence of tail feathers, but the right figure has something, possibly a skin, tied about the waist (the "belt" once had white dots), which hangs down to either side

answered my many questions; also to Judith Swaddling for her cheerful help.

13. The Gela Painter was not at his best in decorating this vase, but it is possible that the strokes are intended for the front of the body and indicate the finer feathers of the under-body.

14. Note that this dancer has an incised line at the neck, indicating the top of the garment.

15. *GTP* 35.

Figures 19a–c. No. 16. Cup. Paris, Louvre CA 1924. Photo: Chuzeville.

Figures 20a–b. No. 17. Skyphos. Boston, Museum of Fine Arts 20.18.

from the hips. The ends, which hang down between the legs, have traces of added colour. All one sees on the left figure are the two hanging flaps, and there is no clear sign of the "belt" around the hips. The forward leg of each bird-man has parallel curves coming forward on the thigh. This is not the way the Gela Painter usually shows leg muscles, and for the left figure it is tempting, in the light of the Getty vase, to see it as a phallos even though it has no distinct end. If the interpretation of the right birdman is correct and his forward leg is his right leg seen from the outside, the lines there cannot be a phallos, although one may note that they are more closely spaced and look more like folds in the garment tied about his waist.

These London birds have some general resemblance to cocks, not least from the combs on their heads, and there is good evidence to suppose that ordinarily this was *the* bird to the Greeks.[16] If, therefore, a Greek was composing an imaginary bird, it is not unreasonable that it should have a comb on its head and spurs at the back of the ankles as on the Getty vase.[17] What makes the Getty birds unique and what is the most surprising feature of their dress is the drawers with tail at the back and erect phallos on the front. The similarity to the dress of satyr-players is made clearer by the decorative circle on the hip, apparently a traditional element in satyr-play costume (cf. figs. 22, 24).[18] It is the accepted wisdom of modern scholarship that the chorusmen of comedy, by contrast with the actors, did not wear phalloi,[19] and this is what the monuments by and large seem to confirm.[20] On the other hand, a few scraps of contrary evidence seem to suggest that the rule, if it ever was such, was not invariable. First, it has been argued that Aristophanes' *Wasps* wore phalloi,[21] and if so, a link may be found either in the fact that they are winged creatures (although some have doubted if they

were in fact shown as wasps rather than just waspish old men), or in the undoubted fact that they are aggressive, like cocks. Another case may also be relevant. *Satyroi* is the title of comedies by Ecphantides (perhaps in the 450's), Phrynichus, and Cratinus (produced in 424 b.c., in competition with the *Wasps*). Cratinus' *Dionysalexandros* also had a chorus of satyrs.[22] We have no evidence on the way they were dressed, but it is difficult to imagine satyrs without phalloi.[23] We may also note that the bull-men of figure 8 are shown as naked.

That our birds should be phallic is not so outrageous as it might first seem. The use of cocks as love-gifts to young men is well known, not least from the parabasis of the *Birds* itself (703ff.):

> That we are the children of Eros is abundantly clear, for we fly and accompany lovers. Many a fine young man after rejecting his lover, has been won over in due course by our power, through the gift of a quail or a porphyrion, a goose or a Persian cock. All man's greatest blessings originate with us, the birds. . . .

We can observe it too in the countless representations on pottery of young men being given cocks and occasionally other birds, and in representations of these birds in association with erotes.[24] One key aspect of the cock is clearly its aggressive character, and this spirit seems to have been taken to apply more generally as we see in the *Birds* when the heroes are first introduced to the chorus. There is also a wider association of birds with winged phalloi and phallos-birds.[25] In a powerful recent appreciation of the play, Arrowsmith has developed this theme and emphasized the erotic content of the *Birds* as a whole.[26]

Another piece of evidence which is possibly to be associated with comedy is a curious terracotta from the Schimmel collection.[27] Here a figure, apparently dressed in

16. See, for example, Euripides' *Iphigenia in Aulis* 9f. (?), Theocritus xxiv, 64 and Gow's note *ad loc.*; also *Birds* 481ff., and Σ^{VE} *Clouds* 889.

17. Note that at *Birds* 1364ff., Peisetairos, in fitting out the *Patraloias* as a bird (ὄρνιν), gives him wings, spurs, and a cock's comb.

18. Bonn 1216.183-5; *ARV²* 1180, 3 (Painter of the Athens Dinos); T.B.L. Webster, *Monuments Illustrating Tragedy and Satyr-Play²* (*BICS* suppl. 20, 1967) 49, AV 24.

19. E.g. *DFA²* 222; *DTC²* 169; Webster, *Hesperia* 29 (1960) 262; C.W. Dearden, *The Stage of Aristophanes* (1976) 119.

20. See also the pieces mentioned *supra* n. 8.

21. See MacDowell on *Wasps* 1062 (κατ᾽ αὐτὸ τοῦτο —"so far as *this* is concerned") and p. 11 of his Introduction; W.T. MacCary, *TAPA* 109 (1979) 147.

22. See D.F. Sutton, *The Greek Satyr Play* (1980) 136-137 and E.W. Handley, *BICS* 29 (1982) 109-117. Timocles and Ophelion in Middle Comedy also seem to have written plays with a chorus of satyrs.

23. It is not easy to decide which, if any, representations of satyrs should refer to comedy. One possibility, as Simon suggests (*supra* n. 9) 142 n. 130, is the stamnos in the Louvre by the Eucharides Painter, since the satyrs seem to wear tights in addition to their drawers; however, the

action of the figures is more typical of satyr-plays (Paris, Louvre 10754, *ARV²* 228, 32; *DFA²* 184, fig. 39; *JdI* 97 [1982] 67, fig. 3). Another is the cup in Cambridge mentioned in n. 7 above.

24. See principally H. Hoffmann, *RevArch* (1974) 195-220, esp. 204ff., and for additional references J.-P. Descoeudres, *CVA Basel* (1), text to pl. 26, 3-5. For another representation of erotes in association with cocks, see D.C. Kurtz, *Athenian White Lekythoi* (1975) pl. 16,5.

25. See the useful collection of illustrations in the article mentioned in n. 26 below; see also, because of the theatrical context, the winged phallos on the Early Gnathia fragment in Harvard, A.D. Trendall, *Phlyax Vases²* (*BICS* suppl. 19, 1967) no. 154, pl. 4g; M.E. Mayo and K. Hamma (eds.), *The Art of South Italy. Vases from Magna Graecia* (1982) 263 no. 121. It has a comic actor pursuing a winged phallos in parody of the common human habit of pursuing a bird intended as a love-gift, seen so often on Apulian vases. Note, too, the use of the word πουλί in modern Greek. On the aggressive aspect, note the possibility that in the first version of the *Clouds*, the *logoi* were shown as cocks in cages: see Σ^{VE} 889 and Dover's discussion (ed., 1968) pp. xc-xciii and xcvi.

26. *Arion* n.s. 1 (1973) 119-167.

Figure 21. No. 18. Detail of lekythos. London B 658.
Courtesy of the Trustees of the British Museum.

in the more or less accurate guise of a different bird.[28] What has prompted this assumption, of course, is the way the birds are introduced in the text. On the other hand, even leaving the Getty vase out of account for the moment, the archaeological evidence for differentiated or individualized costume as a general principle is not very encouraging.

The Amsterdam cup (No. 1 in the list above, fig. 4) has half-choruses which differ from each other in the length of the skirt or the wearing of feathers in the cap, but they are identical within the half-chorus and generically similar throughout. The hydria (No. 2, fig. 5) is typical of the rest of the series. The men all wear an identical style of dress but each is decorated differently. Similarly, the Berlin Knights (No. 3, fig. 6) have the crests of their helmets varied but nothing else. The Christchurch Titans (if that is what they are; No. 4, fig. 7) vary in the decoration of the corselets, but the style of dress is otherwise consistent. The London minotaurs (No. 5, fig. 8) are identical, not unnaturally perhaps. Oltos' dolphin-riders (No. 6, fig. 9) differ only in their shield-devices. The Oxford bull-men (No. 7, fig. 10) dance a different step on the two sides of the vase (on A both arms forward, palms up; on B one hand back, the other forward, palm down), but the costume is the same throughout. The London birdmen (No. 8, fig. 11) seem intended as identical. On the Brooklyn amphora (No. 9, fig. 12), the men's himatia differ slightly in the details of the decoration, as do their helmets, but they are homogeneous overall. The slight variation makes the total effect more lively. The three dancers of the Würzburg oinochoe (No. 10, fig. 13) wear identical dress. The Berlin cock-men (No. 11, fig. 14) differ in the form of the beard and no more. The skyphos from Thebes (No. 12, fig. 15) varies the decoration of the dress very slightly but is otherwise consistent. The dolphin-riders (Nos. 13–17, figs. 16–20a) are identical within each set, as are the Boston ostrich-riders (No. 17, fig. 20b). So too the London head-hunters (No. 18, fig. 21). We do not, of course, have any texts for these performances, and most of them are considerably earlier than Aristophanes.[29] On the other hand, they clearly give no support to the idea of distinctively dressed individuals. Minor variation of colour and costume was possible within the standard costume. One could imagine, for example, that it would have been possible to differentiate the Berlin Knights (fig. 6) verbally, with such emphasis on their crests as the performance demanded, but essentially chorus costume seems to have been

something like feathered pyjamas and with a removable mask, has a hole at the front where a phallos must have been attached. We do not know where the terracotta was made or even when (Boeotia and the fourth century have been suggested), but the important point is that it seems to have been a phallic birdman. For all these reasons we can argue that to have a chorus of phallic birds was not outrageous, but we should not lose sight of the fact that it was undoubtedly funny.

To judge by the normal iconographic conventions, our two birds should stand for the chorus as a whole, and we are thus immediately faced with a problem. Most commentators have assumed that each bird was dressed differently,

27. Height 18.7 cm. O.W. Muscarella (ed.), *Ancient Art. The Norbert Schimmel Collection* (1974) no. 49; J. Settgast (ed.), *Von Troja bis Amarna* (1978) no. 89.

28. For the view that individualized choruses were not uncommon, see recently A.M. Wilson, CQ 27 (1977) 278–283. His article may be taken as

typical of the usual approach to the problem.

29. Their evidence is not, however, negated by later pieces such as those mentioned in n. 8.

30. On the form of the name, see B. Marzullo, *Philologus* 114 (1970) 181ff. Russo 235–236 makes a useful assessment of the parts played by

uniform, just as the chorus danced with a uniform step.

To come to the *Birds*, when the chorus proper enters, it is clearly stated to be entering as a flock (lines 295–296), and we are given a string of bird-names that offers no chance of individual identification. The rush of names echoes the rush of the chorus. In one sense it is parallel to the strings of utensils or foodstuffs that one finds not uncommonly in comedy, even if Aristophanes lifts the idea to a higher poetic level. There are only names, not individual identifications at this point.

The more precise identifications come earlier, at 268ff., for the four birds who enter before the main chorus. At the beginning of the play, our two heroes, the rather slow but good-natured Euelpides and his smart friend Peisetairos,[30] have left Athens in search of Tereus, the Hoopoe, to see if he has found any better place to live. By line 50 they find his house and then converse with his servant. Tereus, the Hoopoe, appears at line 92, and the visitors explain their problem. Peisetairos then evolves the concept of founding a city in birdland which would control the traffic between men and gods. The Hoopoe is quickly convinced and from line 209 he sings his song to summon the nightingale and then to call the other birds. The songs are lyrical and exciting, but no birds appear. There is a moment of anticlimax before Peisetairos spots a single bird (268ff.):[31]

Πι. ὦγάθ' ἀλλ' ⟨εἶς⟩ οὑτοσὶ καὶ δή τις ὄρνις ἔρχεται.
Ευ. νὴ Δί' ὄρνις δῆτα. τίς ποτ' ἐστίν; οὐ δήπου ταῶς;
Πι. οὗτος αὐτὸς νῷν φράσει· τίς ἐστιν ὄρνις οὑτοσί;
Επ. οὗτος οὐ τῶν ἠθάδων τῶνδ' ὢν ὁρᾶθ' ὑμεῖς ἀεί,
     ἀλλὰ λιμναῖος. Ευ. βαβαὶ καλός γε καὶ φοινικιοῦς.
Επ. εἰκότως ⟨γε⟩· καὶ γὰρ ὄνομ' αὐτῷ 'στι φοινικόπτερος.
Ευ. οὗτος ὦ σέ τοι. Πι. τί βωστρεῖς; Ευ. ἕτερος
     ὄρνις οὑτοσί.
Πι. νὴ Δί' ἕτερος δῆτα χοὗτος ἔξεδρον χρόαν ἔχων.
     τίς ποτ' ἔσθ' ὁ μουσόμαντις ἄτοπος ὄρνις ὀρειβάτης;
Επ. ὄνομα τούτῳ Μῆδός ἐστι. Πι. Μῆδος; ὦναξ
     Ἡράκλεις·
     εἶτα πῶς ἄνευ καμήλου Μῆδος ὢν εἰσέπτετο;
Ευ. ἕτερος αὖ λόφον κατειληφώς τις ὄρνις οὑτοσί.
Πι. τί τὸ τέρας τουτί ποτ' ἐστίν; οὐ σὺ μόνος ἄρ' ἦσθ' ἔποψ,
     ἀλλὰ χοὗτος ἕτερος; Επ. οὑτοσὶ μέν ἐστι Φιλοκλέους
     ἐξ ἔποπος, ἐγὼ δὲ τούτου πάππος, ὥσπερ εἰ λέγοις
     Ἱππόνικος Καλλίου κἀξ Ἱππονίκου Καλλίας.
Πι. Καλλίας ἄρ' οὗτος οὗρνίς ἐστιν· ὡς πτερορρυεῖ.
Ευ. ἄτε γὰρ ὢν γενναῖος ὑπό ⟨τε⟩ συκοφαντῶν τίλλεται,
     αἵ τε θήλειαι προσεκτίλλουσιν αὐτοῦ τὰ πτερά.
Πι. ὦ Πόσειδον ἕτερος αὖ τις βαπτὸς ὄρνις οὑτοσί.

these two.

31. I use Hall and Geldart's text and the traditional line order, but see L. Koenen in H. Dahlmann and R. Merkelbach (eds.), *Studien zur Textgeschichte und Textkritik* (*G. Jachmann gewidmet*) (1959) 85. On this passage, see also H.L. Crosby, *Hesperia* suppl. viii (1949) 75–81.

Figure 22. Detail of the Getty krater (fig. 3).

Figure 23. Fragments of a hydria. Corinth T 1144. Photo: American School of Classical Studies.

τίς ὀνομάζεταί ποθ' οὗτος; Επ. οὑτοσὶ κατωφαγᾶς.
Πι. ἔστι γὰρ κατωφαγᾶς τις ἄλλος ἢ Κλεώνυμος;
Ευ. πῶς ἂν οὖν Κλεώνυμός γ' ὢν οὐκ ἀπέβαλε τὸν λόφον;
Πι. ἀλλὰ μέντοι τίς ποθ' ἡ λόφωσις ἡ τῶν ὀρνέων;
    ἢ' πὶ τὸν δίαυλον ἦλθον; Επ. ὥσπερ οἱ Κᾶρες μὲν οὖν
    ἐπὶ λόφων οἰκοῦσιν ὦγάθ' ἀσφαλείας οὕνεκα.
Πι. ὦ Πόσειδον οὐχ ὁρᾷς ὅσον συνείλεκται κακὸν
    ὀρνέων; Ευ. ὦναξ Ἄπολλον τοῦ νέφους. ἰοὺ ἰού,
    οὐδ' ἰδεῖν ἔτ' ἔσθ' ὑπ' αὐτῶν πετομένων τὴν εἴσοδον.

Peisetairos:	Look, friend, there's a bird coming now.
Euelpides:	Yes there is, a bird. Whatever sort is it? It's not a peacock?
Peis.:	Let's ask the expert. What sort of bird is this?
Hoopoe:	It is not one of the sort you are used to seeing round here. It's a marsh-bird.
Euel.:	It *is* a fine-looking one and a wonderful purple.
Hoopoe:	You're right. And its name is a purple-wing [flamingo].
Euel.:	Hey, look!
Peis.:	What are you shouting about?
Euel.:	Here's a second bird.
Peis.:	God yes. This one has an inauspicious colour.[32] What is this bird so strange, prophetical, haunter of hill-tops?
Hoopoe:	It is called a Median.
Peis:	A Median? Lord Herakles. If it's a Median, then how did it fly in without a camel?
Euel.:	Here's another with a great crest.
Peis.:	What kind of creature is this? Is it another hoopoe? Aren't you the only one?
Hoopoe:	This one is child of Philokles, grandchild of Hoopoe. I am his grandfather, as if you were to talk of Hipponikos, son of Kallias, and Kallias of Hipponikos.
Peis.:	Oh, so this bird is Kallias. How he's moulting.
Euel.:	Well he's such a noble chap, he's stripped by sycophants, and the women too pluck out his feathers.
Peis.:	Poseidon, look at this other coloured bird. Whatever do you call this?

32. χρόαν is preferable to χώραν, the *lectio facilior* in view of the borrowing from Sophocles' *Tyro*. For a useful assemblage of the evidence, see *TrGF* iv, fr. 654 (Radt), and the comment by H. Lloyd-Jones, *CR* 31 (1981) 177. See also n. 38 below. In line 276, better: ὀριβάτης — see Ed. Fraenkel in Dahlmann and Merkelbach (*supra* n. 31) (= *Kleine Beiträge* [1964] i, 431–432).

33. The point is well demonstrated by Rosenmeyer, *AJP* 93 (1972) 288 n. 11.

34. Athenaeus ix.397 makes a convenient collection of ancient sources on the peacock, many of which make it clear that it was far from common in Athens at this period even if it had gained some notoriety: cf. *Acharnians* 63, but note Starkie *ad loc.* who looks to the peacocks at the Temple of Hera on Samos rather than Persia. Plutarch (*Vit.Per.* 13.10) knew a reference to a comic poet's suggestion that women were procured for

Perikles with peacock feathers from Pyrilampes' aviary. The flamingo may have been known from Egypt and North Africa, but there is little sign of it in Athens. Indeed it is quite possible that the name meant little to most of the audience; *contra* J. Pollard, *Birds in Greek Life and Myth* (1977) 14 who uses this passage as evidence for acquaintance with the flamingo. Cratinus fr. 114 K (from his *Nemesis*) mentions a φοινικόπτερος bird, but we have no idea of the context.

35. *Imagines* II, 31, quoted by Gow in his discussion of Persian dress, *JHS* 48 (1928) 151. Aeschylus fr. 304 uses στικτὸς πτέρυξ of the hoopoe.

36. Corinth T 1144, Beazley, *Hesperia* 24 (1955) 305–319; *ARV²* 571, 74; *Para.* 390 (Leningrad Painter); Webster, *Monuments Illustrating Tragedy and Satyr-Play²* 46, AV 13; about 470–460/50 B.C. A random selection of examples of the later fifth and early fourth centuries: *Oriental king*, pelike, Paris, Louvre, Campana 11164, *AM* 90 (1975) pl. 40,1; *Orien-*

Hoopoe:	This is a gobbler.
Peis.:	If he's a gobbler, he can surely only be Kleonymos?
Euel.:	If he's Kleonymos, how come he hasn't thrown away his crest?
Peis.:	But what is the cresting of all these birds? Have they come for the hoplite race?
Hoopoe:	No, they're like the Carians. They live on crests for safety.
Peis.:	Poseidon, do you see what a plague of birds has gathered?
Euel.:	Lord Apollo, what a cloud of them. Wow, you can't even see the entrance for them flying in.

Each of the four is essentially fictitious, and the two Athenians need the Hoopoe's help to identify them at all. Even the first, the flamingo, is probably more fictitious than real:[33] the description basically rests on the play on words about his purple colour, φοινικιοῦς (line 272), Phoenician and therefore eastern and strange. As the Hoopoe says, it isn't the sort of bird you see round here. In line 269, Euelpides has asked if this same bird is a peacock. Even an Athenian in 414 B.C. might be expected to know that a peacock does not look at all like a flamingo, or at least like this bird.[34] The peacock is an Indian bird (which doubtless arrived via Persia) and therefore also outlandish and foreign, although there is another aspect to the joke to be discussed in a moment. The major point about this bird is that it too is outlandish rather than real. Similarly the second bird, the Median. Persian is the normal description of a cock, but Median is no known bird. As a scholiast put it rather lamely: ζητεῖται δὲ εἰ ὄντως καλεῖταί τις ὄρνις μῆδος. The third is a grandson of the Hoopoe, whom Peisetairos takes as Kallias, the notorious dissolute; the fourth is the gobbler who is compared with Kleonymos. None of these can therefore look like real birds as individualized types, otherwise the jokes would be impossible. If, on the other hand, we envisage them as looking like the birds on the Getty vase, many comments begin to make sense.

When Euelpides asks (line 269) if the first bird is not a peacock, one thinks of the dotted circles on the body of the birdman (in colour rather than the monochrome of the drawing), and it immediately explains a joke that had been incomprehensible before we knew this vase. As Philostratus put it when describing a picture of the Great King, he is στικτὸς οἷον ταῶς.[35] The same joke in fact appears earlier when Euelpides and Peisetairos first meet the Hoopoe. In the present case it is probably safe to assume that the costume was reddish-purple. There may also be some play with the word λιμναῖος: not only of the marsh but of Dionysos, suitable for such a phallic figure. The second bird is literally described by Peisetairos as being outlandish as well (line 275), using, as the scholiast tells us, words borrowed from Sophocles' Tyro; the next line, again according to the scholiast, borrows from Aeschylus' Edonians, adding to the high parody before the down-to-earth joke about the camel. The bird is called a Median, and here again the dot-filled circles are relevant, because it is precisely the same decoration which we see so often on the clothes of easterners on red-figure vases. The hydria fragments from Corinth (fig. 23) are a useful example because they have a theatrical context (an oriental king rising behind a pyre), but there are many others, especially of this period.[36] In fact, on the vases, it probably stands in the first instance for elaborate costume, for we see it also on the clothes of virtuoso musicians, especially pipers, but there can be no doubt that the audience could easily make the eastern connexion. With the third bird (line 280) they emphasize the crest, relate him to the Hoopoe, work in the Kallias reference, and then have the moulting joke. Here the dot-filled circles are used yet another way: the plucked-chicken effect. With the fourth bird (line 287) the stress is on colour, and then the crest (of bird, of helmet, and of hill) with the double joke about Kleonymos as glutton and coward.[37] What is happening, then, is that the dot-filled decoration is used in three quite different ways, as a series of visual jokes, just as the crest is used for verbal jokes.[38] Any differences between the costumes are likely to have been in colour and possibly in the style of the crest, the traditional convention for comedy as we have seen. To sum up, we can demonstrate from the text that the Getty

---

tals, calyx-krater, Athens NM 12489, ARV² 1409, 10 (Meleager Painter), AM 90 (1975) pl 39,1-2; Medea, calyx-krater, Adolphseck 78, ARV² 1346, 2 (Kekrops Painter), CVA pls. 49-50 (distinguished from the other participants in the scene; but note type also used on companion krater for a young woman who may be a daughter of Kekrops); Trojan, calyx-krater frr., Würzburg H 4728, CVA (2) pl. 39,5; frequently for Amazons, as A. Lezzi-Hafter, Der Schuwalow-Maler (1976) pls. 85d, 97e, 114d, 154b,d, 157b, 158, 159a.

37. See MacDowell on Wasps 19 for a good discussion and further references.

38. Dover, Aristophanic Comedy (1972) 145, followed by A.S. Henry, CP 72 (1977) 52-53, explains the crest-joke by supposing that these four birds parade on the roof of the skene. Henry takes the reference to ἐξέδρον χώραν in 275 (where he assumes that is the right reading: see n.32

above) to echo the same point, and also notes ὀρειβάτης (not ὀριβάτης !) and ἄτοπος in the next line. In view of the crests on the Getty birds, Dover's suggestion now seems less necessary. A difficulty in having them on the roof, though not an insuperable one, would be that Peisetairos, Euelpides and the Hoopoe would have to look behind and up to point to and describe these birds, turning away from the audience. It would be easier for the actors to have these birds strut across the orchestra, and easier for the audience to pick out the detail since the birds would be nearer and not outlined against the light of the sky behind. Again, the roof is primarily the theologeion, and its use for birds might be inappropriate when the action on stage and orchestra is fairly specifically midway between heaven and earth.

Figure 24. Fragments of a krater with actors in a satyr-play. Bonn, Akademisches Kunstmuseum 1216.183–5.

vase does illustrate Aristophanes' play. For the rest, and this is surely the important point, Aristophanes shows himself wonderfully capable of turning the sameness of dress to his own comic advantage at a level we have never been able to comprehend before.

We have noticed two references back to the Hoopoe. The joke about the peacock in line 269, which is repeated from line 102, and with the Kallias-bird. If we go back in the play to the point where our heroes first meet the Hoopoe (lines 93–107), it seems clear both from these references (including the Hoopoe's own statement about his relationship to the Kallias-bird), and from the dialogue in the earlier passage, that his costume too must be much the same.[39]

Ευ. ὦ 'Ηράκλεις τουτὶ τί ποτ' ἐστὶ τὸ θηρίον;
    τίς ἡ πτέρωσις; τίς ὁ τρόπος τῆς τριλοφίας;
Επ. τίνες εἰσί μ' οἱ ζητοῦντες; Ευ. οἱ δώδεκα θεοὶ
    εἴξασιν ἐπιτρῖψαί σε. Επ. μῶν με σκώπτετον
    ὁρῶντε τὴν πτέρωσιν; ἢν γὰρ ὦ ξένοι
    ἄνθρωπος. Ευ. οὐ σοῦ καταγελῶμεν. Επ. ἀλλὰ
    τοῦ;
Ευ. τὸ ῥάμφος ἡμῖν σου γέλοιον φαίνεται.
Επ. τοιαῦτα μέντοι Σοφοκλῆς λυμαίνεται
    ἐν ταῖς τραγῳδίαισιν ἐμὲ τὸν Τηρέα.

Ευ. Τηρεὺς γὰρ εἶ σύ; πότερον ὄρνις ἢ ταῶς;
Επ. ὄρνις ἔγωγε. Ευ. Κᾷτά σοι ποῦ τὰ πτερά;
Επ. ἐξερρύηκε. Ευ. πότερον ὑπὸ νόσου τινός;
Επ. οὔκ, ἀλλὰ τὸν χειμῶνα πάντα τὦρνεα
    πτερορρυεῖ τε καὖθις ἕτερα φύομεν.
    ἀλλ' εἴπατόν μοι σφὼ τίν' ἐστόν;

Euelpides:	Herakles, whatever is this creature? what is its plumage? what kind of triple crest?
Hoopoe:	Who is it that wants to see me?
Euel.:	The twelve gods seem to have rubbed you out.[40]
Hoopoe:	Are you two by any chance laughing at my plumage? Let me tell you, friends, I used to be a man.
Euel.:	No, we're not laughing at *you*.
Hoopoe:	What at then?
Euel.:	We find that beak of yours ridiculous.
Hoopoe:	That, I am afraid, is an indignity Sophocles inflicted on me at the tragic festival. I am Tereus.
Euel.:	So you're Tereus? But are you a fowl or a peacock?
Hoopoe:	I am a fowl.
Euel.:	Then where are your feathers?
Hoope:	They fell out.
Euel.:	What, did you catch some disease?
Hoopoe:	No. All the birds moult their feathers in winter

39. I have again used Hall and Geldart's text, but the attribution to speakers is open to serious question: Ed. Fraenkel, *Beobachtungen zu Aristophanes* (1962) 61ff.

40. On τρίβειν in its various forms, see J. Henderson, *The Maculate Muse* (1975) 152 and 176.

41. I have not noticed any evidence that ῥάμφος can have an obscene sense in Greek, but a *double entendre* would fit the context well. ῥύγχος is used at lines 348 (see Σ), 364, 479, 672, 1138, and 1155, which might suggest that there is something special about the use of ῥάμφος here. The primary meaning must of course imply that Sophocles had had Tereus appear in a bird-mask at the end of his play. On the use of ἡμῖν, see Fraenkel, *Beobachtungen* 65ff.

42. See above.

43. Cf. Aristotle *HA* VI, 616 B1, on the hoopoe: τὴν δ'ἰδέαν μεταβάλλει τοῦ θέρους καὶ τοῦ χειμῶνος, ὥσπερ καὶ τῶν ἄλλων ἀγρίων τὰ πλεῖστα. Aristophanes' lines may be a parody of some similar statement. Those who prefer to turn comedy into pedantry may see the moulting joke as necessary to the drama to account for the fact that the Hoopoe, the one individualized "real" bird, does not have its distinctive coat. The crest of course is suitable.

44. For an excellent discussion of repeated patterns and their function in the opening scenes of the *Birds*, see Gelzer, *BICS* 23 (1976) 4ff.

45. It also follows that, despite the lucidity and apparent logic of his arguments, Fraenkel was wrong (*Eranos* 48 [1950] 82–84, = *Kleine Beiträge*

and then we grow others. But tell me, who are you?

First (line 93) we have the crest, then (line 97) the first reference to the plumage, which we now know the audience can see is no plumage. Then there is another reference which now has an added point: "I used to be a man," a gesture to the phallos. Then reference is made to the beak (line 99), clearly so monstrous and absurd in the drawing.[41] Next occurs the first time for the peacock joke; and here, when the Athenian asks if he is a peacock or a fowl, ὄρνις must carry connotations of the domestic fowl. The question makes no sense otherwise.[42] Then we have the first time for the plucked-chicken effect, with the Hoopoe, who is consistently formal, not to say pompous in these scenes, making his nonsense reply in line 105.[43] Aristophanes handles all this quickly and lightly. He is preparing the audience for what comes later, so that he can exploit it more fully.[44] He is allowing time, too, for the audience to recover from what must have been a staggering piece of theatre, to become accustomed to this costume before he puts it to other uses.

The Hoopoe and the four early birds are demonstrably dressed like those on the calyx-krater. As was noted above, the scene on the calyx-krater is the standard way in vase-painting of depicting a chorus. The two birdmen there stand for the chorus as a whole. Whatever else may be said, this cannot be doubted. It follows, therefore, that all the birds had the same basic costume in the terms which we have seen applied to earlier choruses.[45] For the remainder of the play, what we hear about birds in the text is poetry, but even so it is interesting how much of it is general statement and how little particularly applied.

The *Birds* was always the strongest case for the individualization of dress in the chorus. The other most frequently quoted possibilities are the *Poleis* of Eupolis, the *Nesoi* by Archippus or Aristophanes, and the *Konnos* of Ameipsias. We have no visual evidence for the way the choruses of these plays were dressed, nor do the contexts in which fragments of the plays are quoted suggest any knowledge of their staging. From the *Poleis*, we have fragments describing Tenos, Chios, and Kyzikos, apparently in a list or sequence, since the passage about Kyzikos begins

"and last comes . . .;"[46] the fragments do not, however, describe the appearance of the chorus-members but the characteristics of the places themselves, Tenos as full of scorpions and sycophants, Chios as a reliable supplier of ships and men, and Kyzikos as a place to have a good time. There is a fragment from the *Nesoi* which seems to describe the overcast, clouded appearance of what one takes to be a single island, but again the words can hardly describe her dress or appearance in the *orchestra*.[47] For the *Konnos* we are simply told that Ameipsias did not list or number (οὐ καταριθμεῖ) Protagoras in the chorus of philosophers.[48] None of these passages mentions dress, and in two of the three cases (*Poleis* and *Konnos*) there is a suggestion that the chorus-members concerned were not so much dealt with as individual characters or personalities as listed as parts of a group. The evidence of the *Birds* and of all the other representations of choruses examined above makes it likely that any variation of dress within a chorus was minor, within a standard form. The isolation of individuals in a chorus was a matter for the text, as the need arose. Visually the chorus was a coherent group, which at most could be split into two, and the archaeological evidence suggests that even two halves were not dissimilar.[49]

We still have to consider what may have motivated Aristophanes to use elements of the dress of satyr-play for his birds. Two possibilities come to mind. First, that having decided to equip the birds with erect phalloi, the loin-cloth seemed the obvious way to do it. The actors' all-over tights that formed their dramatic skin (which are worn in a decorated version by the birds) only supported a dangling phallos, whether hanging more or less straight or tied up in a circle. It is possible that an erect phallos needed more support from the garment as well as from within the object itself, and it is quite likely that the loin-cloth, which was laced up at the front, was made of stiffer, stronger material that allowed a firmer attachment. Having made that decision, Aristophanes could well have found it convenient to atttach a bird-tail at the back in the manner of the horse-tail of a satyr-player. On the other hand, one has the impression, admittedly subjective, that the recalling of the dress of satyr-play is more deliberate, not least because it is so outspoken, even to the markings

---

[1964] i, 459–460, = H.-J. Newiger [ed.] *Aristophanes und die Alte Komödie* [1975] 263–264) to say that the four early birds have nothing to do with the chorus, although one would agree that they hardly have time to dance: cf. Lawler, *TAPA* 73 (1942) 58–63. See also Russo 248–250 and 256 n.5, and Sifakis, *Parabasis* 126 n.5. The chorus is not, however, a typical one: see the next paragraph.

How Aristophanes dressed the Nightingale, whom Peisetairos found so attractive (665ff.), is open to speculation. A scholiast had one guess: ἑταιρίδιον πρόσεισι, τὰ ἄλλα μὲν κεκαλλωπισμένον, τὴν δὲ κεφαλὴν ὄρνιθος ἔχον ὡς ἀηδόνος. Another guess could be a girl like the one on the stemless cup in Corinth by the Q Painter (*Hesperia* 45 [1976] 396, no. 48, pl. 92, with earlier references [I.D. McPhee]; *JdI* 97 [1982] 87, fig. 25) or on

the Miletos fragments attributable to the Pronomos Painter (*IstMitt* 22 [1972] 79, no. 11, pl. 23, 1; *JdI* 97 [1982] 85, fig. 24). Lines 672–674 are explained if she wore a mask like those on the Getty vase: they are remarkably egg-like.

46. Frr. 231–233 Edmonds.

47. Fr. 395 Edmonds.

48. Fr. 11 Edmonds. There is no need to take the Socrates of fr. 9 as a member of the chorus. He is surely more likely to be on stage, especially since Konnos is his music-teacher.

49. See No. 1 and the Agora relief mentioned in n. 8.

on the hips (compare fig. 24). There are two other aspects of satyr-play which seem to coincide. The *Birds* resembles satyr-play inasmuch as characters, like the Hoopoe, whom one could count as belonging to the chorus or at least to the same stock as the chorus, take a direct and major part in the action.[50] Again, the chorus in this play is remarkably consistent in its character. It is not composed of humans who sometimes act in animal fashion, but of animals who sometimes pretend to human fashion.[51] Another point of similarity is the staging. It seems likely that the rock and thicket from which the Hoopoe's servant and the Hoopoe himself emerge at lines 60 and 92, and behind which the Hoopoe says he will retire at lines 202ff.,[52] were at the central door, which must therefore have been conceived as a cave, the scheme which was standard for satyr-play.[53] Why Aristophanes should have wanted to play this game is unclear. He may have played it for its own sake. On the other hand, it is quite possible that he intended some parody we can no longer appreciate. We do not know anything about the satyr-play which accompanied Sophocles' *Tereus*, an obvious choice given the identity of the Hoopoe, which is stressed from as early as line 15, and the large influence that play seems to have had;[54] but we do know that Aeschylus' nephew Philocles (see line 281 and the Kallias-bird), whom Aristophanes apparently regarded as unoriginal and unlikeable, put on a whole tetralogy called the *Pandionis* some time between Sophocles' *Tereus* and the date of the *Birds*.[55] It may even be that the *Birds* (especially its earlier half) was to some degree intended as a mock satyr-play for the *Tereus* itself. Indeed this is probably the most likely answer.

Whatever the explanation, the unique opportunity that the vase provides of comparing text and costume demon-strates how conscious the poet was of performance. It is doubtful if we shall ever have any external evidence for the details of the staging of a fifth-century comedy, but in this case we can come a little closer to envisaging the performance.

We can also gain a little insight into the poet's creative process. The costume was designed first, and the text written with it in mind. And we can see too how Aristophanes organized the early scenes to ensure the best effect from this costume. Some parts of the text are explicable only in terms of the costume. In the Hellenistic period, when a poet such as Menander was shown at work, he was depicted holding a mask as his source of inspiration because characterization and the plot deriving from the interplay of characters were arguably the most important aspects of a play.[56] When Aristophanes showed Euripides at work, he showed him surrounded by his costumes.[57] For a comedian at this date, the chorus was arguably still the most important element, and its production a vital aspect.

It is always pleasant to have an illustration of something we have only read about before, but the Getty vase tells us many things besides. For one, it gives a not unimportant fixed date in the development of later fifth-century red-figure vase-painting. As our first representation of an extant classical comedy, it prompts us to reconsider seriously our views of chorus costume and especially that of the *Birds*, and it seems to imply that an integral part of the poet's attempt to win the competition was indeed to add something new, interesting, or different in the costuming of a traditional chorus. But the real importance of the vase lies in the way that it allows us to add a new dimension to our appreciation of the genius of Aristophanes.

University of Sydney

τετραλογίᾳ οὗ ἡ ἀρχή· †τσε τῶν πάντων† δεσπότην λέγω'
ἄλλως· Φιλοκλεῖ ἐστι δρᾶμα Τηρεὺς ἢ Ἔποψ
ἄλλως· ὁ Σοφοκλῆς πρῶτος τὸν Τηρέα ἐποίησεν, εἶτα
  Φιλοκλῆς, διὰ τοῦτο δὲ εἶπεν· 'ἐγὼ δὲ πάππος' ἀντὶ
  τοῦ 'πρὸ αὐτοῦ ἐγράφην'
ἄλλως· ἐν ἐνίοις ὑπομνήμασιν ὅτι προκέφαλός ἐστιν
  ὁ Φιλοκλῆς ὡς ὁ ἔποψ, ἀλλ' οὐδαμοῦ κεκωμῴδηται.
  εἴη ἂν οὖν τὸν ἔποπα ἐσκευοπεποιηκὼς τῇ Πανδιονίδι
  τετραλογίᾳ, ἣν καὶ Ἀριστοτέλης ἐν ταῖς Διδασκαλίαις
  ἀναγράφει. κτλ.

In the first notice, the relative οὗ has no obvious antecedent: the gender should exclude τετραλογία or Πανδιονίδι. The possibility that ἔποπα is a title is made unlikely by the verb ἐσκεύασεν which surely means that Philocles dressed him up as a hoopoe. Another, more attractive, possibility is that οὗ . . . λέγω has been transposed from the second notice, where it could refer to δρᾶμα. The consequence would be that the quoted first line would be of *Tereus or Epops*, not the whole tetralogy. One might then speculate that the line was addressed to Hoopoe rather than Helios as has normally been supposed (cf. Snell 141 *ad fin*.), and that he is addressed as master of the bird-world, as in Aristophanes.

50. The *Lysistrata*, the *Ekklesiazousai*, and the *Thesmophoriazousai* also have members of the chorus taking part in the dialogue.

51. Russo 236–237: "Il Coro degli *Ucelli* non è composto di esseri umani che talvolta si paragonano con degli animali e come tali agiscono, sibbene è composto di animali che talvolta si atteggiano a esseri umani o divini, ma sempre coerentemente concepiti come animali; e tutto quanto il Coro dice è quasi sempre intrinsecamente pertinente ad ucelli."

52. For this point it matters little whether he actually does go behind it to sing his song in this notorious passage. See Rosenmeyer, *AJP* 93 (1972) 225ff.

53. See in general W. Jobst, *Die Höhle im griechischen Theater des 5. und 4. Jahrhunderts v. Chr.* (1970).

54. On the *Tereus*, see *TrGF* IV 435ff. (Radt) and Erika Simon, "Tereus. Zur Deutung der Würzburger Satyrspieler-Scherbe," *Festschrift des Kronberg-Gymnasiums, Aschaffenburg* (1968) 155–167. For other possible South Italian representations, see M. Schmidt, *Gnomon* 42 (1970) 826, 830. On satyr-plays' sharing of theme with a tragedy of the same set, see D.F. Sutton, *HSCP* 78 (1974) 132. The same writer suggests (p. 127) that the rejuvenation scene in the *Knights* may have been inspired by Aeschylus' *Dionysou Trophoi*.

55. See *Birds* 281 and the scholia *ad loc.*; *TrGF* I, 139ff. (Snell). There is a problem with the reading of the scholia vett.:

οὗτος ὁ Φιλοκλῆς ἔποπα ἐσκεύασεν ἐν τῇ Πανδιονίδι

56. See my notes in *RevArch* (1982) 246, with its references to earlier discussions.

57. *Acharnians* 412ff.

Parisurteil der Zeit Alexanders des Grossen

Karl Schefold

Die Pelike im J. Paul Getty Museum, die hier vorgestellt wird, gehört zu den bedeutendsten spätklassischen Vasen Athens, die Furtwängler nach dem Fundort der meisten die Kertscher Gattung genannt hat (Abb. 1–4).[1] Sie ist ohne Bruch erhalten, über eine Elle hoch (48,5 cm) und damit eine der grössten Kertscher Vasen; der Mündungsdurchmesser ist fast ein Fuss (29 cm). Die berühmte Eleusinische Pelike ist nur 38 cm hoch.[2] Auf keiner anderen Vase der Gattung sind die Farben so gut erhalten.

Die Vorderseite (Abb. 1, 5) wird durch ihre Farbigkeit ausgezeichnet, an der sogar die vergoldeten Mittelrippen der Blätter auf dem Mündungsrand teilnehmen.

Die Qualität der Zeichnung steht dem feinsten Kertscher Maler, dem Marsyasmaler kaum nach.[3] Die Fassung des Themas der Vorderseite, des Parisurteils, ist für uns das letzte Wort der Klassik zu diesem grossartigen Vorwurf und ein interessantes Zeugnis der Stimmung in Athen der Spätzeit Alexanders des Grossen. Hier wird ein bedeutendes Gemälde des Reichen Stils aus der Zeit des peloponnesischen Kriegs, das Georg Lippold aus Vasenbildern erschliessen konnte, neu gefasst.[4] Man hätte eine gegen den persischen Erbfeind gerichtete Tendenz erwarten können. Statt dessen wird der orientalische Fürst Paris in einer Weise verherrlicht, die uns zu denken gibt. Verehrungswürdig hatte den Perserkönig auch Aischylos in seiner Tragödie dargestellt, und in tragischer Grösse wird ihn bald nach der Entstehungszeit unserer Pelike Philoxenos in seinem Gemälde der Alexanderschlacht sehen.[5]

Für die Datierung der Pelike geht man am besten von der Gefässform und vom Bild der Rückseite aus (Abb. 2). Die Schlankheit der Form wird nur von wenigen etwas jüngeren Peliken übertroffen, wie der des Amazonenmalers

mit der kühn aus dem Bild sprengenden Amazone in Leningrad.[6] Die Szene der Pelike Malibu ist stiller. Die reitende Amazone kämpft gegen einen vom Rücken gesehenen, von rechts angreifenden Griechen. Aber beide stechen nicht zu in diesem fast zeitlosen Gegenüber. Man erkennt vor dem Hals der Amazone die in vergoldetem Tonschlamm aufgelegte Spitze ihres Speers und unter dem rechten Ellbogen des Griechen die metallene Fassung des unteren Endes seines Speers, den sogenannten Sauroter, der ebenfalls vergoldet aufgelegt ist. Schild und Reiterhelm sind weiss, ebenso wie das Nackte der Amazone, deren Hosen- und Aermelgewand farbig war. Hier sind nur Reste des blaugrünen Chitons auf der weissen Grundierung erhalten. Ihren Helm hat sie verloren wie der Alexander des Gemäldes des Philoxenos (Anm. 5). Von den Schultern weht ein einst ebenfalls bemaltes Mäntelchen zurück, durch das eine mit gespanntem Bogen vordringende Amazone teilweise verdeckt wird. Diese überdeckt selbst zum Teil das Henkelornament in kühner, mehr malerischer als zeichnerischer Behandlung der üblichen skythischen Tracht der Bogenschützen (Abb. 4).

Die drei Figuren der Rückseite sind auf der Pelike des Amazonenmalers völlig verwandelt (Anm. 6). Die Reiterin sprengt als Anführerin ihres Heeres in Dreiviertelansicht nach rechts, mit gebietender Gebärde, gleichsam aus dem Bild heraus. Eine zweite Amazone, diesmal mit einem Schild gedeckt, als Hoplitin, begleitet die Reiterin, nach rechts eilend, indes der griechische Hoplit nach links ausweicht. Man hat an die literarisch überlieferten Reiterbilder Alexanders des Grossen gedacht, von denen freilich die erhaltenen keine rechte Vorstellung geben,[7] bei der momentanen Oeffnung der Komposition nach vorn auch

1. A. Furtwängler und K. Reichhold, *Griechische Vasenmalerei* (München, 1904–1932) I,104ff. zu Taf.40.

2. J. D. Beazley, *Attic Red-Figure Vase-Painters* (Oxford, 1963) (im Folgenden ARV²) 1476,1. Zuletzt E. Simon, "Neue Deutung zweier eleusinischer Denkmäler des vierten Jahrhunderts v.Chr.," *AntK* 9 (1966) 72ff., Taf.17f. (Literatur).

3. K. Schefold, *Untersuchungen zu den Kertscher Vasen* (Berlin und Leipzig, 1934) (im Folgenden UKV) 127ff.; ARV² 1474f.

4. G. Lippold, *Antike Gemäldekopien, Abhandlungen der Bayerischen Akademie der Wissenschaften*, Philosophisch-Historische Klasse, Neue Folge Heft 33 (1951) (im Folgenden Lippold) 38ff., Abb.23–26.

5. Literatur bei H. Fuhrmann, *Philoxenos von Eretria* (Göttingen, 1931); B. Andreae, *Das Alexandermosaik* (Recklinghausen, 1977); T. Hölscher,

Griechische Historienbilder des 5. und 4. Jahrhunderts v.Chr. (Würzburg, 1973) 122ff., Anm.674; K. Schefold, *Die Antwort der griechischen Kunst auf die Siege Alexanders des Grossen, Sitzungsberichte der Bayerischen Akademie der Wissenschaften*, Philosophisch-Historische Klasse 1979 Heft 4 (München, 1979). Zum Parisurteil vgl. auch H. Metzger, *Les représentations dans la céramique du IVᵉ siècle* (Paris, 1951) 269ff.,5–15. Literatur im *Lexicon Iconographicum Mythologiae Classicae* (LIMC), s.v. Alexandros 1 (Zürich und München, 1981) 494ff. (R.Hampe). Dazu J. M. Moret, "Le jugement de Pâris en Grande Grèce," *AntK* 21 (1978) 76ff.

6. Leningrad NB 2230. ARV² 1478,6. K. Schefold, *Kertscher Vasen* (Berlin-Wilmersdorf, 1930) Taf.24 a. E. Buschor, *Griechische Vasen* (München, 1969) Abb.269.

7. J. J. Bernoulli, *Die erhaltenen Darstellungen Alexanders des Grossen*

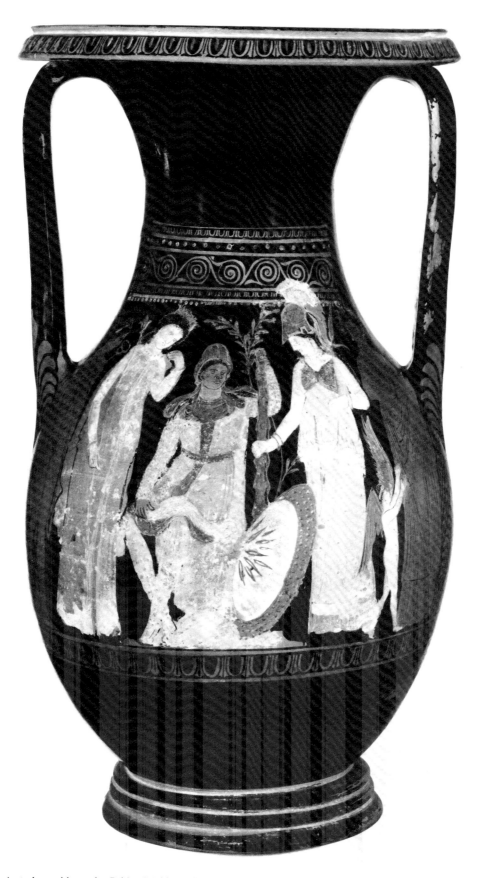

Abb. 1. Attisch-spätklassische Pelike. Malibu, The J. Paul Getty Museum 83.A.E.10. Vorderseite.

Abb. 2. Malibu 83.AE.10. Rückseite.

Abb. 3. Malibu 83.AE.10. Profil.

Abb. 4. Malibu 83.AE.10. Profil.

an eines der letzten, vor dem Verbot von 317 gefertigten Grabreliefs, das des Aristonautes,[8] und bei diesem wieder an die Phantasiai des Theon von Samos, der einer der sieben bedeutendsten Maler der Zeit Alexanders des Grossen war. Er malte einen vorstürmenden Hopliten so, dass man eine ganze Schlacht vor sich zu sehen glaubte.[9]

Unter den Werken des Amazonenmalers gibt es eine noch etwas spätere Stufe. Seine Hydria in Leningrad mit dem figurenreichen Amazonenkampf ist wohl eine der letzten rotfigurigen attischen Vasen überhaupt, und ihre Komposition weicht so sehr von den eben besprochenen Bildern ab, dass sie nur aus dem Vorbild der Alexanderschlacht des Philoxenos von Eretria zu verstehen ist.[10] Wie

auf diesem, im Neapler Mosaik treu überlieferten Gemälde ist die Komposition nicht mehr nach vorn offen, sondern in malerischer Weise dicht zusammengeschlossen. Konnte man die Pelike mit der Reiterin (Anm. 6) als letzte, geradezu barocke Steigerung der spätklassischen Rhythmik auffassen, wird diese Rhythmik jetzt gebrochen in der kristallinen Kompositionsweise, die den beginnenden Hellenismus kennzeichnet. Die nach rechts sprengende Amazone der Hydria (Anm. 10) erinnert an den Darius des Alexandergemäldes bis ins Motiv der Mütze, die wie eine Tiara nach oben steht. Einige Peliken lassen sich an den Stil der Hydria anschliessen, auf denen deren heftige Bewegung noch mehr erstarrt ist.[11]

(München, 1905) 11ff.,98ff.; E. Neuffer, *Das Kostüm Alexanders* (Diss. Giessen, 1929), Nr.40.

8. H. Diepolder, *Die attischen Grabreliefs* (Berlin, 1931) Taf.50; Schefold, *Antwort* a.O. (oben Anm.5) 17; S. Karouzou, *Nationalmuseum:*

Illustrierter Führer durch das Museum (Athen, 1979) 97.

9. Schefold a.O. nach H. Brunn, *Geschichte der griechischen Künstler* 2 (Stuttgart, 1889²) 252f.

10. Hydria Leningrad St.1810 *ARV²* 1480,36; E. Pfuhl, *Malerei und*

Abb. 5. Malibu 83.AE.10. Detail der Vorderseite.

Auf den sorgfältigeren der späten schlanken Peliken erhält der Hals ein breiteres Ornamentband, weil er nicht mehr ins Bild einbezogen werden konnte, so schon um 330 auf dem Spätwerk des Marsyasmalers, der Athener Pelike mit dem Parisurteil.[12] Der Zweig über dem Amazonenbild der Pelike in Malibu ist eher noch feiner als der jener Pelike in Athen. Das Spiralband auf der Vorderseite der Pelike in Malibu ist eine Neuerung, die der Marsyasmaler noch nicht kennt, die aber vom Amazonenmaler nachgeahmt wird.[13] Die Pelike des Marsyasmalers wurde bald nach 330 datiert; man kann unter den Grabreliefs die der Demetria und Pamphile, die Stele vom Ilissos und die bekannte von Rhamnus vergleichen.[14] Etwa um 325 würde

die Pelike in Malibu folgen, um 320 die aus dem Bild sprengende Amazone (Anm. 6) und um 315 die mit der Alexanderschlacht des Philoxenos verglichene Hydria (Anm. 10).

Man kann fragen, warum ein so wenig kriegerisches Bild wie das Parisurteil in der Zeit des peloponnesischen Krieges so beliebt war, und weiter, warum das Thema in der Spätklassik zunächst zurücktritt und in der Zeit der Kriege Alexanders eine neue Bedeutung gewinnt, ja, warum unser Maler sich durch ein Gemälde von neuem anregen lässt, das schon Maler der Zeit des peloponnesischen Kriegs beschäftigt hatte. Die erste Frage hat der feinste französische Vasenforscher der älteren Generation,

Zeichnung der Griechen (München, 1923) Abb.603; *JdI* 73 (1958) 47; K. Schefold, "Das Ende der Vasenmalerei," *Hommages à Marcel Renard* 3 (1969) 511ff.

11. *ARV²* 1478,9.1479,24.27.

12. *UKV* Taf.36.37,1. *ARV²* 1475,5.
13. *UKV* Taf.37,2.
14. Diepolder a.O. (oben Anm.8) Taf.48.51,1.54.

Charles Dugas, bald nach dem ersten Weltkrieg und vielleicht in Vorahnung des zweiten gestellt. Warum konnte ein blosser Streit um den Preis der Schönheit als Anlass eines gewaltigen Ringens, des troianischen Kriegs, so wichtig genommen werden? Dabei ist zu bedenken, dass Paris von der antiken Kunst "nie im negativen Sinn gezeichnet wurde, wie ihn moderne Kritiker gelegentlich beurteilt haben."[15] Dass er über höchste Göttinnen richten durfte, wurde als unerhörte Auszeichnung empfunden. Diese alte hohe Auffassung wurde von der neuplatonischen Deutung vorausgesetzt, die Sallustius, der Freund das Kaisers Julian, überliefert in seiner Schrift über die Götter (Kap. 4): Die Göttinnen sind die lenkenden Kräfte, die zum Wohl der Welt wetteifern. Paris spricht der Schönheit, dem höchsten Wert, den Preis zu und wird damit zum Symbol der Unsterblichkeit. Schon auf dem um 630 gefertigten Elfenbeinkamm aus Sparta ist Paris ein thronender Fürst, und ein Königssohn bleibt er auch später als Hirt, als Sieger im Wettkampf, als nie fehlender Bogenschütze, der den Achill tötet, auch wenn er dem Menelaos unterlegen ist und nicht den gleichen Rang wie Hektor hat. Als Bogenschütze trägt er seit dem späten sechsten Jahrhundert oft das skythische Hosen-und Aermelgewand.[16] Schon Polygnot scheint diese Tracht auf seinem Unterweltsbild zu orientalischem Prunk gesteigert zu haben, wie ihn Euripides in seinem Spätwerk, der aulischen Iphigenie um 410 schildert (71.74): "bunt im Prachtgewand, von Goldschmuck strahlend, prunkend nach Barbarenart." So verkörpert Paris die Herrlichkeit des Orients, wenn er Aphrodite den Preis gibt, und dieser Orient begann für die Athener damals aus dem gefährlichen Feind zu einem möglichen Bundesgenossen zu werden.

Besser verstehen wir unser Bild, wenn wir zuerst das Vorbild betrachten, das am besten auf der Hydria in Karlsruhe von einem dem Meidiasmaler verwandten Meister überliefert ist.[17] Die Haltung des Paris und die Andeutung des Hains findet sich schon hier. Hermes und Eros sprechen dem Paris zu, der mit seiner antwortenden Gebärde, den leise sich berührenden Fingern die Feinheit seiner Wahl andeutet. Ein zweiter Eros muss von Aphrodite gehalten werden—so sehr strebt ihr eigenes Lieben zu Paris hin. Athena ist im vollen Waffenschmuck reicher ausgestattet, und bei Hera finden sich zwar dieselben Attribute wie auf der Pelike, aber alles ist feierlicher und vielgestaltiger. Der Hund zu Füssen des Paris kennzeichnet ihn

nicht als Hirten, denn wo wäre die Herde? Solche Tiere, oft Felinen, begleiten den orientalischen Herrscher, so im Fries von Gjölbaschi.[18] Dann ist auch die Keule des Paris, die auf unserer Pelike fast mannshoch ist, nicht die Wurfkeule des Hirten sondern ein Attribut seiner Würde.

Die ganze "himmlische" Sphäre der Karlsruher Hydria hat der Meister der Pelike der klassischen Einheit und inneren Bewegung seines Bildes geopfert, aber wir verstehen die Bedeutung seines Bildes besser, wenn wir die Aussage jener Sphäre hinzudenken. Das Gemälde des Reichen Stils, das Lippold erschlossen hat, war nach dem Vorbild des Pheidias, z.B. im Ostgiebel des Parthenon, von Sonne und Mond umrahmt.[19] Auf der Hydria erhebt sich rechts das Gespann des Helios, wie sich alles grosse Geschehen in griechischer Vorstellung am Morgen vollzieht. Auf dem Krater in Wien, der auf dasselbe Vorbild zurückgeht, fehlt links die scheidende Reiterin Selene nicht.[20] Ueber Aphrodite sind auf der Hydria zwei Göttinnen bereit, Paris zu bekränzen: Eutychia, die Wunscherfüllung, ist inschriftlich benannt. Mit ihrer Gefährtin könnte Euthymia gemeint sein, der frohe Mut, denn solche Heilbringerinnen sind in der Zeit des Reichen Stils ein häufiges Motiv.[21] So ist wohl auch die inschriftlich benannte Klymene hinter Hera als Spenderin des Ruhms zu verstehen.

Aber wichtiger ist die unheimliche Eris, die über Paris hinter einem Berg auftaucht, mit wildem gorgonenhaftem Ausdruck. Sie und Themis "sind die beiden Göttinnen, die über dem ganzen Geschehen walten, die Anstifterinnen des Zwistes, des grossen Krieges sind . . . Oben auf dem Ida aber sitzt Zeus, der erste Lenker des Ganzen" (Lippold). So sind diese Bilder des Parisurteils zu verstehen aus der tiefen Einsicht der Klassik, dass mit dem Geschenk des höchsten Gutes, der vollkommenen Schönheit Verhängnis verbunden ist, hier der furchtbare Krieg. So sah man auf Polygnots Bild der Zerstörung von Troia Helena, die vollkommen Schöne, unberührt unter all den unglücklichen Frauen; so sah man auf der Basis des Zeus in Olympia die Geburt der Pandora, auf der Basis der Athena Parthenos in Athen die Schmückung der Pandora, auf der Basis der Nemesis in Rhamnus die Hochzeit der Helena, und erhalten ist in Berlin-Charlottenburg die zauberhafte kleine Spitzamphora des Heimarmenemalers, auf der die Verführung der Helena durch Paris gerahmt ist durch gewaltige Göttinnen des Schicksals, Nemesis, Tyche und Heimarmene.[22]

15. *Recueil Charles Dugas* (Paris, 1960) 59ff; R. Hampe, *LIMC* 1,525.
16. *LIMC* 1,513. Elfenbeinkamm: *LIMC*, s.v.Alexandros Nr.6 (Bild).
17. Lippold a.O. (oben Anm.4) Abb.24. Karlsruhe 259. Furtwängler-Reichhold (oben Anm.1) Taf.30. CVA Taf.22,4.5, Taf.23, Taf.24,1–5. *ARV²* 1315,1(a).
18. F. Eichler, *Die Reliefs des Heroons von Gjölbaschi-Trysa* (Wien, 1950) Taf.19. *Propyläenkunstgeschichte* 1 (1967) Abb.93.

19. K. Schefold, *Die Göttersage in der klassischen und hellenistischen Kunst* (München, 1981) 19f.,101ff. Vgl.auch a.O.84 Abb.105.93f.Abb. 121.
20. Lippold a.O.(oben Anm.4) Abb.25; *ARV²* 1318. Wien 1771.
21. R. Hampe, "Eukleia und Eunomia," *RM* 61 (1955) 107ff.
22. Berlin-Charlottenburg 30036. Furtwängler-Reichhold (oben Anm.1) Taf. 170,2. Lippold a.O. Abb.14. *LIMC* s.v. Alexandros Nr. 45

Auf das vielgestaltige Erzählen und Symbolisieren des Reichen Stils verzichtet die Blütezeit der Malerei im vierten Jahrhundert, die sich darin als die Erfüllung der Klassik erweist. Auf dem wahrhaft kosmischen Gemälde, das auf einer Pelike um die Mitte des vierten Jahrhunderts in Leningrad überliefert ist, berät sich Zeus mit Themis, der Göttin der Rechtsordnung über die Uebervölkerung der Erde und erfährt besorgt von ihr, dass nur ein furchtbares Mittel helfen kann, der Krieg.[23] Neben Zeus steht Athena, von der Siegesgöttin bekränzt, weil die Griechen gewinnen werden. Aehnlich klassisch vereinfacht ist die Szene des Parisurteils auf unserem Bild (Abb. 5). Der Betrachter kannte den Zusammenhang, den wir nun auf der Karlsruher Pelike kennen gelernt haben. Wie auf diesem Vorbild sitzt Paris in grossartiger Vorderansicht auf einem Felsen. Der Hain ist nur durch ein einziges Bäumchen angedeutet, das in vergoldetem Tonschlamm aufgelegt ist, wie er auch für die Keule des Paris, Athenas Schild, Eros' Flügel und Details der Gewänder verwendet ist, so auf dem roten Aermel- und Hosengewand des Paris, auf den Laschen seiner phrygischen Mütze, dem Schulterbesatz und Mittelstreifen seines blaugrünen gegürteten Chitons, der sich von einem rötlich angedeuteten Mantel abhebt.

Paris' weiches, anatolisch üppiges Gesicht ist mit gerunzelter Stirn und leicht geöffnetem Mund etwas mürrisch zu Athena geneigt, die zu seiner Linken steht und ihm mit lebhafter Gebärde der Rechten zuredet. Sie ist durch ihre Grösse ausgezeichnet, sodass ihr Helmbusch ins obere Ornamentband ragt. Mit der Linken hält sie die Lanze. Ueber dem Chiton, von dem unten nur der rote Tongrund sichtbar ist, trägt sie einen grünen, über dem langen Ueberschlag sehr hoch gegürteten Peplos, von dessen farbigem Saum nur die weisse Grundierung erhalten ist. Die braune Aegis auf der Brust war golden, wohl mit Schuppen verziert. Der ebenfalls braune korinthische Helm hatte vergoldeten Rand und der Helmbusch wird von einer metallenen, jetzt bläulichen Fassung gehalten. Athena erinnert in ihrer Haltung und im lockeren Fallen des Gewandes an die herrliche eherne Statue des Kephisodot aus dem Piräus, aber die Proportionen setzen die des Urkundenreliefs von 330 voraus.[24]

Hera steht links von Paris und blickt ihn verdrossen an, offenbar schon abgewiesen. Wie Athena ist sie durch helle Hautfarbe ausgezeichnet. Sie trägt einen Chiton und einen Mantel, der auf ihrem Haupt aufruht, von der Linken

über der linken Schulter gehalten wird, sonst nur über den Rücken herabfällt. Von den Gewändern ist nur der Tongrund und etwas von der weissen Grundierung erhalten, dazu ein vergoldet aufgelegter Mittelstreifen. Sie hält ein Szepter und trägt einen Polos, der wie die Blüte des Szepters vergoldet aufgelegt ist. Der Herrin (Abb. 3) zugewandt steht hinter ihr Hermes, mit beiden Händen das Kerykeion haltend, fast in Vorderansicht, nackt, bis auf die Chlamys, die um den Hals befestigt, hinter dem Körper bis zu den Knien herabfällt. Es ist für den Maler bezeichnend, wie Hermes in keiner Weise mit der Plastik des Gefässes verbunden ist, sondern—als fehlte der Platz, ein Tafelbild zu kopieren—so an den Bildrand gedrängt ist, dass Schulter und Oberarm hinter dem Henkel und der oberen Palmette zu verschwinden scheinen, während der Unterkörper so das Henkelornament bedeckt, dass es nicht so frei spielen kann, wie auf der Rückseite der Vase.

In der Art wie sich Aphrodite am rechten Bildrand mit der Plastik des Gefässes verbindet, ist es dem Maler besser gelungen, seinem Vorbild, dem Marsyasmaler zu folgen.[25] Schon der Maler der Karlsruher Hydria hatte versucht, was dann in der Spätklassik allgemein wird, dass Eroten die Empfindungen der Liebenden verkörpern.[26] Hier wendet sich der Eros des Paris mit ausgestreckten Armen seiner Mutter zu, wie ein Kind, das in den Arm genommen werden will. Aphrodite (Abb. 4) blickt, bis über den Mund verschleiert, mit bannenden, sorgfältig gezeichneten Augen auf Paris, fast wie die eifersüchtige Medea des Timomachos.[27] Ueber der hohen Frisur liegt ein mit spitzigen Blättern teilweise vergoldet aufgelegter Kranz. Sonst hat sich der Maler auf die in der Spätklassik oft so verfeinerte rotfigurige Zeichenweise beschränkt, die sich von den überraschend grellen Farben der Hauptfiguren abhebt und die Gestalt mit der rotfigurigen Ornamentik des Gefässes verbindet. Wie sich der gebeugte rechte Arm und der gesenkte Linke durch den Mantel zeichnen, und wie der Mantel den Chiton bedeckt, der unten sichtbar wird, ist souverän gezeichnet, aber wie alles bei diesem Maler etwa flächiger als bei dem feiner modellierenden Marsyasmeister, dessen Hauptwerk, der Lebes in Leningrad, etwa zehn Jahre früher gefertigt wurde.[28]

Im Ganzen bewundert man die leise, aber deutliche Gebärdensprache, welche die Gestalten verbindet und eine schlichtere klassische Einheit schafft als sie der Reiche Stil kannte. Sie überbrückt die plastische Isolierung der Figur,

(Bild). Zitat: Lippold a.O. 39.

23. Leningrad St.1793. Furtwängler-Reichhold (oben Anm.1) Taf.69. Pfuhl a.O. (oben Anm.10) Abb.597. *UKV* Taf.32,1–3. *ARV²* 1476 unten 2. 1695.

24. K. Schefold, "Die Athene des Piräus," *AntK* 14 (1971) 37ff. Taf.15. M. Robertson, *A. History of Greek Art* (Cambridge, 1975) 386.410, Taf.126b. Urkundenrelief: *RM* 47 (1932) Taf.28,3.

25. Besonders ähnlich die Verschleierte auf dem Lebes in Leningrad Inv. 15592. *ARV²* 1475,1; *Kertscher Vasen* a.O. (oben Anm.6) Taf.20a; E. Simon, *Die griechischen Vasen* (München, 1976) Taf.238f.

26. *Göttersage* a.O. (oben Anm.19) 201.

27. K. Schefold, *La Peinture Pompéienne* (Bruxelles, 1972) 217,227,Pl.50a.

28. Marsyasmeister: *UKV* 127ff.159. *ARV²* 1474–1476. Oben Anm.25.

die nach 340 aus dem Bedürfnis entstanden war, das Ethos zu vertiefen. Dieses Bemühen hatte zu so herrlichen Schöpfungen geführt wie den Grabreliefs vom Ilissos und von Rhamnus (oben Anm. 14). Weniger als auf der Pelike in Malibu ist die Verbindung der Gestalten auf dem ähnlichen Bild einer Hydria aus Alexandria in München gelungen, die ich eine Werkstattarbeit des Malers des Hochzeitszugs genannt hatte.[29] Die Pelike in Malibu stammt von diesem Maler selbst, dessen Eigenart am schönsten auf dem Lebes mit dem Hochzeitzug in Leningrad zu beobachten ist, nach dem er benannt ist, ferner auf der berühmten Hydria mit dem Streit von Athena und Poseidon und in motivreichen Kentauren- und Amazonenkämpfen.[30] Statt wie der Marsyasmaler die plastische Spannung von Figur und Gefäss zu suchen, füllt er die Wölbungen mit flächigen malerischen Formen, die er durch farbig aufgelegte Flächen bereichert, Ueberdeckungen nicht scheuend. Damit steht er gleichzeitiger Monumentalmalerei, wie sie jetzt durch die Gemälde von Vergina in so herrlichen Meisterwerken bekannt geworden ist, näher als der Marsyasmaler.[31] Auch in der Farbgebung bleibt unser Maler flächiger, als man es für die gleichzeitige Monumentalmalerei nachgewiesen hat; besonders fällt an Athenas Peplos das "Froschgrün" auf, das auf einem spätklassischen Kleiderinventar genannt wird (batracheion).[32]

Das Urteil des Paris war im Reichen Stil oft, im Kertscher Stil vor der Alexanderzeit selten dargestellt worden. Umsomehr fallen die vier bedeutenden Bilder auf, die 330/20 entstanden sind: die Pelike des Marsyasmalers (Anm. 12), der Kelchkrater des Erotostasiamalers in Athen,[33] die Pelike in Malibu und die Hydria in München (Anm. 29). Die Auffassung des Paris ist auf diesen Bildern so verschieden, dass sie lebhafte Gespräche im damaligen Athen voraussetzt, so wie für das gleichzeitige Tarent, von der apulischen Perservase in Neapel ausgehend, Diskussionen über das verhängnisschwere Verhältnis von Grie-

chenland und Asien erschlossen worden sind, bei denen der Perserkönig in grosser Würde erscheint.[34] Auf der Pelike des Marsyasmalers sitzt Paris in ernstem Sinnen auf seinem Felsen wie der berühmte Herakles des Lysipp auf seinem Korb, dem Symbol seiner schweren und entwürdigenden Mühen.[35] Eros und Hermes sprechen Paris zu, der trotzdem von der hoheitvollen Gestalt Aphrodites abgewandt ist. Nur leise deutet der Maler den Erfolg Athenas im Kampf gegen die Barbaren an, indem sie wie auf der Themispelike (Anm. 23) von der Siegesgöttin bekränzt wird. Aehnlich ist die Auffassung auf dem Kelchkrater des Erotostasiamalers (Anm. 33). Paris sitzt im Profil nach rechts und schaut zur feierlich sitzenden Hera auf, ohne zu bemerken, dass neben ihm die Siegesgöttin Athena bekränzt und dass Eros von Aphrodite her auf ihn zufliegt.

Der Maler könnte daran gedacht haben, dass Hera in der literarischen Ueberlieferung die Herrschaft über Asien, als Symbol der Weltherrschaft verspricht.[36] Es ist verlockend, sich vorzustellen, dass die Bilder des sorgenvollen Paris unter dem Eindruck der Siege Alexanders und der Katastrophe des Perserreichs geschaffen wurden, denn in Athen waren damals die meisten unter der Führung des grossen Demosthenes gegen Alexander eingestellt. Anders wurde die Stimmung in der Zeit unserer Pelike und der Münchner Hydria nach 325, als Demosthenes verbannt war. Nun erscheint Paris zum erstenmal wieder in grossartiger Vorderansicht, nach dem Vorbild des von Lippold erschlossenen Gemäldes des Reichen Stils (Anm. 4), aber nun im Stil der spätklassischen Erfüllung der Bildeinheit, um die man seit 500 v.Chr. gerungen hatte, gleichzeitig mit dem ebenfalls noch spätklassischen Alexandersarkophag und kurz bevor Philoxenos 317 die tragische Sicht des grossen Geschehens prägte:[37] Der Paris der Pelike wirkt als Inbegriff der Herrlichkeit des nun befriedeten Ostens, als Fürst, der der Schönheit den höchsten Wert zumisst.

Antikenmuseum
Basel

29. Inv.2439. Furtwängler-Reichhold a.O. (oben Anm.1) Taf.40. Pfuhl a.O. (oben Anm.10) Abb.598. CVA München 5 Taf.235f. UKV 134 Nr. 188.

30. UKV 132ff. Taf.28-31.50.Abb.58.62f. Pfuhl a.O. Abb.604. Oben Anm. 29. Besonders nahe steht in Zeichnung, Farbverteilung und Ornamentik der Pelike Malibu die Pelike Athen 1718 CC 1857, die von Semni Karouzou im CVA Athènes 2 III I e Taf.32-34 vorzüglich veröffentlicht und im Führer a.O. (oben Anm.8) 188f. als "wunderbar reiche Pelike in farbiger Vielfalt, weiss, hellblau, gold" gerühmt und, wie schon von mir UKV (oben Anm.3) Nr.338, auf die Ueberreichung der Hochzeitgeschenke an die Braut gedeutet wird; Rückseite dionysisch.

31. M. Andronikos, The Royal Graves at Vergina (Athen, 1978). Ders., in The Search for Alexander, An Exhibition (New York, 1980) 26ff.

32. Vgl. I. Schreibler, "Probleme der griechischen Farbgebung," AA

(1972) 792ff. Dies, "Zum Koloritstil der griechischen Malerei," Pantheon 36 (1978), 299ff. (Zurücktreten blauer und besonders grüner Töne in der Klassik). Zum "Froschgrün" macht mich M. Schmidt aufmerksam auf D. Rössler, "Modetendenzen in der griechischen Tracht," in E. Ch. Welskopf, Hellenische Poleis 3 (Berlin, 1974) 1543,69.

33. Athen 12545. ARV² 1457,11; Kertscher Vasen (oben Anm. 6) Taf. 23a.

34. M. Schmidt, "Asia und Apate," in Aparchai, Festschrift P.E. Arias (Pisa, 1982) 505ff. Moret a.O. (oben Anm. 5).

35. Schefold, "Das Ende . . ." a.O. (oben Anm. 10) 515.

36. Moret a.O. (oben Anm. 5) 92ff.

37. Vgl. Anm. 5 und zur Zeitbestimmung besonders Schefold, Die Antwort a.O. (oben Anm. 5) 7ff.

A Bell Krater by the Branicki Painter

Marit Jentoft-Nilsen

Figure 1. Campanian bell krater by the Branicki Painter. Malibu, The J. Paul Getty Museum 78.AE.255. Obverse.

Figure 2. Reverse of figure 1.

In 1978 a Campanian bell krater by the Branicki Painter was added to the antiquities collection.[1] Although, like his other pieces, it cannot be termed artistically outstanding, it is very representative of work by this painter, who is characterized by Trendall as having "a very individual style."[2]

The obverse shows a wreathed youth driving a quadriga to the left. He is nude except for a chlamys flowing over his shoulders and fastened at his neck by a brooch indicated in added yellowish-white. His facial features are like those of figures on other vases by the same painter; the nose and

mouth are basic and small, and the upper proportions of the face are longer than the lower, resulting in a "top-heavy look."[3] Each of the four horses strikes the same pose and lurches forward with only a single hoof touching the ground. Faint traces of added white remain, as is typical for the Branicki Painter, on their heads,[4] on their lower legs, and to an even lesser degree on the chariot wheels. The surfaces from which added white has disappeared now appear darker than the contiguous red areas. Yellow dilute glaze indicates the team's bridles, and white dots descending from behind the ears and encircling the necks repre-

1. Malibu, The J. Paul Getty Museum, accession number 78.AE.255. Presented by R. Collins. Height 43.8 cm. Ex-Deepdene, Hope 327; Anderson Galleries, *Kevorkian Sale Catalogue*, 19–21 November 1925, lot 356 (ill.); A. D. Trendall, *Red-figured Vases of Lucania, Campania, and Sicily* (Oxford, 1967) 540, no. 775 (hereafter, *LCS*); *Treasures of the Ancients: A Selection of Greek Vases from the J. Paul Getty Museum* (University

of California at Riverside, 1978), no. 25. My thanks to Dr. Jiří Frel for permission to publish this piece.

2. *LCS*, 539.

3. *LCS*, 539.

4. Trendall points out this feature as characteristic of the Branicki Painter, *LCS*, 539.

sent a kind of "horsey" necklace, as it were. Reins in black are held by the charioteer, and heavy applications of black glaze were used for the harnesses. The few physical details of the horses as well as the driver are in both black and dilute glaze, some of it now gone. To the front of the horses is a rhomboid edged in white and containing a saltire cross.

On the reverse appears a common scene, three mantled women to the left[5] alternating with four rhomboids again edged in white and containing saltire crosses. The figures are identically dressed; each wears a himation with a heavy black U at the neck and a stephane in added white. The hair of each woman sticks out from behind a kekryphalos with ties ending in clusters of four yellow dots. One can justly regard the drawing as mechanical and uninspired.

In reserve on the outside of the krater's mouth, just below the lip, is a wreath of laurel. A reserved band im-

mediately below and a parallel one at the bottom of the body form the upper and lower borders for the scenes. The side frames are created by palmettes beneath the handles, and here is preserved some of the added white used for the floral elements. Encircling the lower body of the vase is a wave pattern in reserve, again a standard decorative device used by this painter.

Another bell krater by the Branicki Painter in the British Museum dating to the earlier part of his career, 330–320 B.C., and showing Zeus in a quadriga,[6] provides a close comparison to the Getty piece. Although the poses of the charioteers differ, the horses are so similarly rendered that they almost appear to be the same team, racing a second time. Indeed, the similarities in scene between both pieces are close enough to suggest that the two kraters may well have been painted at the same time.

Malibu

---

5. Very standard, *LCS*, 538.

6. British Museum 1949.9.9–26.2; *LCS*, 540, no. 774, pl. 211.1.

An Apulian Loutrophoros Representing the Tantalidae

A. D. Trendall

The J. Paul Getty Museum has recently acquired an Apulian loutrophoros[1] (figs. 1–4) from the third quarter of the fourth century B.C., which is of exceptional interest for its shape and ornamental decoration as well as for its subject matter. On the obverse are represented two of the children of Tantalus—Niobe, above, mourning at the tomb of her slain children and, below, her brother Pelops in the chariot with his bride Hippodamia. On the reverse is a funerary scene, offerings at a small naiskos in which stands a large white marble lekythos. The loutrophoros must, on stylistic grounds, be attributed to the Painter of Louvre MNB 1148, a close follower and pupil of the Varrese Painter,[2] and it ranks as one of his most important works.

SHAPE

The loutrophoros—the name comes from two Greek words meaning "bath-bringer," i.e. bringer of water for the bath—appears in Athens from the sixth century B.C. onwards in two principal types, one based on the amphora and the other on the hydria.[3] In the fourth century the former usually has a slender, ovoid body with a wide mouth set on top of a tall, funnel-like neck that is flanked by high handles. Such vases, as their name implies, served to carry water for use in nuptial rites; they were also placed on the tombs of those who died unwed. In South Italy the loutrophoros is found only in Apulia,[4] and there only in variants of the amphora form, which are very different from the Attic versions. Two main types occur, and it is interesting to note that both may be seen in the tomb monument on the Malibu vase (figs. 1 and 8), where Niobe grieves for her children, who had died before marriage. In the first type (on the left in the monument), the vase has an ovoid body, a tall, narrow neck, and a wide mouth sometimes (although not here) with a knobbed lid on top; the curving handles take the form of an elongated S, spiraling at the top and bottom, where they are attached to the neck and shoulder. A variant of this type has straight handles (like those on Attic vases) but is perhaps closer to a neck amphora than to a typical loutrophoros[5] (fig. 5). In the second type,[6] which is shown to right in the monument and of which the Malibu vase is itself an excellent example, the body is cylindrical, not ovoid, and slightly concave, spreading outwards at the bottom just above the foot; the handles assume a rather more

I am deeply indebted to Dr. Jiří Frel for inviting me to publish this important vase and for supplying me with photographs of it; also to Dr. Hans Lohmann for the photographs of Naples 2887 (fig. 6) and Louvre MNB 1148 (fig. 16), the Galerie Nefer and Messrs. Sotheby for the photos used for figs. 10 and 11; Dr. Margot Schmidt of the Basel Antikenmuseum for the photo of S. 21 (fig. 12); the Akademisches Kunstmuseum in Bonn for fig. 5; and the Soprintendenza Archeologica of Naples for fig. 7.

In the footnotes below, the standard abbreviations are used for periodicals, etc.; other frequently cited publications are abbreviated as follows:

Ap. Grabvasen	M. Schmidt, A.D. Trendall, Alexander Cambitoglou, *Eine Gruppe Apulischer Grabvasen* (Basel 1976).
Cat. V.E.	*The Art of South Italy: Vases from Magna Graecia.* Catalogue of an Exhibition in the Virginia Museum of Fine Arts (Richmond 1982).
Kossatz-Deissmann	Annaliese Kossatz-Deissmann, *Dramen des Aischylos auf westgriechischen Vasen* (Mainz 1978).
Lohmann	Hans Lohmann, *Grabmäler auf unteritalischen Vasen* (Berlin 1979).
RVAp	A.D. Trendall and Alexander Cambitoglou, *The*

Red-figured Vases of Apulia (Oxford: vol. I, 1978) vol. II, 1982 - with bibliographies on pp. xl-xlv of vol. I and pp. xlv-xlvi of vol. II; see also *Bull. Inst. Class. Studies, Suppl.* 42 (London 1983).

1. Malibu, The J. Paul Getty Museum, accession number 82.AE.16. Height (overall) 98 cm; (neck) 37 cm; (foot) 7.5 cm. Diameter (mouth) 21.9 cm; (shoulder) 27.6 cm; (bottom above foot) 9.4 cm; (bottom) 16.5 cm.

2. The Varrese Painter is discussed in *RVAp* I, 335–358, and the Painter of Louvre MNB 1148 in vol. II, 588–591. A great deal of very important new material concerning the latter has recently come to light and this is dealt with in *Supplement* I, 45–47.

3. See Richter and Milne, *Shapes and Names of Athenian Vases*, 5–6, figs. 40–42, of which fig. 41 shows the hydria type (not found in S. Italy) and fig. 44 a typical fourth-century example, like an elongated neck amphora. See also Kurtz and Boardman, *Greek Burial Customs*, 127, 152.

4. On loutrophoroi in Apulia, see, in particular, Lohmann, 152–153, and Schmidt, in *Ap. Grabvasen*, 81.

5. E.g. Bonn 99; *RVAp* I, no. 13/3, pl. 108,2; Lohmann, 153, type 2, n. 1307 (notes 1306 and 1307 have been interchanged in the text), pl. 53,1.

6. Lohmann, 153, type 3, with typical examples listed in n. 1306 and illustrated on pls. 15,2; 25,1; 29,1–2; 31,1.

Figure 1. Loutrophoros. Malibu, The J. Paul Getty Museum 82.AE.16. Obverse.

Figure 2. Malibu 82.AE.16. Reverse.

Figure 3. Malibu 82.AE.16. Left profile.

Figure 4. Malibu 82.AE.16. Right profile.

Figure 5. Loutrophoros. Bonn, Akademisches Kunst-museum 99.

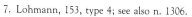

Figure 6. Loutrophoros. Naples, Museo Nazionale 2887. Photo: Hans Lohmann.

elaborate form than in the first type, sometimes with bud-like elements between the curving members at both ends. Loutrophoroi of both types were often placed upon stands, as with the two in the monument, but these, like the lids, tend to become separated from the vases to which they belong and to disappear. In a variant of the second type,[7] the handles are completely omitted, and in this case the

shape is sometimes referred to as a "barrel amphora" to distinguish it from its handled counterpart. The barrel amphora becomes popular in the last third of the fourth century and is found mainly in the Canosan group of Apulian vases, especially those from the workshop of the Baltimore Painter and his followers.

In all, about seventy loutrophoroi and thirty "barrel

7. Lohmann, 153, type 4; see also n. 1306.

8. *RVAp* I, 323, no. 12/55; Lohmann, *Jdl* 97 (1982) 213, fig. 18.

9. Other good examples are Naples 2208 (*RVAp* II, 467, no. 17/60), three on the London market (*Suppl.* I, nos. 18/16 c, d, e), Louvre S 4047

(*RVAp* II, 506, no. 18/105). Cf. also the loutrophoros by the Patera Painter, formerly on the Zurich market (Lohmann, *Jdl* 97 [1982] 213, fig. 19; *RVAp, Suppl.* I, no. 23/125a), and Taranto 61500, by one of his followers (*RVAp* II, no. 23/249).

which the obverse design is remarkably similar; one wonders, in fact, whether the new shape does not represent an experiment in vase design on the part of the potter. The bodies of the two vases are much the same, with variations made on the mouth, now flatter and wider; the neck, now taller and more slender; the handles, now more elaborate and S-shaped; and the foot, now with a much shorter stem. The shape was adopted by the Varrese Painter who, however, preferred a more elongated body (e.g. Naples 3246; fig. 7); this became the standard Apulian form[9] until the time of the Darius Painter, when the second type, with a concave, cylindrical body that seems also to have originated with the Varrese Painter,[10] came into more general use. Both varieties continue until the end of the red-figured style, but in the last third of the century the cylindrical type (with or without handles) is by far the more popular. The handles were usually made and fired separately from the vase and attached to it later. In the later phase the neck tends to become increasingly taller and more elaborately decorated, with both pattern-work and figured scenes; the latter are also found on the shoulders, especially as single figures or heads in a floral setting, when they are not decorated with gadroons in relief, as on the Malibu vase.

The Malibu vase has been skillfully recomposed from numerous fragments by Penelope Potter of the Getty Museum. Small parts of it, especially on the reverse, were missing and have been restored, as have the handles, which had been badly broken.

SUBJECTS

The scene on the obverse (figs. 1 and 8) is not formally divided into two separate registers by a band of ornamental pattern-work, as is often the case on large vases on which two distinct subjects are represented,[11] and it is therefore not unreasonable to see a closer connection between the two subjects than may be apparent at first sight. Above, Niobe is shown mourning at the tomb of her slain children, with four women and various offerings around it; below is Pelops, with his bride Hippodamia, in a four-horse chariot. As Pelops was Niobe's brother, it may well be that the scene depicts his arrival at the tomb where she is mourning, in order to join their father in his attempts to persuade her to desist; this seems to be his role also on the hydria that is presently on the Zurich market (fig. 10), although as yet no other representations of this version, in which Pelops is specifically identified, are known.

Figure 7. Loutrophoros. Naples, Museo Nazionale 3246.

amphorae" are known at present. The earliest loutrophoros would seem to be Naples 2887[8] (fig. 6), which has been attributed to the Painter of Lecce 660, one of the followers of the Snub-Nose Painter. This piece is probably to be dated around the middle of the fourth century. It has a rather squat, ovoid body, not unlike that of the same painter's amphora, Naples 2029 (*RVAp* I, no. 12/54), on

10. Cf. two such loutrophoroi at present on the market, one in California (Intercontinental Antiquity Corporation, inv. 3983), the other in London (*RVAp, Suppl.* I, nos. 13/22 a and b). Another excellent example may be seen in Basel S. 21 (*Ap. Grabvasen*, color plate opp. p. 78, pls.

19–22); here the stand has been preserved, and it should be compared with those of the two vases beside Niobe on the Malibu loutrophoros.

11. E.g. Basel S. 21 (*RVAp*, pl. 171,4); British Museum 1900.5-19.1 (pl. 174,1); New York 11.210.3 (pl. 174,2); Taranto (pl. 179,1); Naples, private

Figure 8. Malibu 82.AE.16. Detail of obverse.

Figure 9. Malibu 82.AE.16. Detail of reverse.

Figure 10. Hydria. Zurich market. Photo: Courtesy of Ms. Tchacos.

The ancient legends concerning Tantalus are somewhat confused, but it is generally agreed that he possessed great wealth and ruled one of the provinces of Lydia near Mt. Sipylus. He was a friend of Zeus, who admitted him to banquets on Mt. Olympus, but he betrayed the hospitality of Zeus by stealing the food of the gods and giving it to mortals. He further outraged the gods by serving to them in a stew the dismembered body of his son Pelops, with the result that Zeus condemned him to eternal punishment in the underworld; he is represented as one of the great sinners on the Underworld Krater in Munich (3297; *RVAp* II, 533, no. 18/282, pl. 194,1). After punishing Tantalus, Zeus

restored Pelops to life by having his body reboiled in the cauldron; Demeter replaced the shoulder she had unwittingly consumed with one of ivory, so that he emerged more beautiful than before. Pelops was hastily carried off to Olympus by Poseidon, whose cup-bearer he became, and the god assisted him in the chariot race against Oenomaus. The descendants of Tantalus, shown in the table below, figure prominently in Greek mythology; their deeds provided the themes for several of the more famous tragedies of the fifth century B.C., as well as being represented on numerous vase paintings, both Attic and South Italian.

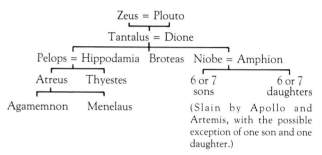

The two best-known children of Tantalus were Niobe and Pelops; reference is made to other sons, especially Broteas,[12] who was a hunter and extremely ugly, but little is known of them and they do not concern us here. Niobe was married to Amphion, King of Thebes, and by him had six (or seven) sons and an equal number of daughters, of whom she was extremely proud. By disparaging Leto for having only two children, she incurred the wrath of the goddess, who straightway dispatched Apollo and Artemis to shoot down the Niobids with their arrows. Apollo slew the sons (with the possible exception of one) while they were out hunting, and Artemis the daughters (again with a possible single exception) while they were spinning in the palace. Thereafter Niobe mourned for nine days and nights at the tomb of her slain children, refusing to yield to the entreaties of her father, Tantalus, to desist; she was subsequently turned to stone by Zeus.

The previously known representations of the mourning Niobe have been the subject of several recent studies,[13] and a possible connection with the lost *Niobe* of Aeschylus has been suggested. Two versions of the scene appear on

coll. 108 (pl. 179,2); Munich 3300 (pl. 200,1); Taranto 9847 (pl. 329,1–3). Cf. also large amphorae such as nos. 18/43–49 and those illustrated on pls. 179; 190; 271,1–3; 284,1–2; 352,1–2. The band of fish on the Andromeda loutrophoros (Naples 3225; *RVAp* II, no. 18/58) serves a rather different purpose.

12. Pausanias III.22,4.

13. See, in particular, A.D. Trendall, "The Mourning Niobe," *RA* 1972/2, 309–316, with earlier bibliography in n. 2; Kossatz-Deissmann, 75–88; Eva Keuls, "Aeschylus' *Niobe* and Apulian Funerary Symbolism," *ZPE* 30 (1978) 41–68; Margot Schmidt, *Ap. Grabvasen*, 40ff.

14. (i) With Tantalus — loutrophoros, Naples 3246 (Trendall, *op. cit.*, 311, fig. 2; Keuls, pl. III, fig. 2; Kossatz-Deissmann, 79, no. K 24, pl. 9,2; here fig. 7); dish, Taranto 8928 (Trendall, 313, fig. 3; Keuls, pl. 2, fig. 3; Kossatz-Deissmann, K 25, pl. 12,1); amphora, Taranto 8935 (Trendall, 315, fig. 5; Keuls, pl. II, fig. 1; Kossatz-Deissmann, K 26, pl. 10).

(ii) With only mourners — Bonn 99 (Trendall, 315, fig. 4; Keuls, pl. III, fig. 5; Kossatz-Deissmann, K 22; here fig. 5).

To this list Kossatz-Deissmann adds the amphora British Museum F 93 (K 23, pl. 9,1 = *RVAp* I, 268, no. 10/53), but I am far from sure that it is meant to represent Niobe, since the other figures do not correspond with

Apulian vases,[14] one in which Niobe is shown at the tomb monument in the presence of the aged Tantalus and a woman in an attitude of dejection—perhaps the nurse or the mother of Amphion—and another in which she is surrounded by four women, as on the Malibu vase. Here we see Niobe (fig. 8) standing in the monument, as on Bonn 99 (fig. 5), but facing in the other direction; her cloak is drawn up over her head like a veil and is held in her left hand a short distance from her head, which is slightly inclined towards it. She is shown in three-quarter view, with a sorrowful mien; beneath the cloak she wears a long garment, the lower portion of which is painted white to symbolise her coming petrification.[15] On either side of Niobe is a loutrophoros, painted in white, perhaps to indicate that the originals were in marble; both have lids and rest upon stands. The one to left has an ovoid body while that of the other is cylindrical, like the actual vase; it is decorated with three figures in diluted glaze. The naiskos itself stands on a low base; the roof, of which the ceiling beams are just visible, is supported by four Ionic columns, the two in front painted white, the two behind with white capitals. A massive architrave supports a low pediment, which has a white disk in the centre, flanked by floral motifs similar to those which terminate the handles of the actual vase. Around the naiskos stand four women, two on each side; all wear chitons, with cloaks wrapped across their bodies and over their shoulders or arms. The two on the left appear to be conversing and those on the right bear offerings: a phiale with a leafy spray in it and a wreath. Beside the top of the monument are disposed two citharae in white and a *kalathos* (wool basket); similar offerings may be seen in front of the monument on Naples 3246 and the hydria on the Zurich market (figs. 7 and 10), but on the Malibu vase they have been moved upward to clear the space below for the arrival of Pelops.

Two other vases with more detailed representations of the Niobe legend have recently come to light. One is a large Apulian hydria on the Zurich market (Galerie Nefer, *Cat. 2*, 1983, no. 52; ht. 59 cm; here fig. 10), which was published in *RVAp Supplement* I (70, no. 18/11a, pl. 9,1), where it was placed as close in style to the Actaeon situla in the Indiana University Art Museum.[16] This is still the case, but the appearance on the New York market of a sec-

Figure 11. Lekythos by the Painter of Louvre MNB 1148. London market. Photo: Courtesy of Sotheby's.

those on the above vases.

A Campanian hydria of the Libation Group gives an excellent representation of the first version (Sydney 71.01: Trendall, 310, fig. 1; Keuls, pl. II, fig. 4; Kossatz-Deissmann, K 27, pl. 11; Lohmann, K 145, pl. 7,2); it is possible that Berlin inv. 4284, by the Caivano Painter (Kossatz-Deissmann, K 21, pl. 12,2, where it is erroneously numbered F 3282), also represents Niobe, since the supporting figures correspond more closely, even if the tomb monument is replaced by a mound.

15. As on Naples 3246, Taranto 8928, Bonn 99, and (in Campanian) Sydney 71.01. See Margot Schmidt, *Ap. Grabvasen*, 48.

ond hydria, which is clearly by the same hand as the one in Zurich, now shows that both are in fact to be attributed to the Ganymede Painter, as is also the Actaeon situla. The new hydria represents on the shoulder Pan with syrinx and *pedum*, Apollo and Artemis, with a bow and quiver, between two small Paniskoi, one at each end, and on the body a woman and youth on either side of·a naiskos, in which is a seated woman. The figures of the youths and women beside the naiskos are in the typical manner of the Ganymede Painter, and show without doubt that the vase is to be attributed to his hand, and with it the other two. The resemblance between the Artemis on the situla and the one on the Zurich hydria was pointed out in *Suppl.* I, 70; she appears again in very similar form on the new hydria.

In the centre of the Zurich hydria is the tomb monument in which Niobe is standing. She is veiled and rests her head on her right hand; the lower part of her garment is painted white, as on the Malibu vase. Beside her, and this is without parallel on the other Niobe vases, stands a young girl on a rather smaller scale; she is painted entirely in added white, like the figures normally found in naiskoi, and she holds up an alabastron. To right is a white-haired and bearded man, presumably Tantalus, leaning on a knotted staff and holding his head with his right hand; behind him stands a white-haired woman in an attitude exactly like that of Niobe. On the other side is a young man wearing a Phrygian cap, holding two spears in his left hand and a phiale in his right. He is surely Pelops, the brother of Niobe, and therefore the woman standing behind him holding an oinochoe in her left hand should be Hippodamia; this scene is the sequel to the one on the loutrophoros. Above to left are Artemis, with spears and bow, and Apollo; to right are a seated nude youth and a woman holding two distaffs of wool above a *kalathos*. These may well be the son and the daughter of Niobe who, according to some versions of the legend (cf. Pausanias V.16.3), survived the slaughter. The presence of the distaffs and wool basket reminds us that Artemis was reputed to have killed the daughters while they were spinning. In front of the naiskos is a row of offerings, including two open boxes, three citharae, and two *kalathoi*; beneath the left handle is a seated woman holding a mirror and a

cista, while on the other side a woman comes running up with a *kalathos* in her hands. This is one of the fullest representations of the Niobe legend and the only one which apparently shows both Pelops and the two surviving children.

The second vase is in a very fragmentary state and I owe my knowledge of it to the kindness of Drs. Maurizio Gualtieri and Helena Fracchia, who most kindly sent me photographs of it. It comes from Tomb 24 at Roccagloriosa[17] and was found during the excavations in the summer of 1980. It has not yet been recomposed, but the fragments show Niobe standing in the typical attitude of mourning on a square plinth, which appears to be decorated with painted figures. The lower portion of Niobe's drapery may well have been painted white, but this is difficult to determine from the available photographs. To left is the kneeling figure of the aged Tantalus, his right hand raised in a gesture of entreaty; behind him is a bearded man wearing a pilos, who supports him with both hands. To right is the aged woman, veiled and white-haired. Above to left Artemis stands beside a stag, and to right Apollo rides on a swan. Until the vase has been cleaned and recomposed, it is difficult to establish precisely to what fabric it belongs and to whose hand it may be attributed. The excavators thought it to be Apulian, and they may well be right; but the rendering of the drapery, especially the dot-stripe and wave-pattern borders, is also reminiscent of Paestan vase-painting.

Below the Niobe scene on the Malibu loutrophoros is a representation of her brother Pelops with Hippodamia in a four-horse chariot. He is dressed in Oriental costume, wearing a garment with long purple sleeves and a Phrygian cap. Beside him stands Hippodamia, wearing a crown and holding up a portion of her cloak behind her head; her drapery is patterned with white dot clusters. She has a remarkably composed air, and Pelops turns his head to gaze upon her with a rather soulful look.

Oenomaus, the father of Hippodamia, was extremely reluctant to give his daughter in marriage to any of her numerous suitors, either because of his own love for her or because of an oracle which foretold his death at the hands of his son-in-law. He, therefore, used to challenge the suitors to a chariot race on a long course from Pisa to Cor-

---

16. Inv. 70.97.1. Schauenburg, *JdI* 84 (1969) 34ff., figs. 4–6; Kossatz-Deissmann, 156, K 47, pl. 31,1; *RVAp* II, 478, no. 18/11; Leach, *RM* 88 (1981) 310, pl. 131,1; *LIMC* I, 464 (*Aktaion*, 111), pl. 361,3; *Cat. V.E.*, no. 54, ill. on pp. 140–141.

17. On the excavations at this site see *NSc* 1981, 103–109 (campaign of 1978) and *Expedition*, vol. 22, no. 3 (Spring 1980) 34–42.

18. E.g. on the fragmentary calyx-krater Taranto 7104 by the Iliupersis Painter (*RVAp* I, 194, no. 8/15); the amphora B.M. F 331 by the Varrese Painter (*RVAp* I, 338, no. 13/5, pl. 109,2); the volute-krater, Naples, private coll. 370 (*RVAp* II, 866, no. 27/27, pl. 325,2); and the amphora in

Bari, De Blasi Cirillo coll. 15 (*RVAp* II, 868, no. 27/40, pl. 327).

19. It is a popular subject on the necks of large volute kraters, e.g. Taranto, *RVAp* I, 169, no. 7/29; Naples 3255 and 3256 (*RVAp* II, 496, nos. 18/42 and 40).

20. 4604; *RVAp* I, 164, no. 7/2; Degrassi, *BdA* 50 (1965) fig. 52.

21. For the significance of these offerings, see H.R.W. Smith, *Funerary Symbolism in Apulian Vase-painting* (Berkeley 1972) s.v. Chattel: Symbolism in the index, 292–294; Eva Keuls, *The Water Carriers in Hades* (Amsterdam 1974) 97–103.

22. See, in particular, Lohmann, *Grabmäler* and *RVAp* II, 1287–78, for

inth, and, since he was possessed of wind-begotten horses of magical swiftness, he invariably overtook his opponents and transfixed them with his spear. The heads of the unsuccessful suitors are sometimes shown on Apulian vases above the altar where Oenomaus sacrificed to Zeus before setting out on the race.[18] Oenomaus insisted that Hippodamia ride beside each suitor, perhaps to distract his attention, and many vases represent the race, with her father in hot pursuit.[19] Pelops, however, bribed Oenomaus' charioteer Myrtilos to remove the lynch pins from his master's chariot and replace them with wax, so that the wheels fell off and Oenomaus, entangled in the wreckage, fell to his death; Pelops was then free to marry Hippodamia. The scene on the Malibu vase can hardly be intended to show the actual race, when Pelops might be expected to appear more intent on winning, as he is on the hydria in Taranto by the Sarpedon Painter.[20] Rather, the painter shows us the aftermath, with Pelops triumphant, and he has taken the opportunity of giving a new turn to the legend by letting Pelops pay a visit to his mourning sister, as on the hydria (fig. 10), although there would appear to be no literary authority for this version of the story.

The design on the reverse (fig. 9) is more directly related to the funerary purpose of the vase. It shows five women, holding a variety of offerings,[21] grouped around a small naiskos in which stands a large white marble lekythos, on either side of which a white fillet is suspended from above. Of the five women, two are standing, one on each side of the naiskos, and the remaining three are in front of it; two are seated, one with her hand on the other's shoulder, and the third is bending slightly forward over her raised right foot, which rests upon a white rock pile. All five hold offerings—mirror, cista, patera, open box, wreath, or ball. The woman to left of the naiskos stands in a relaxed, almost Praxitelean, pose and rests her left arm on some sort of eminence on the ground, which is indicated by lines of dots, as is the higher ground upon which the two women are seated below. She wears a short-sleeved chiton and holds up a mirror in her right hand. The woman on the other side is similarly dressed but wears a short cloak draped diagonally across her body and over her left shoulder. The women below all wear similar drapery; the

central figure also has a cloak across the lower part of her body. On the ground in front of them are some pebbles and a small flowering plant, with an open box and a phiale. The upper part of the body and drapery of the woman on the right is missing and has been restored.

Naiskos scenes are extremely common on Apulian vases,[22] but it is more usual to find in the naiskos one or more human figures, painted in white to simulate the marble or stuccoed limestone of the actual grave monuments. Many such monuments survive from Athens and other sites on the Greek mainland, as well as numerous fragments from Taranto itself.[23] However, vases occur not infrequently, although lekythoi are rare; few other examples of their use are presently known.[24] In Athens marble lekythoi sometimes served as grave monuments,[25] and such a practice may well have been followed in Apulia. It is perhaps of interest to note that the painter of the Malibu vase also decorated a large red-figured lekythos (fig. 11), which has only recently come to light and was sold at Sotheby's in London on December 13, 1982 (lot 297, ill. on p. 103; *RVAp Suppl.* I, 101, no. 20/278d, pl. 19,3–4). In shape it is very similar to the vase in the naiskos, although its shoulder is more sloping and there is a rosette at the upper handle-join. The figured decoration is divided into two registers, an Amazonomachy above, and women below; there is a white female head in a floral setting on the shoulder. Three other large red-figured lekythoi from this period are also known; two are now in Richmond (*Cat. V.E.*, 128–136, nos. 50–51) and a third, depicting the rape of Persephone, is at present on the London market. The use of such large lekythoi for funeral purposes is well illustrated on an Early Ornate bell-krater in Taranto.[26] The scene represented is the meeting of Orestes and Elektra at the tomb of Agamemnon; it includes a woman approaching the tomb bearing just such a vase, which she rests upon her shoulder.

ORNAMENTAL DECORATION

The tall slender neck of a loutrophoros lends itself to elaborate ornamental decoration (see *RVAp* II, 486), and the painter has here taken full advantage of the opportunity offered him. On the obverse numerous bands of pattern-work, in which added white is frequently used,

lists of Apulian vases depicting naiskoi. Relevant bibliographies will be found in *RVAp* I, xliii–xliv; II, xlvi; see also Margot Schmidt n *Cat. V.E.*, 23–26.

For representations of vases in naiskoi see Lohmann, 138–161 and 319, *Nicht-figurliche Naiskoi*, 4; *RVAp* II, 1288, s.v. Naiskoi - vases.

23. On the sculptured fragments from Taranto see, in particular, L. Bernabò Brea, "I relievi tarantini in pietra tenera," *RivIstArch* n.s. 1 (1952) 5–241; J.C. Carter, "Relief Sculptures from the Necropolis at Taranto," *AJA* 74 (1970) 125–137 and *The Sculpture of Taras* (American Philosophical Society, *Transactions*, vol. 65, part 7, Dec. 1975).

24. E.g. on Taranto 61500, from Ruvo = *RVAp* II, 758, no. 23/249; Lohmann, 261 , no. A 716; Margot Schmidt, *Cat. V.E.*, 31 and 35, n. 19. The Taranto vase is a loutrophoros with ovoid body, associated in style with the work of the Patera Painter, and depicts a woman in a naiskos resting her left hand upon a large white (marble) lekythos.

25. See, especially, B. Schmaltz, *Untersuchungen zu den attischen Marmorlekythen* (Berlin 1970); Kurtz and Boardman, *Greek Burial Customs*, 127–129.

26. Inv. 4605 = *RVAp* I, 164, no. 7/3 (with bibliography).

Figure 12. Neck of loutrophoros. Basel, Antikenmuseum S.21.

Figure 13. Malibu 82.AE.16. Detail of reverse neck.

lead down to a figural representation at the lower end (fig. 14). Here the neck broadens out as it joins the shoulder, which is decorated with gadroons in black glaze. On the reverse a similar scheme is followed, except that in the top panel pattern-work is replaced by a figure of Eros (fig. 13), as on the obverse of the Basel Alcestis loutrophoros (fig. 12). This vase might well have been one of the sources of inspiration for the painter of our vase. Most of the patterns—ovoli, rosettes, scroll-work, zig-zags, rays, tongues, etc.—are standard in Ornate Apulian, but one or two deserve special mention. The lozenge pattern which fills the panel at the top on the obverse is of particular interest. We see it first, in a somewhat simpler form, on the neck of a pelike associated with the Iliupersis Painter,[27] and it may well have been derived from the decoration on some Apulian imitations of the Saint-Valentin class (see Beazley, *EVP*, 219, n. 1). The later form, as on the Malibu vase, is rather more decorative, in that the contrast be-

tween the black and the white is given greater emphasis; this scheme is used extensively as a subsidiary decoration on vases from the workshop of the Darius and Underworld Painters.[28] The swastika maeander with hollow squares is also a popular motif; it is of architectural origin (see *RVAp* I, 223) and appears frequently on the necks of volute kraters, as a dividing band between the two registers on loutrophoroi or amphorae, and as a decoration for the bases of naiskoi, especially on vases by the Darius and Baltimore Painters.[29]

Of much greater interest is the strange creature (fig. 14) shown at the bottom of the neck on the obverse, consisting of the upper part of a winged female figure. She wears a crown and rises from an acanthus-like lower portion with spiralling tendrils on either side, which she grasps in each hand. Similar figures are to be seen elsewhere: on the neck of a volute krater in Edinburgh (*RVAp* I, 171, no. 7/45, pl. 56,4), there without wings; on the

27. Taranto, Baisi coll. 38 = *RVAp* I, 200, no. 8/72, pl. 64,5.

28. E.g. on the loutrophoroi New York 11.210.3 (*RVAp* II, 489, no. 18/20), Zurich Market (*Suppl.* I, no. 18/20a), Naples 3225 (*RVAp* II, no. 18/58), Naples 3233 (no. 18/62), Munich 3300, and Berlin F 3262 (*RVAp* II, 535, nos. 18/297–8).

29. E.g. on necks of volute kraters: *RVAp* II, no. 23/231 = pl. 280,1; 27/7 = pl. 321,1; 27/22A = pl. 325,1; as a dividing band: 18/45, 49, 59 = pls. 178,2–3 and 179,2; 18/297 = pl. 200,1; 27/44 = pl. 329,1–3; on the base of a naiskos: 18/297 = pl. 200,1; 27/44 = pl. 329,1–3; on the base of a naiskos: 18/290 = pl. 199,1; 27/5 = pl. 320,2. Cf. also the lekythos by the

Figure 14. Malibu 82.AE.16. Detail of obverse neck.

Figure 15. Malibu 82.AE.15. Detail of reverse neck (female head).

plinth of the Niobids' tomb monument on Naples 3246 (fig. 7); on the feet of two volute kraters by the Darius Painter (*RVAp* II, 496, nos. 18/40 and 42); and as the main decoration on an oenochoe by the White Saccos Painter (*RVAp* II, 971, no. 29/124, pl. 380,8), where she wears a Phrygian cap. A sculptural parallel may be seen on a capital from Cyprus, now in the British Museum,[30] which has been dated around the middle of the fourth century. The identity of the figure remains obscure; she reminds us of the winged sphinx, wearing a crown, perched upon the flower of a large plant on the neck of the Patroclus krater in Naples by the Darius Painter (3254; *RVAp* II, 495, no. 18/39 = Anna Rocco, *ArchCl* 5 [1953] pl. 85,2). However, it is more probable that the painter is using her primarily as a decorative motif, with no very precise concept of what

she may represent. She has been associated with Nike but, in view of her appearance without wings or wearing a Phrygian cap, this does not seem very likely.

The corresponding area on the reverse of the Malibu vase is filled by the head of a woman (fig. 15) in profile to left, rising from a campanula flower amid spiralling tendrils.[31] It is in red-figure, which is perhaps more normal than added white for the heads which appear in subsidiary position on the reverses of large vases, or as the sole decoration on vases of smaller dimensions. Again, it is not always clear whom they are intended to represent (see *RVAp* II, 647); when the head is flanked by erotes, it is almost certainly that of Aphrodite, and when it wears a crown it may be that of Persephone, who would be appropriately represented on a funerary vase. In the majority of

Painter of Louvre MNB 1148, fig. 11.

30. A.H. Smith, *Cat. Sculpt.* ii, 263–264, no. 1510, pl. 27. Somewhat similar figures, but of bearded males in Persian costume, appear as the decoration on the backs of marble *thronoi* (see Richter, *The Furniture of the Greeks, Etruscans and Romans* [New York 1966] 32–33, figs. 154–155,

159–160, 165); the fact that one of the creatures like that on the Malibu vase wears a Phrygian cap suggests a possible Oriental origin.

31. Cf. the heads on the necks of the reverses of the volute kraters nos. 18/17–18 or the loutrophoroi nos. 18/19–21 by the Darius Painter.

Figure 16. Loutrophoros. Paris, Louvre MNB 1148. Detail of obverse. Photo: Hans Lohmann.

cases, however, there is nothing to indicate the particular identity of the female figure whose head is shown, and it is likely that in this context it has again become something of a stock decoration.

Below the handles is an elaborate palmette design (figs. 3–4), which consists of superposed palmette fans, one upward and the other downward, above another palmette fan, surrounded by scrolls and smaller fans, all enlivened with touches of white. Beneath the pictures, running right around the vase, is a band of maeanders, interspersed with the characteristic Apulian quartered and dotted squares. The body of the vase swells out just above the stem that joins it to the foot, and, like the shoulder, is decorated with gadroons in relief in plain black. The handles, recomposed and restored from small fragments, are not decorated, except for a white border and a white diamond in the centre of each of the "buds."

ATTRIBUTION

The Malibu loutrophoros was attributed in *RVAp Supplement* I (99–100, no. 20/278a pl. 19, 1–2), to the Painter of Louvre MNB 1148 and must rank among the more important of his extant works; a list of these, together with some account of the painter's style, is given in *RVAp* II, 589–590, and a further six vases are added in Supplement I.[32] The new material shows the painter to be an artist of considerable stature, whose importance had earlier not been fully appreciated; he should perhaps have been given a section to himself in chapter 18 of *RVAp*, along with the Darius and Underworld Painters, rather than grouped together in chapter 20 with the lesser painters from their workshop.

The painter takes his name from what was formerly considered his major work, a large loutrophoros in the Louvre, MNB 1148 (fig. 16).[33] This vase has a tall, ovoid body and curving handles with a double volute at the top. The neck, however, is shorter, with rather less elaborate decoration than the Malibu vase; on both shoulders is a female head in a floral setting, but no gadroons. It is a slenderer version of Naples 3246 by the Varrese Painter (fig. 7), from whom as we shall see the painter derived a number of the characteristic features of his style, which both the Louvre and the Malibu loutrophoroi illustrate well. Among these we may note, in particular:

The drawing of the head and face

The women's heads have a heavy appearance, due partly to their squareness and partly to the large mass of curly hair which emerges from the *kekryphalos* at the back. The mouth often has a downward curve, which tends to produce a rather determined look—his women are obviously not people to trifle with, as may also be seen in their strongly pronounced chins. Excellent examples of these characteristics are seen on figures 8, 9, 11, and 16. We should also compare his treatment of the seated figures on figs. 9, 11, and 16, which are remarkably alike. The Malibu vase has only one male figure upon it, and that in no way typical, but the painter's other vases (e.g. fig. 16) show his youths to have similar characteristics, and we may note his regular practice of drawing one nipple in profile as a small circle projecting outward from the chest.

The rendering of the drapery

On women's drapery the lines to indicate the folds are boldly and clearly drawn; on standing figures they often fall vertically in groups of two or three (cf. fig. 9); on seated figures one leg is normally visible in outline beneath the drapery (cf. figs. 9, 16), and this is often also the case with standing figures. Most noteworthy, however, is the treatment of the drapery over the breasts, where it has obviously been strongly influenced by the work of the Varrese Painter. The drapery appears to be drawn tightly across; one breast is generally rounded, the other is shown in profile, pointing slightly upward and outward (as on the seated women on figs. 9 and 16). Between them runs a series of horizontal fold lines, sometimes connecting the nipples, just as with the Varrese Painter; these lines are intersected by a single or double black line which runs vertically down the front of the garment (as on the central seated women on figs. 9 and 16). This practice is found on almost all the painter's vases, and, together with his characteristic drawing of the profile face, is one of the distinguishing elements in his work.

We may also note the constant repetition of stock filling ornaments—trees, flowering plants, fillets, bunches of grapes, etc.—as well as his remarkably uniform treatment of adjuncts such as rocks and cistae. This, together with the characteristic elements of his style referred to above, enables us now to attribute more than twenty vases to his hand.

32. These include, apart from the Malibu loutrophoros, two dinoi with Dionysiac scenes at present on the London market; the Amazonomachy lekythos (fig. 11), a calyx krater in a Belgian private collection; and a stamnos once on the California market (*Suppl.* I, nos. 20/278 a–d, 283a, 286b).

It may be noted that his dish in Lugano (no. 20/280a) has been published by Paola Porten-Palange in *NAC* 9 (1980) 70–79, with a full discussion of the attribution; the situla in a private collection (no. 20/286a) by

K. Schauenburg in *Meded* 43 (1981) 83–89, with illustrations of it and other vases on pp. 181–188; and that the dish formerly in Bari (no. 20/282a, pl. 225,3) appeared subsequently on the Basel market (Kunsthaus zum Gellert, *Cat.* 24, 26–28, November 1981, no. 2279, ill.).

33. Height 81.5 cm. *RVAp* II, 589, no. 20/278, pl. 225,1; Lohmann, 243, no. A 572, pl. 43,1; Schauenburg, *Meded* 43 (1981) 83 and figs. 7–8 on 182, pl. 25.

The strong influence of the Varrese Painter, who was active around the middle and early second half of the fourth century B.C., and the parallels with the work of the Darius and Underworld Painters, suggest a date for the Painter of Louvre MNB 1148 in the third quarter of the fourth century, with a floruit around 330 B.C.

La Trobe University
Bundoora

A New Etruscan Vase Painter at Malibu

Jiří Frel

In 1983 an anonymous donor presented the J. Paul Getty Museum with a huge ensemble of ceramic fragments, alleged to be a homogenous group. While the overwhelming mass consists of fourth-century Etruscan black ware, there are examples of Attic fourth-century cups, some earlier ones, and a large quantity of Faliscan red-figure. Several bell kraters are fairly complete, but the core of the group is formed of fragments of cups. The general impression is that the group is from a favissa, composed to a great extent from the products of one potter's workshop, including some collector's items (for example, a cup attributed by M. True to the Brygos Painter), some Attic models for the workshop, and the products of the same. Many cups are decorated and probably also potted by one man, who may be named the Del Chiaro Painter after the California scholar who has contributed more than anyone since Beazley to the study of Etruscan red–figure.

About fifty fragmentary cups and fragments of cups may be attributed to this modest craftsman, an unprecedented case in the present knowledge of Etruscan vase painting. Since the mending of the fragments continues, an exhaustive study will require much more time. However, a kind of preliminary report, illustrated with thirty-one cups and fragments representing successive stages of the career of the Del Chiaro Painter, may be justified. This unpretentious decorator, who seems at first to be limited to repeating some standard compositions taken over from Attic vases, becomes on closer examination a creative personality. His drawing style seems to change radically with the change of technique—the early style is drawn, the late done with brush strokes—but this apparent diversity covers a surprising unity of style.

During the first four well-defined stages of his career (Standard Styles I, II, III, Intermediary Stage), the Del Chiaro Painter decorated two variants of the same cup shape (figs. a,b) with the same profile of the foot with a reserved bottom often with a black fillet. Both variants

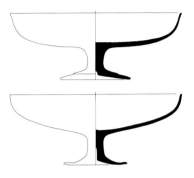

Figures a, b. Drawing by M.B. Bredemeyer.

share a steep vertical lip curved abruptly from the body. The inside of the cup is slightly concave in one variant and flat like a plate in the other. In the very last stage of his career, the painter seems to have decorated exclusively the concave variant; numerous cups of this period have been identified, but, as of this date, none of the flat type. Throughout the whole activity of the painter, the potting remains essentially the same. The only notable change is that the cups become increasingly more massive, although some rather heavy cups already occur during Standard Style II). Hence it may be correct to assume that potter and painter were the same man. Of course, the current evidence may be purely accidental, being limited to a single homogenous lot of material, however large. Vases from other collections and from other finds attributable to our painter may settle this point.

As is usual in Etruscan red–figure, the cups of all stages were given a creamy light red wash to cover the pale ocher color of the clay. It is a substitute for the miltos of the Attic vases which is rather resilient: the Etruscan wash is easily abraded. Added white is limited in the earlier stages of the Del Chiaro Painter's career to discrete "landscape" elements; later it is more strikingly applied for abundant jewelry. The hair, especially for women, is done with a brush in thinner glaze.

The author owes thanks to Mario A. del Chiaro for friendly help, to Marit Jentoft-Nilsen and Karen Manchester, who helped to mend the fragments, to Cynthia Hoyt whose patient work in mending changed many vases and brought to light others; to Lisbet Trevise and Maya Barov, always ready to interrupt their own tasks to reconstruct the cups; to Sandra Knudsen Morgan for unfailing patience and careful editing, to Faya Causey Frel and to Janos Gy. Szilagyi for inspiring discussions.

A preliminary survey of the painter was presented in a class at the University of Southern California, October 1983. All the fragments are registered under accession number 83.AE.368; no further subdivision of this number is given in the text and in the captions, as the mending continues.

Figure 1a. No. 1. Dionysos and maenad (Ariadne?), detail of the interior.

Figure 1c. No. 1. Detail of side A.

Figure 1b. No. 1. Interior, Dionysos and maenad (Ariadne?).
Diam. of tondo: 12.5 cm.

Figure 1d. No. 1. Detail of side B.

Figure 2a. No. 2. Fragment of the interior. Est. diam. of tondo: ca. 12 cm.

Figure 2b. No. 2. Detail of side A. L: 8.5 cm.

Figure 2c. No. 2. Detail of side B. Est. diam.: ca. 17 cm.

Some conventions in the following descriptions may be stated. Youths are nude and females draped, unless stated otherwise. Diadems are mostly doubled with pearls in added white (sometimes only pearls, sometimes turned unintentionally into a spiky diadem). Crossbands are two strings of large pearls in added white on the chest (sometimes only one band is seen, but the crossband was intended). Youth or satyr bent forward means with one foot on a support. Satyrs are bearded, unless otherwise stated. (Description of the subject): only partly preserved.

STANDARD STYLE I

The main feature, unusual in Etruscan red-figure cups, is the systematic use of relief line both inside and outside. But the tondos are clearly the major concern of the painter

and they even have relief contours (very extensive on No. 1, but also on the remnants of Nos. 2 and 8; Nos. 3–7 preserve only the outsides, but their style classifies them here). Also, the drawing of the tondos is more careful, and there are more relief lines than on the outsides. The palmette and volute patterns in the handle zones are mostly brushed in. While in general the drawings are disciplined and carefully executed, there is some evolution toward free lines, with a greater progression in the next stage.

Under the outside top edge of cups Nos. 1, 2, 4, 5, and 9 there is a fine incised line, probably intentional.

No. 1. (figs.1a–d; some fragments with pattern only are not reproduced). I, Dionysos with thyrsos and maenad (Ariadne?), both standing on a maeander exergue (very extensive relief contours). A/B, woman with torch between

Figure 3. No. 3. Fragment of side A. L: 4.5 cm.

Figure 4. No. 4. Two fragments of side A. L of small fragment: 2.1 cm; L of large fragment: 6.5 cm.

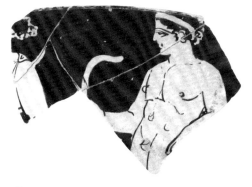

Figure 5. No. 5. Fragment of side A. L: 6.5 cm, H: 4.5 cm.

Figure 6. No. 6. Fragment of side A. L: 4.3 cm.

Figure 7. No. 7. Fragment of side A. L: 3.8 cm.

Figure 8c. No. 8. Fragment of side A. L: 8 cm.

Figures 8a–b. No. 8. Two fragments of the interior. Est. diam. of tondo: ca. 12.5 cm.

Figure 8d. No. 8. Fragment of side B. L: 8.8 cm.

Figure 9a. No. 9. Interior, Nessos abducting Deianeira. Diam. of tondo: 14 cm.

Figure 9b. No. 9. Side A. Max. H. of left figure: 13.5 cm.

Figure 10. No. 10. Fragment of side A. Max. L of top row fragment: 9.8 cm; bottom row fragments from left: 3.5 cm, 3.4 cm, 3 cm.

youths (one of the four youths bent forward, another youth with a chlamys holds an aryballos [not shown in fig. 1c]).

No 2. (figs.2a–c; a big fragment with pattern is not reproduced). Variant of the last. From I, only the top of the thyrsos, one foot of Dionysos and one foot of the maenad remain, both standing on the exergue. A/B, woman with torch between youths.

No. 3. (fig.3; two more fragments not reproduced). From the outside, draped female torso in profile to the right. The general scheme was like No. 1.

No. 4. (fig.4; two more fragments with palmette are not reproduced). Two fragments of: a, female face to the right; b, bust of youth in the opposite direction and a palmette.

No. 5. (fig.5). Fragment of the outside: back part of a woman, hair to the left, and an athlete.

No. 6. (fig.6). A, torso of a youth to right.

No. 7. (fig.7). A, female head to left.

No. 8. (figs.8a–d). Inside of one fragment: (head of a small Eros), of the other: (female foot on an exergue of egg pattern). One fragment each of A and B: running woman and Eros flying after her.

STANDARD STYLE II

No more relief contours, otherwise like Standard Style I.

No. 9. (figs. 9a–b, 32). I, Nessos abducting Deianeira. A/B, woman running and looking back at a satyr bent forward (without support) trying to retain her.

No. 10. (figs.10a–d). Four fragments with outside represen-

tations: a, crowned head of a satyr with a thyrsos facing a maenad. Perhaps the best drawing by the Del Chiaro Painter; b, head of a satyr; c, head of a female satyr.

No. 11. (figs. 11a–b). A fine drawing, closely associated with No. 8. Two fragments of I, Artemis; outside of the smaller fragments (not reproduced), a leg of a youth in matte line.

No. 12. (figs. 12a, b; several small sherds of B are not reproduced). I, seated Dionysos with thyrsos and satyr bent forward (both with diadem and crossband). A (and B), youth bent forward and youth in mantle. The drawing of the outside is done in cursory lines, partially in relief; in spite of the difference in quality, the profile of the bent youth is the same as the satyr on No. 10.

STANDARD STYLE III

The use of relief lines continues in the tondos while on the careless exteriors it appears only occasionally (No. 13). Usually the figures on the outside are rendered in matte brush strokes (cf. especially No. 14).

No. 13. (fig. 13). Several fragments of outside (only one reproduced): A, youth facing a maenad, B, the same reversed. Debased drawing in matte brush lines, but the woman's hair looks exactly like the women on the outside of Nos. 1, 2, 5 and Deianeira, Artemis, and Eros inside of Nos. 9, 11, and 14. Very fine make.

No. 14. (figs. 14 a, b; several small scraps are not reproduced). I, seated Aphrodite to whom Eros is handing a phiale (some relief lines, even a few relief contours, but the sketchy drawing is not early). A/B, youth and maenad in

Figures 11a–b. No. 11. Two fragments from the interior:
Artemis. Est. diam. of tondo: 17 cm.

Figure 12a. No. 12. Interior, Dionysos and satyr. Diam. of
tondo: 10.5 cm.

Figure 12b. No. 12. Side A. Max. H of left figure: 8 cm.

Figure 13. No. 13. Side A. L: 12 cm.

Figure 14a. No. 14. Interior, Aphrodite and Eros. Diam. of tondo: 9 cm.

Figure 14b. No. 14. Outside. Diam. of tondo: 7.5 cm.

Figure 15. No. 15. Interior. Eros and Dionysos. Est. diam.
of tondo: 18 cm.

Figure 16. No. 16. Interior. Herakles. Max. L: 10.5 cm.

Figure 17. No. 17. Interior. Eros. Diam. of tondo: 11 cm.

Figure 18. No. 18. Interior. Dionysos and satyr. Diam. of
tondo: 13 cm.

Figure 19. No. 19. Fragment of the interior, head of a woman. W: 9.2 cm.

Figure 20. No. 20. Fragment of the interior, head of a satyr. H: 5.8 cm.

brush outline (many other fragmentary pieces, not included here, are in the same style, which is characteristic of the later Faliscan).

INTERMEDIARY STAGE

The same figures and subjects continue, but the potting is more massive, the glaze poorer, and the lines collapse. Relief line appears sometimes in the tondos (Nos. 16, 18) without improving the quality of the drawing. Exceptionally, a very lively piece (No. 17), with a surprising use of brush painting in dilute glaze, achieves a truly pictorial effect. A new element appears among the patterns of some later pieces of the group: chevrons around the tondos. At the same time, the poor figures on the outsides are replaced by schematic olive wreaths. The cups decorated with female heads begin here; both known samples are of the flat variant.

No. 15. (fig. 15). I, Eros turned away from seated Dionysos with diadem and crossbands. A/B (not reproduced), two figures, cf. No. 14 above.

No. 16. (fig. 16). I, seated Herakles with crossbands. A/B, tiny remnants of figures as on No. 15 (not reproduced).

No. 17. (fig. 17). I, seated Eros with crossband. Outside, olive wreath.

No. 18. (fig. 18). I, seated Dionysos and satyr bent forward, both with diadems and crossbands; tondo frame, chevrons. Outside was an olive wreath. Some relief lines and even contours, especially in both heads, which are still comparable to the satyr on No. 10 and to the youth on the outside of No. 12.

No. 19. (fig. 19; several fragments not reproduced). I, head of woman, around her, wave pattern; cf. the head of Dionysos No. 15 (fig. 15).

No. 20. (fig. 20). I, head of satyr; cf. No. 19.

LATE STAGE

At first glance, this seems to be the lowest point of the whole production. The pottery is still heavier than in the Intermediary Stage, the glaze pitiful, the chevrons and the olive crowns irregular, and the figures clumsy. Often unrelated accessories (circular phialai) fill the space. But, in spite of the weak work, the scenes are full of life; and the large brush strokes mark a clear transition from linear drawing toward free painting. The hair and beards are painted by brush strokes in more or less diluted glaze, and the extensive use of added white suggests the possibility that the Del Chiaro Painter may have decorated some cups in white and/or red on black; indeed he did (cf. No. 31 below). On several cups of this stage, the letters **HE** are painted in added white, which may be an abbreviation for dedications to Herakles.

Several cups of the concave variant are decorated with female heads roughly sketched wearing spiky stephanai in added white. Only the subject connects these cups with the same representations belonging to the previous stage (Nos. 19 and 20 above). The waves on their outsides correspond to the same pattern around the tondos of Genucilia plates, and it is evident that these cups are the immediate forerunners of the Genucilia plates—a proper conclusion for the painter named after the man who studied this last offspring of Etruscan red-figure.

Figure 21. No. 21. Interior, head of a woman. Est. diam. of tondo: 12 cm.

Figure 22. No. 22. Interior, head of a woman. Diam. of tondo: 12.5 cm.

Figure 23. No. 23. Interior, Eros. Diam. of tondo: 12 cm.

Figure 24. No. 24. Interior, rider. Diam of tondo: 13.5 cm.

Figure 25. No. 25. Interior, Lasa and youth. Diam. of tondo: 14.5 cm.

Figure 26. No. 26. Interior, Lasa and youth. Diam. of tondo: 15 cm.

Figure 27. No. 27. Interior, satyr courting a girl. Diam. of
tondo: 16 cm.

Figure 28. No. 28. Interior, Aphrodite and a satyr. Diam.
of tondo: 15 cm.

Figure 29. No. 29. Interior, Aphrodite and a satyr. Diam.
of tondo: 16.5 cm.

Figure 30. No. 30. Interior, satyr and a goat. Est. diam. of
tondo: 20 cm.

Figure 31. No. 31. Interior, two goats. Est. diam. of tondo: 17.5 cm.

No. 21. (fig. 21). I, head of woman with white spiky stephane; cf. the head of Dionysos No. 15.

No. 22. (fig. 22). Replica of the last.

No. 23. (fig. 23). Eros. Transition from the Intermediary Stage.

No. 24. (fig. 24). Rider with diadem holding spear (in white). Cf. the profile with Dionysos on No. 15.

No. 25. (fig. 25). Lasa with diadem and crossband seated on the lap of a youth.

No. 26. (fig. 26). Replica of the last.

No. 27. (fig. 27). Satyr courting a nude girl (both with crossbands).

No. 28. (fig. 28). Aphrodite (?) exposing herself for the admiration of a satyr (both with diadems and crossbands).

No. 29. (fig. 29). Replica of the last.

No. 30. (fig. 30). Satyr and a goat.

A CUP IN ADDED WHITE
(actually rather pink).

No. 31. (fig. 31). Two heraldic goats (male and female). Inscribed IVL·IVINIO. The attribution is supported by comparison with the goat on No. 30.

Some characteristic features of the Del Chiaro Painter remain the same throughout his career. He draws a hand which is fleshy, especially on the side of the thumb, with fingers that are sometimes so schematic that their tips seem cut off. Sometimes the toes are very carefully detailed. The collarbones touch together in the middle under the neck. Female breasts appear more generous from the frontal view than in profile. The painter uses two patterns to draw nipples: in profile they protrude like doorbell buttons; seen frontally (bare or covered by the drapery), they form a neat circle which is also used to draw the belly button. The real signature of the painter is given by the female chignons and by the profiles of all the heads with their small but solid chins, sketchy lips, large eyes, rather long noses with the point protruding slightly forward. The profiles confirm the unity of the painter's work from his standard style through the late stage and help to connect the tondos with female heads with the rest of the painter's work; the spiral locks before the ears on these heads are the same as on an earlier Dionysos (No.15).

Two stock figures are characteristic of the painter: a seated figure (usually Dionysos, but also Herakles and others) and a standing figure (satyr or a youth) bent forward, the raised foot on a support. Often the seated figure and the standing one are united in a standard composition, a kind of *sacra conversazione*. Particularly successful are the satyrs (and a centaur of the same kin). From his early stages to his latest work, their hirsute profiles enhance the best scenes the Del Chiaro Painter drew. The female nudes, which all belong to the late stage, were painted with a manifest gusto.

Using well-established and conventional compositions, the Del Chiaro Painter repeated many Dionysiac scenes. Other traditional subjects also occur, but the most lively work from his earlier period is the tondo with Nessos abducting Deianeira (fig. 32). The eloquent gesture of Herakles' wife brings to mind the wisdom of Herodotos: men of common sense do not care about abducted women. In his last stage, new life breaks through the old schemas, the subjects and the treatments are new: a courting scene becomes a surprising readaptation of an archaic motif; the Aphrodite who overestimates her beauty; the seductive Lasa; and also the satyr with the goat are all resplendent with a joy and vitality reminiscent of Picasso's old days.

The Del Chiaro Painter must have learned his craft from Attic cups from the workshop of the Jena Painter dating

Figure 32. No. 9. Detail of Nessos and Deianeira. Actual
size of image shown: H: 5.3 cm, W: 5.5 cm.

from the early second quarter of the fourth century. Some charming drawings compete well with the models, but in general the early production does not rise above the standard of Etruscan red-figure. Following the general trend of the time around the middle of the century, and perhaps also pushed by progressive farsightedness, the painter substituted large brush strokes for the earlier lines. Giving up the calligraphic precision, the artist reached something more like true painting. Without aspiring to masterworks, he created scenes pleasant to remember.

Malibu

A Faliscan Red-figure Bell Krater

Mario A. Del Chiaro

This study of a Faliscan red-figure bell krater in the J. Paul Getty Museum (No. 1, figs. 1 and 2)[1] is offered in honor of Dietrich von Bothmer for three reasons: because of the special concern for Faliscan vase painting by one of his most influential tutors, Sir John Beazley;[2] the presence of an instrumental Faliscan stamnos in the Metropolitan Museum of Art (No. 3, figs. 4 and 5), an institution which Bothmer has so dutifully served these many decades; and the original publication by him of two small Faliscan bowls which are included in this presentation (Nos. 8 and 9, figs. 11–13).[3]

Beazley, in his pioneer investigation of Etruscan red-figure vase painting, associated seven vases—four skyphoi, a stamnos, a bell krater, and an oinochoe—on the evidence of a decorative detail these vases shared in common; namely, the "cauliflower tendril" (e.g., fig. 5),[4] the description aptly applied by Beazley to the spiny or thorny character of the detail located within the floral/vegetal scrolls which frame the figured scenes. All seven of these vases were assigned by Beazley to his "Later Red-Figure II" of Faliscan vase painting; i.e., within his "Fluid Group."[5] It is the intention of the present paper to call attention to the Getty bell krater; to provide additional examples for Beazley's original list; and, more significantly, to demonstrate that the cauliflower tendril need not serve as the sole criterion to attract additional vases. In this last instance, it should be noted that on the small bowls (Nos. 8 and 9, figs. 11 and 12), the style of drawing for the satyrs—not the presence of the cauliflower tendril—is the key to attribution.

It has been clear from the very start that the vases here assigned to the "Cauliflower Class," a designation which recognizes Beazley's observation and one with which to make a distinction between "Class" and "Group,"[6] are not the work of a single painter but rather, quite clearly, the creations of a number of individual artists who share the cauliflower tendril as a decorative detail. The vases which comprise this class must, consequently, be considered products of a single Faliscan workshop active in the *Ager Faliscus*, specifically at Cività Castellana (*Falerii Veteres*, approximately forty kilometers north of Rome) or in its environs, during the second half of the fourth century B.C.[7]

THE CAULIFLOWER CLASS

The Painter of Copenhagen H 153

The following nine vases of different shapes can be attributed to a Faliscan artist named by Beazley the "Painter of Copenhagen H 153" after a bell krater in the Ny Carlsberg Glyptotek (here No. 2). Together with the Getty bell krater (No. 1), it marks the largest vase shape utilized by the painter.

Bell Kraters

1. Malibu, The J. Paul Getty Museum (figs. 1 and 2)
Anonymous loan, acc. no. L.78.AE.10
Height, 40 cm; diam. of mouth, 42 cm; diam. of foot, 20 cm
Mended from numerous fragments.
Side A: draped maenad striding to the right between two confronting, bearded satyrs.
Side B: seated nude maenad between two confronting, bearded satyrs.

On side A, the satyr at the left stands with his upraised foot placed on a reserved rock which is decorated with a black dotted-rosette. His arms and hands are outstretched toward the maenad, the right straight forward, the left lowered. The companion satyr at the right stands upright

1. I wish to thank Dr. Jiří Frel, curator of antiquities of the J. Paul Getty Museum, for permission to study and publish the bell krater (inv. no. L.78.AE.10) which he has already attributed to the "Copenhagen H 153 Painter" (Museum label).

2. J.D. Beazley, *Etruscan Vase-Painting* (Oxford, 1947)—henceforth, Beazley, *EVP*.

3. I am grateful to Dr. Joseph Veach Noble for photographs and permission to publish the two small bowls in his private collection.

4. Beazley, *EVP*, 160f. I have been unable to consult the skyphos listed by Beazley (*EVP*, 160): Rome, Principe del Drago from Nazzano.

5. *Ibid.*, chapter VIII.

6. "Class" rather than "Group" in conformance with Beazley's "Fluid Group" of his "Later Red-Figure II" (*supra* n. 5) wherein he lists the vases with cauliflower tendril. However, one of these—the name piece, No. 2, fig. 3 in this paper—was placed by Beazley within "Later Red-Figure I" (*EVP*, chapter VII, see p. 135).

7. *Falerii Veteres* (present-day Cività Castellana) is the focal point of the *Ager Faliscus*, a region inhabited by an Etruscanized Italic, Latin-speaking people well known for a prolific and impressive production of Etruscan art: sculpture (chiefly terracotta) and red-figure vases. Some of the better-known centers other than *Falerii Veteres* are Narce, Capena, Corchiano, Vignanello, and Rignano Flaminio.

Figure 1. No. 1. Bell krater attributed to the Painter of Copenhagen H 153. Side A. Malibu, The J. Paul Getty Museum L.78.AE.10.

Figure 2. Side B of figure 1.

Figure 3. No. 2. Bell krater by the Painter of Copenhagen H 153 (name piece). Side A. Copenhagen, Ny Carlsberg Glyptotek H 153.

and gestures toward the maenad with the open palm of his right hand while his upturned left hand balances an upright tympanum. The maenad, whose flesh is rendered in white paint and who wears bracelets and earring, moves swiftly to the right as she looks back to the left. An obscure round object (ball or fruit?) can be seen in her upraised right hand. In the field beneath her lowered left hand there is a cursorily painted basket of cage-like form which, on the evidence of a similar but more clearly depicted form present on a skyphos in Edinburgh (see fig. 14), may have been intended as a cornucopia. In the field at the top left is a recurrent detail—broad sash with internal (embroidered?) decoration.

Side B of the Getty bell krater shows the two confronting satyrs in a near heraldic composition with their inside legs raised, the feet resting on relatively high white rocks which, through their elaborate internal modulations (hatching), seem more like tree stumps than rocks. Between the raised and lowered outstretched hands of each satyr, there must have once appeared, or originally been intended, a long beaded necklace or wreath, as known from a myriad of such representations.[8] Owing to the

fugitive nature of the white paint used to indicate these necklaces and wreaths, such details may seem altogether absent or at times only faintly visible (see the right-hand satyr, fig. 2). Both satyrs, and their counterparts on side A, wear long beaded necklaces which run over the shoulder, across the chest, and round the waist, an especially common fashion in Faliscan and Caeretan red-figure ware of the second half of the fourth century B.C. More often than not the bushy-tailed satyrs affect a rather intense stare through somewhat slanted eyes. Also more often than not, the satyrs wear soft slippers.

In sharp contrast, the more carefully drawn maenad, whose white flesh is remarkably well preserved, is seated on a mantle which cushions a rock that is only implied. The details of the face, anatomy, and the jewelry which are painted in black over the white flesh color are clear and precise. The upright tympanum balanced in the maenad's left hand echoes that of the satyr at the opposite side in its decoration—alternating "O" and "X" motif, etc. In the field, broad sashes appear at the upper corners; the sash at the left is painted white. Behind the rock and below the maenad's right hand is a "patera" for which there are traces of a bordering pattern of three triangularly placed dots which, in their pristine condition, would have appeared at three to four places along the edge of the "patera" (see fig. 4).

2. Copenhagen, Ny Carlsberg Glyptotek (fig. 3)
Inv. no. H 153
Height, 37 cm
Beazley, *EVP*, 161, no. 2; *Bildertafeln des Etruskischen Museums der Ny Carlsberg Glyptotek* (Copenhagen, 1928), pl. 53,1.
Side A: draped maenad striding to right between two confronting, bearded satyrs.
Side B: replica.

In the shape (especially the high torus foot) and the horizontal decorative bands above and below the picture field (note the short vertical stripes or dashes in the laurel pattern at join of stem and leaves), the Malibu and Copenhagen bell kraters are identical. Within the picture field of the Copenhagen vase, the left-hand satyr, despite the absence of a rock beneath his raised foot, is very much the same as the left-hand satyr on sides A and B of the Getty vase (see figs. 1 and 2). The companion satyr on the Copenhagen bell krater, however, assumes a more dance-like attitude with the high kick of his right leg and the backward tilt of his body. In her attire, posture, and move-

8. See for example, Etruscan red-figure vases attributed to Caeretan artists: M. Del Chiaro, *Etruscan Red-Figured Vase-Painting at Caere* (Berkeley, 1974)—henceforth, Del Chiaro, *ERVC*.

Figure 4. No. 3. Stamnos attributed to the Painter of Copenhagen H 153. Side B. New York, The Metropolitan Museum of Art 91.1.441.

Figure 5. Side view of figure 4.

ment, the maenad can be regarded as a true sister of the maenad on side A of the Getty vase. The two "paterae" in the field, one to each side of the maenad, possess the same triangular dotted configuration mentioned earlier for the Getty vase.

Stamnos

3. New York, The Metropolitan Museum of Art (figs. 4 and 5)
Inv. no. 91.1.441
Height, 24.5 cm
Beazley, *EVP*, 301; M. Del Chiaro, *ERVC*, fig. 17 (side A).
Side A: draped maenad striding to the right while looking round. Both arms held out to the sides with the palms of the hands outstretched.
Side B: replica (here fig. 4).

On the evidence of her short and squat proportions, one may hesitate at the outset to accept the maenad on the New York stamnos (fig. 4) as the creation of the painter responsible for the taller and far more elegant maenads on the Getty and Copenhagen bell kraters (see figs. 1 and 3). However, close scrutiny of the rendering of the heads, hands, and feet will readily disclose the hand of the Painter

of Copenhagen H 153. The chiton of his maenads is essentially the same on vases Nos. 1 to 3 except for the wave pattern—also found at the hem of the chiton on the Copenhagen bell krater and the New York stamnos— which is added diagonally at the right breast of the maenad on the stamnos (fig. 4). The well-preserved pattern of triangular white dots to the "patera" serves to make this filler-motif the clearest example on vases thus far known for the Cauliflower Class.

On the shoulder and directly above the picture field of the New York stamnos, a lazy wave pattern has been painted running from left to right, a decorative motif which recalls that painted above and below the picture field on the skyphos in Siena (No. 4, fig. 6), and, in a tighter form, above the picture field for the two Milan skyphoi (Nos. 6 and 7, figs. 8–10). The decorative band below the picture field on the New York stamnos, however, bears a segmented maeander or key pattern interrupted by crossed-metopes. This motif is also employed on other vases by the Painter of Copenhagen H 153 and in the Cauliflower Class: see the Getty and Copenhagen bell kraters (Nos. 1 and 2); one of the skyphoi in Milan (No. 7, fig. 10); the two small bowls in New York (Nos. 8 and 9,

Figure 6. No. 4. Skyphos attributed to the Painter of Copenhagen H 153. Side A. Siena, Museo Archeologico, Chigi Zondadari Collection. Photo: Foto Grassi, Siena.

Figure 7. No. 5. Skyphos attributed to the Painter of Copenhagen H 153. Side A. Copenhagen, National Museum 6577.

figs. 11 and 12); a small fragment of a "schalen" in Frankfurt;[9] and, at times, without the crossed-metope as on the Michigan oinochoe (figs. 17 and 18).

Skyphoi

At least two skyphoi (Nos. 4 and 5) may be attributed to the Painter of Copenhagen H 153, each of which shows a broad-shouldered, narrow-waisted bearded satyr who is seated on a rock covered with an animal skin (probably panther).

> 4. Siena, Museo Archeologico (fig. 6)
> Chigi Zondadari Collection
> Height, 30.4 cm; diam. of mouth, 30.8 cm
> Side A: bearded satyr seated on a rock while reaching back to place his arm around the waist of a nude maenad.
> Side B: replica; much damaged.

> 5. Copenhagen, National Museum (fig. 7)
> Inv. no. 6577
> Height, 26.5 cm; diam. of mouth, 24.5 cm
> Beazley, *EVP*, 161, no. 2; CVA, fasc. 5, pl. 220, 4.
> Side A: lone, bearded satyr seated on a rock with an upright tympanum grasped by his left hand.
> Side B: replica.

The satyrs, each sporting that characteristic intense look, are depicted with a double rather than a single

strand of long beads which are worn "bandolier" fashion across the chest. The animal skin (panther?) upon which each satyr is seated, facing to the right, is painted in white with scattered, short hatching to indicate spots. The head of the animal is represented frontally. No filler oramentation is found in the field of the Siena skyphos, but that on the Copenhagen specimen shows a relatively large dotted-rosette in white on the black ground. A tympanum, which is present only on this latter vase, is not enhanced with the "O" and "X" motif noted for the tympanum on the Getty bell krater and one of the bowls in New York (No. 8, fig. 11) but is treated instead with an encircling wave pattern, a decorative detail also known for one of the Milan skyphoi (No. 7, fig. 10).

Although the nude maenad who stands with right arm akimbo in so wholly relaxed and nonchalant pose on the Siena skyphos (fig. 6) is a far cry from her counterpart on side B of the Getty bell krater (fig. 2), she is nevertheless closely related by reason of the detailing which, unfortunately, is now very faint. In place of the wave pattern located above and below the picture field on the Siena skyphos, the Copenhagen skyphos carries two decorative motifs not noted thus far on vases of the Cauliflower Class: i.e., a series of small, neatly spaced chevrons facing to the left below the picture field and a pattern of inter-

---

9. P. Bol, *Liebieghaus-Museum alter Plastik. Guide to the Collection of Ancient Art* (Frankfurt am Main, 1981) 189, fig. 268. A photograph of the fragment was not available at the time of writing this paper.

Figure 8. No. 6. Skyphos attributed to the Painter of Copenhagen H 153. Side A. Formerly on the art
market in Milan.

Figure 9. Side B of figure 8.

locked, striated triangles—the last a distinctive motif
which is found on an Etruscan red-figure skyphos I have
assigned to contemporary Tarquinian production.[10]

The two following skyphoi (Nos. 6 and 7) may be challenged as works of the Painter of Copenhagen H 153
because of their obvious slovenly drawing and, perhaps
more poignantly, because of the lack of figural criteria
when compared to that encountered on the vases thus far
presented. Regardless, there is an unquestionable common
stamp to the satyr heads, the filler motifs (broad sash and
"patera"), etc. which should at the least arouse strong sus-
picion that the two skyphoi may be products of his hand.
Note, for example, the character and drawing of the rather
obese satyr at side A of the Milan skyphos, No. 6 (see fig.
8). It should be pointed out that his female companion
shows signs of repainting at breasts and head. It should be
also noted that she, like the nude maenad at the opposite
side of the vase (fig. 9), holds an obscure roundish object
(ball or fruit?) in her upraised right hand, a gesture and object which should recall the maenad on side A of the Getty
bell krater (fig. 1).

    6. Formerly Milan art market (figs. 8 and 9)
Height, 30 cm; diam. of mouth, 30.9 cm
A. Stenico, *Finarte 5* (Milan, March 1963),

Figure 10. No. 7. Skyphos attributed to the Painter of Copenhagen H 153. Side A. Formerly on the art
market in Milan.

pl. 67, no. 129.
Side A: obese bearded satyr standing at the left facing a
draped maenad who moves swiftly away to the right while
looking back to the left. A portion of the upper body and
the head of the maenad has been repainted.
Side B: satyr chasing a nude maenad off to the right.
"Patera" in the field between the legs of the maenad.

10. See M. Del Chiaro in *RM* 73/74 (1966/67) 257 and pl. 93, figs. 1–2.

Figure 11. No. 8. Shallow bowl attributed to the Painter of Copenhagen H 153. Interior. New York, J.V. Noble Collection.

Figure 12. No. 9. Shallow bowl attributed to the Painter of Copenhagen H 153. Interior. New York, J.V. Noble Collection.

Figure 13. Profile of figure 12.

7. Formerly Milan art market (fig. 10)
Height, 38 cm; diam. of mouth, 28.8 cm
A. Stenico, *Finarte 5* (Milan, March 1963),
pl. 66, no. 128.
Side A: satyr moving to the right in a crouched position
with tympanum in left hand and a long fillet (*tenea*) over
his left forearm. Broad sash in the field at upper left.
Side B: replica.

Shallow Bowls

Two fragmentary but mended small bowls in the private
collection of Dr. Joseph Veach Noble, first published by
Bothmer,[11] provide examples of vases which do not bear
the "cauliflower tendril" but, on stylistic grounds, are
nevertheless attracted to the vases here assigned to the
Cauliflower Class.

8. New York, J.V. Noble Collection (fig. 11)
Height, 5.5 cm; diam. of bowl, 21.5 cm
D. von Bothmer, *Ancient Art from New York Private Collections* (New York, 1961), no. 263, pl. 99.
Interior: bearded satyr standing to the right with his left
foot raised and resting on a rock. A tympanum is held
basket-like in his left hand. A sash, "patera," and plant in
the field.

9. New York, J.V. Noble Collection (figs. 12 and 13)
Height, 5.2 cm; diam. of bowl, 21.3 cm
D. von Bothmer, *op.cit.*, no. 264, pl. 99.
Interior: bearded satyr leaning against or sitting on an up-
right storage amphora. A filleted thyrsos is supported with
his left hand.

These two bowls rest on a relatively high ring base (see
fig. 13) which is reserved but for traces of black originally
painted as a band nearest the resting surface. The under-
sides are reserved except for a large central dot and two
concentric circles painted in black. The entire exterior of
the bowls is painted black and carries no decoration.
Within the bowl, the medallions are encircled by a broad
reserved band enhanced with a motif already encountered
on some vases previously discussed; i.e., a segmented
maeander interrupted by crossed-metopes (see figs. 1–5,
and 10). The hard stare of the satyrs, to which attention
has been called as characteristic of the Painter of Copenhagen H 153, is especially evident on bowl No. 9 (see fig.
12). A detail which merits consideration is well preserved
and rendered with clarity on this last bowl, namely, the
narrow white fillet which is tied around the satyr's head
with loops and top-knot. This peculiar manner of depicting a head-fillet—now made comprehensible for the satyr
on this New York bowl—helps explain the more obscure

Figure 14. No. 10. Skyphos assigned to the Cauliflower
Class. Side A. Edinburgh, Royal Scottish
Museum.

parallels present on other vases by the same painter: see
the Getty and Copenhagen bell kraters (figs. 1–3) and the
Copenhagen skyphos (fig. 7).

Kylix

A small fragment of a kylix ("schalen") in Frankfurt
(Liebieghaus-Museum alter Plastik, inv. no. 1623)[12] presents an adequate glimpse of its medallion decoration—
torso and head of a bearded satyr with filleted thyrsos and,
in the field, a broad sash, the whole originally encircled by
a decorative band with segmented maeander and crossed-
metope—to place it within the Cauliflower Class on the
evidence of the New York bowl (No. 9, fig. 12). There is
sufficient reason to believe, however, that the skyphos is
not the work of the Painter of Copenhagen H 153, although it must stand very close to him. A special feature
within the thyrsos itself—the "w" forms—are solid black
shapes in the New York bowl but thin and somewhat
trident-shaped on the kylix fragment. Provocatively, such
detailing may eventually attract additional vases to the
Cauliflower Class or to the hand of the Painter of Copenhagen H 153.

Skyphoi

Like the kylix fragment in Frankfurt, the following two
skyphoi are not attributable to the Painter of Copenhagen
H 153, but, on the basis of the cauliflower tendril present
in the vegetal/floral framing motifs beneath the handles,

11. D. von Bothmer, *Ancient Art from New York Private Collections* (exhibition catalogue, The Metropolitan Museum of Art, New York, 1961),
nos. 263 and 264.

12. *Supra* n. 9.

Figure 15. No. 11. Skyphos assigned to the Cauliflower Class. Side A. Geneva, Musée d'art et d'histoire MF 274.

Figure 16. Side B of figure 15.

can be assigned to the broader Cauliflower Class.

10. Skyphos (fig. 14)
Edinburgh, Royal Scottish Museum
Side A: draped maenad striding to the right as she looks round. The arms are down to the sides, the left slightly raised. In the field: cornucopia below the left hand, pendant triangular wreaths or sashes to each side of the maenad's head.
Side B: replica but for differences in the field: "patera" at the left, shell-like form at the right, and pendant sash or wreath at top left.

11. Skyphos (figs. 15 and 16)
Geneva, Musée d'art et d'histoire
Inv. no. MF 274
Height, 29.9 cm; diam. of mouth, 30 cm
Beazley, *EVP*, 161; *RevArch* (1916) 253f.
Side A: draped maenad striding to the right while looking back. Left hand down, right hand raised. Unusual plant-like form in the field at left.
Side B: young satyr (clean shaven) leaning precariously forward with left foot raised and resting on a large rock. Large "patera" in the field at lower right; plant between his legs.

Although the Edinburgh skyphos does not display decorative bands above and below the picture field, the Geneva skyphos possesses bands of evenly spaced but somewhat shoddy chevrons facing to the right, a motif already noted for one of the Milan skyphoi (No. 6, see figs. 8 and 9) but running to the left. Granted that the garment of the

maenads for these last two skyphoi are "stylistically" unlike, the common character and details of the garment (note the dart motif) cannot be denied. Of the two skyphoi, the Edinburgh example shows a chiton which approximates more closely the type preferred by the Painter of Copenhagen H 153.

Oinochoe, Shape VII

An oinochoe of characteristic Etruscan Shape VII (figs. 17 and 18) must be included here because of the cauliflower tendril which appears within the floral/vegetal scroll at its neck. On the neck and body of the vase may also be found a new element in the decorative repertory for vases of the Cauliflower Class—a large swan moving slowly to the right while looking back with an expression that, on the neck of the vase, seems rather nasty and onerous. On the body of the Michigan oinochoe a partially draped female stands to the left of the swan with her left foot raised and resting on a rock decorated with small black dots. Although her garment, which disguises or contributes to the strange proportions of the figure, does not bear the dart or wave motifs, it is at least consistent in character with the wardrobe of the other draped maenads of the class. As is clearly evident, the pose and gesture of the partially draped female also strongly recall those of a number of satyrs on vases of the class (e.g., figs. 1 and 2). The shoulder of the oinochoe is decorated with a carefully rendered tongue pattern, whereas the decorative band directly below the picture field bears the segmented

Figure 17. No. 12. Oinochoe, Shape VII, assigned to the Cauliflower Class. Front. Ann Arbor, University of Michigan, Kelsey Museum of Archaeology 2609.

Figure 18. Profile of figure 17.

maeander pattern, but without crossed-metopes.

12. Oinochoe, Shape VII (figs 17 and 18)
Ann Arbor, University of Michigan, Kelsey Museum of
Archaeology
Inv. no. 2609
Height, 21.3 cm
Beazley, *EVP*, 156, no. 10 and pl. XXXVI, 5 and 6; *CVA*,
fasc. 1, pl. XXIV, figs. 4a–b.
Neck: swan moving to right while looking back.
Body: partially draped female at left facing to the right
toward a swan which moves off to the right while looking
back.

Spouted Lebes

A last vase to be assigned here to the Cauliflower Class
is, like the oinochoe Shape VII, a characteristic Etruscan
type and one that has received my attention in an earlier
study.[13] Once again, the key to attribution is found in the
cauliflower tendril within the framing motifs at each side
of the vase. At the front of the lebes, below the lion-head
spout, is a bird (pigeon?) painted in white. The bird faces
to the right with its head sharply upraised and its body set
close to the ground, its wings seemingly fluttering as if to
indicate a bird bathing rather than one about to take
flight.

13. See M. Del Chiaro, "One Vase Shape, Three Etruscan Fabrics,"
RM 76 (1969) 122–127.

Figure 19. No. 13. Spouted lebes assigned to the Cauli-flower Class. Front. Paris, Musée du Louvre S 4183.

Figure 20. Profile of figure 19.

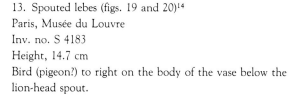

13. Spouted lebes (figs. 19 and 20)[14]
Paris, Musée du Louvre
Inv. no. S 4183
Height, 14.7 cm
Bird (pigeon?) to right on the body of the vase below the lion-head spout.

The present study based on the Getty bell krater (No. 1, figs. 1 and 2) has attempted to place the vase in its proper Etruscan setting and to illustrate that Etruscan red-figure vases which bear the distinctive cauliflower tendril need not be ascribed to a single artist—i.e., solely to the Painter of Copenhagen H 153—but may very well be products of other painters who, needless to say, were members of the same workshop. In addition, it has been possible to show that some vases, without the cauliflower tendril, can be associated on stylistic grounds alone, thereby not only increasing the scope of the Cauliflower Class but also of Faliscan red-figure vase painting as a whole during the second half of the fourth century B.C.

University of California
Santa Barbara

14. A current study based on seven spouted lebetes in Paris, Musée du Louvre—of which the only example with cauliflower tendril is given here (figs. 19, 20)—should appear in a future number of the *Revue Archéologique.*

Polychrome Vases and Terracottas from Southern Italy in the J. Paul Getty Museum

Frederike van der Wielen-van Ommeren

The antiquities collection of the J. Paul Getty Museum includes some very nice polychrome vases and terracotta figurines from southern Italy.[1] The exact provenance of these objects is not known. Nevertheless, the askos (No. 1), the head vases (Nos. 2, 3, 4), the stand (No. 5), the pyxis (No. 6), and the birds (Nos. 7, 8) can be assigned to workshops at Canosa in Apulia or to workshops in the neighborhood of this Daunian town. The other terracottas (Nos. 9, 10, 11) could also have been produced in ceramic centers located elsewhere in Apulia.

The objects here presented, in particular Nos. 1–6, are typical of the vase production of the Canosan workshops in the Hellenistic period. This production is not only characterized by special shapes, such as askoi, head vases, and pyxides, but also by the polychrome and plastic decoration of the objects. It began at the end of the fourth century B.C. (last quarter) and probably lasted for about a century.[2]

This ware was specially made for funerary purposes and has been found in great numbers in the chambered tombs that have been excavated in the bedrock around Canosa.[3]

1. Askos (figs. 1–2)
   Malibu, The J. Paul Getty Museum, accession number 78.AE.372. Total height approximately 54.0 cm; height to rim 42.2 cm, diameter base 15.0 cm, diameter mouth 8.2 cm.
   Condition: vase body intact with traces of polychromy; handle and left figurine missing, the other two figurines refixed break on break with heads missing, also right forearm and left hand of central figurine; ears and part of legs of horse protomes missing.

Light orange clay, white slip, polychromy: black (originally blue?), purple or violet (originally pink?).

Wheel-turned vase body with pierced bottom; the joint of the lateral sides forms a crest that ends in an upraised point at the back side; wheel-turned neck fixed on an opening cut in the joint with mouth of slightly convex profile. The plastic ornaments have been molded (relief heads, horse protomes, figurines) or hand-modeled (handle) and placed on the vase body with the help of liquid clay before the firing of the object. The white slip and polychromy have been applied after the firing.

Painted decoration: the entire vase body, apart from the bottom, has been covered with white slip. On this, a second ground of pink color had probably been applied (partly, cf. traces of purple or violet around the plastic head under the mouth). On the front of the vase, the outstretched wings of the large relief head have been outlined in black: details of the head had originally been touched up (red lips, black eyes, brick or rust-red hair), neck and shoulders indicated by contour lines. The small plastic head on the neck also has traces of polychromy (black contours of left eye). The lateral sides of the vessel show traces of a winged horse or seahorse (black outlines) moving toward the winged head, and of a wave pattern along the crest. The back side seems to have carried a large palmette (traces of black).

1. I wish to express my gratitude to Prof. Jiří Frel for allowing me to publish these vases and terracottas and for supplying me with photographs and detailed information on the objects.

2. On the production of Canosan vases in general, see O. Elia, "Canosini, vasi," in *EAA* II (1959) 317f. with lit.; K. Van Wonterghem-Maes, *De polychrome en plastische keramiek van Canosa di Puglia gedurende de Hellenistische periode* (Louvain, 1968); A. Oliver, Jr., *The Reconstruction of Two Apulian Tomb Groups, Antike Kunst*, Suppl. 5 (1968); F. van der Wielen et al., "Céramique insolite de l'Italie du Sud: les vases hellénis-

tiques de Canosa," *Genava*, n.s. 26 (1978) 143ff.

3. On Canosa and Canosan chamber tombs: N. Jacobone, *Canusium. Un'antica e grande città dell'Apulia* 3rd ed. (Lecce, 1962); O. Elia, "Canosa di Puglia," in *EAA* II (1959) 315ff.; F. Tiné Bertocchi, *La pittura funeraria apula* (Naples, 1964) 15ff. with lit.; Oliver, *op. cit.*, 21ff.; G. Andreassi, "Note sull'ipogeo 'Varrese' di Canosa," *Archivio Storico Pugliese* 25 (1972) 233ff.; Van der Wielen et al., *op. cit.*, 142f; J.-L. Lamboley, "Les hypogées indigènes apuliens," *MEFRA* 94 (1982) 91ff.

Figure 1. No. 1. Askos. Malibu, The J. Paul Getty Museum 78.AE.372.

Figure 2. Profile of figure 1.

Plastic decoration: of the large winged bust on the front, only the oval face and undulating hair have been modeled in low relief; the hair is parted down the middle with a small disk above the forehead; the earrings are composed of a button (rosette?) and an oval-shaped pendant. A much smaller head has been placed under the mouth of the vessel: also in frontal position, it has a modeled neck and the same type of face and hairdress as the large head beneath it, but no wings. From the shoulder of the vase the foreparts of a galloping horse emerge at both sides of the small head: the manes end in a forelock on top of the head;

details once indicated in paint, such as eyes, head-stall with phalera, and probably also the harness. A draped female figurine was originally fixed behind either horse protome (left figurine missing): the one at the right is wrapped in a chiton and himation, with the right hand placed on the hip and the lowered left hand holding a flap of the himation. A third female figurine, of larger size, has been placed behind the vessel's mouth: she is dressed in nearly the same way as the figure at her left; the forearms are free and were extended forward, probably holding an object. The handle, of which the attachments have been preserved

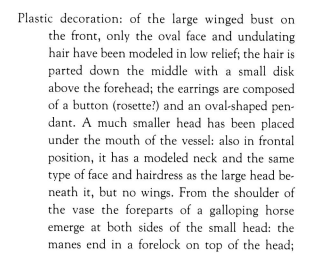

4. On Scylla askoi, see K. Schauenburg, "Skylla oder Tritonin? Zu einer Gruppe canosinischer Askoi," *RM* 87 (1980) 29ff.

5. Cf. Van Wonterghem-Maes, *op. cit.*, 1ff.

5a. A fifth polychrome askos without horse protomes can now be

added: Sotheby's, New York, 1 March 1984, lot 89 (ill.): total height 43.2 cm; plastic ornaments; wings flanking mouth, small gorgoneion, draped female figurine with fish tail of the same type as the lateral figure on the Malibu askos.

Figure 3. Askos. Paris, Louvre CA 3241.

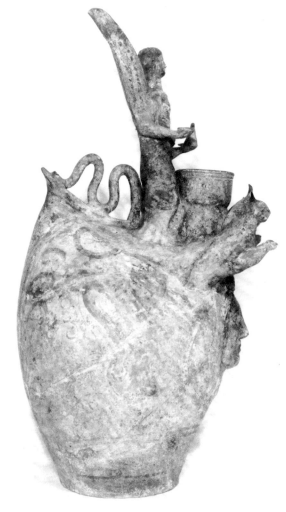

Figure 4. Profile of figure 3.

on the crest of the askos, presented a sea monster's tail, forming one or two bows before
ending in a caudal fin above the rear point of
the crest.

This type of askos is of great importance for the study of
Canosan polychrome vases, since it forms the link between the so-called Scylla askoi[4] and other series of askoi
with polychrome and plastic ornaments.[5] The following
are the examples known to me.[5a]

a. Paris, Louvre CA 3241 (figs. 3–4). From the Lagrasta I
hypogeum, acquired by Biardot in 1845. Total height 56
cm, height to rim 37.2 cm. One mouth. Polychromy:
dolphin and stylized rosette on lateral sides, palmette on
back side. Plastic ornaments: same types of relief heads as

on Malibu 78.AE.372 (same molds?), large head with neck
in relief, two horse protomes, one draped and winged
female figurine behind the mouth (himation covering left
arm and lower part of body, hands carrying phiale and
pigeon), sea monster's tail forming two bows.[6]

b. Malibu 78.AE.372 (figs. 1–2). Unpublished.

c. Bari, Archaeological Museum 6005. From the Mazza
group discovered in 1902 in the Varrese hypogeum. Total
height 86 cm, height to rim 58 cm. Four mouths, no handle. Polychromy: pink ground on upper half of vase body;
palmette on back side with elaborate floral pattern and stylized rosettes on lateral sides; running wave on mouths.
Plastic ornaments: two heads in high relief (the larger,
male, with wreath; the smaller, female, with wings, wreath,
earclips, buttons on border of dress), four horse protomes,

6. E.P. Biardot, *Les terres-cuites grecques funèbres dans leur rapport avec
les mystères de Bacchus* (Paris, 1872) 414ff., pl. 43; Tiné Bertocchi, *op. cit.,,*
22 n. 40; Schauenburg, *op. cit.,* 31 no. 21. I should like to thank Prof. R.
Villard and in particular Dr. A. Pasquier for their permission to publish

this askos.

7. M. Jatta, "Tombe canosine del Museo Provinciale di Bari," *RM* 29
(1914) 105f., pl. X,2a; Van der Wielen et al., *op. cit.,* 147, fig. 8; R.
Striccoli, in P. Malagrinò, *I musei di Puglia* (Fasano, 1980) pl. I,3.

three female figurines (the larger one winged) on false mouths, and horse's head surmounting rear point of crest.[7]
d. Warsaw, National Museum 195. Also from the Lagrasta I hypogeum and acquired by Biardot. Height to rim 45 cm. Four mouths, no handle. Polychromy: pink ground; chariot on mouth with two wheels on shoulder, winged seahorse and dolphin on lateral sides, large palmette on back side, stylized rosettes and florals in the field; friezes of running waves, egg-and-dart and triangles around base, mouths, and crest. Plastic ornaments: one female head in low relief of the "friendly looking" gorgoneion type with painted wings and draped shoulders, four horse protomes. This vessel inspired Bachofen to write his treatise on funerary symbolism.[8]

These four vases form a special category among the Canosan askoi, not only because of their very rich polychrome and plastic decoration but also from the technical point of view. They constitute the only askoi with horse protomes (items a, b, c, d) and figurines (items a, b) that have been fired with the vessels; moreover, the Malibu askos is the only one so far known with two figurines fixed on the *shoulder* (without making holes in the vase body) before firing took place.[9]

The shape of these wheel-turned vessels clearly follows that of the Apulian red-figure askoi[10] and the polychrome Canosan Scylla askoi,[11] which are of smaller size, with the widest diameter normally situated in the lower half of the vase ("ascoid" body).

The polychrome decoration is also inspired by the Scylla askoi, a number of which carry a Pegasus, a winged hippocamp, or a dolphin on the lateral sides. A palmette decorates the back side of nearly all Apulian red-figure and of many polychrome askoi.

As regards the plastic decoration, female heads in low relief are already found on several Scylla askoi, where they substitute the painted heads borrowed from the red-figure askoi; they are nearly always of the same type as on Warsaw 195 (item d), but without neck or wings.[12] The type of large head on the Paris and Malibu askoi (items a,

b; figs. 1, 3) has also been used for the first series of Canosan polychrome plastic vases in the shape of a woman's head (cf. Malibu 80.AE.73, *infra* No. 2, fig. 5).[13] The small head under the mouth on the same vessels is a miniature replica (without wings) of the large head beneath it. On the Varrese askos (c), the head above the four horses presents itself as the abbreviation of a winged female charioteer, crowned with a wreath of vine leaves. The prancing foreparts of horses occur for the first time on askoi of this type as an integrated part of the vessels. On the Warsaw askos (d), the chariot of the quadriga appears on the neck of the vase with a wheel beside the first and the fourth horse. The figurine behind the mouth very clearly derives from the Scylla or Triton figure on the Scylla askoi: from a female half figure, accompanied or not by dog protomes, it has developed into a complete female figurine wearing chiton and himation, even wings (a, c), holding objects in her hands (phiale, bird), with a sea monster's tail in her back (a, b; figs. 2, 4). Of the three figurines which originally decorated the Malibu askos, the lateral ones were most probably identical, represented in a stance and drapery inspired by well-known Tanagras.[14] On the Varrese askos (c), the separately fired figurines have been placed on false mouths; the lower part of the central figure even had to be partly removed due to lack of space; on the crest, the sea monster's tail has been replaced by a horse's head on the rear point. On the second Lagrasta askos (d), there is apparently no trace left on the four mouths of any figurine, nor has the crest been surmounted by any plastic ornament; only the type of the relief head recalls the Scylla askoi.

Of the other types of askoi, those with globular, hand-modeled vase bodies carry separately fired appliques.[15] Those with egg-shaped, wheel-turned bellies are sometimes decorated with "incorporated" gorgoneia, whereas the horse protomes and figurines have always been glued on these vases after firing.[16]

The friability of the polychromy and the presence of

8. J.J. Bachofen, *Die Unsterblichkeitslehre der orphischen Theologie* (Berlin, 1867) 3ff., pl. opposite p. 7; Biardot, *op. cit.*, 366ff., pl. 40; *CVA* Poland I, pl. 50.5a-b; K. Meuli, in *J.J. Bachofens Gesammelte Werke* VII (Basel, 1958) frontispiece and "Nachwort" pl. Q; Van der Wielen et al., *op. cit.*, 147, figs. 9–11 (different states of preservation).

9. On techniques employed in Canosan ceramic workshops: A. Rinuy, P. Hartmann, and F. Schweizer, *Genava*, n.s. 26 (1978) (cf. *supra* n. 2), 149ff.; F. van der Wielen-van Ommeren, "Deux vases à entonnoir au Musée de Leyde et un groupe funéraire de Canosa," *OMRO* 63 (1982) 80f.

10. On Apulian red-figure askoi, see J.D. Beazley, *Etruscan Vase-Painting* (Oxford, 1947) 272; Van der Wielen-van Ommeren, *op. cit.* P10 n. 98 with lit.

11. Cf. *supra* n. 4.

12. Cf. Schauenburg, *op. cit.*, nos. 2, 16, 19. On the "friendly looking" gorgoneion type, see A. Levi, "La evoluzione della testa di Medusa," *BdA*

5,3 (1925) 1ff.; E. Buschor, *Medusa Rondanini* (Stuttgart, 1958) 32ff.; J. Floren, *Studien zur Typologie des Gorgoneion* (Munster, 1977) 177ff.

13. Cf. also the frontal head painted on the red-figure askos New York 96.18.58 framed by a pair of vertical wings: Schauenburg, *op. cit.*, no. 14 pl. 22,2. Another askos carrying both types of relief heads: Christie's, London, 19 October 1970, lot 54 (ill.). The head vases, Sotheby's, London, 5 July 1982, lots 331–332 (ill.), present the same types of head and draped figurine as the Malibu askos.

14. Cf. F. Winter, *Die Typen der figürlichen Terrakotten* II (Berlin-Stuttgart, 1903) 25,2.4; G. Kleiner, *Tanagrafiguren. Untersuchungen zur hellenistischen Kunst und Geschichte*, *JdI* Suppl. 15 (1942) pls. 22,2. 23; S. Besques, *Catalogue raisonné de figurines et reliefs en terre cuite au Musée du Louvre* III (Paris, 1971/2) pl. 21,d.e.

15. Cf. Bari 6006 (Varrese): Jatta, *op. cit.*, 106, pl. IX,1; Rinuy et al., *op. cit.* (*supra* n. 9), 150ff., figs. 12ff. (Geneva 15052, 15051).

16. Cf. *CVA* British Museum 7, IV Da pl. 15,1. 16.

Figure 5. No. 2. Head vase. Malibu, The J. Paul Getty Museum 80.AE.73.

Figure 6. Profile of figure 5.

plastic ornaments, as well as the open bottom, made any practical use of these vessels impossible.[17] Their find place also indicates the purely funerary destination of this class of objects: furnishing of chamber tombs.[18] Their iconographic "program" expresses the current belief regarding afterlife: voyage to the Islands of the Blessed (biga, quadriga, sea monsters, dolphin, Pegasus), persons accompanying the dead's soul (figurines, relief head), demons of the other world (gorgoneion, relief head).[19]

The material from the Varrese-Mazza find and from the Lagrasta I hypogeum acquired by Biardot is generally dated at the very end of the fourth century B.C.[20] The Malibu askos, because of its close resemblance with one of the Biardot askoi (a), clearly belongs to the same period (around 300).

2. Head vase (figs. 5–6)

Malibu, The J. Paul Getty Museum, accession number 80.AE.73. Total height 36.2 cm, diameter base 10.0 cm.

Condition: handle recomposed, firing crack in bottom, white slip and polychromy partly worn off.

Buff-colored clay; black glaze on neck, mouth and handle; white paint on neck; white slip and polychromy (pink, red-brown, dark brown, blue) on head.

Closed bottom, base and neck of head wheel-turned, head molded in two parts, oinochoe neck wheel-turned, oinochoe handle hand-modeled.

The flaring neck has been mounted on a conical, stepped base ring, which carries traces of polychromy. The oval-shaped face has large eyes (set off in dark brown), a long nose, a small sensual mouth which is placed slightly diagonally, and ears of which only the lower part has been modeled. The red-brown hair is parted down the middle and dressed in undulating bandeaux; the sakkos which covers the back is rendered in pink lattice design, decorated with a pink wave band along the edge, a range of pink dots inside, and blue rosettes at intervals.

The head is surmounted by the neck of the vase with trefoil mouth and the ribbed handle of a late Apulian red-figure oinochoe; the neck is decorated with white rays framed above by two lines.

The Canosan ceramic workshops produced several series of head vases, starting with a red-figure imitation of the Attic plastic oinochoai attributed by Beazley to Group N.[21] The next product is represented by this Malibu head vase, which combines two ceramic techniques: a) the neck, mouth, and handle are executed in red-figure technique with superimposed white rays on the neck; b) the head has been drawn from two molds, mounted on a base rim, and decorated with white slip and polychromy after the firing. It belongs to the initial phase of the polychrome ceramic production of Canosa, for which only this type of mold is known.[22] It also illustrates the close collaboration which existed between potters and coroplasts. The same archetype was used in the next phase, producing entirely polychrome head vases,[23] of which the pair Malibu 81.AE.156–157 (*infra* Nos. 3–4, fig. 7) presents more elaborate specimens.

The best preserved examples of this type of head vase belong to the Varrese-Mazza find, which yielded four of them with a flaring polychrome base and open bottom.[24] The stepped base ring of the Malibu head vase occurs also on a pair in the Barletta Museum[25] and on another example in an American private collection[26] (the latter also with closed bottom, all three with plastic earrings).

This type of head vase, which had the same funerary[27] purpose as No. 1., has been dated in the last quarter of the fourth century B.C.[28]

3–4. Head vases (fig. 7)[29]

Malibu, The J. Paul Getty Museum, accession numbers 81.AE.156–157. Total height 36.5 and 37.2 cm, diameter base 8.7–8.9 and 9.2–9.3 cm.

Condition: 81.AE.156: intact, nose of figurine broken; 81.AE.157: recomposed, nose and part of wreath of figurine missing; polychromy well preserved.

Buff-colored clay, white slip, polychromy (pink, pink incarnate, brick-red, blue, black).

Open bottom; head molded in two parts, leaves and figurine molded; base, diadem, and handle hand-modeled.

Both objects, drawn from the same molds and forming a pair, are composed of a stepped base, a

17. On vases with open bottom, see H. Lohmann, "Zu technischen Besonderheiten apulischen Vasen," *JdI* 97 (1982) 210ff.; Van der Wielen-van Ommeren, *op. cit.*, n. 120 (bibl.).

18. Cf. *supra* n. 3.

19. Cf. E.P. Biardot, *Explication du symbolisme des terres cuites grecques de destination funéraire* (Paris, 1864); Bachofen, *op. cit.*; Biardot, *op. cit.* (*supra* n. 6); Meuli, *loc. cit.*; Van der Wielen et al., *op. cit.*, 148f.

20. Oliver, *op. cit.*, 22f.; A. Riccardi, "Vasi configurati a testa umana di

provenienza o produzione canosina nel Museo di Bari," in *Canosa* I (Bari, 1980) 10; Van der Wielen-van Ommeren, *op. cit.*, 110 nos. III. V.

21. Cf. Bari 1424–1425: Riccardi, *op. cit.*, 9f., nos. 1–2, pl. I.

22. For the type of face, cf. also *supra* no. 1, fig. 1, and n. 13.

23. Cf. Bari 796–799: Riccardi, *op. cit.*, 13ff., nos. 7–10, pls. IV–V.

24. Bari 6033–6036: Jatta, *op. cit.*, 109, fig. 11; Riccardi, *op. cit.*, 10ff., nos. 3–6, pls. II–III.

25. Riccardi, *op. cit.*, 11, fig. 1.

Figure 7. Nos. 3–4. Head vases. Malibu, The J. Paul Getty Museum 81.AE.156–157.

woman's head with flaring neck, a figurine, and an oinochoe handle.

The upper, horizontal part of the base has been painted pink. The short neck has a brick-red lower contour line and carries traces of a necklace. The oval-shaped face has pink lips, and black brows, eye lashes and pupil. The clearly modeled ears are painted pink and wear disk-shaped earrings. The black hair is dressed in bandeaux and surmounted by a very large crescent-shaped diadem, which is decorated with a painted white maeander in a pink field and three disks in relief, each one carrying a smaller blue disk. The back of the head has lost its polychromy (sakkos). The neck is framed by two long, vertical leaves with molded veins, the inner half painted pink and the outer blue. The flat loop handle placed on top of the head has dark contours (originally pink or red) and is

decorated, on the loop above the figurine, with a stylized rosette (dark contour lines and polychrome rings) in a pink field. The figurine, which has been placed against the handle, represents a woman standing with her weight on her left leg and draped in a chiton (81.AE.156: pink; 81.AE.157: white) and long himation covering both arms (white with pink borders and hanging fold); the right forearm crosses the bust at the waist; the left arm seems to be lowered; the head (pink incarnate face, brick-red hair) is slightly lifted toward the left shoulder and wears a vine wreath.

For the creation of this composite product, the potter or coroplast has replaced the oinochoe neck of the foregoing type of plastic vase (cf. *supra* No. 2, figs. 5–6) by a figurine which leans against the oinochoe handle; the latter is the only part which recalls the initial oinochoe, and tends also to disappear.[30]

26. Louis Beck Collection (with the same richly decorated sakkos): F. van der Wielen-van Ommeren, in M.E. Mayo, *The Art of South Italy. Vases from Magna Graecia* (Richmond, 1982) no. 155.

27. On the signification and destination of head vases, see M. Trumpf-Lyritzaki, *Griechische Figurenvasen* (Bonn, 1969) 128f.; Riccardi, *op. cit.*, 7ff.

28. Oliver, *op. cit.*, 7, 24; Riccardi, *op. cit.*, 10f.

29. F. van der Wielen-van Ommeren, "Un corredo funerario da

Canosa," *Canosa* II (1982) 106 fig. 13.

30. Cf. Bari 6007 (Varrese): Jatta, *op. cit.*, 106f., pl. X,1, with loop of oinochoe handle fixed in back of figurine; Naples 16173: A. Levi, *Le Terrecotte figurate del Museo Nazionale di Napoli* (Florence, 1926) no. 283, pl. IV,2, figurine without handle.

Figure 8. No. 5. Stand. Malibu, The J. Paul Getty Museum
80.AD.36.

Figure 9. No. 6. Pyxis. Malibu, The J. Paul Getty Museum
81.AE.125.

The head has a relatively short neck and a face of
rounder shape than on the preceding head vase. The hair
in front of the diadem is modeled in the melon-coiffure
that became so popular in Hellenistic times.[31] There are no
traces left of the red or pink sakkos which covers the back
of similar pieces (cf. *supra* No. 2, fig. 6). The rigid diadem,
decorated with maeander and disks, is also a new invention, as are the two leaves dressed at both sides of the
neck; the latter seem to recall the link existing between
this type of head and vegetation (cf. heads in kalyxes of
leaves or flowers).[32]

The figurine shows another variant of draped woman,[33]
of rather poor execution, lacking the freshness and quality
of the figurines on the Malibu askos (*supra* No. 1, figs. 1–2).

A pair of identical objects in an Italian private collection
and a third similar head vase (with diadem of different
shape), at one time on exhibition in Japan,[34] are placed on
separate stands of exactly the same shape as the Malibu
stand 80.AE.36 (*infra* No. 5, fig. 8). These head vases are
also known with a wreath of long leaves (identical to those
framing the neck) in the place of the rigid diadem.[35]

This type of head vase is very close to one found in a
burial comprising four minor red-figure vases and nine
polychrome vessels. This group has been dated around 300
B.C.[36] The Malibu pair of head vases should be dated in the
very beginning of the third century B.C.

5. Stand (fig. 8)

Malibu, The J. Paul Getty Museum, accession number 80.AD.36. Height 11.5 cm, diameter base
14 cm, diameter rim 6.6 cm.

Condition: intact, with crack and chip at rim; polychromy partly worn off. Buff-colored clay,
light-colored slip, polychromy: pink, rust-red,
pale blue, gray.

Thrown on the wheel.

The stand is composed of a large, dome-like base, a
cylindrical stem with molded ring between base
and stem and slightly concave wall, a rim with
offset carinated lip.

The lower part of the base is painted rust-red, the
horizontal upper part shows a frieze of pink
and pale blue triangles; the molded ring is

31. G. Kleiner, *op. cit.*, 15; D. Burr Thompson, *Troy. The Terracotta
Figurines of the Hellenistic Period* (Princeton, 1963) 38f.

32. Cf. K. Schauenburg, "Zur Symbolik unteritalischer Ranken-
motive," *RM* 64 (1957) 198ff.; H. Jucker, *Das Bildnis im Blätterkelch*
(Olten, 1961) 195ff.; Van der Wielen-van Ommeren, *op. cit. (supra* n. 9),
n. 105 (lit.).

33. Cf. Kleiner, *op. cit.*, 19,2; Besques, *op. cit.*, pl. 19,b (with right hand
resting on left hand).

34. Catalogue, *Exhibition of Greek and Etruscan Arts* (Tokyo, 1973) no.
76.

35. Cf. Christie's, London, 20 May 1981, lots 249a–b (ill.).

painted rust-red; the stem carries friezes separated by gray lines: from bottom to top, gray band, pink maeander, rust-red lattice pattern.

Polychrome stands of different shapes and varying sizes have been found in the tombs in the region around Canosa:

a. Low ring with offset edges, height approximately 3 cm, diameter approximately 18 cm.[37]

b. Pedestals of different sizes with molded flaring base, short stem and upper disk, height range 8.9–14.5 cm, upper diameter range 12.6–22 cm.[38]

c. The types of support presented here, already mentioned above as stands for head vases, of variable height (10–16 cm), all decorated with the same polychrome patterns; the Malibu example seems to be too small to serve as a stand for a head vase of the size of Malibu 81.AE.156–157 (*supra* Nos. 4–5, fig. 7: diameter of base 8.7 and 9.2, against 6.6 cm for the Malibu stand).

Similar types of high stands are found under polychrome vases from Centuripe.[39]

This stand belongs to the same period as the preceding head vases (beginning of third century B.C.).

6. Pyxis (fig. 9)

Malibu, The J. Paul Getty Museum, accession number 81.AE.125. Total height of box with lid approximately 27.2 cm, height box 22.3 cm, height lid 7 cm, diameter box at rim 19.4 cm, maximum diameter lid 25.6 cm.

Condition: one leg broken off (only bird preserved), surface box chipped at several places, polychromy partly preserved.

Buff-colored clay with a darker shade for the box, white slip, polychromy: red, red-brown, pale blue, azure blue.

Box and lid wheel-turned; four feet in the shape of hand-modeled birds which are attached to the box with the wings. Box with slightly concave wall, offset rim and inset ledge for lid. Domed lid with flange beneath, two moldings and conical disk knob with relief decoration. The flange of the lid slips over the ledge of the box.

The in- and underside of the box and the underside of the cover have been left undecorated. The wings of the bird-shaped legs carry a red palmette. The wall of the box is divided into at least three zones of variable width and separated by red lines; from bottom to rim: red cross-hatches; two red lines; figured frieze presenting in its actual state of preservation three figures to the left outlined in red-brown, with details rendered in the same color: from left to right, figure in three-quarter view, followed by winged male figure in profile (nude, bracelet around left thigh, bandolier, pale blue wings), and female flutist in profile (drapery with azure blue panel); two red lines; the inside of the rim and inset ledge painted red. Of the lid, the inside of the rim and the flange are painted red; on the domed part, the moldings are bordered by red lines; the lid knob is decorated with a molded gorgoneion which is surrounded by a red band.

Three types of Apulian pyxides with polychrome and/or plastic decoration are so far shown:

a. Large polychrome pyxides (diameter 20–30 cm) with relief scene on the lid.[40]

b. Rather small pseudo-pyxides (height approximately 6–10 cm) with relief medallion, the lid and the box forming one piece without bottom, often provided with three feet in the shape of lion's paws or stubs.[41]

c. The type of polychrome pyxis presented here, of which only a few examples are known:

c.1. Richmond, The Virginia Museum of Fine Arts 79.14.3/4: total height 19.7 cm, diameter of box 19.3 cm, three feet in the shape of disks, large egg-and-dart frieze on box.[42]

c.2. Malibu 81.AE.125 (fig. 9): unpublished.

c.3. Swiss market, 1980: total height 16.5 cm, maximum diameter 22 cm, three feet in the shape of birds, vine branch on box.[43]

c.4. Italian market, 1981: total height approximately 15–20 cm; six feet (lion's paws alternating with stubs), vine branch on box.[43a]

36. Cf. *supra* n. 29.

37. Cf. *CVA University of Michigan*, IVD, pl. XXX,1a–b; Van der Wielen-van Ommeren, *op. cit.* (*supra* n. 9), P18–19.

38. Cf. Jatta, *op. cit.*, 108,k fig. 16,3; M. Borda, *Ceramiche apule* (Bergamo, 1966) pl. XXIII; Van der Wielen-van Ommeren, *op. cit.* (*supra* n. 9), P13; Head., *op. cit.* (*supra* n. 29), nos. 5–7.

39. Cf. U. Wintermeyer, "Die polychrome Reliefkeramik aus Centuripe," *Jdl* 90 (1975) fig. 1ff. On stands in general, see K. Schauenburg, in W. Hornbostel, *Aus Gräbern und Heiligtümern* (Mainz, 1980) no. 116, 200ff.; Lohmann, *op. cit.* 195ff.

40. Cf. P. Wuilleumier, *Le trésor de Tarente* (Paris, 1930) 109ff. nos.

12–13, 16–21; Oliver, *op. cit.*, 9f.; Hornbostel, *op. cit.* (*supra* n. 39), no. 123, 215ff. F.L. Bastet, *BABesch* 57 (1982) 155ff.

41. Cf. Wuilleumier, *op. cit.*, 107ff., nos. 1–11; H. Sichtermann, *Griechische Vasen in Unteritalien* (Tübingen, 1966) 61, K107–108, pl. 155; O.-M. Jentel, *Les gutti et les askoi à relief étrusques et apuliens* (Leyde, 1976), figs. 99–102,104, pp. 18, 110, 141.

42. Van der Wielen-van Ommeren, *op. cit.* (*supra* n. 26), no. 153.

43. Laforêt S.A., Geneva, 11 December 1980, lot 70.

43a. Add c.5. Sotheby's, London, 11 July 1983, lot 300 (ill.): ht. 21.6 cm, two bird-shaped feet and one stub, egg-and-dart frieze on box.

Figure 10. Nos. 7–8. Birds. Malibu, The J. Paul Getty Museum 80.AD.38a–b.

The shape of these four pyxides recalls that of the Attic type A,[44] which is similar to that of the pseudo-pyxides mentioned under b. The lid knob carries (in three cases) a relief gorgoneion (c.2, 3, 4). The domed lid and box are both decorated with friezes of patterns also found on the large Canosan pyxides (a): kymation, wave pattern, debased tongue, wreath of vine leaves; plus saltire squares, cross-hatches, and triangles. All four have feet, like many of the pseudo-pyxides (b): lion's paws (c.4), birds (pigeons?) (c.2, 3), disks (c.1), a kind of triangular stub (c.4).

The Malibu pyxis is the only example with a painted figurative scene on the box. A kind of Dionysiac procession seems to be represented, with an Eros (second from left) and a female flutist (at right) among the participants.[45]

Pyxides were used by women for their toilet articles and may have followed their owners into the grave; they are also found in burials of warriors.[46]

The pyxis in the Virginia Museum of Fine Arts (c.1) was reported to have been found together with two poly-

chrome oinochoai and a terracotta bird.[47] The oinochoai have been dated in the beginning of the third century B.C. This date should also be assigned to the Malibu pyxis.

7–8. Birds (fig. 10)

Malibu, The J. Paul Getty Museum, accession number 80.AD.38A–B. Left bird: height 8.7 cm, preserved length 15.5 cm; right bird: preserved length 13.7 cm.

Condition: left bird: beak missing; right bird: head missing; polychromy partly worn off.

Buff-colored clay, white slip, polychromy: rust-red, purple, azure blue. Hand-modeled solid body, wings added separately, cylindrical hole in bottom. Ovoid body with flat ogival wings, slightly upturned fan-shaped tail, long neck, and small head with probably a rather long beak (missing). The wings have an azure blue contour line and a rust-red pattern (feathers). The left bird

44. S. Rutherford Roberts, *The Attic Pyxis* (Chicago, 1978) 109ff.

45. Cf. W.D. Albert, *Darstellungen des Eros in Unteritalien* (Amsterdam, 1979) 49ff. ("Der dionysische Eros").

46. Oliver, *op. cit.*, 9f., pl. 6,1–2 (warrior's burial).

47. Van der Wielen-van Ommeren, *op. cit.* (*supra* n. 26), nos. 151–154.

48. J. Neils, in A.P. Kozloff, *Animals in Ancient Art from the Leo Mildenberg Collection* (Cleveland, 1981) no. 151.

49. Cf. *CVA* British Museum 7, IV Da, pl. 13,2; and Geneva 15050, Rinuy et al., *op. cit.* (*supra* n. 9), 157f., figs. 23f., 27 (funnel kraters); Tarentum 10128, L. von Matt-U. Zanotti-Bianco, *La Grande Grèce* (Zurich-Paris, 1962) fig. 249 (head vase).

50. Cf. K. Van Wonterghem-Maes, "Une tombe à chambres et son matériel funéraire," *Ordona* 3 (1971) 133ff. nos. 61–65, pl. LIV.

51. Boys or Eros riding animals: Winter, *op. cit.* 298ff.; Burr Thomp-

carries a rust-red collar and other patterns in purple on the neck. On the right bird, there are only traces of painted decoration.

An identical, intact bird in a private collection[48] shows a long beak; nevertheless, the shape of the body and the tail are clearly that of a pigeon.

Similar birds of smaller size were fixed with a wooden plug on large Canosan vases.[49] This pair of pigeons may have been placed in a tomb as separate offerings as part of a larger set.[50]

As indicated above, a terracotta bird with painted wings in the Virginia Museum of Fine Arts was found together with a pyxis of the same type as Malibu 81.AE.125 (*supra* No. 6, fig. 8). The Malibu pigeons should therefore also be dated in the beginning of the third century B.C.

9. Riding Eros (fig. 11)

    Malibu, The J. Paul Getty Museum, accession number 80.AE.37. Preserved height 6.2 cm.

    Condition: fragmentary: head, arms, wings and lower part of legs missing; polychromy partly preserved.

    Brown-orange clay, white slip, polychromy: pink, rust-red. Molded, without vent-hole; small round hole on bottom. There are traces of rust-red paint on the baldric and of pink on the fold of the chlamys.

Figure 11. No. 9. Riding Eros. Malibu, The J. Paul Getty Museum 80.AE.37.

The fragmentary figurine originally presented an Eros riding some animal,[51] with a baldric crossing his chest and a chlamys covering his back with flaps on his thighs. The arms were very probably outstretched; the hands may have held some object.

The Eros figure became very popular in the Hellenistic period, changing from a slender ephebe into a chubby, putto-like child.[52]

Third century B.C.

10. Sitting Eros (fig. 12)

    Malibu, The J. Paul Getty Museum, accession number 81.AE.160. Preserved height 7.8 cm.

    Condition: fragmentary: most of arms, legs, and right wing missing; white slip and polychromy worn off.

    Light brown clay, white slip, polychromy (rust-red, blue, blue-violet). Molded, without vent-hole.

son, *op. cit.,* 137f. with lit. Cf. also Sotheby's, London, 14 December 1981, lot 307 (ill.): a group of four riding Eros figures wearing helmet and chlamys (approx. ht. 15.9 cm).

52. Kleiner, *op. cit.,* 170ff.

Figure 12. No. 10. Sitting Eros. Malibu, The J. Paul Getty Museum 81.AE.160.

Figure 13. No. 11. Lion's paw. Malibu, The J. Paul Getty
Museum 81.AD.126.

Like the foregoing figurine; head bent to the left carrying
a wreath of vine leaves, the arms outstretched, a chlamys
on the back with one flap on the right upper arm.[53]
Third century B.C.

11. Lion's paw (fig. 13)
Malibu, The J. Paul Getty Museum, accession number 81.AD.126. Height 5.6 cm, length approximately 9.0 cm, maximum width at the attachment 7.2 cm.
Conditon: recomposed, with a few chips.
Light brown clay, white slip, no traces of polychromy. Molded, two attachment holes at the
back.

This lion's paw was attached to some object at the
back. It probably served as a foot of a large vessel or
stand.[54] Third century B.C. (?).

Geneva

53. *Supra* n. 51. Cf. also Sotheby's, London, 14 December 1981, lots
304–306 (ill.): four sitting Eros figures (ht. 11.2–12.1 cm).
54. Cf. Sichtermann, *op. cit.*, K78, pls. 136–137; G. Schneider-Herr-
mann, *Apulian Red-Figured Paterae with Flat or Knobbed Handles*, BICS
Supplement 34 (1977) pl. III,2.

Herakles und Theseus auf Vasen in Malibu

Frank Brommer

Herakles und Theseus sind die beliebtesten Helden in der griechischen Vasenmalerei. Von dem einen haben sich etwa 3500, von dem anderen etwa 900 Vasenbilder erhalten. Damit kennen wir von diesen beiden griechischen Helden etwa so viel Vasenbilder, wie von allen übrigen zusammen. Kein Wunder, dass beide Helden auch in der Vasensammlung des J.P. Getty Museums reich vertreten sind. Ich verdanke J. Frel die Einladung zu einem Aufenthalt dort im Januar und Februar 1981, an den ich mit Freude und Dankbarkeit zurückdenke, und zugleich die Aufforderung, die Vasen mit Herakles und Theseus vorzustellen. Dies geschieht hier so, dass erst Herakles, dann Theseus behandelt wird, beide in der alphabetischen Reihenfolge ihrer Gegner oder Partner. Neben Darstellungen, deren Typus bereits bekannt ist, kommen auf den hier vorgestellten fünfzig Bildern auf vierundvierzig Gefässen auch ganz ungewöhnliche Themen vor, wie Herakles mit Omphale in archaischer Zeit, oder Herakles mit Philoktet, Theseus mit Minos oder Poseidon. Dazu kommt eine provinziell-rotfigurige Kopie nach einem attischen Vorbild.

HERAKLES UND ALKYONEUS

Das schwarzfigurige Bruchstück stammt vom oberen Rand eines Volutenkraters, der mit zwei Bildzonen geschmückt war (Abb. 1). Im oberen Streifen sieht man den Oberkörper eines bärtigen, auf einem Felsen schlafenden Riesen. Rechts vom Felsen ist der Vorderteil eines stehenden Tieres zu sehen. Im unteren, niedrigeren Streifen ist gerade noch ein nach rechts sprengendes Viergespann erhalten, rechts davon ist eben noch ein Stück des schwarzen Bildrandes zu sehen. Daraus ergibt sich, dass wir auch vom oberen Bild den rechten Rand vor uns haben. Das Tier muss den rechten Abschluss der Bildzone gebildet haben, weitere Gestalten müssen sich links angeschlossen haben.

Es kann kein Zweifel daran bestehen, dass die Tötung des schlafenden Alkyoneus durch Herakles[1] hier dargestellt ist und dass rechts ein Tier aus der Rinderherde wiedergegeben ist, die der Riese dem Helios gestohlen hatte.

Die Sage begegnet seit 520 v.Chr. in der attischen Vasenmalerei und ist dort bis 480 v.Chr. auf insgesamt 29 Bildern belegt, wurde aber nach dieser Zeit nicht mehr dargestellt. Sie ist also ganz auf die spätarchaische Zeit beschränkt.

Nach Pindar (Isthm. VI 31ff.) tötete Herakles den Riesen mit einem Pfeilschuss. Die Bilder zeigen ihn so,[2] aber noch öfter mit Schwert oder Keule auf den Schlafenden eindringend. So müssen wir uns auf dem Bruchstück links von dem Riesen seinen Gegner Herakles vorstellen, der mit seinen Waffen auf ihn einstürmt. Vielleicht kam auch Athena dabei vor.

Nahe steht das Bild auf einer Lekythos in Toledo (Ohio),[3] das der Leagrosgruppe angehört und um 510 v.Chr. geschaffen wurde. Nach ihm dürfen wir uns das gleichzeitige Bild in Malibu ergänzen.

HERAKLES UND DIE AMAZONEN

Der Zug des Herakles gegen die Amazonen gehörte zu den kanonischen Taten des Herakles. Die Sage ist eine der beliebtesten in der griechischen Vasenmalerei. Mehr als 440 Vasenbilder sind von ihr erhalten. Natürlich ist die Sage auch in Malibu mit mehreren Beispielen vertreten.

Eine fragmentierte Bandschale[4] ist zwischen den Henkelansätzen mit "Amasis" ohne Verbum signiert (Abb. 2). Auf beiden Seiten war der Amazonenkampf dargestellt. Unter den etwas über 100 bekannten Vasen des Amasismalers ist diese die einzige mit einer Amazonomachie. Unter den zehn bekannten Amasis-Signaturen ist diese die einzige, die das epoiesen weglässt.

Auf der einen Seite sieht man einen nach rechts gerichteten Krieger, dann einen nach links fliehenden, der sich

---

1. Die Bilder der Sage bei F. Brommer, *Vasenlisten zur griechischen Heldensage*[3] (1973), im folgenden VL[3] 5ff. Zur Sage: B. Andreae, *Jdl* 77 (1962) 130ff. Das Bruchstück, Malibu acc. no. 81.AE.10.5, anonymes Geschenk, fehlt in *LIMC* I s.v. Alkyoneus, dort ist mit Nr. 21 offenbar dieselbe Lekythos gemeint, wie mit Nr. 24. Die Nr. 23 ist zu streichen. Von dem Skyphos ist zu wenig erhalten, um die Deutung zu sichern. Gegen die Deutung auf Alkyoneus sprechen die Beifiguren.

2. VL[3] 5 A 2,6.
3. VL[3] 6 A 20.
4. Malibu acc. no. 79.AE.197 von J. Frel dem Amasismaler zugeschrieben. Weder diese noch die folgenden Amazonenvasen sind bei D. von Bothmer, *Amazons in Greek Art* (1957) enthalten. Zum Thema: F. Brommer, *Herakles. Die zwölf Taten des Helden in antiker Kunst und Literatur* (1982) 35ff.

Abb. 1. Bruchstück eines attisch-schwarzfigurigen Voluten-kraters. Malibu, The J. Paul Getty Museum 81.AE.10.5. L: 12.6 cm.

Abb. 2. Fragmentierte attisch-schwarzfigurige Bandschale. Malibu, The J. Paul Getty Museum 79.AE.197. Diam.: 22.1 cm.

nach hinten gegen eine ihn verfolgende Amazone verteidigt. Es folgt Herakles nach rechts mit dem Köcher auf
dem Rücken, dem Schwert in der Rechten, der Scheide in
der Linken. Er trägt ein kurzes rotes Gewand, darüber das
Löwenfell. Er eilt einer von ihm nach rechts fliehenden
Amazone nach, die sich nach rückwärts mit der Lanze
verteidigt. An sie schliesst sich ein nach links fliehender
Krieger an, der zu einer ihn verfolgenden Amazone zu-
rückblickt. Den Abschluss des Bildstreifens bildet rechts
ein stehender Lanzenjüngling. Sicher war es bei dem verlorenen linken Ende genauso. Die das Bild rechts und
links rahmenden Lanzenmänner kommen beim Amasismaler öfter vor.[5]

Auf der anderen Seite bildet wieder ein stehender Lan-
zenmann den Beginn. Es folgt ein Bogenschütze nach
rechts, ein Krieger nach rechts, eine Amazone nach links.
Die Amazonen tragen wie die Griechen Rundschilde. Die
Schildzeichen sind mehrfach plastisch herausspringend
wiedergegeben. Es ist viel Rot und Weiss verwandt worden. Namen sind nicht beigeschrieben worden. Alle
kämpfen zu Fuss. Das Bild ist um die Jahrhundertmitte
gemalt worden und gehört somit zu den Frühwerken des
Amasismalers. Es steht in der Tradition der älteren Ama-
zonenbilder und gehört zu der Gruppe der Bilder, in
denen drei oder mehr Gruppen mit Herakles die Amazonen bekämpfen.[6]

Das Bruchstück einer Halsamphora[7] (Abb. 3) bewahrt
einen Teil des Kopfes und den linken Oberarm des Herakles,
der an seinem Löwenfell kenntlich ist, das den Kopf und
die Schulter bedeckt. Der Kopf ist nach unten geneigt und
blickt zu einem rechts unter ihm befindlichen weiteren
Kopf, von dem ausser dem attischen Helm nicht viel erhalten ist. Ein Rest von Weiss aus dem Gesicht und auf
der Hand, die die Lanze waagrecht hält, sichert das weibliche Geschlecht der zweiten Gestalt. Zweifellos handelt
es sich um eine zu Boden gesunkene Amazone, die von
Herakles mit dem gezückten Schwert oder der Keule in
der Rechten bedroht wird. Der Arm des Herakles wird
überschnitten vom roten Rand des Rundschildes der
Amazone. Rot ist auch das Band an ihrem Helm, sowie
am Aermel und Haar des Herakles. Weiss ist an drei
Stellen beim Helmbusch der Amazone. Das Kampfschema
ist nicht von diesem Vasenmaler erfunden worden, sondern begegnet schon früher.[7bis] Herakles packt meist den
Helm seiner Gegnerin, oft fasst er aber auch, wie hier,
tiefer. Rechts von der Amazone kommt schon das Palmet-

Abb. 3. Attisch-schwarzfiguriges Fragment. Malibu, The
J. Paul Getty Museum 81.AE.10.7. L: 17.5 cm.

Abb. 4. Attisch-schwarzfiguriger Kyathos. Malibu, The J.
Paul Getty Museum 76.AE.94. H: 8.4 cm.

5. Lanzenmänner rahmend bei Amasis: Beazley, *ABV* 150ff. Nr. 2, 7,
9, 10, 14, 15, 30, 49, 64, ferner *AntK* 3 (1960) Taf. 3,3.4; 4,1–3; 5,1.3;
6,2.4; 10; 11. *JdI* 71 (1964) 110 Abb.1–3, 9, 19, 20.
6. D.v.Bothmer a.O. 30–35.
7. D.v.Bothmer a.O. Taf. 3 oben, 11 oben, 15 unten, 29,1.
7bis. Malibu acc. no. 81.AE.10.7.

Abb. 5a. Attisch-rotfigurige Schale. Malibu, The J. Paul Getty Museum 79.AE.127. Diam.: 41.3 cm.

Abb. 5b. Malibu 79.AE.127. Einzelheit.

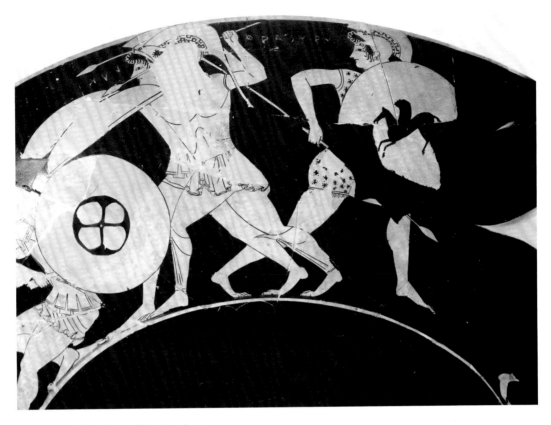

Abb. 5c. Malibu 79.AE.127. Einzelheit.

Abb. 5d. Malibu 79.AE.127. Einzelheit.

Abb. 6. Fragmentierter Rand eines attisch-rotfigurigen Volutenkraters. Malibu, The J. Paul Getty Museum 77.AE.11. H: 14.5 cm.

tenornament. Hier kann also keine weitere Gestalt dargestellt gewesen sein. Es ist anzunehmen, dass es links genauso war und die Szene also auf Herakles und seine Gegnerin beschränkt war. Auch dieses Vasenbild, das etwa um 530 bis 520 v.Chr. entstanden ist, bietet also nichts Ungewöhnliches.[8] Ein drittes Bild des Amazonenkampfes[9] befindet sich auf einem flüchtig gemalten schwarzfigurigen Kyathos (Abb. 4). Herakles ist von zwei Amazonen eingerahmt, von denen ihn die linke nicht wahrnimmt. Jenseits der beiden apotropäischen Augen folgt noch jeweils ein Krieger, aber ein Kampfzusammenhang besteht nicht. Der Vasenmaler des späten 6. Jh. v. Chr. hat die Teilnehmer am Kampf gedankenlos gruppiert.

Etwa gleichzeitig mit dem schwarzfigurigen Kyathos wird die rotfigurige Schale[10] sein, die von J. Frel dem Oltos zugeschrieben wurde (Abb. 5a–d). Links laufen zwei Amazonen nach links. In der Mitte greift Herakles mit gezücktem Schwert eine zu Boden gefallene Amazone an und packt mit der Linken ihren Helm. Von rechts greifen zwei Amazonen mit erhobenen Lanzen Herakles an. Am rech-

ten Bildrand läuft eine sechste Amazone nach rechts davon. Ihr Schild hat als Zeichen einen Pegasos. Sie und die äusserste Amazone links hat keine Namensbeischrift. Alle übrigen Gestalten, auch Herakles, tragen Namensbeischriften. Die zweite Amazone von links heisst Leontiche, die Gegnerin des Herakles ist als Andromache bezeichnet, die vierte Amazone heisst Lyk(op)i(s) und die fünfte Thrasybule. Von diesen Namen ist Andromache als Gegnerin des Herakles geläufig. Die Ergänzung des Namens Lykopis ergibt sich durch drei andere Vasen,[11] von denen zwei vom selben Maler Oltos wie die Schale in Malibu stammen. Die Amazonennamen Leontiche und Thrasybule waren bisher noch nicht belegt.[12] Der Bildtypus ist nicht von Oltos erfunden, sondern kommt schon vor ihm vor.

Eine fünfte Darstellung des herakleischen Amazonenkampfes befindet sich auf dem Rand eines Volutenkraters des Kleophradesmalers[13] und zieht sich dort um den ganzen Rand herum (Abb. 6). In der oberen Bildzone ist auf der einen Seite die Vorbereitung der Amazonen zum Kampf dargestellt, auf der anderen Seite sieht man Hera-

8. Vgl.D.v.Bothmer a.O. 42 Taf.34,1.4;35.

9. Malibu acc. no. 76.AE.94. Erwähnt Getty MJ 4 (1977) 76 Nr.18, dort von J.Frel der Leafless group, Caylus painter zugeschrieben.

10. Malibu acc. no. 79.AE.127. Fuss und Teil des Bildfeldes ergänzt. B, Zug von Komasten I, Musikerin.

11. VL³ 22,42; 23,7.8.

12. Die Namen fehlen auch in der Liste von Amazonennamen in *LIMC* I 653.

13. Malibu acc. no. 77.AE.11. A.Greifenhagen, *Neue Fragmente des Kleophradesmalers* (SbHeidelberg 1972) 24–41. J. Frel, Getty MJ 4 (1977) 63ff.; *Painting on Vases in Ancient Greece* Nr. 21. J. Neils, *AJA* 85 (1981) 177 Anm.6. Dass der Maler nicht mehr als Epiktetos II bezeichnet

kles im Begriff, eine bereits zu Boden gefallene Amazone zu töten, während hinter dieser nicht weniger als sechs weitere Amazonen anrücken, vier mit erhobenen Lanzen und die sechste mit gespanntem Bogen. Hinter dem Rücken des Herakles kämpfte einer seiner Gefährten, wohl Telamon, gegen eine zu Boden stürzende Amazone. Nach einer Lücke trägt am linken Rand eine Amazone eine andere verwundete Amazone vom Schlachtfeld.

Auffallenderweise ist diese Heraklestat, die so ausführlich geschildert ist, im unteren Fries mit drei weiteren Heraklestaten verbunden und zwar mit Hydra, Geryones und Hesperiden. Die vier Taten gehören zu denen, die später kanonisch wurden. Aber auch hier ist kein Versuch gemacht worden, die zwölf Taten wiederzugeben, obwohl durchaus Platz dafür gewesen wäre, denn die ganze Rückseite ist mit dem Kampf zwischen Peleus und Thetis gefüllt. Es ist bemerkenswert, dass die eine Tat des Amazonenkampfes hier so viel Platz einnimmt, wie die drei anderen Heraklestaten zusammen. Beazley hat die Vase kurz vor 490 v.Chr. datiert. Eine sechste Vase, eine fragmentierte Schale aus der Werkstatt des Euphronios, sei nur kurz erwähnt, da sie schon veröffentlicht wurde.[14]

Alle sechs Amazonenvasen in Malibu gehören also in die archaische Zeit, in der die Sage auch am beliebtesten war.

HERAKLES UND ATHENA

Auf einer schwarzfigurigen Bauchamphora[15] sitzt Herakles in der Mitte des Bildes auf einem Schemel nach rechtshin (Abb. 7). Er ist mit einem kurzen Untergewand bekleidet, das etwa zur Mitte der Oberschenkel reicht, und trägt darüber das über den Kopf gezogene Löwenfell. Ueber diesem trägt er ein Schwert und einen offenen Köcher, aber keinen Bogen. Er hat die Linke zum Gruss erhoben und die Rechte waagrecht ausgestreckt. Zu seiner Rechten steht Athena mit einer Lanze in der Rechten, einem Schild in der Linken und einem Helm auf dem Kopf. Eine Aegis hat sie nicht. Das weisse Schildzeichen gibt eine sitzende Sphinx wieder. Links entfernt sich nach links der bärtige Hermes mit kurzen Gewand, Pilos und Schuhen, aber ohne Kerykeion. Er hat, wie Herakles, die Linke zum Gruss erhoben.

Die Vereinigung der beiden Götter mit dem Helden in einem Bild kommt ziemlich häufig vor.[16] Dieses im Jahrzehnt 560–50 v.Chr. in Athen entstandene Bild scheint

Abb. 7. Attisch-schwarzfigurige Bauchamphora. Sammlung Bareiss 4, Leihgabe im J. Paul Getty Museum S.80.AE.3. H: 37.2 cm.

jedoch das früheste erhaltene dieses Themas zu sein. Die Bilder gehören meist der zweiten Hälfte des 6. Jh. v.Chr. an. Meist stehen die drei Gestalten, aber auch der sitzende oder liegende Herakles kommt vor. Gelegentlich schenkt ihm Athena ein. Es ist die Frage, was für eine Vorstellung hinter dem Bild steht. Herakles genoss den Schutz von Athena und Hermes beispielsweise beim Kerberosabenteuer, einer Sage, die in der gleichen Zeit beliebt war, wie unser Thema. Man könnte auch an die Fahrt in den Olymp denken. Aber die gelegentlich bei den drei Gestalten vorkommenden Tiere, wie Panther, Löwe, Ziege, Rind und Hund bleiben dabei unerklärt. So sieht man die drei Gestalten am besten für sich und nicht in Verbindung mit einem Abenteuer des Herakles.

Die von Nikosthenes als Töpfer signierte Schale, deren Fuss ergänzt ist, ist bereits oft in der wissenschaftlichen

---

werden kann, hat J. Boardman, *AA* 1981, 329 erwiesen.

14. Malibu acc. no. 79.AE.19. M. Ohly-Dumm, Getty *MJ* 9 (1981), 5–21.

15. Sammlung Bareiss 4, Leihgabe, Malibu S.80.AE.3. Auf der Rückseite Athena zwischen zwei bärtigen Männern, alle drei stehend. Am unteren Rand des Fusses zwei dicke rote Ringe. Zu dem eigenartigen

Lotospalmettenornament über dem Bild vgl. die Bauchamphora Würzburg 359 Beazley, *ABV* 306,35.

16. *VL*[3] 30. Dort 16 Beispiele, die sich inzwischen auf 32 vermehrt haben.

Abb. 8a. Attisch-schwarzfigurige Augenschale. Einzelheit, Seite A. Sammlung Bareiss 82, Leihgabe im J. Paul Getty Museum S.80.AE.300. H: 11.3 cm.

Abb. 8b. Bareiss 82. Einzelheit, Seite B.

Abb. 9. Attisch-schwarzfigurige Halsamphora. Sammlung Bareiss 13, Leihgabe im J. Paul Getty Museum S.80.AE.5. H: 25.3 cm.

Literatur behandelt worden (Abb. 8a, b).[17]

Auf der einen Seite sind zwischen den apotropäischen Augen die Köpfe von Herakles mit Keule und von Athena wiedergegeben. Bei dem engen Verhältnis, in dem die Göttin zu dem Helden stand, ist diese Verbindung keineswegs auffallend. Bemerkenswert ist die technische Seite: Der Kopf von Athena—mit bekränztem attischen Helm—ist in rotfiguriger Technik ausgespart, der Kopf des Herakles ist rot gemalt, das Löwenfell schwarz und dessen Zähne und Krallen weiss.

Rätselhafter sind die drei Büsten auf der anderen Seite. Der vorderste weibliche Kopf ist wie die Athena in rotfiguriger Technik gemalt. Der Kopf hat lange Haare und trägt ein Blattdiadem. Der zweite, ebenfalls weibliche Kopf ist in schwarzfiguriger Technik gemalt und mit Deckweiss versehen. Er trägt einen Polos. Der dritte, männliche Kopf

17. Sammlung Bareiss 82, Leihgabe, Malibu S.80.AE.300. Beazley, *ABV* 231,30 (Roman market); Schefold, *Meisterwerke* (1960) Nr. 144 (Schweizer Privatbesitz); 22.*MM Auktion Basel* (1961) Nr. 133; Beazley, *ARV*² 122 u.,1627 (München, Bareiss 82); H. Metzger, *Recherches* Taf. 4 oben; K. Schauenburg in *Weltkunst in Privatbesitz* (Köln 1968) A 17 Taf. 4; K. Schefold, *AntK* 1968, 118; D. v.Bothmer, *Greek Vases and Modern Drawings from the Collection of Mr. and Mrs. W. Bareiss* (im folgenden: *Bareiss*) Nr. 38 (New York 1969. L 68,142,7); Beazley, *Para* 109 O. von Vacano. Zur Entstehung und Deutung gemalter seitenansichtiger Kopfbilder auf sf. *Vasen des griech. Festlandes* (1973) 234 A 170.; G. Riccioni, *Mél. Heurgon* II (1976) 903ff.; K. Schauenburg, *AA* 1981, 340 Anm. 29. Zu vergleichen ist die Schale Bonn-Heidelberg: Greifenhagen, *AA* 1935, 479 unter Nr. 45 O. von Vacano 234 A 172.; *CVA Heidelberg* (4) Taf. 159,5 und die Schale: *MM Auktion* 34 (1967) Nr. 131 Taf. 37 O. von Vacano 233 Nr. 169. Sammlung Bareiss Nr. 94.

Abb. 10a. Fragmentierter attisch-schwarzfiguriger Napf. Sammlung Bareiss 125, Leihgabe im J. Paul Getty Museum S.80.AE.24.

Abb. 10b. Bareiss 125.

Abb. 10c. Bareiss 125.

Abb. 10d. Bareiss 125.

Abb. 11. Attisch-schwarzfiguriges Fragment. Malibu, The
J. Paul Getty Museum 81.AE.10.4. Grösste L: 6.8
cm.

ist wieder in schwarzfiguriger Technik gemalt. Er trägt
einen kurzen Bart und in die Stirn gestrichene Haare. Unter dem einen Henkel befindet sich ein Eber, unter dem
anderen ein Hahn.

Umstritten ist, wer mit dem männlichen und den beiden
weiblichen Köpfen gemeint ist. Beazley hatte erst gar keinen Namen genannt. Schauenburg und von Bothmer
haben es ebenso gehalten. Schefold nannte sie Hades, Persephone und Demeter. Der Basler Auktionskatalog führt
die Deutung von A. Bruckner auf Zeus, Hebe und Hera
an. Später deutete Beazley: Hebe und Hera und meinte, in
dem Mann würde man Zeus erwarten, aber der Bart sei zu
ärmlich dafür. Die Deutung muss offen bleiben. Bei Sche-
folds Deutung wäre "eine Einführung des Herakles in
einen eleusinisch charakterisierten Olymp" gemeint. Aber
für einen solchen gibt es keinen Hinweis. Bei der anderen
Deutung würde auf die Einführung des Herakles in den
Olymp ohne eleusinischen Hintergrund angespielt, aber
dabei bleibt die Schwierigkeit, dass der männliche Kopf
nicht wie Zeus aussieht.

Verwandt ist eine Augenschale der Villa Giulia.[18] Auch
da ist es schwer zu sagen, wen die beiden Kriegerköpfe
meinen, die Herakles einrahmen. Vielleicht ist an Ares
und Kyknos gedacht. Ferner lässt sich eine Augenschale
im Vatikan[19] vergleichen mit den drei Köpfen von Herakles, Athena und Hermes.

Die Schale in Malibu ist um 530 v.Chr., zur Zeit, als die
rotfigurige Technik aufkam, entstanden.

Auf einer schwarzfigurigen Halsamphora[20] ist gerade
noch soviel auf der einen Seite erhalten, dass man Herakles, Athena, Dionysos und eine Frau, also Semele oder
Ariadne, vereint sitzend erkennt (Abb. 9). Herakles trägt
ein Gewand um den Unterkörper und blickt nach rechts.
Athena mit Helm blickt zu ihrem Schützling und hält die
Lanze. Dionysos ist bekränzt und blickt nach rechts zu der
ebenfalls bekränzten Frau. Bei ihm wächst ein Weinstock.
Ueber den Köpfen findet sich die Inschrift *Kalias kalos.*
Wieder ist kein bestimmter Sagenaugenblick bekannt, auf
den sich die Darstellung beziehen könnte, aber die Aus-
wahl dieser vier Gestalten ist nicht abwegig. Die gleiche
Auswahl und zusätzlich Hermes kommt vor auf einer
Halsamphora im Vatikan. Die beiden Gottheiten sind mit
Herakles und Iolaos (statt der Frau) vereint auf einer
Hydria in Athen[21] und mit Hermes statt der Frau auf
einer Halsamphora im Vatikan[22] und mit Hermes und
Ares statt der Frau auf einer Lekythos in Berlin.[23]

Auf einem fragmentarisch erhaltenen schwarzfigurigen
Napf[24] hält der liegende Herakles eine geritzte Blüte in der
Rechten mit überlangem Finger (Abb. 10a–d). Ueber ihm
hängen links Bogen, Köcher und Gewand, sowie rechts
das Löwenfell. Rechts von ihm sitzt auf einem Block ihm
zugewandt und weit vorgeneigt, Athena mit eigentüm-
lichem Helm ohne Busch und mit Aegis. In der Linken
hält sie eine Lanze. Weiter rechts schöpft eine nur teilweise erhaltene männliche Gestalt mit einer Kanne aus
einem Kessel oder Krater. Weiter rechts sitzt wieder auf
einem Block eine bärtige männliche Gestalt barhaupt,
aber mit Schwert, die Keule in der Linken haltend. Der
Mann, sicher Iolaos, der Gefährte des Herakles, sitzt mit
dem Unterkörper nach links hin, mit dem Oberkörper
frontal und blickt mit dem Kopf nach rechts zu Herakles
hin. Er hat Rot an den Brustwarzen. Ebenso ist der grosse
rote Fleck über der Rechten von Herakles zu deuten. Das
Gefäss ist um 520/10 v.Chr. zu datieren.

Die fünfte Darstellung von Herakles und Athena in
Malibu[25] findet sich auf einem schwarzfigurigen Fragment,
das um 510 v.Chr. entstanden sein wird (Abb. 11). Es
stammt von einem Gefäss mit scharfem Schulter-Knick
und ist innen ohne Glanzton. Für eine Lekythos ist es
wohl zu gross, also wird es von einer Amphora oder
Hydria stammen. Erhalten ist ein Teil des Kopfes von
Herakles mit dem Löwenfell. Auf dem Rücken trägt er
Köcher und Bogen. Er blickt nach rechts zu Athena, von
der nur die mit der Aegis bedeckte Schulter erhalten ist
und darüber ein roter Strich, der wohl das Ende des
Helmbusches bezeichnet. Es lässt sich nicht sagen, ob

18. Rom, Villa Giulia 6313; O. von Vacano 234 A 172.; Schauenburg,
AA 1974, 152f. Abb. 5; Riccioni, *Mél. Heurgon* II (1976) 903ff.; Proietti, *Il
museo naz. Villa Giulia* fig. 59; Schauenburg, *AA* 1981, 342 Abb. 21.
19. Vatikan 456 Albizzati S.208 fig. 156 O. von Vacano 234 A 171.
20. Sammlung Bareiss 13, Leihgabe, Malibu S.80.AE.5. Auf der

anderen Seite Herakles und der Löwe. Hier S.122 Beazley, *ARV*[2] 1588,
damals Zürich, Vollmöller, derselben Hand wie Berlin 1841 (Beazley,
ABV 320,6) zugeschrieben, Beazley, *Para* 140,6 bis. Zum Lieblingsnamen
Kallias: *Para* 317.
21. Athen, NM.564 CC764 Beazley, *ABV* 329,4.

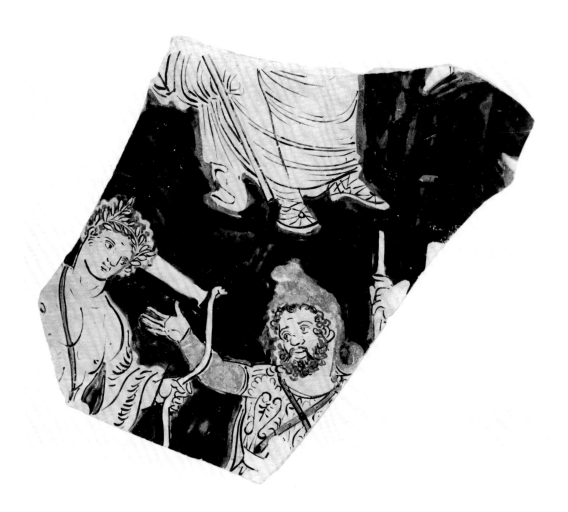

Abb. 12. Apulisch-rotfiguriges Kelchkraterbruchstück. Sammlung Bareiss 192 a,b, Leihgabe im J. Paul Getty Museum S.80.AE.263. Grösste L: 16.1 cm.

Herakles und Athena—und andere—allein für sich wiedergegeben wurden in einem blossen Zusammensein, oder ob eine bestimmte Sage gemeint ist.

HERAKLES UND BUSIRIS

Auf der Scherbe eines apulischen Kelchkraters in Malibu[26] bedroht der jugendliche, bekränzte Herakles mit der Keule einen orientalischen König (Abb. 12). In der Linken hält er den Bogen und über den linken Arm ist das Löwenfell gelegt. Der König hält in der Linken das Zepter und streckt die Rechte flehend zu Herakles aus. Er trägt ein Gewand mit langen Aermeln und eine spitze Mütze. Ueber der Kampfhandlung sitzt eine Gestalt, von der nur der bekleidete Unterkörper erhalten ist. Sie hält in der Rechten ein Zepter. Herakles und ein orientalischer König: Das

kann nur der Streit mit dem ägyptischen König Busiris oder mit dem trojanischen König Laomedon sein. Da von Laomedons Rossen nichts zu sehen ist, die Sage auch in der Vasenmalerei unbekannt ist, wird es sich um Busiris handeln.

Die Geschichte von Herakles und Busiris ist bildlich nur innerhalb der griechischen Vasenmalerei dargestellt worden. Zeitlich reichen die Darstellungen von 560–320 v.Chr. Die meisten Bilder sind archaisch und zwar attisch oder jonisch. Während der Klassik kommen die Bilder nur in Attika vor, während der Spätklassik auch in Unteritalien. Insgesamt sind nicht weniger als dreissig Vasenbilder bekannt.[27] Umso merkwürdiger ist es, dass die Sage ausserhalb der Vasenmalerei nicht in der bildenden Kunst zu beobachten ist. Dagegen ist es nicht auffällig, dass Vasen

22. Vatikan 379 Albizzati Taf. 60.

23. Berlin 1961. Beazley, *ABV* 379,273.

24. Sammlung Bareiss 125, Leihgabe, Malibu S.80.AE.24. Innen Glanzton. Athena, Hermes, Herakles und Mundschenk sind auf der Bauchamphora München 2301 Beazley *ARV²* 4,9 dargestellt.

25. Malibu acc. no. 81.AE.10.4, anonymes Geschenk.

26. Sammlung Bareiss 192a,b, Leihgabe, Malibu S.80.AE.263. D.v. Bothmer, *Bareiss* Nr. 107: Fragment of krater. Herakles and Busiris. Attributed to the Darius painter. About 325 B.C.

dieses Themas der Auseinandersetzung der Griechen mit dem Ausland hauptsächlich ausserhalb Griechenlands gefunden wurden.[28]

Die früheste literarische Erwähnung der Sage findet sich in der ersten Hälfte des 5. Jh. v.Chr., also erst ein Jahrhundert nach den frühesten Bildern. Nach Pherekydes tötete Herakles den Busiris, den Sohn des Poseidon, mit seinem Sohn Iphidamas, dem Herold Chalbes und den Opferdienern. Nach Herodot (2,45) haben die Aegypter den Herakles bekränzt und in Prozession weggeführt, um ihn dem Zeus zu opfern. Herakles habe so lange Ruhe gehalten, aber als sie bei dem Altar angekommen waren, alle getötet.

Nach Isokrates (Or. 11) kann die ganze Geschichte nicht stimmen, da Busiris mehr als 200 Jahre vor Herakles gelebt habe.

Aehnlich wie Pherekydes berichtet Apollodor (2, 5, 11): Neun Jahre lang habe in Aegypten Dürre geherrscht, da sagte der Seher Thrasios aus Zypern, die Dürre würde aufhören, wenn sie jedes Jahr dem Zeus einen Fremden opfern würden. Busiris liess zunächst ihn töten und dann die vorbeikommenden Fremden. Auch Herakles wurde festgenommen und zu den Altären gebracht. Dort zerriss er seine Fesseln und tötete Busiris mit seinem Sohn, der hier Amphidamas heisst.

Hygin (Fab. 56) weiss auch von der neunjährigen Dürre und dem Seher Thrasios. Herakles (Fab. 31,2) habe sich mit Opferbinde zum Altar führen lassen, dort aber den Busiris samt Opferdienern mit der Keule erschlagen.

Die Sage blieb der römischen Literatur,[29] beispielsweise Ovid und Vergil bekannt, ja sie war noch im 4. Jh. n.Chr. Autoren wie Macrobius und Servius vertraut, also 700 Jahre, nachdem die letzte uns bekannte bildliche Darstellung entstand.

In der Vasenmalerei wird Busiris nur dreimal mit der Uräusschlange charakterisiert.[30] Zweimal ist nur sein Kopf, sonst nichts von der Szene erhalten. Alle drei Bilder gehören noch dem 6. Jh. v.Chr. an. Auf den späteren Bildern ist Busiris nicht mehr eindeutig zu erkennen. Meist vermutet man ihn in dem Gegner des Herakles, aber dieser Gegner ist in mehreren Fällen unbärtig,[31] hält einen

Opferkorb, eine Hydria oder ist nackt. Der bei Pherekydes und Apollodor erwähnte Sohn des Busiris ist auf den Bildern ebenso wenig zu erkennen, wie der Herold Chalbes.

Mit Ausnahme der frühesten ganz erhaltenen Szene[32] sind die Rassemerkmale der Aegypter und Neger im allgemeinen deutlich wiedergegeben. Im allgemeinen findet der Kampf beim Altar statt, wie es auch Herodot, Hygin und Apollodor schildern. Nur selten[33] fehlt der Altar. Herakles kämpft meist mit der Keule,[34] wie es bei Hygin heisst, aber auch mit dem Schwert,[35] oder ohne Waffen.

Um die Mitte des 5. Jh. v.Chr. kommt eine neue Darstellungsweise auf. Herakles wird gefesselt vor den König geführt,[36] der in einem Fall auch dargestellt war. Aber leider ist der Oberkörper des Thronenden verloren. Immerhin erkennt man das Zepter und die langen orientalischen Hosen.

Auf zwei unteritalischen Vasen ist Herakles noch gefesselt, hat sich aber losgerissen[37] und bedroht den König mit der Keule. Einmal liegt dieser vor dem Altar. Der grösste Teil seines Körpers ist weggebrochen, aber man erkennt die langen orientalischen Aermel. Das andere Mal[38] sitzt er auf dem Thron und hält in der Linken das Zepter. Zum erstenmal ist er mit der spitzen Mütze bekleidet.[39] Darin kommt dieses Bruchstück dem in Malibu am nächsten. Das Fragment in Malibu ist die einzige Darstellung, wo Herakles, wie es Herodot schildert, zum Opfer bekränzt ist. Er gebraucht die Keule und hält in der Linken den Bogen, wie auch sonst.[40] Nur auf dem Fragment in Malibu ist über der Kampfszene eine sitzende Gestalt mit Zepter wiedergegeben. Auf den übrigen Bildern kommt diese Gestalt ebenso wenig vor, wie in der antiken Literatur zu der Sage. Man könnte an Zeus denken, für den das Opfer bestimmt war,[41] oder an Poseidon, der der Vater des Busiris war, wie Pherekydes und Hygin[42] berichten. Das Bild auf der Scherbe in Malibu ist die späteste erhaltene antike bildliche Darstellung, die wir von der Sage kennen.

HERAKLES BEIM DREIFUSSRAUB
Als dem Herakles in Delphi das Orakel verweigert wurde, raubte der Held den Dreifuss aus dem Heiligtum, gab ihn aber nachher auf Befehl des Zeus wieder heraus. So be-

27. VL³ 34ff. Dabei ist D 3 zu streichen und durch die hier vorgelegte Scherbe in Malibu zu ersetzen. Bedenken gegen die Deutung von D 3 äusserten: K. Schauenburg, Perseus Anm. 719; A.D. Trendall, LCS 113; Webster-Trendall, Illustrations III 6,3; A. Kossatz-Deissmann, Dramen des Aischylos 101.

28. 21 Vasen stammen aus Italien, 2 aus Afrika, 6 sind unbekannter Herkunft und nur zwei wurden in Griechenland gefunden.

29. Ovid, Met. 9,183; Vergil, Georg. III,5; Macrobius, Sat. 6,7,4; Servius, Georg. 3,5; Aen. 8,30.

30. A 1, C 3 (nur Kopf) und C 1.

31. B 1, 3 (mit Opferkorb), 5 (mit Hydria), 6 (nackt), 8, 9, 11, 20, 22.

32. A 2.

33. B 5, 16, 22.

34. B 1, 5, 6, 9, 12, 16, 22, D 1–3.

35. B 3, 4.

36. B 13, 14 (mit König).

37. D 1, 2.

38. D 2.

39. Wenn die Haare am Bruchrand der New Yorker Fragmente (D 1) rechts vom Kopf des Herakles zu Busiris gehören, dann trug dieser kaum die spitze Mütze.

40. B 5, 12.

41. Herodot 2,45; Apollodor 2,5,11.

42. Hygin, Fab. 56, 157.

richten es Apollodor und Hygin.[43] Das Thema ist schon auf einem spätgeometrischen Dreifussbein aus Olympia dargestellt worden.[44] Der antiken Literatur entsprechend mit Zeus als Schlichter in der Mitte ist es im Giebel vom Schatzhaus der Siphnier in Delphi wiedergegeben.

Die Sage begegnet seit 560 v.Chr. in der attischen Vasenmalerei. In den hundert Jahren bis 460 v.Chr. sind rund 200 Vasenbilder geschaffen worden, die uns erhalten sind.[45] 190 von ihnen sind attisch. Damit gehört die Sage zu den in der Vasenmalerei am meisten dargestellten. Auf den attischen Sagen ist es zum Unterschied von den Angaben der Literatur Athena, die den Streit schlichtet. Zeus kommt nur sehr selten vor.[46] Wenn nicht die beiden Gegner allein für sich wiedergegeben werden, dann sind meist aus Symmetriegründen noch mindestens je eine weitere Gestalt rechts und eine links dargestellt. In Malibu ist das Thema auf der sogar einschliesslich des Deckels ganz erhaltenen rotfigurigen Bauchamphora 79.AE.139 behandelt, die um 480 v.Chr. entstanden ist (Abb. 13).

Der Held trägt über seinem Gewand das Löwenfell. Ein Köcher mit Bogen hängt vor seinem Bauch. In der Rechten schwingt er eine Keule, mit der Linken hat er den waagrecht gehaltenen Dreifuss gepackt und entfernt sich nach links nicht ohne sich dabei umzublicken. Denn auf dem Fuss folgt ihm Apollon in kurzem Gewand, hohen Stiefeln, einem Lorbeerkranz im Haar, Köcher auf dem Rücken, Bogen und Pfeilen in der Linken. Er hat Herakles eingeholt und dessen Keule mit der Rechten gepackt. Ein Reh begleitet den Gott. Am linken Bildrand steht Athena mit einer Lanze in der Linken, dem Helm in der Rechten, mit einer Aegis über dem Oberkörper. Sicher hält sie den Helm in der Hand, damit er nicht mit dem Bildrahmen in Konflikt kommt. Verdünnter Glanzton findet sich auf dem Streifen am Helm der Athena, sowie am Löwenfell und den Stiefeln des Apollo.

Zwischen den beiden Köpfen der männlichen Gestalten steht in weissen Buchstaben die Inschrift: HAISIMIΔES/ KAΛOS. Die gleiche Lieblingsinschrift ist noch von zwei weiteren Vasen bekannt.[47] Aber, da die gemeinte Persönlichkeit nicht historisch bekannt ist, verhilft sie nicht zu einer Datierung.

Abb. 13. Attisch-rotfigurige Bauchamphora. Malibu, The J. Paul Getty Museum 79.AE.139. H, mit Deckel: 66 cm.

Die Darstellung weist einige Besonderheiten innerhalb der grossen Menge der Bilder gleichen Themas auf. Einmal sind drei Gestalten, wie auf unserer Vase, selten.[48] Meist fasst Apollon nach dem Dreifuss. Der Griff nach der Keule des Herakles ist ebenfalls sehr selten.[49] Ein Reh

43. Apollodor, *Bibl.* II 6,2; Hygin, *Fab.* 32. Die antiken Zitate bei J. Defradas, *Les thèmes de la propaganda delphique* (1954) 126ff.

44. E. Kunze, *Schildbänder* Beil. 8.

45. Die letzte Zusammenstellung durch D.v.Bothmer, *Festschrift Brommer* 51–63 enthält 186 Vasen. Dazu kommen 12 weitere, nämlich sechs att.-sf. Halsamphoren: Fiesole, Costantini *CVA* 11,4; Los Angeles, Dechter, Sotheby 17.5.76 Nr. 364; Ch. Ede, *Pottery from Athens* IV (1977) Nr. 19; *RA* 1978, 228 fig. 1.2; Helgoland, Dr. Kropatscheck, Hornbostel, *Aus Gräbern und Heiligtümern* Nr. 55; Rom, Villa Giulia 74921 Fragment, Proietti, *Il museo nazionale della Villa Giulia* fig. 278; Kunsthandel Palladion März 1981. Ferner zwei att. sf. Lekythen: Essen, Ruhrlandmuseum Ausstellung 1975 Nr. 27; Mainz, Pb. Dazu ein Kyathos: Kunsthandlung

Arete 1980. Ein Rhyton: Serajewo *CVA* (4) 27. Schliesslich die hier behandelte Amphora in Malibu und ebendort das Bruchstück 79.AE.212.1. Bei v. Bothmer 51 sind die Nrr. 8 und 9 als Skyphos-Fragmente bezeichnet, aber auf derselben Seite richtig den Kantharoi zugerechnet.

46. Zeus auf *VL*³ 39, 33.37; 42,8.9; 43,29; 44,9.

47. Beazley, *ARV*² 1559f.

48. Drei Gestalten: *VL*³ 38,20; 39,10.35; 43,21; 44,25.

49. *VL*³ 39,9; 42,2.

Abb. 14. Attisch-schwarzfigurige Halsamphora. Sammlung Bareiss 143, Leihgabe im J. Paul Getty Museum S.80.AE.232. H: 43 cm.

kommt auf den schwarzfigurigen Vasen in diesem Zusammenhang zwar oft vor, auf rotfigurigen ist es hingegen selten.[50]

Das grossfigurige, sauber gezeichnete Bild hat also durchaus seine eigenwilligen Besonderheiten.

HERAKLES UND DER ERYMANTHISCHE EBER

Zu den zwölf kanonischen Taten des Herakles gehörte die Aufgabe, den wilden Eber, der im Erymanthos-Gebirge hauste, zu fangen und lebend dem König Eurystheus zu bringen.

Etwa um 560 v.Chr. setzen die Bilder dieser Sage ein, die sich in ansehnlicher Zahl erhalten haben. Etwa 170

attisch-schwarzfigurige Vasen dieses Themas sind bekannt, aber nur 4 attisch-rotfigurie und 3 ausserattische archaische. Doch bezeugen verschiedene andere Denkmäler die Bekanntheit der Sage auch ausserhalb Attikas. Das zeitliche Schwergewicht der Vasen liegt eindeutig in der zweiten Hälfte des 6. Jh. v.Chr.

Gleich zu Anfang hat sich ein Darstellungstyp herausgebildet, bei dem Herakles den Eber zu Eurystheus bringt, der sich voll Schreck in ein grosses, in den Boden eingelassenes Fass verkrochen hat. Diesem Typus gehört etwa die Hälfte der erhaltenen Darstellungen an. Die andere Hälfte verteilt sich auf die Bilder vom Fang und vom Transport des Ebers.

Das Bild der Halsamphora in Malibu[51] hält sich ganz an das übliche Schema (Abb. 14). Herakles trägt über seinem kurzen Gewand das Löwenfell, hat das Schwert an der Seite und den Köcher auf dem Rücken. Sein rechtes Knie ist ergänzt, der Bart ist rot. Er kommt von links und tritt mit dem linken Fuss auf das Fass, in das sich Eurystheus verkrochen hat. Nur der bärtige Kopf und die abwehrenden Arme ragen heraus. Herakles hebt den Eber über den König.

So in fast genau gleicher Weise ist das Thema auf allen bekannten Darstellungen wiedergegeben. Nur die Beifiguren wechseln. Hier steht links Athena mit Aegis und Helm, die Lanze in der Rechten. Die Linke berührt den auf dem Boden stehenden Schild. Dessen weisses Schildzeichen ist verblasst. Rechts steht eine attributlose weibliche Gestalt. Athena und eine weibliche Gestalt begegnen bei dieser Sage auch auf anderen Vasen.[52] Man[53] hat die weibliche Gestalt als Nymphe oder als die Mutter des Eurystheus aufgefasst. In anderen Darstellungen nehmen an dem Vorgang Iolaos, Hermes, mehrere Frauen, Artemis, ein Greis und ein Jüngling teil.[54]

Die Vase ist bereits von Schauenburg der Leagrosgruppe zugewiesen und um 510 v.Chr. datiert worden. In dieser Gruppe ist das Thema nicht selten behandelt worden.

HERAKLES UND GERYONES

Das Thema kommt in Malibu vor auf den bereits erwähnten Fragmenten eines Volutenkraters des Kleophrademalers (Abb. 15).[55]

Herakles hält in der Rechten die Keule. Die vorgestreckte Linke hielt wohl den Bogen. Der Hirt Eurytion

50. Reh: D.v.Bothmer a.O. 61 Mitte. Rotfigurig *VL*³ 44,9.21.24; 45,31; 46,5. Zürich, Kunsthandel 1968 Kelchkraterfrr.

51. Sammlung Bareiss 143, Leihgabe, Malibu S.80.AE.232. K. Schauenburg in *Weltkunst aus Privatbesitz* (Köln 1968) A 26 Taf. 9. D.v. Bothmer, *Bareiss* Nr. 20: 520–510 v.Chr. Zum Thema: Brommer, *Herakles* 18ff.

52. *VL*³ 47,1.25; 48.40.47; 49,14.

53. G. Beckel, *Götterbeistand* 116 Anm. 466. Einmal (*VL*³ 53 B 1) be-

gegnet die Namensbeischrift Kaliphobe.

54. Mehrere Frauen: *VL*³ 47,18. Artemis: *VL*³ 48,16. Greis und Jüngling: *VL*³ 49,2.

55. Hier unter Herakles und Amazonen, Malibu acc. no. 77.AE.11. *VL*³ 62 B 6. Zu den dort aufgeführten Geryonesvasen kommen hinzu: S.59 A 24 Dublin 1921.95 Halsamphora Johnston *Cat.* S.371 Nr. 328; S.61 A 25 Würzburg 246 Bauchamphora *ABV* 296,8; S.62 A 22 Tessin, Privatbesitz Stamnos Isler-Kerenyi, *Stamnoi* 24ff.; J. Frel, *Stamnoi* Nr. 6;

Abb. 15. Fragmentierter Rand eines attisch-rotfigurigen Volutenkraters. Malibu, The J. Paul Getty Museum 77.AE.11. H: 7.6 cm.

liegt bereits tot am Boden. Ein Pfeil steckt in seinem Leib, sein Auge ist gebrochen. Die drei linken Füsse des dreileibigen Geryones sind gerade noch erhalten. Der zweiköpfige Hund Orthros liegt tot links hinter Herakles am Boden. Die Sage wurde schon im 7. Jh. v.Chr. dargestellt und war in der zweiten Hälfte des 6. Jh. besonders beliebt. Damals war der Darstellungstypus bereits fest ausgebildet. Man hielt sich allgemein an ihn. Das hat auch der Kleophradesmaler getan. Wahrscheinlich war der dritte Leib des Geryones tot heruntersinkend dargestellt.

HERAKLES IN GIGANTENKAMPF

Die schwarzfigurige Augenschale[56] hat innen—nicht aussen—einen abgesetzten Rand (Abb. 16). Sie ist dem Töpfer Nikosthenes zugeschrieben worden. Auf der einen Seite ist Athena mit Helm, Schild und Lanze nach rechts stürmend dargestellt. Aus dem linken der beiden apotropäischen Augen entspringt ein bärtiger Kopf mit skythischer Mütze, sowie eine Hand mit Bogen, aus dem rechten Auge ein behelmter Kopf und eine Hand mit Lanze. Beide wenden sich gegen Athena. Offenbar ist ein Ausschnitt aus der Gigantomachie gemeint.

Auf der anderen Seite kämpft eine unbehelmte, schildlose Frau mit der Lanze gegen einen zu Boden sinkenden Krieger. D. v. Bothmer hat die Frau ebenfalls für Athena gehalten; aber das Fehlen von Helm, Schild und Aegis spricht dagegen, ausserdem ist das Fell auffällig, das sie über dem Gewand trägt und das bei Athena ganz ungewöhnlich wäre. Eher schon wäre an eine Amazone zu denken, die, wenn auch selten, mit einem Fell bekleidet sein können.[57] Noch wahrscheinlicher ist, dass es sich um Artemis handelt und damit ebenfalls um einen Ausschnitt aus der Gigantomachie. Rechts und links beider Henkel kämpfen Herakles und ein Krieger mit Lanzen gegeneinander. D. v. Bothmer hielt den Gegner für Kyknos oder einen Giganten. Wir werden der zweiten Deutung den Vorzug geben, zumal sowohl Zeus, wie Ares fehlen. Somit ist das Thema der ganzen Schale die Gigantomachie.

Unter dem einen Henkel ist, kleiner gebildet, ein Mann wiedergegeben, der sich nicht benennen lässt, unter dem anderen eine Frau, die D. v. Bothmer ebenfalls nicht benannte. Da sie in der Rechten ein Lanze trägt, wird es sich um Athena handeln. Die Schale ist um 530 v.Chr. entstanden.

A 23 Brit.Mus. 1895.10–29.1 Lekythos Brize, *Geryoneis* Taf. 4; A 24 Ann Arbor, Kelsey Mus. 29200 Bruchstück; A 25 Budapest Bruchstück; B 7 Verschollen Schalenbruchstück *AZ* 1846, 342 Nr. 13; *CVA* Ashby S.VI. Zum Thema: Brommer, *Herakles* 39ff.

56. Sammlung Bareiss 83, Leihgabe, Malibu S.80.AE.229 (früher New York L 69.11.69). Innen laufende Nike oder Iris nach rechts, sich umblickend. D.v.Bothmer, *Bareiss* Nr. 37. Zu Schalen mit abgesetzten Rand innen: H. Bloesch, *Formen att. Schalen* 137f. und Anm. 219, sowie J.Mer-

tens, *MetMusJ* 9 (1974) 96ff. Zum Herauswachsen aus den Augen: Boston, MFA 10.651 Schale *ABV* 157,86; Boardman, *Athenian Black Figure Vases* (1974) 82; London, Brit.Mus. B 215 Halsamphora *ABV* 286,1; Boardman a.O. fig. 195.

57. Amazone mit Fell: Athen, Kerameikos 76 Dinosfragment D.v. Bothmer, *Amazons* 14 Taf. 17,1.

Abb. 16. Attisch-schwarzfigurige Augenschale. Sammlung Bareiss 83, Leihgabe im J. Paul Getty Museum S.80.AE.229. H: 12.9 cm.

Dasselbe Thema ist vielleicht auch auf einem Bruchstück, wohl einer Oinochoe,[58] gemeint (Abb. 17). Erhalten ist der Ausschnitt aus einer Kampfszene mit dem Unterkörper des Herakles, der ein rotes Gewand, ein Löwenfell und darüber einen roten Gürtel trägt. Das Bruchstück stammt aus dem späten 6. Jh. v.Chr.

HERAKLES UND DIE HESPERIDEN

Das Thema ist auf dem bereits erwähnten fragmentierten Volutenkrater[59] des Kleophradesmalers dargestellt (Abb. 18).

Herakles—der Kopf ist im Louvre—steht vor dem von der Schlange bewachten Apfelbaum. Drei Köpfe dieser Schlange sind sichtbar. Herakles hält in der Linken Bogen und Keule und greift mit der Rechten offenbar nach einem Apfel. Hinter ihm steht Athena und rechts vom Apfelbaum steht Atlas. Eine Hesperide ist nicht wiedergegeben. Als dieses Bild gemalt wurde, war die Sage in der Bildkunst seit sieben Jahrzehnten bekannt. Drei Versionen wurden dargestellt, nämlich Herakles entweder beim Apfelbaum oder bei Atlas[60] oder mit den Aepfeln weglaufend.[61] Hier sind zum bisher einzigen Mal in der Vasenmalerei die beiden ersten Versionen in ein Bild zusammengezogen. Aber offensichtlich gab es das schon vor dem Kleophradesmaler, denn die Gruppe des Theokles in Olympia umfasste nach Pausanias (VI 19,8) Atlas, Herakles, den Apfelbaum und die Hesperiden. Athena wird nicht erwähnt und sie kommt auch auf den Vasen sonst

in diesem Zusammenhang nicht vor. Hier bietet der Kleophradesmaler also etwas besonderes. Auch, dass die Schlange (mindestens) dreiköpfig ist, ist ungewöhnlich. Sie ist normalerweise einköpfig[62] oder zweiköpfig.[63]

HERAKLES UND HYDRA

Auf dem dünnwandigen, innen mit Glanzton versehenen Bruchstück wohl einer Schale[64] sieht man einen grossen geschuppten Leib, ferner einen Schlangenleib mit Kopf (Abb. 19). Aus dem grossen Leib fliesst Blut in Strömen heraus. Damit ist bereits ausgeschlossen, dass es sich um den Kampf mit dem Meerwesen handelt, denn der verläuft immer unblutig. Es kann hier nur die Hydra gemeint sein, die Herakles mit Keule, Schwert, Bogen oder Sichel bekämpft, wobei ihm Iolaos manchmal mit Fackeln hilft.

Trotzdem ist der Kampf auf den 51 uns bekannten attischen Vasen im allgemeinen unblutig dargestellt. Aber zu den attischen Darstellungen kommen verhältnismässig viele ausserattische archaische hinzu, darunter elf korinthische und vier lakonische. Dabei fliesst auf dem korinthischen Aryballos in Basel und dem korinthischen Kesselfragment[65] das Blut in Strömen.

Das Thema kommt auch auf den Kraterfragmenten des Kleophradesmalers vor (Abb. 20).[66]

Die Hydra befindet sich in der Mitte. Von rechts kommt Iolaos mit Helm und Beinschienen. Er hält in der Linken einen Schild, der mit dem beim Kleophradesmaler belieb-

58. Malibu acc. no. 76.AE.130.57. Innen ohne Glanzton.

59. Unter Herakles und Amazonen Malibu acc. no. 77.AE.11. Hier S.111. Zum Thema: Brommer, *Herakles* 47ff.

60. *VL³* A 4, D1, 2, 7, 15 und Schale Bern, Jucker, *Festschrift Brommer* 191ff. Taf. 53.

61. *VL³* A 6, B 9.

62. *VL³* A 1,5; B 2, 4, 5, 11, 13 (jetzt in Champaign-Urbana).

63. *VL³* A 3. Zu den in *VL³* aufgeführten Vasen kommen hinzu ausser der in Anm. 2 erwähnten Schale: B 23 München, Kunsthandel 1929 Kelchkrater DAI Rom 51.110; B 24 diese Vase in Malibu.

64. Malibu acc. no. 81.AE.10.3, anonymes Geschenk.

65. *VL³* 81 C 8.

66. Hier unter Herakles und Amazonen erwähnt, Malibu acc. no. 77.AE.11.

Abb. 17. Bruchstück einer attischen Oinochoe. Malibu, The J. Paul Getty Museum 76.AE.130.57. L: 8 cm.

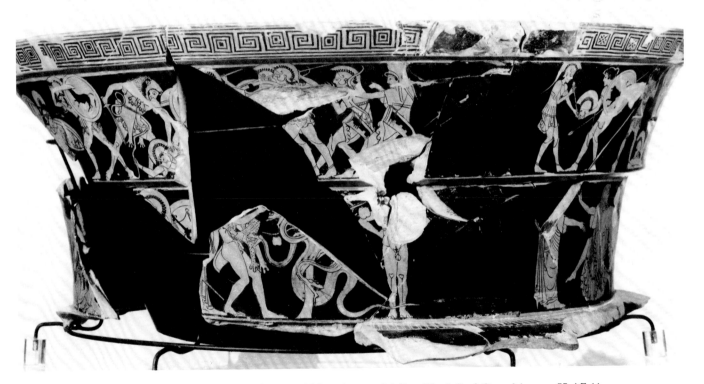

Abb. 18. Fragmentierter Rand eines attisch-rotfigurigen Volutenkraters. Malibu, The J. Paul Getty Museum 77.AE.11.

Abb. 19. Bruchstück einer Schale. Malibu, The J. Paul
Getty Museum 81.AE.10.3. L: 5.4 cm.

ten Zeichen des Pegasos geschmückt ist, und eine Lanze.
In der Rechten hält er eine brennende Fackel, um die
Hälse der abgeschnittenen Hydraköpfe auszubrennen.
Von links kommt symmetrisch Herakles, von dem sich
nur der Teil eines Fusses erhalten hat. Dieses so beschrie-
bene Kampfschema ist alt und lässt sich mehrfach bele-
gen.[67] Der Kleophradesmaler hat sich also auch hier an
das Uebliche gehalten.

HERAKLES UND KERBEROS

Die Amphora aus der Sammlung Bareiss[68] ist von Beazley der Leagrosgruppe zugesprochen worden (Abb. 21a, b).
Man sieht links den unbekleideten Herakles, der ein
Schwert an einem weissen Band umgehängt hat und in
der Rechten eine Keule hält. Am unteren Ende der Backe
sind Haare durch Ritzung wiedergegeben, aber das Kinn
ist bartfrei. Ihm wendet sich mit dem Oberkörper Athena
nach links zu, während der Unterkörper und die Füsse
nach rechts gerichtet sind. Sie trägt über ihrem Gewand
eine Aegis, dazu einen Helm und hält in der Linken eine
Lanze. Die Rechte hat sie zum Gruss erhoben. Hinter ihr
steht nach rechts Kerberos, der zwei Köpfe hat, wie auf
den attischen schwarzfigurigen Vasen immer.[69] Er hat rote
Flecken am Hals und blickt auf zu Hermes, der am rechten
Bildrand ihm zugewandt steht. Seine Arme sind vom
Mantel bedeckt, aber ein Stab, sicher das Kerykeion,
kommt hinter seinem Körper zum Vorschein, ist also in
der Rechten gedacht. Er trägt eine Kopfbedeckung und

Stiefel. Er hat einen roten Bart. Offenbar besänftigt er den
Höllenhund, den Herakles entführen soll.[70]

Die Kerberossage erfreute sich in der archaischen Zeit
grosser Beliebtheit. Mehr als einhundert attisch-schwarzfigurige Vasen mit dem Thema sind erhalten. Die attisch-
rotfigurigen machen nur ein Zehntel dieser Zahl aus, aber
auch sie gehören sämtlich in die archaische Zeit. Auf archaischen Vasen ist die Sage ferner belegt in Korinth,
Sparta, Caere und Etrurien. Im 4. Jh. v.Chr. kommt sie
vor allem auf den grossen apulischen Volutenkrateren vor.

Die Wiedergabe der Sage auf der Amphora in Malibu
hält sich durchaus an das Uebliche, sieht man davon ab,
dass dem Herakles Bart und Löwenfell fehlen. Dieselben
drei Gestalten begegnen oft bei Kerberos. Auch ist die Bewegung des Kerberos im allgemeinen nach rechts gerichtet.

Nicht selten ist auf den Kerberosbildern durch eine
Säule der Palast des Hades bezeichnet und dann auch
Kore oder der Unterweltsgott selbst wiedergegeben. Der
Palast befindet sich meist am rechten Bildrand und die Bewegung geht daher dann nach links.[71] Ein Rest von einer
solchen Szene ist offenbar auf dem attisch-schwarzfigurigen
Amphorenbruchstück in Malibu[72] erhalten (Abb. 22).
Hinter der Säule ist der Hinterkörper des Kerberos bewahrt, links davon Schulter und erhobener Arm von
einer bekleideten männlichen Gestalt, vielleicht Hermes.
Rechts von der Säule steht eine bekleidete bärtige Gestalt
mit ursprünglich weissen Haaren. Sie hält in der Rechten
einen Stab. Vielleicht ist Hades mit dem Zepter gemeint.[73]
Auf der Kanne[74] zieht Herakles mit in der Rechten erhobener Keule den Kerberos nach rechts (Abb. 23). Hinter
diesem steht mit einer Lanze in der Hand die helmlose
Athena. Auf sie folgt Hermes mit Petasos, Kerykeion und
Flügelschuhen. Den Beschluss bildet ein Jüngling mit
Speer. Das flüchtige Bild ist im letzten Jahrzehnt des 6. Jh.
v.Chr. gemalt worden.

Die Kerberossage ist noch ein viertes Mal auf einer Vase
in Malibu dargestellt, auf den Bruchstücken einer rotfigurigen Schale (Abb. 24a, b).[75] Von Kerberos ist zwar nichts
erhalten, wohl aber die Oberkörper von Herakles und
Hermes mit Resten ihrer Namensbeschriftungen. Hermes
hält einen roten Stab, das Kerykeion, in der Rechten. Die

67. VL³ 79ff. A 1, 5, 6, 13, 24, 35; B 6, 13; C 1, 3, 6, 9, 13. Zum
Thema: Brommer, Herakles 12f.

68. Sammlung Bareiss 12, Leihgabe, Malibu S.80.AE.230. Beazley,
Para 166,113 bis; VL³ 91,4; Weltkunst aus Privatbesitz A 27; D.v.Bothmer,
Bareiss Nr. 21 (L 68.142.13). Zum Thema: Brommer, Herakles 43ff.

69. Dreiköpfiger Kerberos: VL³ 95 B 6; 96 C 5,6,7, sowie unteritalische
Bilder. Einköpfig: 96 C 3.

70. Zur Besänftigungsgeste des Hermes bei Kerberos: VL³ 92,23; 93 A
9, 10; 95 B 1,3. Die gleiche Anordnung von Herakles, Athena und Hermes: VL³ 91 A 3; 94 A 1 u. und Christie Sale 2.VIII.1980 Nr. 82 = Castle
Ashby CVA 20.

71. Palast rechts: VL³ 91 A 4, 5, 11, 13, 14; 92 A 4, 5; 93, 4, 8, 10, 11,

13; 94 7, 13; 95 A 19; B 1, 3, 4. Palast links 91 A 18; 92,8, 10, 11, 21, 25;
93,15.

72. Sammlung Bareiss 18, Leihgabe, Malibu S.80.AE.86.

73. Auf den Kerberosvasen kommen ausser den genannten Gestalten
noch vor Apollon (VL³ 92,7), ein Jüngling mit einem Speer (93,1), ein
Viergespann (93 4,10), ein Krieger (94 13 o.), zwei Männer und drei
Frauen (92,6), Iolaos (93,16).

74. Malibu acc. no. 79.AE.21. Von A. Clark der Altenburg class zugewiesen.

75. Malibu acc. no. 77.AE.94. J. Frel, Painting on Vases in Ancient
Greece Nr. 6, dem Oltos zugeschrieben.

Abb. 20. Fragmentierter Rand eines attisch-rotfigurigen Volutenkraters. Malibu, The J. Paul Getty Museum 77.AE.11. H: 17.5 cm.

Abb. 21a. Attisch-schwarzfigurige Halsamphora. Seite A. Sammlung Bareiss 12, Leihgabe im J. Paul Getty Museum S.80.AE.230. H: 46.2 cm.

Abb. 21b. Bareiss 12. Seite B.

Abb. 22. Bruchstück einer attisch-schwarzfigurigen Amphora. Sammlung Bareiss 18, Leihgabe im J. Paul
Getty Museum S.80.AE.86. L: 11.9 cm.

Abb. 23. Attisch-schwarzfigurige Kanne. Malibu, The J.
Paul Getty Museum 79.AE.21. H: 22.8 cm.

Abb. 24a. Bruchstück einer attisch-rotfigurigen Schale.
Malibu, The J. Paul Getty Museum 77.AE.94.
L: 9.4 cm.

Abb. 24b. Malibu 77.AE.94. Bruchstück.

Mitwirkung des Hermes bei dieser Heraklestat macht es wahrscheinlich, dass hier ebenfalls dieses Heraklesabenteuer dargestellt war.

Alle vier Vasen sind zeitlich nahe bei einander entstanden im letzten Viertel des 6. Jh. v.Chr., in der Zeit, in der überhaupt die meisten Kerberosbilder geschaffen wurden.

HERAKLES UND DIE KERKOPEN

Die Kerkopen waren zwei nichtsnutzige Gauner. Ihre Mutter hatte sie vor einem Mann mit einem schwarzen Gesäss gewarnt. Eines Tages fanden sie Herakles unter einem Baum schlafend. Sie wollten ihm seine Waffen stehlen. Herakles erwachte, band sie kopfüber mit den Füssen an ein Tragholz und trug sie davon. Die Kerkopen sahen in dieser Lage sein Gesäss und machten darüber so tolle Witze, dass Herakles sie laut lachend freiliess.

Auf den attischen Vasen ist das Thema während des Zeitraums von 520–450 v.Chr. öfter dargestellt worden. In anderen Gegenden kam das Thema jedoch schon früher vor. Das früheste Zeugnis ist ein mittelkorinthisches Schalenfragment aus dem ersten Viertel des 6. Jh. Die rotfigurige Pelike, die sich als Leihgabe in Malibu befindet,[76] ist in Lukanien entstanden (Abb. 25). Ueberhaupt spielt Unteritalien in dieser Sage eine verhältnismässig grosse Rolle. Nur hier ist das Thema auch in der grossen Kunst dargestellt worden, nämlich auf einer Metope von Selinunt und auf einer zweiten von Foce del Sele. Aber die Pelike ist später entstanden als die beiden Metopen und als alle attischen Vasen. Sie unterscheidet sich auch in der Darstellung der Kerkopen von allen früheren Bildern, in denen sie immer in rein menschlicher Gestalt wiedergegeben sind.

Hier haben sie beide riesige Phallen[77] und tierische Köpfe. Der linke hat Spitzohren und der rechte hat ein Affengesicht. Bei der Vase ist wohl einiges übermalt, aber diese tierischen Züge sind doch sicher. Es gibt noch ein zweites unteritalisches Vasenbild der Sage, einen Krater in Catania,[78] welcher zeigt, dass die Sage in Unteritalien auch in der Phlyakenposse behandelt wurde. Auf diesem Krater trägt Herakles an einem Tragholz zwei Käfige, in dem die Kerkopen sitzen. Er bringt sie zu einem König, wohl zu Eurystheus. Insofern weicht die Theaterfassung von der sonst bekannten Sage ab. Es kann sein, dass auch auf dem

Krater in Catania die Kerkopen als affenartige Wesen gedacht sind, jedenfalls sind sie klein und schwarz wiedergegeben.[79] Später sollen die Kerkopen auch versucht haben, Zeus zu betrügen. Nach Xenagoras[80] habe sie dieser in Affen verwandelt und auf die Pithekusen-Inseln (Ischia und Procida) versetzt, die daher ihren Namen erhielten. Damit ist wieder eine Verbindung zu Unteritalien gegeben.

Offenbar hat man seit dem frühen 4. Jh. v.Chr. die Kerkopen mit den Affen verbunden und zwar, wie die Geschichte mit den Affeninseln zeigt, gerade in Unteritalien. Eine Affenart hiess sogar Kerkopen. So ist das affenartige Aussehen der Kerkopen auf der Pelike von Malibu, die im frühen 4. Jh. v.Chr. entstanden sein wird, nicht überraschend.

HERAKLES UND KYKNOS

Kyknos war ein Sohn des Ares, der an der Strasse von Tempe zu den Thermopylen den Wanderern auflauerte, um aus deren Schädeln seinem Vater einen Tempel zu erbauen. Herakles tötete den Kyknos und verwundete den Ares. Von den 143 Vasen dieses Themas, die bekannt sind, sind 135 attisch und gehören der archaischen Zeit an. Damit ist das zeitliche und landschaftliche Schwergewicht der Sage klar bezeichnet. Das Thema kommt in der Vasenmalerei im zweiten Viertel des 6. Jh. v.Chr. auf und hält sich in Attika bis in das erste Viertel des 5. Jh. v.Chr.

Die uns hier beschäftigende Vase[81] trägt mit einer Amphora in Tarent[82] eine der allerfrühesten Darstellungen der Sage in der Vasenmalerei. Herakles und Kyknos sind mit ihren Lanzen im Zweikampf begriffen (Abb. 26). Herakles mit grossem Köcher auf dem Rücken, aber ohne Bogen, fasst mit seiner Linken den Helm des Kyknos und drückt damit seine Ueberlegenheit aus. Kyknos trägt ein rotes Gewand, einen roten Helm und einen böotischen Schild mit einem weissen Dreifuss als Zeichen. Der Krieger, der hinter Kyknos diesem zu Hilfe kommt, ist zweifellos sein Vater Ares. Er trägt ein ursprünglich weisses Gewand, einen roten Helm, rote Beinschienen und einen roten Schild ohne Zeichen. In der Frau hinter Herakles wird man Athena erkennen können. Sie hält einen Kranz in ihrer Rechten. Hinter ihr steht ein Bärtiger mit Petasos, wohl Hermes.[83] Hinter Ares steht eine Frau, deren Gewand mit Punktrosetten geschmückt ist, die aussen weiss

76. Malibu acc. no. 81.AE.189, Geschenk von Mr. and Mrs. Milton Gottlieb. Christie Genf 5.IV.1979 Nr. 118. Auf der Rückseite drei Jünglinge. *The Art of South Italy: Vases from Magna Graecia* (ed. M. Mayo) Richmond 1982/83, 67 n. 7.

77. Dies ist auch der Fall bei einem der beiden Kerkopen der Kanne in Brüssel VL³ 98,1.

78. VL³ 99 D 1.

79. Einen Schwanz haben die Kerkopen jedoch auf keiner der 26 bekannten Darstellungen, obwohl ihr Name von κέρκος (= Schwanz) abge-

leitet wird.

80. Bei Harpokration s.v. Kerkops.

81. Sammlung Bareiss 237, Leihgabe, Malibu S.80.AE.253. *Weltkunst aus Privatbesitz* (Köln 1968) A 13; D.v. Bothmer, *Bareiss* Nr. 14 (L 68.142.3); VL³ 103,18; *Aachener Kunstblätter* 44 (1973) 26 Abb. 33–36. Rückseite: Ein bärtiger Mann eingerahmt von zwei Frauen und zwei sitzenden Sphingen.

82. VL³ 103,13 o.

83. VL³ 104,9; 105,16,17; 106,1.

Abb. 25. Rotfigurige Pelike. Malibu, The J. Paul Getty Museum 81.AE.189. H: 28.5 cm.

und in der Mitte rot sind. Ihre Benennung wird sich durch die zweite Vase dieses Themas in Malibu ergeben.

Am Hals sind zwei sitzende antithetische Löwen. Im Fries unter dem Hauptbild ist eine stehende männliche Gestalt zwischen zwei sitzenden antithetischen Löwen, danach rechts und links je ein stehende, der Mitte zugewandte Sirene, ganz aussen links ein stehender Löwe mit zurückgewandtem Kopf.

Die Vase gehört in das Jahrzehnt 570–60 v.Chr.

Bald nach den frühesten Vasen, noch vor der Jahrhundertmitte, kommt Zeus in dieser Szene vor. Entweder in Person[84] oder in Gestalt eines Blitzes[85] sucht er die Kämpfer zu schlichten, ist aber keineswegs bei allen Darstellungen anwesend. Der Kampf ist meist, wie hier, in vollem Gang dargestellt, oft bricht Kyknos bereits zusammen, oder liegt schon tot ausgestreckt am Boden.[86]

Die grossartigen Kelchkraterbruchstücke mit der Malersignatur des Euphronios[87] bringt die Zahl der mit diesem Meisternamen und *egrapsen* signierten Gefässe auf sieben. Ausser seinem eigenen Namen hat der Meister auch die Namen der Dargestellten aufgeschrieben. Kyknos, der frontal aus dem Bild herausblickt, ist vor dem Ansturm des Herakles bereits zu Boden gesunken. Er trägt einen Schuppenpanzer mit je einem Löwen links und rechts auf den beiden Schulterklappen und zieht vergeblich sein Schwert, das an zwei roten Gurten hängt. Er blutet bereits heftig aus einer Wunde, die ihm Herakles mit der Lanze im ungeschützten rechten Oberschenkel beigebracht hat. Von dem Schild hinter ihm ist nicht mehr viel zu sehen. Sein Bart ist in verdünntem Glanzton wiedergegeben.

Herakles stürmt mit gewaltig ausgreifendem Schritt nach rechts vor, hat aber sein an zwei über die Schulter geführten roten Gurten hängendes Schwert noch in der Scheide. Er trägt ein kurzes Gewand, darüber in verdünntem Glanzton das Löwenfell. In der vorgestreckten Linken hält er den Schild.

Angegriffen wird Herakles von Ares mit hoch erhobener Lanze. In der Linken hält er einen Schild mit einem Gorgoneion in der Mitte und darüber und darunter je einen springenden schwarzen Löwen, ähnlich denen auf den Schulterklappen des Kyknos. Aber Athena tritt dem Gott entgegen und deckt ihren Schützling Herakles mit weit vorgestreckter Aegis. Hinter Ares steht seine namentlich bezeichnete Gemahlin Aphrodite. Ihre Namensbeischrift erlaubt uns, die auch sonst[88] im Kyknoskampf hinter Ares erscheinende Frau, beispielsweise auf der schwarz-

Abb. 26. Euboeisch-schwarzfigurige Halsamphora. Sammlung Bareiss 237, Leihgabe im J. Paul Getty Museum S.80.AE.253. H:36.7 cm.

figurigen Amphora in Malibu, als Aphrodite zu erkennen. Ihre erhobene Rechte mit gespreizten Fingern ist leer, ihr linker Arm gesenkt, die Hand nicht erhalten. Sie trägt zwei rote Reifen im Haar. Ganz links wird das Bild ebenfalls von einer Frau beschlossen, von der nur der Unterkörper erhalten ist mit langem Gewand und Füssen, die nach rechts in weitem Schritt gewandt sind. Eine Namensbeischrift hat sich bei ihr leider nicht erhalten.[89]

Von der anderen Seite des Gefässes hat sich ein Flötenspieler nach links und ein Speerwerfer nach rechts erhalten, sowie links Füsse, die nach links gewandt sind.

Die beiden Kyknosdarstellungen in Malibu sind durch ein halbes Jahrhundert voneinander getrennt. Es springt in die Augen, wieviel das spätere Bild gegenüber dem früheren an dramatischer Wucht und an Eindringlichkeit der Darstellung gewonnnen hat.

84. *VL³* 103,1.11.14; 104,9.14.15.16; 105,18.2; 106,1.10.

85. *VL³* 105,3.10.

86. *VL³* 106,10.

87. Sammlung N.B. Hunt, Leihgabe in Getty Museum in 1980/82. M. Robertson, Getty *MJ* 9 (1981) 22ff. Zu den fünf bei Beazley, *ARV²* 13 aufgeführten Signaturen kommt der New Yorker Sarpedonkrater und

jetzt diese Vase.

88. *VL³* 103,13 o. 18 o. 2 u. 6 u. 16 u.; 104,6; 105,15 o. 20 o; 107 B 3.

89. Namensbeischrift auch nicht bei den übrigen Bildern der hinter Herakles stehenden Frau: *VL³* 105,18; 103,13 o. 7.6u. (mit Lanze); 103,2.18 (mit Kranz); 107 B 3.

HERAKLES UND DER LÖWE

Die Erlegung des Löwen von Nemea ist die erste kanonische Tat des Herakles. Sie ist nicht nur die beliebteste Tat des Herakles in der griechischen Vasenmalerei, sondern es ist die bekannteste griechische Sage überhaupt. Mehr als 900 Vasenbilder dieser Sage sind bekannt.

Kein Wunder, dass auch in Malibu diese Sage am meisten vertreten ist. Es gibt dort nicht weniger als sechs Beispiele, die alle attisch sind. Die älteste Darstellung findet sich auf einer Dreifusspyxis, die aus der Sammlung Schweizer in die Sammlung Bareiss kam (Abb. 27). Die Vase[90] ist um 540 v.Chr. entstanden. Es ist die einzige bisher bekannte Dreifusspyxis, die mit diesem häufigen Thema geschmückt ist. Der bärtige Herakles steht nach rechts gewandt und hat den Hals des Löwen umklammert. Links steht ein Jüngling, rechts ein Mann, beide sind mit langem Gewand bekleidet und halten je einen Kranz. Der linke ist schwarz, der rechte weiss. Rot sind die Haare aller drei Männer und die Zunge des Löwen, der seinen Kopf zurückgewandt hat. Rot liegt auch auf den Gewändern. Gewand hängt im Grund.

Auf den beiden übrigen Füssen des Gefässes sind der Kampf zwischen Theseus und Minotauros, sowie Erastengruppen dargestellt. Auf dem Deckel sind Sportler wiedergegeben. Die Themen haben also keinen Zusammenhang untereinander.

Die zeitlich nächste Darstellung ist etwa ein Jahrzehnt später entstanden. Es handelt sich um ein Amphorafragment[91] mit ebenfalls dem Löwenkampf im Stehschema (Abb. 28). Erhalten sind der Kopf und die rechte Schulterpartie des bärtigen Herakles, der ebenfalls nach rechts gewandt ist, sowie ein Teil des Löwenkopfes. Der Löwe hat seine Vorderpranke auf die Schulter des Herakles gelegt. Links ist ein weiterer, bärtiger Kopf zu sehen, der gewiss dem Iolaos gehört. Rechts ist über dem Kopf des Herakles noch eine Lanzenspitze erhalten, die zu einer dritten Gestalt gehören muss, von der sonst nichts erhalten ist. Dies könnte ein Krieger oder Ares gewesen sein,[92] aber häufiger ist in diesen Szenen Athena und so wird sicher sie die dritte Person gewesen sein. Das Bild ist also etwa so zu ergänzen, wie die Bilder auf einigen Amphoren.[93] Be-

sonders aber stehen zwei Amphoren[94] nahe, auf denen die Kampfszene ebenfalls links von Iolaos und rechts von Athena eingerahmt wird und der Löwe seine rechte Vordertatze auf die Schulter des Herakles gelegt hat. Das Bruchstück gibt also einen bekannten Bildtypus wieder. Die nächste Vase[95] ist wieder ein Jahrzehnt später entstanden und stellt wieder den Kampf im Stehen dar (Abb. 29). Diesmal ist Athena mit der Lanze links und Iolaos, der die Keule hält, rechts. Trotzdem schwingt Herakles seine Keule in der Rechten und hat mit der Linken den Hals des Löwen umklammert, dessen Maul er aufreisst. Eine Keule schwingt er im Löwenkampf nicht eben oft.[96] Insofern hat sich der Maler, der sich auch durch sorgfältige Zeichnung auszeichnet, etwas Besonderes einfallen lassen. Dabei ist allerdings die Keule mit dem Kopf des Iolaos zusammengestossen.

Wieder zwei Jahrzehnte später, um 500 v.Chr., wurde die Oinochoe[97] geschaffen, die Herakles im Liegeschema wiedergibt (Abb. 30). Es ist nur der Unterteil des Gefässes erhalten, aber mit ihm das Wesentliche des Bildes. Die Oberfläche ist angegriffen, wie man besonders in den Ritzungen bemerkt. Der bekränzte, bärtige Held hat mit dem linken Arm den Hals des Löwen umklammert, der sein Maul weit geöffnet hat. Der Löwe sucht mit seiner linken Hintertatze den Kopf des Herakles zu erreichen. Hinter der Gruppe wächst ein Baum auf. Rechts vom rechten Hinterbein des Löwen ist **SATE** . . . zu lesen. Der Name kommt unter den von Beazley aufgeführten Namen nicht vor, auch nicht in retrograder Lesung.

Die beiden folgenden Bilder sind rotfigurig und halten sich wieder an das Liegeschema. Dieses beansprucht einen langen, schmalen Streifen und ist daher auf Schultern von Hydrien beliebt.

Das frühere der beiden rotfigurigen Bilder befindet sich auf der Schulter einer Lekythos (Abb. 31).[98] Der Bauch scheint unbemalt gewesen zu sein. Normalerweise ist es umgekehrt, doch gibt es eine Anzahl von rotfigurigen Lekythen, bei denen auch die Schulter figürlich bemalt ist,[99] und weitere, bei denen, wie hier, ausschliesslich die Schulter mit Figuren verziert ist.[100] Herakles ist unbärtig dargestellt. Es handelt sich ja um die erste Tat, die er voll-

90. Sammlung Bareiss 433, Leihgabe, Malibu S.80.AE.322. *VL²* 97 Nr. 123; MM *Auktion* 40 (1969) Nr. 64 Taf. 20; *VL³* 15,79. Zum Thema: Brommer, *Herakles* 7ff. Sehen Anmerkung Nr. 145.

91. Malibu acc. no. 81.AE.10.8.

92. Vgl. die Bauchamphoren Kassel T 384, Würzburg 247, 248.

93. Amphora Würzburg 185,254, Vatikan 355, Boston 97.205.

94. Privatbesitz VL³ 122,33; Genf 14989.

95. Sammlung Bareiss 13, Leihgabe, Malibu S.80.AE.5. Bareiss Nr. 13, vorher Zürich, Vollmöller, *ARV²* 1588; *Para* 140.

96. S. aber Würzburg 306 Hydria, St. Louis 677 Lekythos, Tarent I.G. 4342 Schale.

97. Malibu acc. no. 76.AE.103, Geschenk von Gordon McLendon.

98. Malibu acc. no. 77.AE.43.

99. Besonders beim Berliner Maler (*ARV²* 211f. Nr. 207 bis, 209, 209 bis, 210, 211) und seinem Schüler Hermonax (*ARV²* 490,114–116), aber auch bei anderen Malern (*ARV²* 640,77; 993,91; Sotheby 1.VII. 69 Nr. 88; Cleveland 78.59 *Midwestern Collection* Nr. 105) Vibo Valentia Inv. 403 (*Bd'Arte* 15 [1982] 61ff.).

100. Ebenfalls beim Berliner Maler (*ARV²* 211 Nr. 199, 200), vor allem aber beim Phialemaler (*ARV²* 1022,133–137), aber auch bei anderen Malern: *ARV²* 557,119; 1003,24, sowie Melbourne, Univ. V 18 *JHS* 71 (1951) 187 Nr. 92; *AthenInstNeg.* Calvert 11; MM *Auktion* 26 (1963) Nr. 134; Oxford 1932.733 *ARV²* 1644 zu 308; Mainz, Privatbesitz Klemm Palmetten auf Schulter.

Abb. 27. Attisch-schwarzfigurige Dreifusspyxis. Sammlung Bareiss 433, Leihgabe im J. Paul Getty Museum S.80.AE.322. H: 8.5 cm.

Abb. 28. Bruchstück einer attisch-schwarzfigurigen Amphora. Malibu, The J. Paul Getty Museum 81.AE.10.8. Grösste L: 11.8 cm.

Abb. 29. Attisch-schwarzfigurige Halsamphora. Sammlung Bareiss 13, Leihgabe im J. Paul Getty Museum S.80.AE.5. H: 25.5 cm.

Abb. 30. Attische Oinochoe. Malibu, The J. Paul Getty
Museum 76.AE.103. H: 10.7 cm.

bringt. So meint der Maler, ihn jugendlich wiederzugeben zu
können. Dass Herakles mit seiner Rechten die linke Hin-
terpranke des Löwen packt, ist ein Motiv, das bereits in
der schwarzfigurigen Vasenmalerei häufig vorkam. Wie
bei den anderen Bildern vom Kampf im Liegeschema
wächst auch hier hinter der Gruppe ein Baum. Das Bild
ist etwa um 480 v.Chr. entstanden.

Etwa ein Jahrzehnt später ist das Bild auf der Hydria[101]
wahrscheinlich vom Aegisthosmaler gemalt worden (Abb.
32). Der linke Arm des bärtigen Helden verschwindet
völlig hinter dem Löwen. Der rechte Arm ist angezogen
und noch nicht zur Umklammerung bereit. Der Löwe hat
seine rechte Vordertatze auf die linke Schulter des Herakles gelegt. Hinter dieser Gruppe wächst ein Baum und
umrahmt den Vorgang. Irgendwelche Waffen oder Attribute des Herakles sind nicht zu sehen, auch nicht aufge-
hängt. Dass die Bilder des Löwenkampfes in Malibu bald
nach der archaischen Zeit aufhören, ist kein Zufall. Sie
werden nach der Archaik allgemein selten.

HERAKLES IM KAMPF MIT DEM MEERWESEN

Um 580 v.Chr. kam in der attischen Vasenmalerei das
Thema von Herakles im Ringkampf mit einem Meerwesen
auf und hat sich dort ein halbes Jahrhundert lang grosser
Beliebtheit erfreut. Fast zweihundert attisch-schwarzfigurige Vasen mit dem Thema sind erhalten, hingegen nur ein
einziges sicher gedeutetes rotfiguriges Gefäss, ebenfalls aus
der archaischen Zeit. Ausserhalb Athens spielt das Thema
kaum eine Rolle. In Athen kam es hingegen sogar auch in
zwei archaischen Giebeln von der Akropolis vor.

Der Gegner des Herakles wird in der wissenschaftlichen
Literatur Triton, Nereus oder Halios Geron genannt. Wegen dieser verschiedenen Benennungen wird hier der neu-
trale Name Meerwesen gewählt. Tatsächlich kommen die
drei Namen in antiken Beschriftungen vor.[102] Dabei
gehören die Beschriftungen Nereus und Halios Geron in
das zweite Viertel des 6. Jh. Sie beziehen sich jeweils auf
ein glatzköpfiges Meerwesen, das sich auch in Schlangen-
oder Löwenleiber verwandeln kann.[103]

Die Tritonbeischriften befinden sich auf Vasen aus der
zweiten Hälfte des 6. Jh. Diese Tritonbilder zeigen nur

101. Sammlung Bareiss 27, Leihgabe, Malibu S.80.AE.233. Beazley,
Para 381; D.v.Bothmer, *Bareiss* Nr. 57 (L 69. 11.27); Burke-Pollitt, *Greek
Vases at Yale* Nr. 55.
102. Triton: Cambridge G 54 Hydria *VL*³ 147,18; London, Brit.Mus.
B 223 Halsamphora *VL*³ 144,20; Berlin F 1906 Hydria *VL*³ 146,1; Tarent
Hamsamphorafrr, Brize, *Geryoneis* 162,40. Hingegen nicht auf Brit.Mus.
B 312, wie I. Raubitschek, *The Hearst Hillsborough Vases* 26 behauptet.
Nereus: Samos Hydriafragmente *VL*³ 147,7.
Halios Geron: Olympia Schildband. E. Kunze, *Schildbänder* 31,213 Nr.
4 Taf. 54.
103. Verwandlungsfähigkeit ist auch angezeigt auf Athen NM 12587
Stangenkrater *VL*³ 149,37 und Louvre CA 823 Lekythos *VL*³ 148,2 und
auf dem korinthischen Bruchstück *Perachora* II Nr. 411 Taf. 22.

Abb. 31. Schulterbruchstück einer attisch rotfigurigen Lekythos. Malibu, The J. Paul Getty Museum 77.AE.43. Diam.: 7.1 cm.

Abb. 32. Attisch-rotfigurige Hydria. Einzelheit. Sammlung Bareiss 27, Leihgabe im J. Paul Getty Museum S.80.AE.233. H: 27.5 cm.

Abb. 33. Bruchstück. Malibu, The J. Paul Getty Museum
81.AE.10.6. H: 11 cm.

einen menschlichen Oberkörper mit Fischleib, keine
Schlangen und keine Glatze. Sicher ist bei all diesen Meerwesen aus der zweiten Hälfte des 6. Jh. immer Triton gemeint, denn oft genug sieht der weisshaarige Nereus dem
Kampf zu,[104] kann also nicht mit dem Meerwesen gemeint
sein. Gelegentlich sehen auch Poseidon oder Amphitrite
zu.[105]

Ueber die Sage unterrichten Zeugnisse von Pherekydes
und Apollodor.[106] Nach beiden Autoren hat Herakles
von Nereus mit Gewalt den Aufenthaltsort der Hesperiden erfahren, dabei hat sich Nereus in verschiedene Gestalten verwandelt. Die Episode mit Nereus hat auffälliger-
weise in der archaischen Zeit viel mehr Darstellungen gefunden als das Hesperidenabenteuer selbst. Sicher war es
der Kampf und noch dazu mit einem mischgestaltigen
Wesen, der die archaischen Künstler reizte.

Buschor[107] hat richtig gesehen, dass seit der Mitte des
6. Jh. das von Herakles bekämpfte Meerwesen Triton ist

und dass seit Klitias Nereus als ein ehrwürdiger Greis dargestellt wurde. Aber er nahm an, dass die Meerwesen bis
zur samischen Hydria Nereus darstellen. Dies führte zu der
merkwürdigen Folge, dass er im Meerwesen des kleinen
Tritongiebels Nereus und in dem des grossen Tritongiebels
Triton sah. Er sah Triton auch in dem Meerwesen auf dem
Klitiaskrater und dem Sophiloskessel, wo inzwischen statt-
dessen Okeanos gesichert ist.[108] Er sah ferner in dem Dreileibigen des grossen Tritongiebels Nereus, obwohl es sich
bei ihm gewiss um kein Meerwesen handelt, denn es hat
keine Fischflossen.[109]

Eher muss man annehmen, dass Nereus ursprünglich
auch in Fischgestalt dargestellt werden konnte, wie Triton.
Nach der Mitte des 6. Jh. v.Chr. wurde aber nur noch
Triton so dargestellt.

Das übliche Kampfschema ist der einfache Ringkampf,
bei dem Herakles auf dem Meerwesen reitet. Dabei ist die
Gruppe meist nach rechts gerichtet. Es kommt aber auch
die entgegengesetzte Richtung vor. Einmal ist auf einer
Schale[110] auf einer Seite die eine Richtung und auf der
anderen Seite die andere Richtung gewählt.

Wegen der Häufigkeit und im allgemeinen gleich blei-
benden Gestaltung des Themas lässt sich das Fragment in
Malibu (Abb. 33),[111] auf dem das rechte Bein des Herakles
und ein Teil der geschuppten Fischwindung zu sehen ist,
leicht zu einem Bild, wie es etwa auf zwei Halsamphoren[112]
vorkommt, ergänzen.

OMPHALE

Auf den ersten Blick meint man auf der fragmentierten
schwarzfigurigen Amphora,[113] die sich durch eine besondere Fussform auszeichnet,[114] Herakles im Löwenfell auf
einem Thron sitzen zu sehen, den Bogen mit zwei Pfeilen
in der Linken (Abb. 34). Beim zweiten Blick freilich be-
denkt man die weisse Hautfarbe, das lange Gewand und
die geflochtenen Sandalen, die Herakles niemals trägt,
und kommt zu dem Schluss, dass es sich nicht um Herakles handeln kann, sondern um eine Frau in seiner Tracht
also um Omphale.

Das ist überraschend, denn die Lehrmeinung ist: "In der
Kunst vor Alexander lassen sich keine sicheren Darstellungen der Omphale nachweisen"[115] und "der berühmte

---

104. Nereus dabei beispielsweise: *VL³* 144,13, 14, 20, 22; 145,28, 32,
55; 146,3, 5, 8, 10; 147,19, 20, 26, 29, 33, 34; 148,38, 39, 40, 45, 8;
150,43. Als Nereus beschriftet: London, Brit.Mus. B 223 Halsamphora
VL³ 144,20; Louvre F 298 *VL³* 147,10.

105. Poseidon dabei: *VL³* 146,16; 147,26; 148,40; 149,21; 145,34. Amphitrite dabei: *VL³* 147,10.

106. Pherekydes *FrGHist* I F 16 a Jacoby. Das von Pherekydes
erwähnte Binden wird auf den Bildern nicht dargestellt. Apollodor, *Bibl.*
II 5,11.

107. E. Buschor, *Meermänner* 1941. Ihm schloss sich an E. Kunze,
Schildbänder 109. Auch K. Schefold, *Götter- und Heldensagen* (1978) 128

nannte den Dreileibigen Nereus. Dagegen R. Glynn, *AJA* 85 (1981) 128
Anm. 60, wobei ihr mein hier in Anm. 8 erwähnter Aufsatz unbekannt
ist.

108. Verf., *AA* 1971, 29f. Von R. Glynn a.O. Anm.37 werde ich
zitiert, als ob ich hier Eurynome sähe.

109. Verf. *MarbWPr* 1947, 1ff. und in *Lissarrague—thelamon, image et
céramique* 103ff.

110. Kampf nach links gerichtet: *VL³* 144,22; 145,33.34; 146,10.16;
149,20.

111. Malibu acc. no. 81.AE.10.6.

112. Würzburg 263 *VL³* 146,10 und Vatikan 346 *VL³* 146,16.

Rollen- und Kleidertausch ist erst in der hellenistischen Zeit aufgekommen."[116]

Die Vase aber gehört der Mitte des 6. Jh. an, ist also mehr als zwei Jahrhunderte älter. Tatsächlich kannten wir bisher keine einzige attische Vase mit Omphale, weder archaisch, noch klassisch, noch spätklassisch. Auch ausserhalb Attikas ist vor der spätklassischen Zeit kein Gefäss mit Omphale bekannt.

Doch sehen wir weiter, was auf dem Gefäss dargestellt ist. Da die rechte Schulter der Omphale so überaus stark gegenüber der linken erhoben ist, ist denkbar, dass der verlorene rechte Arm nach oben geführt war, vielleicht um einen dritten Pfeil aus dem Köcher zu holen. Der Rest eines Gegenstandes dicht unter dem oberen Bildrand—am Fragmentkomplex mit den Reitern unten links—könnte die senkrecht offenstehende Klappe eines Köchers[117] sein.

Vor Omphale steht, mit dem Rücken zu ihr, ein Mann in langem rotem Gewand und weissem Untergewand. Er ist barfuss, der Oberkörper ist verloren. Wohl aber ist der rechte herabhängende Unterarm erhalten, der ein Plektron hält, das an einer schwarzen Schnur hängt. Es handelt sich also um den Spieler eines Saiteninstrumentes. Vor seinem Unterkörper hängt ein mit geritzten Kreuzen versehenes Tuch herab. Dieses Tuch, welches in Bildern von Kitharen oft herabhängt, aber nicht bei Leiern, lehrt uns, dass der Mann in der Linken eine Kithara trug.

Vor ihm sitzt eine Frau. Der rechte erhobene weisse Unterarm, die weisse linke Hand und die weissen Füsse mit dem Rest des Sandalengeflechts wie bei Omphale sind erhalten. Deutlich ist die schräge Linie des Oberschenkels. Sie trägt einen karierten Peplos. Unter ihrem linken Ellbogen ist gerade noch der Rest eines nach rechts gewandten Kinderkopfes erhalten.

Hinter Omphale befinden sich die Enden von zwei Stuhlbeinen. Wenn Herakles dargestellt war, dann muss er entweder hinter Omphale auf diesem Stuhl gesessen haben, oder er muss in dem Kitharaspieler gemeint sein.

Die Rückseite verhilft nicht zu einer Deutung, denn sie hat ein anderes Thema, nämlich einen Zug von mindestens fünf nach links ziehenden Kriegern.

Auf der Schulter sind über der Omphaleszene mindestens drei Reiter nach rechts mit sinnlosen Inschriften.

Ueber der anderen Seite ist ein Rennen von mindestens zwei Viergespannen nach rechts, am rechten Ende ein stehender Mann und ein Siegesdreifuss wiedergegeben. Unter dem Hauptbild ist ein Tierfries: Hahn, Panther, Schaf, Hahn und Löwe sind auf der Vorderseite zu erkennen, auf der Rückseite Panther und Schaf.

Das Bild, zweihundert Jahre älter als die älteste bisher bekannte Omphaledarstellung der Vasenmalerei, ist aufregend und gibt Rätsel auf.

Die bisher bekannten Bilder von Herakles bei Omphale[118] zeigen ihn in weiblicher Tracht mit der Spindel in der Hand oder trunken, jedenfalls nicht als Kitharaspieler. Sie tragen nichts zur Deutung des Amphorenbildes bei.

In der antiken Literatur sind die Zeugnisse des Diodor (IV 31) und Apollodor (*Bibl.* II 6,3) die ausführlichsten. Beide Autoren berichten übereinstimmend, dass dem Herakles ein Orakel weissagte, er werde von seiner Krankheit geheilt werden, wenn er sich als Sklave verkaufen liesse. So kam er in die Dienste der Omphale nach Lydien. Dort nahm er die Kerkopen fest und tötete den Syleus, der die Vorbeigehenden gezwungen hatte, Weinstöcke auszugraben. Nach dem Dienst bei Omphale zog er gegen Ilion.

Diodor berichtet darüberhinaus, dass er die Stadt der räuberischen Itoner zerstörte, dass ihm Omphale die Freiheit gab und ihm den Sohn Lamos gebar.

Apollodor erzählt ferner, dass er den Leichnam des Ikaros, der auf Doliche angespült wurde, bestattete und die Insel Ikaria nannte. Während seines Dienstes bei Omphale habe der Argonautenzug, die kalydonische Eberjagd und des Theseus Zug von Troizen nach Athen stattgefunden.[119] Nach Sophokles (*Trach.* 247ff.) hat der Aufenthalt bei Omphale ein Jahr gedauert, nach Herodor (Schol. Soph. *Trach.* 253) drei Jahre. Von dem Sohn Lamos berichtet auch Ovid (*Her.* IX 55). Nach Lukian (*Dial. deor.* XIII 2) hat Herakles bei Omphale Wolle gekämmt, einen Weiberrock getragen und wurde von Omphale mit einer Sandale geschlagen. Von der Sandale berichtet der gleiche Schriftsteller auch an anderem Ort (*Quomodo hist. scrib.* 10). Von seiner Wollarbeit berichten auch Ovid (*Her.* IX 75), Statius (*Theb.* X 646-649) und Seneca (*Her. Oet.* 371ff.). Nach Hygin (*Poet. astr.* II 74) hat Herakles in Lydien beim Fluss

113. Malibu acc. no. 77.AE.45. Von J. Frel der Group E zugeschrieben mit überzeugendem Hinweis auf München 1471 (J.476) Halsamphora CVA (7) 347,1; *ABV* 137,60; *Tübinger Studien* 4 Taf. 25: Waffenläufer.

114. Zum Fuss: Brit.Mus. B 295 Halsamphora *ABV* 226,1.

115. J. Sieveking, Roschers ML III 1, 887.

116. C. Robert, *Die griech.Heldensage* II (1921) 594. Demgegenüber hat K. Schauenburg, RhM 103 (1960) 62,64 auf eine vorhellenistische Münze von Phokaia hingewiesen, die den Kopf der Omphale im Löwenfell wiedergibt. Dazu *Ephem.* 1899 Taf. 4.

117. Zur Köcherklappe: London B 167 pan. Amphora CVA GrBr 154,1; *ABV* 382, 1 u.; Louvre F 272 Halsamphora CVA 56,4; Toledo,

Ohio 1958.69 pan. Amphora VL³ 76,12. Napf Malibu acc. no. S.80.AE. 24 (= Bareiss 125) (hier unter Herakles-Athene).

118. VL³ 174ff.; DL I 127ff.

119. E. Suhr, *AJA* 57 (1953) 252 stellt dies fälschlich so dar, als ob Herakles während dieser Zeit am Argonautenzug und der kalydonischen Eberjagd teilgenommen hat. Auch er meint a.O. 251 "Except for its (sc., legend of Herakles and Omphale) appearance in literature, especially in comedies, it was completely ignored until Hellenistic and Roman times."

Abb. 34. Fragmentierte attisch-schwarzfigurige Amphora. Malibu, The J. Paul Getty Museum 77.AE.45. Diam. von Boden: 15.0 cm.

Saganis eine Schlange erlegt, die viele Menschen getötet hatte. Nach Pherekydes (Schol. Homer *Od.* 21, 22) hat Hermes den Herakles für drei Talente verkauft. Dass Herakles von Hermes verkauft wurde, berichtet auch Hygin (*Fab.* 32). Nach Plutarch (*Quaest. graec.* 45) hat Herakles der Omphale das Beil geschenkt, das er der Hippolyte abgenommen hat.

Der früheste Autor, der über Omphale berichtet, ist Pherekydes. Mit ihm kommen wir in das frühe 5. Jh. v.Chr., also später als in die Zeit unserer Vase. Leider wissen wir nur zu wenig über seine Kenntnis der Sage. Mit Sophokles, ein halbes Jahrhundert später, ist es nicht viel besser. Die Kerkopensage ist jedenfalls für das 6. Jh. und zwar mehrfach belegt. Wenn sie damals schon mit dem Dienst bei Omphale verbunden war, wäre dies ein weiterer Hinweis für die Kenntnis der Omphalesage im 6. Jh. Aber schon das Zeugnis des Pherekydes allein genügt hierfür.[120] Insofern ist also die Amphora in Malibu nicht überraschend. Wir hatten es in der Omphalesage mit einer der wenigen griechischen Sagen zu tun, bei denen bisher die literarische Ueberlieferung in frühere Zeit hinaufreichte, als die bildliche. Nun ist es umgekehrt.

Aber das Bild gibt trotz Untersuchung der übrigen bildlichen und schriftstellerischen Darstellungen der Sage noch immer Rätsel auf. Was beabsichtigt Omphale mit den bereitgehaltenen Pfeilen zu tun? Warum holt sie wahrscheinlich einen dritten Pfeil aus dem Köcher? Thronende pflegen doch nicht zu schiessen. Wo ist Herakles? Wer ist die sitzende Frau? Wer ist der Kitharaspieler? Ist in dem Kind Lamos zu sehen? Wir wissen es nicht.

Fragen über Fragen tauchen auf, aber unsere bisherige Kenntnis der Sage reicht nicht aus, sie zu beantworten. Wir müssen auf neue Funde hoffen, wie es die Vase selbst einer ist.

HERAKLES UND PHILOKTET

Die Deutung und Meisterzuschreibung der Bruchstücke eines herrlichen und einzigartigen Kelchkraters des Achilleusmalers[121] hat J. Frel gefunden (Abb. 35a–c). Auf der Vorderseite sind drei Gestalten wiedergegeben: In der Mitte die waffenlose Athena mit Aegis, aber ohne Helm, Schild und Lanze. Sie trägt auf dem Haupt ein Diadem und weiteren Schmuck im Ohr und am rechten Unterarm. Ihr langes Gewand ist unten mit einem Tierfries und einem Palmettenfries geziert. Rechts von ihr steht der bärtige Herakles, der an seinem Kräuselhaar und der Keule in seiner Linken kenntlich ist. Er trägt eine Binde im Haar und ein über die linke Schulter geschlagenes Gewand,

Abb. 35a. Fragmentierter attisch-rotfiguriger Kelchkrater. Malibu, The J. Paul Getty Museum 77.AE.44.1. Diam.: 59 cm.

aber kein Löwenfell. Links steht ein behelmter und gerüsteter Krieger, der in der Linken Schild und Lanze hält. Er trägt Beinschienen und Sandalen. Athena, die zu ihm hinblickt, reicht ihm mit der Rechten einen Köcher, der eigentlich nicht zu seiner Hoplitenausrüstung gehört, vielmehr zusätzlich dazukommt. Der Köcher kann nur von Herakles stammen. Sicher hielt sie in der Linken den Bogen, den sie von Herakles übernommen hatte, um ihn weiterzureichen. Damit ist die Deutung des Kriegers gegeben. Es handelt sich um Philoktet, der dem Herakles den Scheiterhaufen für dessen Flammentod errichtete und zum Dank dafür oder für das Anzünden von ihm seinen Bogen und die Pfeile erhielt, wie viele antike Autoren berichten. Das früheste Zeugnis, aus dem sich schliessen lässt dass Philoktet die Waffen von Herakles erhalten hat, findet sich im Vers 262 des Sophokleischen *Philoktet*, der 409 v.Chr. aufgeführt wurde.[122] Unser Vasenbild ist vier Jahrzehnte früher entstanden und ist somit der früheste überhaupt bekannte Beleg für die Uebergabe der Waffen des Herakles an Philoktet. Die Vase ist ferner der bisher einzige Beleg dafür, dass die Uebergabe durch die Vermittlung der Athena erfolgt ist. Die zahlreichen literarischen Stellen berichten nichts davon.

Auf der schlechter erhaltenen Rückseite stehen sich ein Krieger mit Helm und Lanze und ein wie Herakles auf der Vorderseite gekleideter Mann gegenüber. Vielleicht handelt es sich wieder um Herakles und Philoktet.

---

120. Vgl. Schauenburg, *RhM* 103 (1960) 57 Anm. 6: "Da die lydischen Herrscherhäuser sich von Herakles und Omphale ableiteten, muss die Sage schon im 6. Jh. in Lydien verbreitet gewesen sein."

121. Malibu acc. no. 77.AE.44.1.
122. Vgl. Bakchylides fr.7.

Abb. 35b. Athena. Malibu 77.AE.44.1.

Abb. 35c. Herakles. Malibu 77.AE.44.1.

Es gab bisher nur wenige Vasen, auf denen Herakles mit Philoktet dargestellt ist:[123] Eine Schale in New York, die um 490 v.Chr. entstanden und somit die früheste attische Darstellung des Philoktet ist, gibt ihn als Knappen des Herakles wieder, wie dies in der antiken Literatur erst mehr als sechs Jahrhunderte später überliefert ist.[124] Ein Krater in S. Agata dei Goti aus dem Anfang des 4. Jh. v.Chr. zeigt Philoktet bei der Himmelfahrt des Herakles, aber ohne Bogen, Köcher und Pfeile.

Es fällt auf, dass nur eine einzige Darstellung von Philoktet aus der unteritalischen Vasenmalerei erhalten ist.[125] Das ist überraschend angesichts der antiken Nachrichten, dass der Held in Unteritalien gestorben sei.[126] Hingegen gibt es bemerkenswert viele Gemmen[127] mit Philoktet.

Das Thema der Vase in Malibu ist singulär in der antiken Kunst. Der Achilleusmaler hat in seinem reichen Werk Philoktet nicht wieder dargestellt und Herakles auffallend selten. Für dieses Bild muss ein besonderer, uns noch unbekannter Anlass vorgelegen haben. Alle drei grossen Tragiker haben das Philoktet-Thema gestaltet. Aber auch das Drama des Euripides, das 431 v.Chr. aufgeführt wurde, ist erst beträchtliche Zeit nach dem Vasenbild entstanden.

HERAKLES UND PHOLOS

Auf seinem Weg zum erymanthischen Eber kehrte Herakles bei dem Kentauren Pholos ein, nach dem das Pholosgebirge benannt ist. Dieser öffnete ein Weinfass für seinen Gast. Von dem Duft angelockt kamen andere Kentauren, um Wein zu rauben. Sie griffen mit Fichten, Steinen, brennenden Fackeln und Beilen an. Herakles tötete die meisten und trieb den Rest in die Flucht. So berichtet Diodor die Sage. Apollodor erzählt sie ganz ähnlich und fügt noch hinzu, dass Pholos in einer Höhle wohnte.[128]

Die früheste Darstellung der Sage befindet sich auf einem korinthischen Skyphos aus dem ersten Viertel des 6. Jh. v.Chr.[129] Die attischen Vasenbilder setzen erst um 530 v.Chr. ein, also ein halbes Jahrhundert später, dann aber in grosser Zahl—etwa 100 sind erhalten—während die ausserattischen Bilder spärlich bleiben. Die attischen Vasenbilder reichen bis in das zweite Viertel des 5. Jh. v.Chr., erstrecken sich also über einen Zeitraum von 60 bis 70 Jahren. In diesen Zeitraum gehört auch die Halsamphora in Malibu (Abb. 36a, b).[130] Herakles mit rotem

Bart, rotem Kopfband, mit Panzer, den er hier auffallenderweise trägt,[131] und Schwert an weissem Band, mit einem rot gepunkteten Mantel über dem Panzer, aber ohne Löwenfell hält in der Rechten die Keule und hat mit der Linken einen Kentauren gepackt, der mit einem weiss gepunkteten Fell bekleidet und mit einem Ast bewaffnet ist. Er steht hinter dem in den Boden eingelassenen Fass und blickt zu Herakles zurück und streckt ihm dabei abwehrend die Linke entgegen. Die Höhle und Trinkgefässe sind nicht wiedergegeben. Zwischen den Füssen des Herakles liegt ein Stein, sicher eine Waffe des Kentauren. Die Darstellung setzt sich auf der anderen Seite des Gefässes fort. Ein Baum bezeichnet die freie Natur. Vor ihm sind zwei Kentauren, die beide in der Rechten einen Ast halten. Der vordere wendet sich zu dem anderen um und gebietet mit der Linken Halt. Der hintere trägt auf dem linken Arm ein Fell, wie einen Schild. Offensichtlich ist der Kampf ganz an seinem Anfang dargestellt. Die Kentauren sind gerade erst dabei heranzukommen.

Unter den Bildern ziehen sich fünf dicke Ringe um das Gefäss. In dieselbe Zeit, oder etwas später, um 510 v.Chr., gehört eine schwarzfigurige Lekythos (Abb. 37).[132] In der Bildmitte ist ein Weinfass in den Boden eingelassen, rechts und links steht je ein zur Mitte gewandter Kentaur. Der linke ist bekleidet und hält einen Ast über der linken Schulter. Ueber dem Fass befindet sich ein Kantharos. Ganz links oben ist eine Höhle angedeutet. Der Fuss des Gefässes ist ergänzt, ebenso beim rechten Kentaur drei Unterschenkel, dazu ein unbemaltes Stück hinter dem linken Kentaur, wohl auch dessen zu langer Pferdeschweif.

Herakles ist nicht dargestellt. Das Bild liess sich ohne ihn symmetrischer gestalten und so ist es auch noch auf weiteren Lekythen[133] geschehen.

THESEUS UND ATHENA

Auf der fragmentierten rotfigurigen Hydria[134] steht links Athena (Abb. 38). Sie hält in der einen Hand den Helm, in der anderen, ebenfalls verlorenen, die Lanze. Ihr Gewand ist am Oberkörper mit senkrechten Streifen aus verdünntem Glanzton geziert, auf dem Unterkörper mit Punktsternen. Der unterste Teil des Unterkörpers ist ergänzt, aber die Zehenspitzen sind antik. Sie trägt die Aegis, darüber einen Mantel und auf dem Haupt ein Blattdiadem. Ihr gegenüber steht ein Jüngling in gegürtetem Chiton und Mantel. Er trägt den Petasos im Nacken und hat

123. New York 12.231.2 Schale *ARV*² 319,6; S. Agata dei Goti Krater *ARV*² 1420,5. New York 52.11.18 Kelchkrater, *AJA* 66 (1962) 305, Taf. 81 und Psykter Privatbesitz (Guy in *Lissarrague-thelamon, image et céramique und reliefvasenfr. déchelette, vas. cér.* II 167 Nr. 60.

124. Philostrat, *Her.*, p. 171 (Kayser).

125. *VL*³ 463 D 1.

126. H.H. Schmitt in *Bonner Festgabe J. Straub* (1977) 55–66.

127. *DL* III 469ff.

128. Diod.Sic. IV 12,3; Apollodor *Bibl.* II 5,4. Zur Sage: B. Schiffler, *Die Typologie des Kentauren* (1970) 37–41.

129. *VL*³ 182 C 1.

130. Sammlung Bareiss 134, Leihgabe, Malibu S.80.AE.65. K. Schauenburg, *Aachener Kunstblätter* 44 (1973) 32 Abb. 44, 45. Von D.v. Bothmer der Group of Würzburg 221 zugeschrieben. Keule beim

Abb. 36a. Attisch-schwarzfigurige Halsamphora. Seite A.
Sammlung Bareiss 134, Leihgabe im J. Paul
Getty Museum S.80.AE.65. H: 41.3 cm.

Abb. 36b. Bareiss 134. Seite B.

ein Schwert umgegürtet. In der Linken hält er zwei Speere.
Im Haar trägt er eine Binde. Er wendet sich nach rechts
zum Abschied und blickt zu Athena zurück.

    D. von Bothmer hat die Vase dem Berliner Maler zuge-
schrieben, C. Burke und Beazley haben sich angeschlossen. Alle drei haben den Jüngling nicht benannt, wenn
auch C. Burke es für möglich hielt, dass es sich um Theseus handelt. Sie meinte, Athena böte ihm den Helm als
Schutz an und er griffe nach ihm.

    Es kann wohl kein Zweifel daran bestehen, dass es sich
bei dem Jüngling um Theseus handelt. Es ist sicher sein
Aufbrechen zu der Wanderung nach Athen gemeint, auf

der er immer in der hier dargestellten Ausrüstung erscheint. Die Göttin ist mit Theseus zwar nicht so oft dargestellt worden, wie mit Herakles, aber doch mehrfach.[135]
Es kann jedoch keine Rede davon sein, dass sie ihm ihren
Helm anbietet. Dafür haben wir kein Beispiel, auch trägt
Theseus hier schon den Petasos, ferner hat er überhaupt
nur sehr selten einen Helm.[136] Schliesslich fasst seine
Rechte gar nicht nach dem Helm, sondern sie ist weit unter ihm zum Abschiedsgruss ausgestreckt. Athena wohnt
einfach helmhaltend seinem Abschied bei, so wie sie,
ebenfalls helmhaltend, anderen Szenen beiwohnt.[137] Die
Vase ist 480/70 v.Chr. gemalt worden.

Pholoskampf auch. *VL*³ 179, 10.
  131. Zu Herakles im Panzer: K. Schauenburg, *AA* 1971, 174f. Anm.
68.
  132. Sammlung Bareiss 107, Leihgabe, Malibu S.80.AE.19, von D.v.
Bothmer dem Gelamaler zugeschrieben. *Greek Vases in the J. Paul Getty
Museum* 1, OPA 1, 65.
  133. *VL*³ 180 A a 1–3, dazu 4. Hamburg 1952,143; *CVA* (1) 32,1–3.

  134. Sammlung Bareiss 29, Leihgabe, Malibu S.80.AE.185 D. v. Bothmer (L 69.11.25); Burke-Pollitt, *Vases at Yale* Nr. 47; Beazley, *Para*
345,183. Zu Theseus allgemein: F. Brommer, *Theseus, Die Taten des
Helden in der antiken Kunst und Literatur* (1982).
  135. *VL*³ 219. Zu Theseus und Athena: J. Boardman, *JHS* 95 (1975) 2f.
  136. Zu Theseus mit Helm: Verf., *AM* 97 (1982).
  137. Beim Stierkampf des Theseus: Brüssel R 303 Spitzamphora *ARV*²

Abb. 37. Attisch-schwarzfigurige Lekythos. Sammlung
Bareiss 107, Leihgabe im J. Paul Getty Museum
S.80.AE.19. H: 23.2 cm.

THESEUS UND KENTAUREN

Auf der rotfigurigen bauchigen Lekythos,[138] die etwa im
letzten Jahrzehnt des 5. Jh. v.Chr. (Abb. 39) in Athen geschaffen worden sein mag, hält ein bärtiger, nach rechts
gewandter Kentaur über dem linken Arm ein Fell wie
einen Schild zum Schutz. In der rechten, nach hinten aus-
holenden Hand schwingt er den Oberteil eines zer-
brochenen Kruges.

Zweifellos handelt es sich um einen Auszug aus der bekannten Sage vom Streit der Lapithen mit den Kentauren,
der bei der Hochzeit des Peirithoos, des Freundes von
Theseus, ausbrach. Bei diesem Streit werden oft Gefässe
von den Kentauren als Waffen verwendet.

Der Kentaurenkampf des Theseus wurde schon im zweiten Viertel des 6. Jh. v.Chr. dargestellt.[139] Aber da handelt es sich um eine Feldschlacht mit gerüsteten Kriegern.
Der andere Kentaurenkampf, der hier gemeint ist und der
im Saal ausbrach, wobei man Behelfswaffen verwandte, ist
erst ein halbes Jahrhundert vor diesem Vasenbild aufgekommen und hat nicht viele Darstellungen in der attischen Vasenmalerei gefunden. Dieses Bild ist eins der letzten Attikas.

THESEUS UND MINOS

In der Bildmitte[140] sitzt ein weisshaariger und -bärtiger
König, dessen Zepter zwischen seinen Beinen steht und
von der linken Hand gehalten gedacht ist (Abb. 40). Der
König ist, wie alle neun Gestalten des Bildes, bekränzt. Er
trägt Hosen oder hohe Stiefel und ein Gewand mit langen
Aermeln. Er sitzt auf seinem Mantel und blickt nach links
zu einem vor ihm stehenden Mädchen, das barfuss ist, wie
alle Gestalten ausser dem König. Mit der Linken zieht sie
einen Gewandzipfel von der Schulter in einer koketten
Geste, wie sie seit dem letzten Viertel des 5. Jh. v.Chr. in
der Vasenmalerei oft beobachtet werden kann. Sie trägt,
wie auch die übrigen Mädchen, ein ärmelloses Gewand
und an beiden Armen und am Hals Schmuck. In der
rechten Hand hält sie etwas Weisses, vielleicht ein Ei. Sie
blickt zu dem König hin. Beide Gestalten werden durch je
eine sitzende weibliche Gestalt eingerahmt, die zur Bildmitte hinblicken. Die linke lüpft einen Gewandzipfel und
die rechte—die Partie ist da nicht ganz erhalten—tat es
wohl auch. Bei der rechten ist auch das Gesicht verloren.
Unter dieser rechten sitzt ein viertes nach unten blicken-
des Mädchen, rechts entfernt sich ein fünftes Mädchen
und blickt sich um. Unter der Mitte zwischen König und
stehendem Mädchen sitzt ein unbekleideter Jüngling auf

249,6. Bei Erichthonios: Brit. Mus. E 372 Pelike *ARV²* 1218,1.

138. Malibu acc. no. 71.AE.216.

139. Florenz 4209 Krater des Klitias *ABV* 76,1; Baltimore, WAG
48.198 Exaleiptron. Verf., *JWalt* 38 (1980) 108–112. Zu Theseus im Ken-

Abb. 38. Fragmentierte attisch-rotfigurige Hydria. Sammlung Bareiss 29, Leihgabe im J. Paul Getty Museum S.80.AE.185. H: 21 cm.

seinem Mantel. Er hält in der Rechten eine Keule und blickt zu einem links sitzenden Jüngling, der mit einem Himation bekleidet ist und einen Petasos im Nacken hat. Ueber ihm steht am linken Bildrand nach rechts gewandt ein weiterer Jüngling im Himation. Einen Anhalt zur Deutung liefert die Keule. Ihretwegen kann in dem unbekleideten Jüngling nur Herakles oder Theseus gemeint sein. Das jugendliche Alter des Helden, der wenig athletische Körperbau, das Fehlen des Kräuselhaares und des Löwenfelles sprechen gegen Herakles und für Theseus.[141]

Aber wer ist der König? Mit drei Königen hatte Theseus zu tun: Mit Pittheus, Aigeus und Minos. Bei den beiden

ersten sind die anwesenden Mädchen nicht zu verstehen, bei Pittheus hatte zudem Theseus auch seine Keule noch nicht. Also Minos? Dann könnte die neben ihm stehende Frau Ariadne sein und die übrigen Gestalten könnten die attischen Jünglinge und Mädchen sein. Dass es nicht vierzehn sind, überrascht nicht. Diese Zahl wird in der Bildkunst kaum genau wiedergegeben.[142] Es kann ein Augenblick vor dem Kampf oder nach dem Sieg gemeint sein. Wahrscheinlich ist das Letztere. Die Bekränzung spricht dafür, auch hätte es nicht viel Sinn, einen Augenblick vor dem Kampf wiederzugeben. Allerdings fehlen sowohl eine Nike, wie der tote Minotauros. Ein Augenblick

taurenkampf: Brommer, *Theseus* 104ff.

140. Malibu acc. no. 71.AE.254; erwähnt *AA* 1982, 80. Auf der Rückseite Mänade zwischen zwei Bärtigen.

141. Zum sitzenden Theseus mit Keule: Adolphseck, Kelchkrater

CVA 49. Brommer, *Theseus* Taf. 45.

142. Zur Zahl der attischen Jünglinge und Mädchen: Verf., *AA* 1982, 79ff.

Abb. 39. Attisch-rotfigurige bauchige Lekythos. Malibu,
The J. Paul Getty Museum 71.AE.216. H der
Figur: 6.1 cm.

gabe ist in einem sehr geläufigen Schema[146] erfolgt. Theseus greift von links her an, der Minotauros sucht nach
rechts zu entkommen und blickt zurück, dabei hält er in
der erhobenen linken Hand einen Stein. Theseus hat ihn
mit der Linken an einem Horn gepackt und bedroht ihn
mit dem Schwert in der Rechten. Das Besondere dieses
Bildes ist, dass der Minotauros, obwohl er im Knielauf-
schema wiedergegeben ist, die gleiche Grösse hat wie Theseus. Aber auch dafür gibt es Parallelen.[147] Eingerahmt ist
die Szene durch zwei Manteljünglinge, von denen der
rechte einen Kranz hält.

Ungefähr gleichzeitig mit der Pyxis ist eine fragmentierte
Amphora entstanden,[148] auf deren einer Seite ein Krieger
dabei ist, eine Beinschiene anzulegen. Eingerahmt wird er
auf jeder Seite von je zwei Gestalten. Auf der anderen
Seite ist Theseus im Minotauroskampf dargestellt (Abb.
42). Das Ungeheuer ist auf sein rechtes Knie gesunken
und blutet bereits aus dem Rücken. Es ist dem Theseus
zugewandt und hält den linken Arm hoch. Theseus hat es
mit der Linken am linken Unterarm gepackt und setzt
ihm mit der Rechten das Schwert, dessen Spitze gerade
noch erhalten ist, auf die Brust. Der Held ist mit einem
kurzen Gewand bekleidet, das bis zur Mitte der Oberschenkel reicht. Eingerahmt ist das Bild rechts von einer
Frau im Peplos, die ihre Rechte ohne Attribut ausstreckt,
und einem unbekleideten männlichen Wesen. Ganz am
linken Rand ist wieder ein unbekleidetes männliches Wesen zu sehen. In der Lücke zwischen ihm und Theseus be-
fand sich vielleicht wieder eine Frau. Vom Gefäss fehlen
ausserdem der Fuss bis zur Mitte des Strahlenkranzes,
sowie der Hals und die Mündung mit dem oberen Teil des
Bildfeldes, dabei sämtlichen Köpfen auf beiden Seiten bis
auf einen.

Auch dieser Bildtyp mit dem auf das Knie gesunkenen
und dem Helden zugewandten Minotauros ist überaus
häufig vertreten. Ueber einhundert attisch-schwarzfigurige
Vasen dieses Bildtyps sind bekannt. Dabei kommt es auch
häufig vor, dass Theseus den Minotauros, wie hier am linken Arm gepackt hat.[149] Meist hält Minotauros in diesem
einen Stein. So mag es auch hier gewesen sein. Die Inschrift hinter Minotauros—es ist die einzige, die sich auf
dem Gefäss erhalten hat—ist sinnlos. Das Gefäss wird in
der Mitte des 6. Jh. v.Chr. entstanden sein.

Die rotfigurige Pelike[150] wurde nach Kunsthandelsanga-
ben in Sizilien gefunden (Abb. 43). Der Glanzton deckt
sehr schlecht, der zum Vorschein kommende Ton ist gelb-

nach dem Kampf, nach der Erlegung des Ungeheuers ist
schon seit der archaischen Zeit dargestellt worden, wenn
auch selten.[143]

Das Besondere dieses Bildes, das etwa um 370 v.Chr. in
Athen gemalt wurde, ist, dass jeder Hinweis auf Minotauros fehlt. Insofern ist das Bild singulär. Da der Maler
zwar gut, aber nicht sehr gut ist, hat er kaum den Gedan-
ken zu der Komposition aus sich selbst geschöpft. Er muss
seine Anregung sich irgendwo geholt haben. Die bunte
Tracht des Königs weist auf das Theater. Von dort könnte
die Anregung zu dem einzigartigen Bild kommen.

THESEUS UND MINOTAUROS

Die attisch-schwarzfigurige Pyxis[144] wurde bereits bei
Herakles und dem Löwen behandelt, dem Thema eines
ihrer drei Beine (Abb. 41). Auf dem zweiten Bein ist der
Kampf zwischen Theseus und dem Minotauros wiedergegeben, ein Thema, das in der attischen Vasenmalerei archaischer Zeit ausserordentlich beliebt war.[145] Die Wieder-

143. Toter Minotauros: VL³ 240,46; 241,74.

144. Sammlung Bareiss 433, Leihgabe, Malibu S.80.AE.322. Hier
S.122 und Anm.90, VL³ 231,70. Zum Thema: Brommer, *Theseus* 35ff.

145. Ueber 320 attisch-schwarzfigurige Vasenbilder des Themas sind
bekannt.

146. VL³ 228 A b.

147. VL³ 229,21; 230,42.

148. Sammlung Bareiss 364, Leihgabe, Malibu S.80.AE.224.

149. VL³ 231 A c, dabei Minotauros am linken Arm gepackt: 2, 3, 26,
35, 37, 38, 39, 44, 56, 69, 70 und Christie 10.VII.1974 Nr. 113.

150. Malibu acc. no. 76.AE.19.

Abb. 40. Attisch-rotfiguriger Krater. Malibu, The J. Paul Getty Museum 71.AE.254. H: 36.9 cm.

Abb. 41. Attisch-schwarzfigurige Dreifusspyxis. Sammlung Bareiss 433, Leihgabe im J. Paul Getty Museum S.80.AE.322. H: 8.5 cm.

Abb. 42. Fragmentierte attisch-schwarzfigurige Halsamphora. Sammlung Bareiss 364, Leihgabe im J. Paul Getty Museum S.80.AE.224.
H: 20.1 cm.

Abb. 43. Rotfigurige Pelike. Malibu, The J. Paul Getty Museum 76.AE.19. H: 22 cm.

Abb. 44. Attisch-rotfigurige Pelike. Sammlung Bareiss 347, Leihgabe im J. Paul Getty Museum S.80.AE.235. H: 36 cm.

braun, aber bei den Figuren rot grundiert. Auch die Töpferarbeit ist nicht sehr gut. Die Mündung verläuft unregelmässig. Es handelt sich um eine provinzielle Arbeit. Das häufige Thema des Kampfes zwischen Theseus und Minotauros ist auf eigenwillige Weise gestaltet. Theseus greift ungewöhnlicherweise von rechts her an.[151] Ferner fällt auf, dass er das Schwert in der Linken hält. Das Bild wirkt, als hätte der Maler ein Vorbild spiegelbildlich kopiert. Theseus fasst mit der Rechten zum Hals des Ungeheuers. Am Oberkörper des Helden sind scharf eingeritzte Vorzeichnungen zu sehen. Das Horn des Minotauros ist teilweise von Glanzton übermalt, der Kopf ist ziemlich misslungen. Auf der anderen Seite der Vase ist eine andere Theseustat, der Kampf mit Sinis wiedergegeben. Die Vase ist etwa im Jahrzehnt 460–50 v.Chr. entstanden.

THESEUS UND POSEIDON

Die rotfigurige Pelike mit dem sitzenden Poseidon[152] ist

dem Triptolemosmaler zugeschrieben worden und in die Zeit von 480/70 v.Chr. datiert worden (Abb. 44). Der bärtige Gott, am Dreizack in seiner Linken leicht kenntlich, ist mit langem Chiton und Himation bekleidet. Er sitzt nach rechts gewandt auf einem Block, der die Inschrift ΚΑΛΟΣ trägt. Er ist umgeben von einem stehenden Jüngling links und einem stehenden Bärtigen rechts. Beide sind mit kurzem Chiton und Chlamys bekleidet, halten in der Linken je zwei Speere, haben ein Schwert umgehängt und tragen einen Petasos auf dem Kopf. Der Bärtige ist barfuss, der Jugendliche trägt Stiefel und fast bis zum Knie reichende Strümpfe. Genauso wie er ist sehr oft Theseus dargestellt. Da Poseidon sein göttlicher Vater ist, gibt die Gruppierung einen Sinn. Doch wer ist der bärtige Petasosträger? Schauenburg und von Bothmer dachten an Aigeus, Schefold und Beazley an Peirithoos.

Tatsächlich wird weder Aigeus, noch sonst ein attischer König jemals mit dem Petasos auf dem Haupt wiedergegeben. Es kann sich also nicht um den menschlichen Vater

151. VL³ 235,19; 236,28; 239,15.16.

152. Sammlung Bareiss 347, Leihgabe, Malibu S.80.AE.235 (und früher

Abb. 45. Rotfigurige Pelike. Einzelheit. Malibu, The J. Paul Getty Museum 76.AE.19.

Abb. 46. Fragmentierte rotfigurige Schale. Sammlung Bareiss 1D, Leihgabe im J. Paul Getty Museum S.80.AE.268. Grösste Breite: 21.5 cm.

des Theseus, sondern muss sich um einen seiner Gefährten handeln.

Sowohl Peirithoos, wie sein anderer Gefährte, Phorbas, werden meist bärtig wiedergegeben. Aber welcher Augenblick ist gemeint? Wir wissen, dass Theseus zweimal seinen göttlichen Vater um Hilfe bat. Einmal auf der Fahrt nach Kreta wegen des Ringes des Minos.[153] Damals begab sich Theseus in das Meer in den Palast seines Vaters. Gewiss war er dabei nicht mit Petasos und Speeren versehen, war auch allein. Diese Begegnung kann also nicht gemeint sein. Das zweite Mal bat Theseus seinen Vater um die

Bestrafung des Hippolytos. Auch das wird hier nicht gemeint sein. Es gibt einige wenige Vasenbilder[154]—sie sind alle attisch-rotfigurig—die Theseus bei Poseidon wiedergeben. Ein besonderer Grund für das Zusammentreffen ist meist nicht zu erkennen. So ist es auch hier. Eine literarische Nachricht, die uns Aufschluss geben könnte, ist jedenfalls nicht erhalten.

THESEUS UND SINIS

Die hier schon unter "Theseus und Minotauros" behandelte rotfigurige Pelike[155] stellt auf der anderen Seite eine

New York L 68.142.20); K. Schauenburg in *Weltkunst in Privatbesitz* (Köln 1968) A 36: 480/70; K. Schefold, *AntK* 11 (1968) 118; D. v. Bothmer, *Bareiss* Nr. 42: 470 v.Chr.; Beazley, *Para* 364,21 bis. Auf der Rückseite überreicht ein Mann einem Jüngling einen Hasen. Zwischen beiden ein Hund. Beide Bilder sind nicht gerahmt.

153. Brommer, *Theseus* 77ff. ebenda 140f. zu Theseus und Poseidon.
154. *VL³* 244f.
155. Malibu acc. no. 76.AE.19. Zum Sinisthema: Brommer, *Theseus*

6ff.

156. *VL³* 250,30; Brommer, *Theseus* Taf. 38.
157. Plaoutine, *JHS* 57 (1937) 22ff.; Musée Rodin *CVA* 28–30; Beazley, *EVP* Taf. 4, kopiert nach *ARV²* 451,1.
158. Lullies, *AM* 65 (1940) 1ff.
159. B. Shefton, *WissZeitschrift Rostock* 16 (1967) 529ff. Taf.86/7 Stamnos in Vich, kopiert nach Spitzamphora Cab. med. 357 *ARV²* 987,2, also auch unter Wechsel der Gefässform, wie bei dem Sinisbeispiel.

weitere Theseustat dar, nämlich den Kampf gegen Sinis (Abb. 45).

Die Körper der beiden Gegner sind unproportioniert: Der rechte Fuss des Theseus ist riesig, der linke verkümmert. Die rechte Hand des Sinis ist ebenfalls sehr gross, sein Auge misslungen. Der Körper des Theseus hat reiche Innenzeichnung in verdünntem Glanzton mit etwas wirrer Muskulatur. Die Rückenlinien des Sinis gehen über den Bruch hinüber, sie sind also mindestens teilweise nachgezogen. Dies gilt auch für den Theseus derselben Seite. Sinis hält in der Linken einen Stein, ist also Linkshänder wie Theseus auf der anderen Seite der Vase. Beim Baum waren die Blätter weiss gemalt.

Das Bild ist nicht zu denken ohne das Vorbild der Münchner Schale,[156] wo allerdings der Baum in harmonisch ausgewogener Weise das Rund füllt, auch Sinis von vorn gesehen und daher Rechtshänder ist. Komposition und Zeichnung der älteren Münchner Schale sind ungleich besser. Der provinzielle Maler hätte sein schwaches Produkt nicht ohne das Vorbild zustande gebracht.

Es handelt sich um einen ähnlichen Fall wie bei der etruskischen Kopie nach einem Werk des Oedipusmalers,[157] wie bei den von Lullies[158] beobachteten böotischen Kopien nach attischen Vasen und bei der etruskischen Kopie nach einem Werk des Achilleusmalers.[159] Entweder müssen die Kopisten die zufällig erhaltenen Vorbilder gekannt haben, oder Repliken von ihnen, oder ein Musterbuch. Der provinzielle Meister der Pelike muss entweder in Böotien zu Hause sein, oder auf der Insel, auf der das Gefäss gefunden wurde. War das letztere der Fall, dann läge hier zum erstenmal eine sizilische Kopie nach Attischem vor.

Abb. 47. Bruchstücke einer attisch-schwarzfigurigen Amphora. Malibu, The J. Paul Getty Museum 78.AE.305. Grösste L.: 9.8 cm.

THESEUS UND STIER

Auf der einen Seite der fragmentierten Schale[160] ist dargestellt, wie ein unbekleideter Mann, der sein Gewand auf einem Baum hinter sich abgelegt hat, dabei ist, einen Stier zu fesseln, dessen Vorderfüsse er schon zu Boden gezwungen hat (Abb. 46). Mit dem linken Knie stemmt er sich auf Kopf und Nacken des Stieres. Rechts und links schliessen je eine Palmette das Bild ab. Weitere Gestalten waren also nicht dargestellt. Der Kopf des Mannes ist verloren. Man kann daher nicht sagen, ob er bärtig war oder nicht. Einen Stier hat sowohl Herakles wie Theseus bezwungen. Während wir von Herakles bei dieser Tat viele schwarzfigurige und nur wenige rotfigurige Bilder kennen, ist es bei Theseus genau umgekehrt. Die Wahrscheinlichkeit spricht also dafür, dass es sich hier um Theseus handelt. Die wird noch verstärkt durch die Tatsache, dass weder Löwenfell, noch Keule oder Köcher und Bogen zu sehen sind. Sie erhöht sich noch mehr dadurch, dass von dem gleichen Maler, dem Euergidesmaler, das Thema noch weitere zweimal belegt ist.[161] Das Kampfschema ist ähnlich bereits belegt.[162] Die Schale ist um 510 v.Chr. zu datieren.

---

160. Sammlung Bareiss 1D, Leihgabe, Malibu S.80.AE.268. Auf der anderen Seite schleppt der inschriftlich bezeichnete Silen Briachos einen Weinschlauch. Derselbe Name begegnet für einen Silen in der gleichen Zeit noch zweimal: Brit.Mus. E 253 Bauchamphora ARV² 35,2; Cambridge 163 Oinochoe ARV² 10,3. Das Innenbild mit Hahn ist fast ganz verloren. D. v. Bothmer, *Bareiss* Nr. 73 hat die Schale dem Euergidesmaler zugeschrieben. Beazley hat die Vase nicht in *Para* aufgenommen. Hahn innen beim gleichen Maler auch: ARV² 88ff. Nr. 10, 121. Es ist

bemerkenswert, dass Beazley zu der ersten Briachosvase bemerkt hat: "Many details recall the Euergides painter."
161. VL³ 254,18 und *Para* 330 Maplewood. Noble, Schale. Zum Thema: Brommer, *Theseus* 27ff.
162. VL³ 254ff. B 4, 6, 18, 23, 24, 28, 29.

AKAMAS

Akamas—die Namenbeischrift ist bis auf den letzten Buchstaben erhalten—steht auf zwei aneinanderpassenden Bruchstücken einer attisch-schwarzfigurigen Amphora[163] nach rechts gewandt da (Abb. 47). Auf dem Kopf trägt er einen korinthischen Helm, der über das Gesicht gezogen ist, sodass nur der Bart darunter zum Vorschein kommt. In der Linken hat er einen Rundschild gefasst wobei die Ritzung der Hand in den Körper hineinragt. Die Rechte hängt gerade herab. Die Finger fehlen, man kann nicht sehen, ob sie etwas hielten. Sonst trägt er noch einen kurzen Schurz, dessen oberer Abschluss etwa in Höhe des Bauchnabels waagrecht verläuft. Der untere Rand hat Fransen. Vor der Körpermitte ist eigenartigerweise ein Zipfel des Schurzes hochgezogen, sodass das Glied freiliegt.[164] Der Schurz ist mit lauter kleinen Quadraten gemustert, in denen sich je ein Kreis befindet. Dieses Gewandmuster ist bei Exekias ausserordentlich häufig. Von ihm ist das Vasenbild auch bemalt worden,[165] und zwar um 540 v.Chr. Einen ähnlichen Schurz trägt einer der beiden Diener Memnons auf der Londoner Halsamphora und ihrer New Yorker Replik.[166] Dort kommt er unter dem Panzer zum Vorschein, aber Akamas trägt keinen Panzer.

Mit Akamas ist sicherlich der bekannteste Träger dieses Namens, der Sohn des Theseus, gemeint, zumal auf einer attischen Vase. Aber auch von diesem Akamas haben wir nicht viele Darstellungen.[167] Er kommt vor bei der Fortführung der Aithra aus Troja durch ihn und seinen Bruder Demophon und wieder mit seinem Bruder Demophon Pferde führend bei Diomedes und Odysseus mit dem Palla-

dion, bei Pandion, bei Philoktet und wieder mit Demophon und einem alten Mann. Von diesen wenigen Bildern und Themen ist wieder eins von Exekias gemalt. Von dem gleichen Maler stammt auch der mit Namensbeischrift versehene Theseus auf einer Amphorascherbe in Lund. Beazley[168] hat vermutet, dass weiter auf der Vase Akamas und Demophon ihre Pferde führend dargestellt waren, wie auf der Berliner Exekiasvase.[169] So erhebt sich die Frage, ob die beiden Bruchstücke in Malibu und Lund zu demselben Gefäss gehören können.[170] Leider ist von beiden Fragmenten die Herkunft nicht bekannt. Akamas hat auf dem Fragment in Malibu allerdings sicher kein Pferd geführt. Wegen des hohen Luftraums über Theseus ist anzunehmen, dass er sass[171] und dass eine häusliche Szene[172] dargestellt war. Die Rückseite der Scherbe in Malibu ist verrieben, Drehspuren sind nicht zu erkennen, Reste von Erde sind erhalten. Die Rückseite der Scherbe in Lund soll anders aussehen.[173]

So kann die Zusammengehörigkeit der Scherben in Malibu und Lund nicht mit Sicherheit behauptet werden. Aber auch die Deutung muss offen bleiben. Keins der bisher bekannten Akamasthemen scheint gemeint zu sein. Am rechten Ende der Scherbe ist über der Namensbeischrift ein schwarzer Strich erhalten. Es könnte sich um die Spitze eines schräg oder waagrecht über die Schulter gelegten Speeres handeln, so wie sie Akamas und Demophon auf der Berliner Exekiasamphora halten.[174] In diesem Fall müsste Demophon vorangegangen sein, wie auf der Berliner Amphora. Aber der Akamas in Malibu führt weder ein Pferd, noch einen Speer.[175]

Mainz

---

163. Malibu acc. no. 78.AE.305. Erwähnt *AJA* 84 (1980) 433 Anm. 125; Brommer, *Theseus* 129 (dort allgemein zu Akamas). Fehlt in *LIMC* unter Akamas. E.A. MacKay in *Greek Vases in the J. Paul Getty Museum* I 39f.

164. Vergleichbar ist die Art, mit der der Panmaler auf seiner Athener Busirispelike (Beazley, *Panmaler* Taf. 7-11) die Glieder der Aegypter freilegt, hier mit der offenkundigen Absicht, die Beschneidung zu zeigen. Seitlich offener Chiton auf Bauchamphora Krefeld, *CVA* Taf. 11.2.

165. Zuschreibung von J. Frel. Vgl. die Tafeln bei W. Technau, *Exekias.*

166. Technau, *Exekias* Taf. 26 und New York 98.8.13, von Beazley, *ABV* 149 als "near Exekias" bezeichnet.

167. *VL*³ 214, 260, 390, 391. Ein anderer Akamas auf der Euphroniosschale mit Sarpedon in Malibu: Getty *MJ* 9 (1981) 230.

168. Beazley, *Development* 68 Taf. 27,3. Ihm schloss sich Kron, *Phylenheroen* 148f. und K. Schefold, *Götter- und Heldensagen d.Gr. in d. spätarch. Kunst* 161f. Abb. 214 an.

169. Technau, *Exekias* Taf. 2.

170. Wie D. v. Bothmer mündlich vermutete.

171. M. Robertson, *JHS* 34 (1954) 230.

172. J. Boardman, *AJA* 82 (1978) 15.

173. Freundliche Mitteilung von J. R. Bengtsson.

174. Technau, *Exekias* Taf. 2.

175. Die Sagen von Herakles und Theseus sind behandelt vom Verf. in *Herakles*, vierte Auflage (Köln, 1979) und *Herakles* (New Rochelle, 1984) sowie in *Theseus* (1982).

Methodology in Vase-Profile Analysis

E. Anne Mackay

In 1940 the systematic study of vase profiles was born; in that year Hansjörg Bloesch published his *Formen attischer Schalen*,[1] a work devoted to the contours of cups. Twelve years later he followed it with an article entitled "Stout and Slender in the Late Archaic Period,"[2] in which he mapped out the potential of shape analysis both for chronology and for attribution. The intervening years have seen a gradual recognition of the importance of such a study, until pages of foot- and lip-profiles are now regarded as a standard feature of any new fascicle of the *Corpus Vasorum Antiquorum*—though unfortunately not yet of the initial publication of every vase. In recent decades some few scholars, Dietrich von Bothmer not least among them, have felt confident in proposing attributions of certain vases as the handiwork of specific potters.

Several obstacles impede the progress of the profile analyst. First and foremost is the necessity that every vase be examined "in the flesh." Valid judgements may *not* be made from photographs: there is the risk of misleading distortion resulting from an oblique or obtuse angle of camera to object, or its proximity—a danger recognized by Bloesch, who described the ideal conditions for vase photography[3]—or, even in photographs which fulfill Bloesch's criteria, many important details may be unclear, such as the underside of the lip on a one-piece amphora or the articulation points on a neck-amphora, while of course the inside of the lip and the underside of the foot are quite inaccessible in a photograph.

Even when the vase is out of the vitrine (not all museums are helpful in this regard) and stands before the student, problems remain: how to draw a scientifically exact profile and how, assuming this is done, to compare the profiles of several vases which, even within a given shape, can differ considerably in height. Comparison may be

made in terms of proportion, involving the ratio of greatest diameter to height, but this is a crude method which takes little cognizance of the curving subtleties of form. Bloesch, while using this basic ratio as a framework, concentrated his attention primarily on the development of lips and feet as the most readily compared elements of vase-form. Nevertheless, there is increasing evidence that these details, important though they be, cannot be divorced from the vase as a whole in comparative analysis; and it has become necessary to devise a means first of drawing up a consistently accurate profile, and then of comparing in detail the profiles of vases which, while of similar shape, may differ in height.

THE APPARATUS[4]

A pole of duraluminium (A–B),[5] 720 mm in length and 22 mm in diameter,[6] built to very close tolerances and joined in the middle with a spigot-type ferule, is set vertically onto a spigot on an aluminium base-plate of dimensions 6.5 x 153 x 156 mm. Through the pole, at right angles to its length, is drilled a series of holes of 3.1 mm in diameter at intervals of 10 mm from the centre of one to the centre of the next, measured from the bottom of the base-plate. A small rod (C–F), 377 mm in length and 3 mm in diameter, can be passed through the holes in the pole with minimal play (the rod is perspex with a rounded tip, for the greater protection of the vase). The third component is a steel metre rule, marked off in millimetres.

THE PROCEDURE

The vase to be studied is placed on a level surface. The maximum height and diameter are recorded. The pole is positioned in such a way as to touch the vase at its widest point (G),[7] with the holes perpendicular to the vase's sur-

It is with great pleasure that I offer this paper to Dietrich von Bothmer as a humble token of gratitude for his encouragement and support of my research into vase-profiles in the past few years.

1. Berne, 1940.

2. *JHS* 71 (1951) 29–39.

3. Bloesch (*supra* n. 2) 29 n.3.

4. The present writer is not the first to be obsessed with the need for strict accuracy in the taking of profiles: to her knowledge, at least two other devices are in existence. One, based on the template principle, is cumbersome and cannot easily be taken from museum to museum; it was

demonstrated by Bothmer in the Metropolitan Museum of Art, New York. The other, devised by Janine Bourriau of the Fitzwilliam Museum, Cambridge, while extremely portable, was designed for use primarily with sherds. The principal attraction of the present device is not its novelty but its portability and the ease with which the resulting profiles can be mathematically manipulated for comparison.

5. Letters in parentheses refer to figure 2.

6. The specific measurements are for the most part arbitrary but are included here for the sake of offering a complete description.

7. The centre of one side of the vase is the most obvious point, as be-

Figure 1a. Type A amphora attributed as "Related to the Painter of the Vatican Mourner" and to Exekias as potter. Malibu, The J. Paul Getty Museum 72.AE.148.

Figure 1b. Malibu 72.17E.148. Reverse.

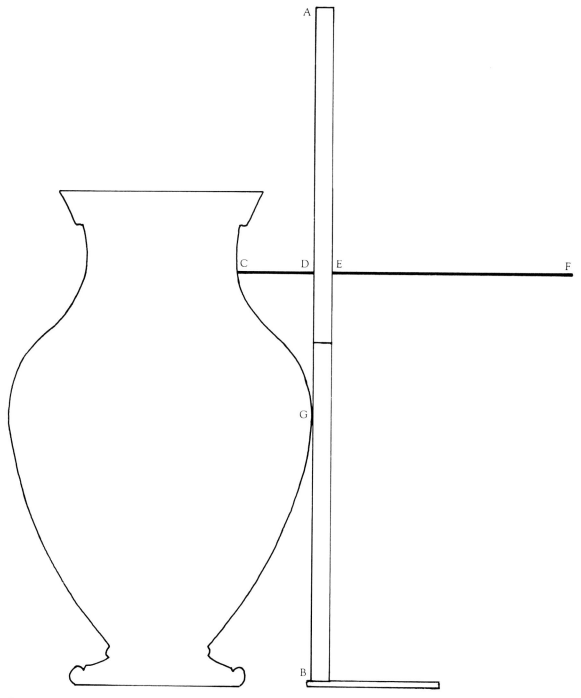

Figure 2. The apparatus. Scale 1:4.05.

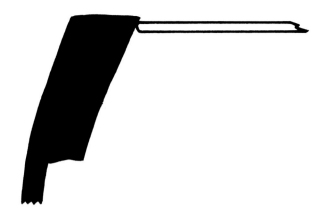

Figure 3. Rim of a vase that does not coincide precisely with one of the holes of the measuring apparatus. Scale 1:1.

face at that point. Starting at the bottom, the rod is inserted in turn into each hole and is pushed through until it touches the surface of the vase (C); the remaining length of the rod (E–F) is measured and the measurement recorded in each case, working up hole by hole to the full height of the vase. Often the rim of the vase does not coincide precisely with one of the holes:[8] in this case an approximate measurement should be recorded and marked as such. The height of the point of contact between vase and pole (that is, the height of the point of greatest diameter) should be recorded, as it is seldom irrelevant. "Thumbnail" sketches should be made to indicate the placing of recorded measurements in relation to the important articulations in the profile.

As very few vases are symmetrical, the procedure should be repeated on the other side of the vase. The mean of the two sets of measurements may be taken as indicative of the vase's overall contour. A markedly irregular vase is unsuited to this type of analysis.

THE PROCESSING[9]

In order to allow the systematic comparison of vases of similar shape but different heights, all profiles should be scaled to a common height, while retaining their original proportions. A height of 230 mm has been chosen here as being of convenient size to fit into publication format.

The data are evaluated by means of the formulae $x = (((A + B) \div 2) - J) \times I$; $y = H \times I$,[10] where x and y are the rectangular coordinates, and A and B are the variables (the two recorded measurements at any given point of the

vase's height). J represents the correction to the central axis of the vase (a positive rather than the negative contour recorded by the measurements), and is calculated by subtracting the radius of the vase at its widest point (that is, half its greatest diameter) from the maximum average profile readings[11]—here $355 - D/2$. I represents the proportional reduction factor, calculated by dividing the maximum height of the vase into 230 (or into the desired height of the scaled-down profile). H represents the height on the pole at which any given pair of measurements was taken: at the start of the calculation process, H should be given the value of the highest hole for which a measurement was recorded; the calculations then follow from top to bottom, with the third part of the programme automatically reducing the value by 10 each time (that is, specifying the height of the next hole down).[12]

THE EXAMPLE

The method will perhaps be clearer if its application to a specific vase is described. The vase selected is Malibu 72.AE.148, a Type A amphora attributed as "Related to the Painter of the Vatican Mourner" (Frel) and to Exekias as potter (Bothmer)—see figure 1.

The maximum height and diameter are recorded: height 532 mm, diameter 337 mm. The apparatus is set up as in figure 2, and the measurements are recorded as in figure 4: first, column A, representing the profile of the obverse, and then column B, the reverse. Column H gives the height on the pole of each measurement. Thumbnail sketches indicate the placing of the recorded measurements in relation to the important articulation points on the amphora—lip and foot.

Next the statistics specific to the vase are programmed into the calculator:

$$H = 530 \text{ (the topmost hole used)}$$
$$I = 230/532$$
$$= .432330827$$
$$J = 355 - (337 \div 2)$$
$$= 186.5$$

At this point the calculations begin, and the calculator is set to round all answers to the nearest millimetre. Starting at the top, at $H = 530$, A and B are valued at 298.5 and 298.5 respectively, and the first set of answers emerges: $x = 48$; $y = 229$; $H = 520$—that is, the x-coordinate, the y-coordinate, and the new value of H (now the second

---

ing least warped by the pressure applied by the potter in attaching the handles. However, care must be taken to avoid including any dents or other accidental irregularities in the profile.

8. See figure 3.

9. Note that all measurements are in millimetres to avoid confusion.

10. This was all programmed into a Sharp EL 5100 Scientific Calcu-

lator as follows: $(((A + B) \div 2) - J) \times I$; $H \times I$; $H - 10$ STORE H.

11. That is, the full length of the rod, less that portion contained within the diameter of the pole (D–E): here 377 mm less the pole's diameter of 22 mm, hence 355 mm.

12. Note that measurements are taken from bottom to top, while calculations are worked from top to bottom.

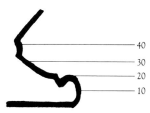

Figure 4. Data and coordinates for profile of Malibu 72.AE.148.

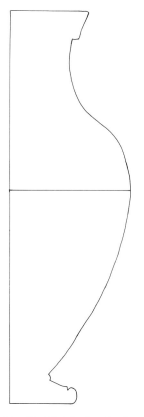

Figure 5. Malibu 72.AE.148. Graph of scaled profile.
Scale: 1:5.14. * marks point of greatest diameter.

H	A	B	X	Y
530	298.5	298.5	48	229
520	294	294	46	225
510	289.5	289	44	220
500	285.5	285	43	216
490	273	271.5	37	212
480	272	270	37	208
470	271.5	269	36	203
460	271	269	36	199
450	272	270	37	195
440	273	271	37	190
430	276	274	38	186
420	279	277	40	182
410	284	281	42	177
400	291	289	45	173
390	302	298.5	49	169
380	314.5	311	55	164
370	327	323	60	160
360	336	333	64	156
350	342	340	67	151
340	347	345	69	147
330	350	349	70	143
320	352	352	72	138
310	353.5	354	72	134
300	354.5	354.5	73	130
*290	355	355	73	125
280	354.5	354.5	73	121
270	354	354	72	117
260	352	352	72	112
250	351	350.5	71	108
240	349	348.5	70	104
230	346	346	69	99
220	344	343.5	68	95
210	340	340.5	66	91
200	337	337	65	86
190	333	333.5	63	82
180	329	329	62	78
170	325	325	60	73
160	320	320.5	58	69
150	316	316	56	65
140	311.5	310	54	61
130	306	305	51	56
120	300	299	49	52
110	294	293	46	48
100	288	287	44	43
90	280	280	40	39
80	274	277.5	38	35
70	266	265	34	30
60	257.5	257	31	26
50	248.5	248	27	22
40	242.5	241	24	17
30	248	247	26	13
20	280	278	40	9
10	283	281	41	4

*Point of greatest diameter.

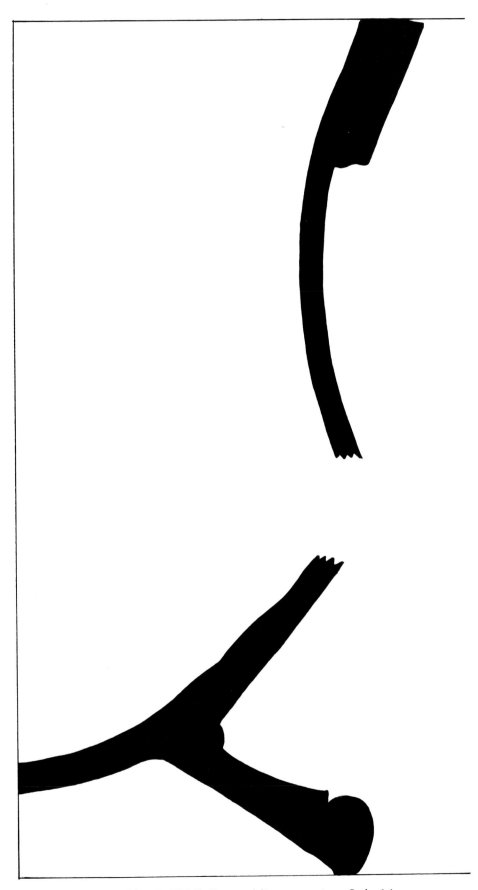

Figure 6. Malibu 72.AE.148. Foot and lip cross-sections. Scale: 1:1.

hole from the top). The *x*- and *y*-coordinates, are recorded in columns X and Y. The process is repeated with succeeding sets of values for A and B until all the data have been evaluated.

At this stage the scaled profile can be graphed using the *x*- and *y*-coordinates, and then drawn on transparent paper for comparison with the profiles of other vases, aligned on the center axis (the *y*-axis of the graph).[13]

While the method described here allows a detailed comparison of the profiles of vases of similar type,[14] it should not be used in isolation: it may augment, but not supersede, the time-honoured analysis of foot and lip cross-sections; all approaches should be used in conjunction. If the extremities of a vase can betoken a potter's identity and development, then it would seem as valid to seek further clues from the vase-profile in its entirety.

University of Natal
Durban

13. See figure 5.
14. Or indeed of any three-dimensional objects of consistent shape, for it could be adapted to suit sculpture, whether relief or in the round, and could be used also for certain architectural elements.

Beazley and the Connoisseurship of Greek Vases

D. C. Kurtz

". . . Beazley has, almost single-handed, transformed the study of Attic vase-painting into a true branch of the history of art, comparable to the study of any documented school of painting."

—Ashmole 453

Sir John Beazley (1885–1970) was Lincoln Professor of Classical Archaeology and Art in the University of Oxford. The ordering of Athenian figured vases of the sixth to fourth centuries B.C., by artists and groups, is but one aspect of his prodigious scholarship. Roughly a thousand painters and groups were listed in publications, and more were recorded privately. The method which Beazley used to attribute vases had been introduced to Italian painting by Giovanni Morelli (1816–1892) and developed by Bernard Berenson (1865–1956), among others, in a large number of influential publications. Outside a rather restricted circle of classical scholarship, Beazley's contribution to connoisseurship is largely unknown. In this article[1] the art historical background to which he came is conjectured, the influence of Morelli and Berenson is assessed, and the nature of the material he worked with is explained—line drawings on fired clay vases.

1. INTRODUCTION

The essence of the Morellian method is careful scrutiny of details, especially those which an artist reproduces so regularly that they can be considered as characteristic of his hand as his handwriting.[2] Morelli recommended the study of drawings by the Great Masters to aspiring connoisseurs, because they reveal characteristic renderings more clearly than paintings. Although we speak of vase-painting, vase–drawings would, in some respects, be more accurate. Preliminary sketches were often made on the clay surface before figures were painted in black silhouette and details incised (black-figure) or outlined in black or brown paint (red-figure). In these two techniques the amount and range of added colour are very restricted, and perspective and shading, as understood by Renaissance artists, are unknown.[3] Just as coloration is not an important consideration technically, landscape and architecture are not important iconographically; man is the dominant subject. The material is well suited to Morellian analysis even though the painting is not on a flat surface; distortion through curvature of the vase is less of a problem than might be supposed. Furthermore, subtleties of shape offer additional information, as does subsidiary pattern-work,

America   J.D. Beazley, *Attic Red-figured Vases in American Museums* (Cambridge, Mass., 1918)

Ashmole   B. Ashmole, "Sir John Beazley," *Proceedings of the British Academy* 56 (1972) 443–461

Brown   D.A. Brown, *Berenson and the Connoisseurship of Italian Painting* (Washington, 1979)

Citharoedus   J.D. Beazley, "Citharoedus," *JHS* 42 (1922) 70–98

Critical Studies   G. Morelli, *Italian Painters—Critical Studies of Their Work (Kunstkritische Studien über italienische Malerei)*, translated by C.J. Foulkes and introduced by A.H. Layard (London, vols. I [1900] and II [1907])

Kurtz   D.C. Kurtz, *The Berlin Painter* (Oxford, 1983)

Robertson   C.M. Robertson, "Beazley and After," *MJb* 27 (1976) 29–46

Rudiments   B. Berenson, *The Study and Criticism of Italian Art*, 2nd series (London, 1902) 111–148 ("The Rudiments of Connoisseurship")

Samuels   E. Samuels, *The Making of a Connoisseur* (Cambridge, Mass., 1979)

Three Essays   B. Berenson, *Three Essays in Method* (Oxford, 1927)

1. Originally a brief introduction to a detailed stylistic study of an Athenian red-figure cup of the late sixth century (published in *JHS* 103 [1983] 68–86), the present article was subsequently rewritten and expanded to suit less narrowly archaeological interests. It was intended to introduce classical archaeologists to the principles and methods of connoisseurship, and art historians to the connoisseurship of ancient Greek vases. I should like to thank Jiří Frel for inviting me to publish it in a journal which covers both fields of art history and then suggesting its inclusion in a volume dedicated to a pupil of Sir John Beazley and a leading connoisseur of Athenian vase-painting. Dr. von Bothmer has an understanding and an appreciation of Beazley's method which could only come to one who had the privilege of working with Beazley over many years. I hope he will accept this article as an expression of my respect for his scholarship.

Bernard Ashmole, John Boardman, Herbert Cahn, Hugh Lloyd-Jones and Martin Robertson read earlier versions of the article in 1980 and offered comments and corrections. Jaynie Anderson, Francis Haskell, Barbara Strachey Halpern, Jane Jakeman, Henri Locard, Luisa Vertova Nicolson, Ernest Samuels, Anna Terni and Margaret Wind kindly offered assistance on the connoisseurship of Italian painting. Brian Cook of the British Museum and Dietrich von Bothmer of the Metropolitan Museum gave permission to publish the photographs in figures 5 and 6. I have also to thank Sandra Knudsen Morgan and Marit Jentoft-Nilsen.

2. See *infra* n. 17.

3. Lekythoi decorated in the white-ground technique can have a broader range of colour, and some late examples have a limited use of perspective and shading: Kurtz, *Athenian White Lekythoi* (Oxford, 1975) 59–60, 68–73.

which can be abstract, floral, or figural. The shapes of vases and their patterns are reliable guides to attribution; their connoisseurship, therefore, combines Morellian analysis of draughtsmanship with observations of potter-work and pattern-work.

The vases may have been found, by chance, almost from antiquity itself, especially in some parts of Italy, where large numbers had been imported and were later buried in tombs which often remained undisturbed by subsequent building, but interest in the vases as works of art did not become established until the eighteenth century.[4] For some time all ancient vases found in Italy were assumed to have been made there, then Greek and Italic wares were distinguished. During the nineteenth century the pace of excavation, and plunder, quickened, greatly increasing the amount of material for study. Archaeological research institutes were established. Great museums of northern Europe formed vase collections and published catalogues. Adolf Furtwängler's of the Berlin collection appeared in 1885, his monumental *Griechische Vasenmalerei* from 1900: large and sensitive drawings, mostly from Athenian red-figured vases, by Karl Reichhold (fig. 2), accompanied Furtwängler's text. This was a landmark in classical scholarship. Germans were in the forefront of research, and their contribution to the study of Greek vases is widely acknowledged.[5] They had searched for artists, but the task was difficult: there were many thousands of Athenian figured vases, many were fragmentary, and very few were signed. Those which were signed bore a proper name or a name and a verb, which indicated that 'x' painted or made it; occasionally both painter and maker sign, and very occasionally the two sign as one.[6] Unlike painters of the Renaissance, these were humble artisans whose accomplishments went unrecorded in contemporary literature. Therefore, scholars who tried to make attributions usually relied upon signed vases. This method produced some good results, but was severely restricted by the scarcity of signatures. Vases without signatures, or of unexceptional style or iconography, tended to remain unassigned.

Furtwängler died in 1907, the year that Beazley completed his undergraduate studies at Oxford.[7] In 1908

Figure 1. Sir John Beazley. Photograph by Cecil Beaton.

Beazley published an article on three Greek vases in the Ashmolean Museum. It reads like his predecessor's work: vases are described iconographically without mention of the artists who painted them.[8] Two years later he published "Kleophrades," in which he respectfully acknowledged the work of his predecessors and then set out on a wholly new course: analyzing the style of a vase bearing the signature of Kleophrades as maker, he identified significant details of draughtsmanship and paralleled them on a good number of unsigned vases.[9] Since Kleophrades signed as "maker" we do not know the name of the

4. R.M. Cook, *Greek Painted Pottery* (London, 1972) 287–331 ("The History of the Study of Vase-Painting").

5. The following may be added to Cook's account: Ashmole 454; Robertson 31; C. Isler-Kerényi, "J.D. Beazley e la ceramologia," *Quaderni ticinesi di numismatica e antichità classiche* 9 (1980) 7–23.

J.C. Hoppin is not singled out in these accounts, but in some respects his approach was sufficiently notable at the time to be mentioned in connection with Beazley. Hoppin took a doctorate in Munich under the direction of Furtwängler; the thesis was published in 1896 with the title *Euthymides*. His better known *Euthymides and His Fellows* (Cambridge, Mass., 1917) reproduced drawings by Reichhold and Beazley. Beazley reviewed the book favourably (*JHS* 37 [1917] 234) but was critical of

Hoppin's means of identifying artists.

6. *BurlMag* (1921) 233 (Beazley); *JHS* 91 (1971) 13f. (R.M. Cook), 92 (1972) 187ff. (Robertson); Robertson 32.

7. Ashmole 444.

8. *JHS* 28 (1908) 313–318.

9. *JHS* 30 (1910) 36–68.

10. *Ibid.* 38.

Compare also: "Nameless, but not unknown: for the name of an artist is the least important thing about him" (*America* p. v) and "Persons who tried to group these vases by means of stylistic criteria were frequently regarded with ingenious disapproval as 'attributing vases to painters who were not known to exist'" (*BurlMag* [1921] 234).

Figure 2. Name–vase (Berlin 2160) of the Berlin Painter. Detail of the obverse, from a drawing by Karl Reichhold.

Figure 3. An early drawing by Beazley in the manner of Reichhold.

painter, but the lack of his name did not trouble Beazley:

> The name of the painter . . . is of little importance; what interests us is himself and his style.[10]

This is a notable change in attitude towards the connoisseurship of Athenian vases. Notable too is the shift in emphasis from a named painter of cups to an unnamed painter of pots ("pot" is the word Beazley used to distinguish cups from vases or other shapes).

In 1911 Beazley took the next step, publishing thirty-

eight vases by a hitherto unrecognized artist whom he named the Master of the Berlin amphora, after an especially elaborate vase in Berlin (fig. 2).[11] Within a few years this artist became the Berlin Painter, and Kleophrades became the Kleophrades Painter.[12] Unlike the 1910 "Kleophrades," the 1911 article dispensed with fulsome descriptions of individual vases.[13] They were listed, as were renderings which Beazley considered characteristic of the painter's style. This spare format was to be retained for almost all his subsequent painter studies.[14] The year 1918

11. *JHS* 31 (1911) 276–295.

12. "Kleophrades" represents early nomenclature, as does "master of the Berlin amphora." Within a few years Beazley standardized terminology. For "maker" signatures Beazley spoke of the x-painter (as Lydos, Psiax, Douris, etc.). Anonymous artists (no works extant bearing the signature of a painter or "maker") were named after some aspect of their work or the location of either a particularly characteristic piece or an especially fine one (as Berlin Painter).

The Kleophrades Painter's pelike in Berlin (2170), which bears two signatures of Epiktetos as painter and gave him the name Epiktetos II (which Beazley did not use to avoid confusion with another Epiktetos recognized previously), has been shown to have modern inscriptions (*AA*

[1981] 329–332 [Boardman]).

13. The format was deliberate. Beazley had written to Martin Robertson's parents: "The article will be a model of conciseness carried *ad absurdum*" (Robertson 32).

14. Beazley departs from the listing of works and renderings in three essays (*Der Berliner Maler* [1930], *Der Pan Maler* and *Der Kleophrades Maler* [1932]) which have recently been reissued by von Zabern (Mainz, 1974) in English.

A bibliography of Beazley's writings can be found in *Select Exhibition of Sir John and Lady Beazley's Gifts—1912–1966, Ashmolean Museum* (Oxford, 1967) 177–188.

saw the publication of *Athenian Red-figured Vases in American Museums* (lists of painters and vases with brief commentary on styles of drawing), 1928 the first compilation of painter-lists—*Athenische Vasenmalerei* (without commentary). The publication of the latter in Germany (Tübingen) is both a tribute to past German scholarship and an indication of the swifter reception which his work received there than in England, where, in 1925 he had been elected to the Oxford professorship. Whatever opposition there may have been initially, at home—his predecessor at Oxford was sceptical about Beazley's "scientific approach"[15]—or abroad,[16] quickly passed. For more than half a century Beazley was the undisputed authority on Greek vases.

2. MORELLI

Morelli has been called the father of modern art history.[17] Details of his life and the controversy which surrounds his work are familiar to art historians. His approach was revolutionary because it was scientific. Morelli was a man of his times—a contemporary of Charles Darwin (1809–81), a contemporary and friend of Louis Agassiz (1807–73), with whom he studied medicine in Germany.[18] Although Morelli showed special aptitude in human and comparative anatomy and an early and continuing interest in the visual arts, he made politics his career and became actively involved in the Italian war of independence. Later, as director of a commission to register national monuments, he studied at first hand the art treasures of his native land. He looked at paintings then as he had for many years—through eyes clinically trained to observe natural forms and their infinite variety. He was a good draughtsman and often sketched significant details of paintings, although apparently not regularly while touring galleries; he probably would have included more drawings in his publications if many had not been anatomical, thus potentially offering fuel to the fire of those who opposed his scientific approach.[19] Whereas his predecessors and contemporaries relied heavily on written documentation, Morelli relied on the lines executed by the artist. He published his first essays on art in the 1870s. They were written in German under the pseudonym Ivan Lermolieff, as was his two-volume *Italian Painters—Critical Studies of Their Work* which appeared from 1880 (English translation, 1883). The text of this influential and controversial work takes the form of a dialogue between Ivan, a young Russian travelling in Italy in search of knowledge about art, and the cognoscenti whom he encounters. In the introduction ("Principles and Method") Ivan is instructed in what we would now call the art of connoisseurship. He is told that only through an accurate knowledge, derived from long and careful study, of the way in which an artist draws details, especially those of the human body, will he succeed in distinguishing the work of one artist from another. The young Russian concludes:

> This matter of fact way of identifying works of art by the help of such external signs savoured more of an anatomist, I thought, than a student of art . . .
>
> *Critical Studies*, I.35

> . . . spare me these details of hands and ears before such a picture.
>
> *Ibid.* 55

Critics, like Wilhelm von Bode, called Morelli a "surgeon" who had done little more than "issue a catalogue of the ears, noses, and fingers, the former property of Sandro (Botticelli), Mantegna. . . ."[20] But Morelli was firm: the "soul of the creator" could only be found through acquaintance with the individual parts which comprise a work of art:

> The study of the individual parts, which go to make up "form" in a work of art, is what I would recommend to those . . . who really desire to find a way through the intricacies of the history of art, and to attain, if possible, to a scientific knowledge of art. For, as there is a language expressed by letters, so there is also a language which expresses itself in form.
>
> *Critical Studies*, I.75–6

Although Morelli was not the first to apply the method, he was the first to publish it. Owing to his position in international art circles, *Critical Studies* had a truly revolutionary effect. Whatever its defects (and these will continue to be debated) the Morellian method offered a scientific basis on which to recognize personal styles. Morelli was probably also the first art historian to make systematic use of another modern tool of research to record what he had seen—the photograph.[21]

Apart from the influence of his method on Beazley,

15. Ashmole 447.

16. Cook, *Greek Painted Pottery* 323.

17. Morelli's life is recounted by A.H. Layard in the introduction to the English translation (1900) of *Critical Studies*. His contribution to modern art history has been assessed by E. Wind, *Art and Anarchy* (London, 1963) 34ff. More recent bibliography has been compiled by Brown 57.

18. E. Lurie, *Louis Agassiz: A Life in Science* (Chicago, 1960) and *Nature and the American Mind: Louis Agassiz and the Culture of Science* (New York, 1974).

19. I owe this information to Jaynie Anderson, who is preparing a publication of drawings by Morelli.

20. *Critical Studies*, vol. 1, Introduction p. 31 (Layard).

21. Brown 44. See also *ArtJ* 39 (1979/80) 117–23 (W.M. Freitag).

22. Samuels 103–104.

BurlMag (1960) 382 (K. Clark): ". . . Morelli's whole approach . . . [was]

Morelli has a personal connection with classical archaeology through Jean Paul Richter, a friend and follower. Richter's role in Renaissance art scholarship, like that of other Morelli pupils, is now overshadowed by Berenson. Richter introduced the young Berenson to Morelli in 1891, the year before the older man died.[22] The correspondence between Morelli and Richter was published by Richter's daughters, Irma and Gisela.[23] Richter's wife was the first to translate *Critical Studies* into English and to use Morelli's name instead of the pseudonym. Irma, the elder daughter, was Morelli's god-child. With her father she edited *The Literary Works of Leonardo da Vinci* (Oxford, 1939). The second edition of this great work was dedicated to Gisela who was already an acknowledged authority in ancient Greek and Roman art. Gisela came to the Metropolitan Museum of Art in New York in 1906, at the age of twenty-four, and was appointed curator in 1925. Most of her prolific writings date from after 1948 when she retired from the museum. She remained a dominant figure in classical art scholarship until her death in Rome in 1972. In her memoirs[24] Gisela recalled the profound effect of her father's teaching upon her appreciation of Greek art, in particular of the scenes painted on Greek vases, and in the introduction to *Red-figured Athenian Vases in the Metropolitan Museum of Art* (New York, 1936) she has written:

> But it is not only a general development that we can trace in Greek vase painting. In the slow unfolding of the history of Greek drawing we can see more than a common advance. Individual personalities stand out as clearly as in Renaissance painting, and they are distinguishable in the same ways. Each artist reveals himself by the general effect of his picture and by his own particular rendering of individual forms; only the differentiation is subtler than in later paintings, for the Greek designer worked with a simpler color scheme and within the narrow restraint of conventionalized design. He could not express his individuality with the same freedom as did a Botticelli and a Titian, who could dip their brushes into rich colours and on vast canvases display the variety of naturalistic form immersed in light and atmosphere.
>
> pp. xix–xx

In view of Gisela Richter's early training in the Morellian method, it is perhaps somewhat surprising that she did not introduce its application to Greek vases. She was,

however, among the first to acknowledge Beazley's contribution publicly.

> The study of Athenian vases has gained enormously during the last decade. . . . Now that Beazley has shown us that we are in no way limited to a few masters with signatures, the study of styles and attributions has become almost as active as in Renaissance paintings.
>
> *AJA* 27 (1923) 265

Owing to J.D. Beazley's epoch-making researches the stylistic study of Greek vases has become the most fascinating of pursuits. More and more Athenian vase painters are emerging into daylight as distinct individualities, whom we can recognize in an increasing number of their works. It matters little that in most cases we do not know their original names, since they live for us as artistic personalities. In such art criticism we must be aware of two things—the general impression of the picture and the individual traits. Each artist's temperament is reflected in the character of his figures—in their attitudes and expressions and composition, in the whole atmosphere so to speak of the picture. We can receive an impression of grandeur, or vivacity, or daintiness, or harmonious monotony, and thereby attribute the work to the Kleophrades painter or the Pan painter or the Dutuit painter or Makron. And we can check these general observations by an analysis of details—the way the collar bones are drawn, or the ankles, or the ear, or the folds of the drapery; for every artist has his own particular way of seeing form and translating it into line. And by these means we can recreate these bygone personalities and make them live vividly for us once more.

> *AJA* 30 (1926) 32

3. BERENSON

Bernard Berenson[25] was twenty years older than Beazley and already well known in London art circles when Beazley was an undergraduate. His writings would have attracted Beazley's attention for several reasons: he was a follower of Morelli and an authority on Italian painting in which Beazley (fig. 4) had early developed an interest. Beazley's family had moved to Belgium in 1897.[26] Trips between home on the continent and school in England were both a necessity and an opportunity to visit museums and galleries. Beazley is said to have had a special liking for Flemish and Sienese painting.

I have not been able to determine whether Berenson and Beazley met or what each knew of the other's work. Each

entirely sympathetic to Mr Berenson. . . . I may add that Mr Berenson never knew him, and only set eyes on him two or three times."

23. I. Richter and G. Richter, *Italienische Malerei der Renaissance im Briefwechsel von G. Morelli and J.P. Richter* (Baden-Baden, 1960). See also Wind, *Art and Anarchy*, 139.

24. *My Memoirs* (Rome, 1972) 14.

25. Brown 41–49.

Berenson's official biographer, Ernest Samuels, is preparing a second

volume. Meryl Secrest's *On Being Berenson* was published in 1979; Berenson's autobiography (*Sketch for a Self-Portrait*) appeared in 1949.

26. Ashmole 433; Robertson 32.

27. I should like to thank Luisa Vertova Nicolson and Anna Terni (Librarian, I Tatti) for confirming that none of Beazley's books bore personal dedications.

28. Beazley is said to have had mixed views on Berenson's scholarship. See also *infra* n. 35.

had some of the other's publications in his personal library,[27] and Berenson is said to have been impressed by Beazley's scholarship.[28] Berenson's background in the classics and in classical art was sound;[29] he also had some association with English classical scholarship, largely through Edward Perry Warren—a man who did a great deal to establish fine collections of classical antiquities in his native New England.[30] Berenson had met Warren when they were both undergraduates at Harvard.[31] Warren soon left Harvard to read classics at Oxford; Berenson left America in 1888 and made his way to Oxford to see his friend and, he hoped, to meet Walter Pater.[32] In time Berenson became a member of Warren's circle and joined others interested in the arts at Lewes House, Warren's country home in Sussex. Both Berenson and Beazley were house guests, but the former's visits were mostly before 1900 (Berenson's trips to England were less frequent after this time),[33] and Beazley's must have been mostly at least a decade or so later. Warren's love was Greek, not Renaissance, art; by about 1900 his collecting declined and his interests became more narrowly Greek. Engraved gemstones especially pleased him.

> Why is it that cosmopolitans like Berenson and Rothenstein tire me now? Because they are not dealing with my problems, problems which spring directly from the study of Greek and of the Bible, from a constant study.[34]

Berenson dedicated *Lorenzo Lotto, An Essay in Constructive Art Criticism* (London, 1895) to Warren. Beazley's *The Lewes House Collection of Gems* (Oxford, 1920) was commissioned by Warren and dedicated to Andrew Gow,[35] Beazley's life-long friend in classical scholarship with whom he shared a love of post-antique painting; together they had bought a "Simone Martini" in 1910.[36] *Athenian Red-figured Vases in American Museums* (1918) had been dedicated to Warren and to Warren's close friend, John Marshall. Beazley also contributed a chapter to Warren's biography.[37]

Berenson's life has been recounted by many, including

himself (*Sketch for a Self-Portrait*). He knew the great contribution Morelli had made to art history.

> . . . his services to the science of pictures are greater than Winckelmann's to antique sculpture or Darwin's to biology.[38]

His personal contribution was a deeper sensitivity for the artistic personality—for the man behind the lines. He often explained how he looked at pictures:

> The aim of these essays is thus to canalize guessing, so to speak. In the beginning was the guess, no doubt. But there is pre-scientific and post-scientific guessing, and we are in the later phase, even in the study of art.
>
> *Three Essays* p. ix

> My aim is . . . to tell younger men what an old explorer like myself has to do when he starts out to find the author of art.
>
> As in hunting, it is a matter of tracking the quarry to his lair, of following the scent. I shall attempt to show the various twists and turns we must take in following it, what we must do to pick it up again where we have lost it, and how we may make sure that it is the right scent and not a wrong one. I shall avoid displays of craft and cunning, and refrain from piling up confusing and distracting directions. . . . Perhaps the quarry may not be worth the pains expended in pursuit, but I, for one, love the sport. Only one must enjoy it for no utilitarian or pretentious reason, but for its own sake and because it exercises eyes, mind, and judgement.
>
> *Ibid.* 45

Berenson often worked with his wife, a scholar of Renaissance art in her own right.[39] As they toured the museums and galleries of Europe and America they made copious notes and recorded their observations in photographs. Neither could draw.[40] Berenson acquired photographs from commercial photographic houses like Anderson in Rome and Alinari in Florence and received them, especially in later years, from dealers in search of information. By 1899 his personal photographic archive had more than 20,000 prints.[41] As he grew older and the cost of

29. Samuels 101; *BurlMag* (1960) 384 (K. Clark); N.Mariano, *Forty Years with Berenson* (London, 1966) 134:

> In later years, when Kenneth [Clark] had already made his reputation as an art critic and writer and as museum director, B.B. and he found themselves again and again in complete harmony while looking together at works of art, and particularly in the contemplation and discussion of classical art.

In his publications, comparisons between Italian painters and ancient Greek artists seemed to come as easily as they did to Beazley. Compare for example: *Rudiments* 120; *Three Essays* 89.

30. O. Burdett and E.H. Goddard, *Edward Perry Warren, the Biography of a Connoisseur* (London, 1941). See also Daniel Robbins' preface to D. Buitron's *Attic Vase Painting in New England Collections* (Cambridge, Mass., 1972) 7–9.

31. Samuels 60–61.

32. *Ibid.* 193.

33. Barbara Strachey Halpern supplied this information.

34. Burdett and Goddard 244; see *supra* n. 30.

35. Gow's obituary for the British Academy (*Proceedings of the British Academy* 64 [1978] 427–441) by F.H. Sandbach documents the friendship with Beazley and their shared interest in the visual arts. Shortly before his death Gow answered some of my questions about Beazley's early years and, in particular, his interest in post-antique painting. Gow said that to the best of his recollection, Beazley did not have a high regard for Berenson personally.

36. Ashmole 446. The painting, later recognized to be a copy of a work by this artist, is now in the Metropolitan Museum, New York.

37. See *supra* n. 30.

38. Samuels 101. Samuels wrote (26 July 1980) that the review was "buried among B.B.'s miscellaneous papers in the I Tatti Archive."

Figure 4. Beazley. Drawing (red conté) by Reginald Wilenski (1911).

travel increased, he came to rely more and more heavily on photographs, and openly acknowledged that most of his work could be done with them in libraries.[42] On some of the prints he wrote suggestions for attributions which would be recorded for posterity in his painter-lists. Artists whose names were unknown were given names, like Amico di Sandro. Berenson's photographs and notes passed to Harvard University on his death and now form the Harvard University Center for Italian Studies, in the Berenson villa near Florence, I Tatti.[43]

4. BEAZLEY

In the course of his work, and as an essential instrument of it, he built up a body of photographs, drawings, and notes on vases surpassing that of any institution in the world; and these passed at his death to the University of Oxford.

Ashmole 453

Comparisons between Berenson and Beazley must not be overemphasized; their lives and their personalities, as recounted by those who knew them, were very different. Yet there are similarities in material and methods of work. There is no fuller published account of Beazley's life than Bernard Ashmole's for the British Academy. Neither he nor Andrew Gow has been able to shed much light on Beazley before 1910. We can only conjecture why he did not mention the names of Morelli or Berenson in print and why he was reluctant to explain his method. Perhaps it was the example of Berenson before him, and the knowledge that he too would work with dealers and collectors. Perhaps he wished to avoid associations which could place him in a compromising position. Perhaps he wished to avoid the type of criticism that had been levelled at Morelli, Berenson, and others. Beazley's public silence did not, however, keep others from making the comparisons. Dame Joan Evans wrote in her memoirs:

> In Greek vases I was Beazley's first pupil and I must confess that I found myself profoundly bored by his Berensonian attributions. I had no particular wish to give a name to a vase painter from the way he drew an ankle.[44]

I asked Bernard Ashmole (25 November 1980) to comment on Dame Joan's remarks.

> You will hardly believe it, but not only do I never remember Jacky mentioning either Morelli or Berenson, but I cannot recall his ever having spoken of his own methods or of the importance of comparing details of drawing on one vase with those on another. This is in spite of what Joan Evans said: although she was of exactly my own age (we were born on the same day) she must have been a pupil of Jacky's at a different time . . . his lectures, apart from a

39. Samuels (see index, p. 464 "Mary Costelloe") emphasizes the important role played by Mary Berenson. He also records (p. 206) that she helped him review a highly significant publication on ancient Greek sculpture—A. Furtwängler's *Meisterwerke der griechischen Plastik* (Leipzig, 1893).

40. Brown 43. Mrs. Halpern (Mary Berenson's granddaughter) assured me that neither could draw.

41. B.S. Halpern, *Remarkable Relations* (London, 1980) 168.

42. Brown 44; Samuels 103.

43. Berenson's personal letters are not part of the archive and may not be consulted until 1984.

44. *Antiquity* 51 (1977) 179.

A fellow student and a pupil of Beazley was Gordon Childe, who wrote ("Retrospect," *Antiquity* 32 [1958] 69):

My Oxford training was in the Classical tradition to which

bronzes, terracottas and pottery (at least if painted) were respectable while stone and bone tools were banausic.

Grahame Clark ("Prehistory Since Childe," *Bulletin of the Institute of Archaeology* 13 [1976] 1–6) expanded upon Childe's works:

He came to Oxford as a classicist and received very little formal training in archaeology. What he did get was an insight into the formal analysis of pottery from Beazley, something which stood him in good stead for the rest of his life. (p. 4)

Such training as he had in Classical Archaeology gave him a keen appreciation of form analysis. Throughout his life he had an amazing visual memory understandable in a pupil of Beazley but all the more remarkable that he found it difficult to represent objects graphically. (p. 6)

Figure 5. New York 56.171.38. Amphora of Type C (obverse). Berlin Painter. Early fifth century B.C.

Figure 6. London E 270. Neck-amphora, with twisted handles (obverse). Kleophrades Painter. Early fifth century B.C.

general chronological scheme and grouping of the vases, consisted of a detailed study of a series of them, one by one, not as you might have expected, of technical or stylistic details, but for the subjects, the way these were arranged and interpreted by the painter, and the quality and expressiveness of the drawing. Little, except in a quite general way, about attributions.

Beazley used Morelli's method and probably benefited considerably from aspects of Berenson's scholarship. Historians of art would find much of value in "Citharoedus" (1922) even though this article is concerned exclusively with drawings on clay vases. (The "citharode vase" is illustrated in figures 5, 7, and 8). It is Beazley's nearest equivalent to an essay on method, a method which employed Morellian principles but was not narrowly morphological. There is a system of forms:

They comprise both the master lines which in archaic art demarcate the several parts of the body and of the drapery, and the minor lines which subdivide or diversify the areas

thus demarcated. We may speak, in fact, of a coherent comprehensive system of representing the forms of the human body naked and clothed.

"Citharoedus" 80–81

The system of renderings described above stands in a certain relation to nature. . . .

Ibid. 83

Memorize the system, and walk through the Louvre or British Museum: you will not be in doubt on which vases it is present or on which it is absent.

Ibid.

A system so definite, coherent, distinctive and in some respects so wilful, is most easily intelligible as a *personal* system: inspired in some measure by observation of nature, influenced and in part determined by tradition, and communicable or prescribable to others; but the child, above all else, of one man's brain and will. The personal character of the system does not necessarily imply that all the works which exhibit it are the work of one hand.

Ibid. 84

Figure 7. New York 56.171.38 (obverse). Youth singing to the music of his cithara. Drawing by Beazley.

Figure 8. New York 56.171.38 (reverse). Judge listening to the music. Drawing by Beazley.

The application of a system of renderings, someone may say, is not sufficient to create a work of art; and the detection of such a system in a number of vases is not equivalent to an exhaustive examination of their content. There are aspects . . . which I have hitherto seemed to be wholly or partly disregarding. There is the material aspect—the nature of clay, glaze, instruments employed, and the like. There are the shape, features and proportions of the vessel itself. There are, finally, those aspects which come under the general heading of design—the arrangement of dark with light, and of line with line, to form a pattern (design in the narrower sense), and to represent something in nature (theme, movement, ethos and pathos).

Ibid. 85

To sum up, we began by speaking about a peculiar system of renderings, through which a certain conception of the human form found expression. . . . The system of render-

ings was not easy to separate from the elements of design: it was, from one point of view, their vehicle, and from another, a collateral expression of artistic will.

Ibid. 90

Beazley's words echo Morelli's and Berenson's: the language of forms, the communication of the language, the detection of a system, the testing of observations. Testing is a recurrent theme of Berenson's "Rudiments of Connoisseurship" (1902) and this underlines the scientific experimental method.

. . . the adequate test is supplied by connoisseurship, which we have defined as the comparison of works of art with a view to determining their reciprocal relationships. It is now time to elaborate the definition, and to discuss the methods of the science.

Rudiments 122

If we, therefore, isolate the precise characteristics distinguishing each artist, they must furnish a perfect test of the fitness or unfitness of the attribution of a given work of a certain master; identity of characteristics always indicating identity of authorship. Connoisseurship, then, proceeds, as scientific research always does, by the isolation of the characteristics of the known and their confrontation with the unknown.

Ibid. 123

References to the scientific method are rare in Beazley's writings, and most of them are early.

The process of disengaging the work of an anonymous artist is the same as that of attributing an unsigned vase to a painter whose name is known. It consists of drawing a conclusion from observation of a great many details: it involves comparing one vase with another, with several others, with all the vases the enquirer has seen. . . . However obscure he may be, the artist cannot escape detection if only sufficiently delicate tests be applied.

America pp. v–vi

Berenson too wrote of the delicacy:

And it is here that Morellianism might be expected to come to our aid, for it is only a more refined and subtler archaeology than we have yet made use of. It is, however, so delicate an instrument, requiring from him who uses it such natural skill, and such elaborate training, that, more often than not, it bends and twists in the hand that wields it, and in some mysterious way blinds and stupefies the practitioner.

Three Essays 83–84

In the preface of this 1927 Oxford publication there seems to be a reference to the man who had been elected to the Lincoln Professorship of Classical Archaeology and Art two years earlier.

The procedure is the one currently and commonly used in Classical Archaeology, but seldom in the study of Italian painting. It demands from the student no magical endowments, no temperamental aptitudes, no special senses. It does require, however, in the first place, good average powers of observation, and concentration and reasoning of the kind that the botanist or anatomist is supposed to have. It calls, besides, for training in the historical method, that method which teaches not only how to weigh evidence in subjects concerned with any bit of the human past, but how to recognize what is relevant when it appears, and how to look for it when it hides.

Beazley knew Italian painting and classical archaeology, and comparisons between the two came easily to him.

The figures [by the Kleophrades Painter; cf. fig. 6], as in the preceding vase, stand firmly with the feet wider apart than in Euthymides, an attitude which reminds us of Signorelli.

JHS 30 (1910) 42–43

He [the Kleophrades Painter] may be said to play a kind of Florentine to the Berlin painter's Sienese [cf. figs. 5 and 6].

America 40–41

All these pictures of music are simple drawings, without shading and without colouring. When we moderns think of a music picture, our minds turn to Signorelli's Pan, to some Dutch interior, to some Venetian landscape, where the impression is determined, in great measure, by the harmony of colour and by chiaroscuro. Such music pictures cannot have existed in the fifth century. But in a later work, the Pan and the Nymphs from Pompeii, colour and landscape combine with composition to make a music picture of memorable charm.

"Citharoedus" 98

It also seems probable that Beazley initially borrowed some terms for expressing relationships between artists from the scholarship (especially German) of Renaissance painting: "school-piece" may owe something to a conception of the ancient workshop as a Renaissance studio. Other examples could be given, but "school-piece" is perhaps the best; Beazley used it frequently in early years.

Thirty-eight vases will be given to the Berlin master's hand. A list of these vases will first be given, arranged according to shape. The characteristics of the master's style will then be indicated.

A further list of twenty-nine vases will follow. These are imitations. To say they show the master's influence would be misleading: they are direct and conscious imitations: they copy his style, some of them so closely that it is difficult to distinguish them from the master's own work. Occasionally stylistic variations and crudity of touch betray the imitator. This list of school-pieces will conclude the study.

JHS 31 (1911) 277

Later, in *Potter and Painter in Ancient Athens* (London, 1946), he described the organization of the ancient workshops, so far as this can be reconstructed: fathers and sons often practised the same trade; senior painters rarely collaborated on a single vase; juniors were rarely employed for subsidiary decoration on a vase. Apprenticeship and patronage, as understood in the Renaissance, did not apply. Terms borrowed from the scholarship of Renaissance painting, therefore, had to be adapted to fit the very different circumstances of the ancient artists.

Morelli and Berenson were often looking at paintings

---

45. Compare *JHS* 31 (1911) 286–288; 34 (1914) 209–215. See also Kurtz 18–46.

Figure 9. "Mantle–figure" on the reverse of an amphora of Panathenaic Type (Munich 2313). Drawing by Beazley.

about which a great deal was already known. A morphological analysis, although recognized to be the most important means of identifying an artist's hand, could be supplemented by contemporary documents, signatures, and the content of the painting itself (landscape, architecture, costume) which gave additional clues to the place and date of manufacture. The morphological analysis of anatomical detail had to rely heavily upon the rendering of ears, eyes, noses, and hands, etc., because these were the features regularly exposed. It is hardly surprising that Morelli's critics spoke in a derogatory manner of the surgeon who issued a catalogue of noses and ears.

Beazley's artists had no contemporary documentation; they rarely signed their work; they did not commonly de-

pict landscape or architecture; and the costume of draped figures was fairly uniform. But many of the figures were shown nude, and features of surface anatomy were often rendered in great detail. In Beazley's method of recognizing styles of individual vase–painters, human anatomy is the single most important aspect of the figure decoration. His essays on painters regularly describe characteristic renderings of parts of the human body,[45] usually in a rather general way, but sometimes in clinical detail. Beazley knew the anatomy and the correct anatomical terms.

> Let us now turn [cf. figs. 8 and 9] to the resemblances: I lay no stress, of course, on the rendering of the nipple as a circle of dots with the centre marked; for this is an extremely common rendering of the nipple; but I would draw attention to the bounding lines of the breasts, with the curvilinear triangle at the pit of the stomach; to the omission of the off clavicle; to the line of the hither clavicle, recurving at the pit of the neck without touching the median line of the breast; to the curved line which runs down from about half-way along the line of the clavicle, separating shoulder and breast; to the smaller arc in the middle of the deltoid; to the indication of the trapezius between neck and shoulder; to the pair of curved lines on the upper right arm; to the projection of the wrist when the position of the hand requires it; to the two brown lines on the neck; indicating the sterno-mastoid; to the marking on the body between the lower boundary of the breast and the himation; to the form of the black lines indicating the ankle; to the pair of brown lines running from each ankle up the leg; to the forward contour of left leg and knee showing through the himation; in the himation, to the peaked folds on the left upper arm, the loose fold in the region of the navel, and the triangle where the inside of the garment shows at the shoulder.

"Citharoedus" 76

Since there is relatively little variety in the costume of draped figures, stylistic analysis relies on the execution of the lines defining folds and hems.[46] On red-figure vases from early in the fifth century there is a draped male (figs. 9 and 10) which is reproduced with near-mechanical regularity—ideal material for Morellian analysis which concerns itself not only with the renderings characteristic of each artist but also with the reproduction of these renderings. The so-called mantle–figures[47] stand alone, or in small static groups, on the reverses of vases of some shapes. They are almost always painted much more hastily, and more carelessly, than the figures on the obverse. Looking at both sides enables us to observe the variations possible within one man's style; it is exceedingly uncommon for the figures on the reverse of the vase not to be painted by the

46. Compare *JHS* 31 (1911) 289–290; 34 (1914) 216–218. See also Kurtz 47–57.

47. Kurtz 48–51.

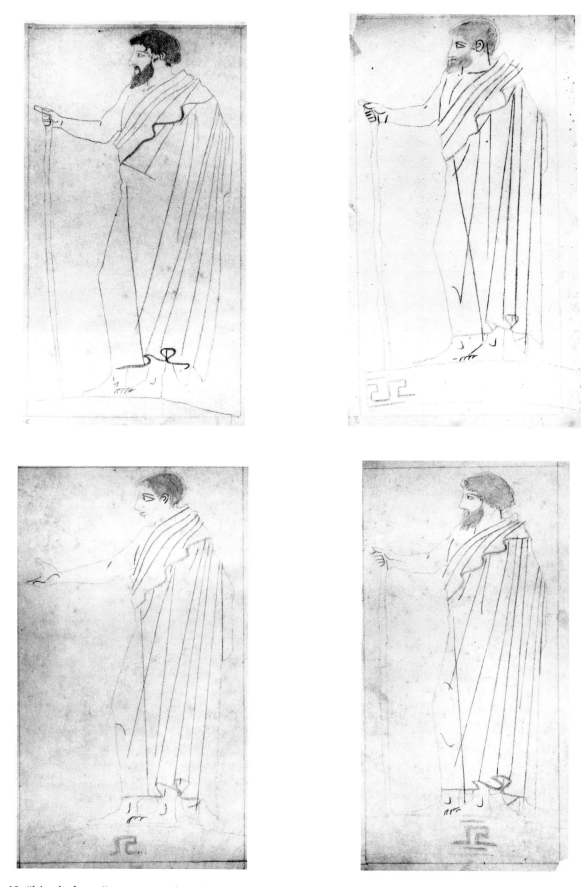

Figure 10. "Mantle–figures" on reverses of vases by a pupil of the Berlin Painter, the Achilles Painter. Drawings by Beazley.

same man as those on the obverse. It is also often easier to detect an artist's system by looking at his mantle-figures, where there are fewer lines reproduced more regularly. At an early stage Beazley felt obliged to defend the stylistic value of the mantle-figure:

> But at this point some reader may cry: of course these himation figures [fig. 10] are as like one another as, short of repetition, fifteen figures could be; but these are mantle figures, and all mantle figures are very much the same: I never look at mantle figures. In answer to this objection, once I have referred the objector to the story of Peter's sheet, I am at a loss; for although I can collect on two pages fifteen mantle figures which are *like* one another, I cannot collect on two others all mantle figures which are *unlike* these fifteen: I can only bid the critic go and look at a roomful of red-figured vases. If he finds any other vases with the same figure on the back I shall be glad to hear of it; for if I turn to the front I shall find that legs, feet, hands, face, clothes are drawn in the same way as on the vases already mentioned, and on other vases in the list I shall presently submit.

JHS 34 (1914) 179

Later he discussed and illustrated mantle-figures without apology. They were not only valuable guides to recognizing an artist's hand, they could also illustrate different phases of his career more clearly than figures depicted with greater care or attention to variety. The mediocre to poor quality of most mantle-figures emphasizes a very significant aspect of Beazley's vase–scholarship: master and hack received equal consideration; the works of both were recorded in the painter-lists, however numerous or unlovely. In these lists we find a "Worst Painter"[48] and even occasional cries of despair:

> In dealing with these trifling objects, not the most delightful of one's tasks, it is not always easy to distinguish the work of the Tymbos Painter from work that is merely in his manner. . . .[49]

Beazley's study of the vases was not restricted to those with figure decoration produced in Athens during the sixth to fourth centuries B.C., nor were his interests in this group narrowly stylistic. Our concern here, however, is connoisseurship, and those unfamiliar with Beazley's stylistic work on Athenian black- and red-figure vases might welcome fuller explanation of methods of study.

The figure decoration is on the curved surface of a vase whose paint can be very glossy; distortion and glare plague even the most skilful photographer. Personal examination of the object is, therefore, essential. Beazley travelled extensively; while handling the vases in museums and private collections, he made copious notes. These recorded essential information (inventory number, iconography, and publication, if the vase had been published) which would be entered in his painter–lists. They also have many sketches of significant details—of shape and of pattern–work, as well as of the figure decoration. The latter were most often of anatomy or of drapery. In addition to these small free-hand sketches, which were personal aides-mémoire and would be filed amongst his working notes, Beazley also often traced off the surface of the vase parts of figures, or whole figures. This is an exceedingly laborious process, as anyone knows who has attempted it. Sometimes he traced in greater detail and worked these tracings up into what is best called a finished drawing (figs. 7–10). These differ from the sketches in accuracy (each line following precisely that executed by the ancient artist) and from his other tracings in recording the technique as well as the form of the lines. In red-figure some lines are painted in black and some are in dilute brown; the latter are not easily captured in photographs and are absolutely essential to a proper understanding of the artist's style (cf. figs. 5 and 7).

Beazley drew all lines in pencil, using heavier strokes for black lines and lighter ones for those rendered in dilute lines. It is hard to believe that these finished drawings, which took a very great amount of time and trouble to complete, were not intended for publication; yet a large proportion was never published. Beazley had been advised by Reichhold on methods of tracing off the surface of the vase. Reichhold's drawings (fig. 2) had set a very high standard of accuracy and sensitivity to ancient draughtsmanship. Almost all of Reichhold's drawings of red-figure vases are set on a black ground to reproduce the effect of the glossy black paint surrounding the figures. Beazley experimented with this type of drawing (fig. 3), but early favoured outlined figures on a light ground because contour lines of the figure decoration were thus revealed.[50] These outline drawings are the best means of studying red-figure vases. It is, however, always necessary to bear in mind the shape of the vase, its subsidiary pattern-work, and the disposition of the figure decoration—the design. For this reason Beazley advocated a combination of finished drawing and photograph for the proper study of the whole

---

48. J.D. Beazley, *Attic Red-figure Vase-painters* (Oxford, 1963) 1353–54.
49. *Ibid.* 753.
50. Beazley made very few "finished drawings" from black-figure vases, and his technique for rendering them was quite different from Reichhold's. Compare *PBSR* 11 (1929) 8, fig. 4 and 14, fig. 7 (Beazley) and

K. Reichhold in A. Furtwängler *Griechische Vasenmalerei* pls. 1–3, 11–13. Working (as on red-figure vases) entirely with pencil, he used heavier strokes for incised lines and lighter for areas painted black on the light ground.

Figure 11. Sir John and Lady Beazley. Photograph
by Dietrich von Bothmer.

recorded on the mount suggestions for attributions and revisions. Photographs of the vases assigned to hands were kept by artist or group; those of vases which could not be assigned were ordered by shape. It is among the latter that some stylistic groups are indicated which were not entered in the published lists—presumably because he felt some degree of uncertainty about the attributions.

The ways in which he gave names to his artists has already been mentioned, and some reference has been made to borrowing of terms from the scholarship of Renaissance painting to express stylistic relationships. Beazley evolved a rather large number of terms, many of which were his own; these were especially chosen to suit the conditions under which the ancient artists worked.[51] He was always cautious, and preferred to keep vases in larger, more general stylistic groups until he could be more certain about their attribution.

No mention has been made, thus far, of attribution to *potters*. This necessitates sensitive observation of subtle variations in shape. Drawings need to be made of the profile of the vase. Although much of the work on potters has yet to be done, excellent models have been set, especially by Bloesch, whose scholarship Beazley greatly admired. Equipped with Beazley's drawings from the figure-work, profile drawings of the vase, and proper photographs, one begins to develop a feeling for the ancient artists. The only better means of studying them is in the gallery with the vases.

Throughout his life Beazley actively sought the opinions of other scholars and generously recorded their contributions. They, in turn, consulted him. Beazley accepted no fees, even from dealers who were keen to have his seal of approval. He established a tradition of generosity in scholarship which was truly remarkable, and which any scholar should be proud to emulate.

vase. Although he built up a very large collection of photographs, which he consulted with his notes when he was working in Oxford, he was not a keen photographer. This task was avidly taken up by his wife (fig. 11), and Beazley took great pride in displaying her prints. There was an exhibition of his drawings and her photographs for the Oxford Art Club in 1928.

Beazley mounted the great part of his photographs and

Beazley Archive
Ashmolean Museum
Oxford

---

51. Martin Robertson very kindly took up the invitation to explain these terms more fully in the introduction (pp. ix–xvi) to the Beazley Archive's first publication—*Beazley Addenda* (Oxford, 1982)—compiled by Lucilla Burn and Ruth Glynn, which brings the references in Beazley's published painter/group lists up to date from about 1965 when he ceased actively compiling his own.